THE INWARD EYE

The Inward Eye

Psychoanalysts Reflect on Their Lives and Work

edited by
Laurie W. Raymond
Susan Rosbrow-Reich

THE ANALYTIC PRESS
1997 Hillsdale, NJ London

Published by The Analytic Press, Inc.
101 West Street, Hillsdale, NJ 07642

The inward eye : psychoanalysts reflect on their lives and work /
edited by Laurie W. Raymond and Susan Rosbrow-Reich /
p. cm.
Includes bibliographical references and index.
ISBN 0-88163-252-X
1. Psychoanalysts--Interviews. 2. Psychoanalysis. I. Raymond, Laurie W. II. Rosbrow-Reich, Susan.
[DNLM. 1. Psychoanalysis--interviews. 2. Psychoanalysis--personal narratives. WZ 112.5.P6.I63 1997]
RC506.I595 1997
616.89'17--dc21
DNLM/DLC
for Library of Congress 96-12694
CIP

To Peter, Maria, and Josh for their love and patience.
L.W.R.

For Kenneth, Elizabeth, and Jennifer
and to the memory of James Rosbrow.
S.R.R.

ACKNOWLEDGMENTS

We want to give special thanks to Paul Stepansky, Ph.D., whose vision of this project greatly influenced our own. His clear thinking was invaluable in helping us finally find a perspective from which to articulate each of our experiences throughout these years of interviewing. We deeply appreciate his understanding of what we were attempting to achieve in these interviews, his willingness to preserve the interviews almost entirely in their original form, and his masterful editing, which turned several unwieldy transcripts into elegant dialogues without in any way corrupting the integrity of the interviews. We want to thank him, Eleanor Starke Kobrin, and The Analytic Press for sustained support and a quality of careful attention that made the last stages of this project, since their involvement, a very gratifying experience for both of us.

We would also like to thank a number of people within the P.I.N.E. (Psychoanalytic Institute of New England, East) community who provided us at critical times with sustained interest and affirmation in what felt like our unending endeavor. James Barron, Ph.D. initiated our original collaboration by inviting us to write for the P.I.N.E. newsletter. He then gave us unrestricted opportunity to publish our initial interviews. Axel Hoffer, M.D. kindly offered encouragement and suggestions at the beginning of this project, which helped us set our direction. Sheldon Roth, M.D. helped guide our expansion of the study and facilitated our considering its publication as a book. His thoughtful questions frequently challenged us to develop a sharper focus.

We want to express appreciation to others at P.I.N.E. who offered useful suggestions and generous support: M. Robert Gardner, M.D., Alfred Margulies, M.D., Evelyne Schwaber, M.D., Robert Pyles, M.D., Ana-Maria Rizzuto, M.D., and Graham Spruiell, M.D. We thank Alice Rapkin for her continued assistance throughout.

From the larger community outside of P.I.N.E., Stephanie Smith, L.I.C.S.W. offered collegial and academic help; Peter Raymond, M.Ed. provided technical assistance and guidance, and Kenneth Reich, Ed.D. gave scholarly attention, all of which enriched our experience.

Finally, we want to thank our interviewees, who made this exceptional learning opportunity possible.

Laurie W. Raymond
Susan Rosbrow-Reich

I wish to make several additional acknowledgments. I want to thank Barbara Pizer, Ed.D., Stuart Pizer, Ph.D., and Diana Kirschner, Ph.D. for their continuing encouraging presence. I thank Sam Kirschner, Ph.D. both for support and for guidance in developing my writing. Finally, I thank Thomas Rosbrow, Ph.D. for enriching my knowledge of the psychoanalytic literature, in this way playing both a direct and indirect role in the evolution of this project.

Susan Rosbrow-Reich

INTRODUCTION

That inward eye
Which is the bliss of solitude
William Wordsworth

Classical psychoanalysis is a deeply intersubjective experience for both analysand and analyst. The intimate bond that develops between the two during years of sustained, committed effort to communicate with each other supports both in the revisiting of earlier experience. According to the tenets of classical analysis, only the analysand's inner dialogue becomes the shared focus of the analytic inquiry. While the analyst must remain open to a complex, emotionally evocative inner dialogue of his or her own, much of that dialogue and self-inquiry remains private, not shared with the analysand. This project was an effort to learn more about that inner dialogue, to see the world from the analyst's inner eye.

That was our intent. At that time we were undergoing classical psychoanalyses, feeling deprived of and curious about the analyst's private experience. This curiosity no doubt stimulated our endeavor. We undertook this study both as a complement and an antidote to our training analyses. We wanted to know how analysts think: what makes people change, what it is like to do the work, how the work affects them. We selected analysts who had done this work for many years and had lived through decades of analytic history. Begun in 1988, this book is a study primarily about classical psychoanalysis as it was practiced by most American analysts until that time. Our specific choices of interviewees were idiosyncratic and highly personal. With several exceptions, we narrowed our sample to psychoanalytic thinkers, almost all now approaching their 80s or older, who viewed the analytic enterprise from a classical, one-person psychology.

We began this book with two particular bonds: we were analytic classmates, and we shared the same analyst. Our backgrounds prior to analytic training were, however, quite different.

SRR: My first experience of the power of the transferential–countertransferential bond occurred during the summers following my sophomore and junior years of college, when I worked as a social worker at a girls' reform school in Delaware. An English major lacking any training in clinical work, I had little awareness of what was transpiring in me, let alone in my clients, except that I felt a remarkably intense, even painful inner response to these girls. I reacted by deciding to become a social worker. (I had no interest in studying hard sciences or attending medical school. Psychology, as it was taught at the University of Pennsylvania at the time, was focused more on rats and lab science than on clinical psychology; psychoanalytic psychology was absent altogether from the undergraduate curriculum.) Almost immediately upon entering social work school and starting a student placement in a social work agency, I became depressed as I grasped the nature of the system. There was a three-rung hierarchical ladder, and social workers occupied the lowest rung. No matter what the work, being a social worker played havoc with my self-esteem. I wanted out. Moreover, I was concerned, even frightened, by my inability to know what to do or how to conceptualize what I was doing in the one-to-one sessions I was conducting with clients. Undertaking my own first psychotherapy experience helped me develop the courage to think of myself becoming a doctor, a role that was conflictual for various reasons.

In 1970 I entered graduate school at Adelphi University's Derner Institute for Advanced Psychological Studies, a rigorously academic program grounded in the psychoanalytic study of development and committed to training clinicians. (The Derner Institute was the first professional school for training clinical psychologists in the country, in distinction to more fundamentally academic programs.) In truth, from the first day at Adelphi I felt I had reached the promised land. It was a first experience of feeling fully immersed in work, study, friendship, professional relations in a community where everyone spoke basically the same language and saw the work from similar perspectives, where openness and personal honesty and use of oneself were key values. For the first time since high school, I developed personal relationships with mentors, teachers with whom I could identify, almost all of them psychologists trained as psychoanalysts outside the American Psychoanalytic Association. In fact, Adelphi had a postdoctoral program in psychoanalysis where most of my faculty taught. Many of my classmates were control patients for analysts in training at this program. Freudian psychology was the underpinning of the curriculum; Otto Fenichel's writings, so we were instructed, were to be "our tools." Enjoying myself tremendously day to day and learning a great deal, I was encouraged to be confident of future success and looked forward to eventually becoming a psychoanalyst at one of the New York institutes, such as Adelphi, that trained psychologists.

I came to Boston in 1973 to pursue a joint internship at Harvard University Health Services and the Cambridge Guidance Center. I chose this particular internship for several reasons; high among them was that at the time psychology was an independent training department at Harvard, with a strong spirit of collegial collaboration between staff and trainees. Completing my Ph.D., I stayed in Boston and by 1975 had developed a full-time private practice. Once settled, I became aware that psychoanalytic training for psychologists did not exist in Boston. There were no institutes run by psychologists. I had some dim knowledge that unusual scholars, for example, Harvard professors, might be able to pursue training at the Boston Psychoanalytic Institute, but that was not an option for me. I was aware of the bitterness of my mentors at the Harvard University Health Services toward the Boston Psychoanalytic Institute (BPSI.) Years earlier, several of them had been invited to train, with the condition that they would sign an agreement that they would practice only under the supervision of an M.D. analyst, a provision that was to remain in effect throughout their lifetimes. I had a short, unsatisfying experience with personal psychoanalysis, leaving me skeptical about its utility for me. So I went on with my career, married, and began raising my children.

In the early 1980s I again began personal psychoanalysis, this time with very different, more favorable results. Early in the analysis, I had a crisis of sorts. Experiencing the power of the psychoanalytic process firsthand, I could no longer ignore the fact that, given that I was treating people intensively, seeing patients two and three times a week for many years, I lacked training that could significantly improve my work and benefit my patients. I was distressed because the path toward training at that point remained tremendously uncertain. Some psychologists had been accepted to begin classwork at either BPSI or the Psychoanalytic Institute of New England, East (PINE), but most failed to obtain the waivers from the American Psychoanalytic Association that permitted them to treat patients. Determined to train, I applied to PINE, where my personal analyst was a training analyst, and was rejected. When asked why, the head of the admissions committee said that I was qualified personally and clinically to become an analyst, but that, since I had not published, the committee was dubious that I could ever obtain a waiver for full training.

Determined to gain admittance, I decided to write a psychoanalytic paper on a subject in which I felt I had particular expertise and could make a contribution—the dynamics of love relations. I had trained at Einstein Family Studies while at Adelphi and from that time had always conducted a significant amount of couples therapy, as well as supervising and teaching on the subject. I made an intensive review of the psychoanalytic literature, searching for formulations that would aid me in articulating certain dynamics I witnessed in clinical practice. Being rejected from one's own analyst's institute during a psychoanalysis is conducive to a most regressive experience. The painfulness of my situation created a sense of urgency that led to an enormous idealization of theory. I needed theory to help me out in a most practical sense. Being able to make use of theory was the necessary step toward admission. With support and encouragement from Dr. William Meissner, a psychoanalytic scholar with whom I was meeting for private supervision, I produced a publishable paper within nine months, reapplied to PINE, and was accepted. At the same time the lawsuit against the American Psychoanalytic Association by the American Psychological Association was nearing its end, with a successful outcome for psychologists looking more probable, so that the larger climate of training had already changed.

Thus I entered PINE and began my training with an immense idealization of theory. Having previously enjoyed intellectual pursuits and the mastery of intellectual challenges, I had now added a new piece of personal history. By writing a publishable paper, I had proved myself worthy to the psychoanalytic community, as represented by the admissions committee. By my incorporation and use of theory, I had turned defeat into victory. I was now poised to become an analyst.

Of course, the story is not so simple. With hindsight, I realize that there was a cost attached to this "victory." I have no question that I have learned an enormous amount and became a much better clinician. For a number of years, however, lingering on even after graduation from PINE, I suffered to some degree from the phenomenon Anna Freud described as identification with the aggressor—that is, I denied and disowned my rage and resentment at being rejected and then forced to meet standards of admission far beyond those of my physician classmates. I reclaimed these feelings, to my surprise, when I was invited to join the admissions committee at PINE. Receiving congratulations from a loved and admired former supervisor, I was confused to find myself less than appreciative and even tempted to make a sarcastic response. Suddenly I recognized that, even though I had complained to friends about the unfairness of the situation, my articulated resentment had been only the tip of the iceberg. In large part, my anger had simply gone underground, remaining unconscious but in full force, only redirected against myself. I had blamed myself for being rejected, for failing to become a great scholar worthy of admission on account of numerous publications. Even after admission, although I did not acknowledge it to myself, I remained intimidated, not by my peer group but by the institution itself and by senior analysts, who, so I thought, had mastered theory.

Looking back at this collection of interviews, I recognize my intimidation particularly in the early interviews, in which idealization somewhat inhibited my responses to a number of the interviewees. Retrospectively, this inhibition seems inevitable. Over half the analysts we interviewed were among those whose work I had studied independently before beginning training. Thus I began this project with a well-consolidated transference to many of our interviewees, and most especially to their writings.

LR: I first thought about becoming a physician when in elementary school I heard stories of Albert Schweitzer and Tom Dooley bringing medicine to people in remote worlds. Their patients suffered from unfamiliar diseases such as "leprosy" and "malaria." I tried to picture how these men managed to communicate with those patients of different languages and customs. While in high school, I spent hours talking to my friends about their concerns and my own, and how we made sense of other people. In retrospect, I realize that I was discovering in those conversations how perplexing we can be to each other, despite sharing the same language and similar cultural backgrounds. Throughout my schooling, I felt most challenged by learning how to think scientifically through hypothesizing and testing inferences; I never envisioned it, however, as a future career without a clinical, personal context in which to practice such scientific thinking.

I spent my college years at Princeton in the independent study of political socialization, trying to make sense of how Soviet children were socialized differently than Americans. In my senior thesis research, I discovered several noteworthy differences in the social organization of Soviet elementary schools: pupils were organized into competitive teams within their classrooms, asked to be responsible for each other, and had one teacher for as long as 10 to 12 years. I wondered how these characteristics of Soviet schooling and our own society's emphasis on individual achievement shaped the moral values of children in both systems. The most interesting aspect of this project was my traveling to the Soviet Union to try to observe these differences firsthand. It was upsetting to discover how difficult it was for my Soviet counterparts to share their experiences honestly, feeling unsafe in their own system about revealing too much. I saw how communication between us was distorted by the larger political conflicts between our respective countries.

I entered Harvard Medical School with the intention of becoming a psychiatrist. It was a rude awakening to see psychiatry condemned and ridiculed as "not real medicine" and "unscientific" by mentors I respected in other medical specialties. At the time, I was not mature enough to withstand this predictable criticism and found myself developing other interests. Being immersed in an intense research atmosphere at Harvard, I became intrigued by Judah Folkman's work on tumor antiangiogenesis factors in mammalian cartilage, that is, his quest to find substances within the body which would stop new vascular growth in tumors. I wanted to explore the possible presence of these factors in the chemically similar bovine eye vitreous. As a medical student, I pored over meticulous illustrations by German scientists of the 19th century; they too had been fascinated by the disappearance of the hyaline artery within the vitreous of various mammals at birth. That we shared this wonder of a particular process in nature across centuries and countries was thrilling to me. As these research interests blossomed, I decided to pursue training in ophthalmology.

I reclaimed my interest in psychiatry after a medical internship at the Massachusetts General Hospital (MGH). I was working part-time in a MGH walk-in medical clinic while raising my first child and undertaking two years of vitreous research. My patients in the walk-in clinic presented an incredible array of human experience. For the first time, I became much more aware of another aspect of communication: I saw how these patients often expressed with their bodies those wishes and needs for which they did not have words. I remember a construction worker, furious with his wife, who developed a right-arm paralysis until their conflict was resolved; I recall as well a lonely engineer whose weekend headaches brought him into regular contact with our clinic staff. I found myself becoming much more interested in the stories behind my patients' symptoms and their ways of imparting meaning to their problems than in diagnosing the symptoms themselves. I again wanted to pursue training in psychiatry and chose an adult psychiatry residency at the MGH rather than starting one in ophthalmology as previously planned.

During my three years of adult psychiatry residency at the MGH, my mentors offered a unique combination of personalities. Thomas Hackett, M.D., our Chief, told us harrowing stories of his experiences with patients in prisons and jails. He taught us how to elicit an entire life history from patients with tattoos by having them describe each tattoo in detail. Ned Cassem, M.D. and George Murray, M.D., both psychiatrists and priests, introduced us to the world of consultation on the medical and surgical floors and brought to us their rare combination of psychiatric skill, humor, common sense, and spiritual perspective. It was during this period of training in a tertiary medical referral center that I also began to learn a new language from my analyst/supervisors, from Gerald Adler, M.D., Ed Messner, M.D., Joseph Schwartz, M.D., Nicholas Kouretas, M.D., and Avery Weisman, M.D. These analysts' attunement to my patients' intuitive world opened up another universe for me. I was intrigued by their ability to listen to my clinical material with a "third ear," hearing emotional refrains in my dialogues with patients to which I had previously been deaf. This marked the beginning of my own psychic awakening, my realization that beyond an "objective" scientific world that included the observable encounter between patient and therapist lay the developmental worlds of both. I began to see that in therapist and patient alike wishes, needs, and adaptations from earlier ages all compete in devising solutions in the present. Only in retrospect can I see that my third-year project on catatonia, of which muteness is a prominent symptom, resulted from my growing interest in the differential causes and nature of nonverbal language. This study allowed me to revisit with renewed fascination old German texts, now the writings of Leonhard, who had meticulously categorized many types of catatonic schizophrenics within German asylums.

I chose to train further in child psychiatry after my adult residency in order to learn more about the nonverbal, intuitive world of communication. I struggled in that training to find words appropriate for my younger patients, as I did at home for my own two children. I realized I needed to do analytic work myself in order to reopen a dialogue with myself, one suppressed by personal history and by my own intensive training as a physician. In this personal and professional context, I decided to pursue psychoanalytic training.

The world of analytic training at PINE presented me with two different languages that I struggled to integrate: the highly personal one of finding words to express, for the first time, the intensely compressed and confused feelings I discovered while on the couch in my own analysis, and the complex verbiage of analytic theoreticians that described intersubjective phenomena I was only beginning to understand. In this new context, I found myself searching intensely for others' experiences in order to learn better how to navigate my own. Training at PINE, however, involved many "invisible" dimensions beyond that of connecting to my analyst through sound rather than sight. PINE, as a small institute without walls, has no common location for informal exchange between faculty and candidates. Being assiduously protective of the privacy of both analysts and analysands so as to safeguard analytic work, PINE provides candidates with only limited exposure to training analysts outside of seminars. I was also aware that many senior analysts at PINE and other institutes were being eliminated from supervisory and administrative positions in the larger community of academic medicine and psychiatric training. This project of interviewing senior analysts mainly from other institutes, then, provided the means by which I could actually see what senior analysts were like as people, to find out what I had in common with them and whether I could identify with them.

SRR and LR: In preparing for these interviews, we made an enormous effort to penetrate and understand the mental processes of each of the analysts through intensive study of their writings. Without articulating it to ourselves, we sought to have the kind of open, intimate dialogue with them we had felt deprived of in our own analyses. The project enabled us metaphorically and actually to get up off the couch, meet the analyst person to person, and formally discuss the psychoanalytic process rather than live it. Our timidity, as well as our reliance on theoretical language in some of the earlier interviews, reflected our sense of ourselves at the time: we did not yet feel like analysts, at most like would-be analysts in the very early stages of professional development. Our attitude toward our interviewees shifted during the course of the interviews, which spanned six years as we completed analysis and then graduated from PINE, Susan in 1993 and Laurie in 1996.

The first interview in this volume, with Arthur Valenstein, was originally intended for and published in the PINE newsletter; it took place before the idea of a book of interviews had taken shape. Having enjoyed collaborating on the interview, we decided to interview senior analysts as they visited PINE, with the plan that, at some unspecified point in the future, we might collect these interviews into a volume. However, within a year, following newsletter publication of several more interviews, we were offered a book contract. Our perspective on the project shifted along with a sense of ourselves. We were now not just would-be analysts in training; we were editors with a mission: to help convey through our questions the person and thinking of our eminent interview subjects. Each interview provided a complex challenge, a time-limited opportunity (sometimes only one hour) to attempt to answer the questions evoked by our reading their work, but also to convey to readers these analysts' respective roles in the history of psychoanalysis.

Although we had not consciously planned it, many of the interviews evolved in a way that in certain respects paralleled an analytic hour. In these interviews, while theory and intellectual ideas remained a central focus, a mode of communication evolved that allowed spontaneity and free association. This happened when certain interviewees recognized that our questions not only mirrored their thinking but also reflected our own. At such moments, we came to feel appreciated as idea-makers in our own right, and the interviews developed a quality of mutuality and play, as interviewees and interviewers together generated a shared space for creative exchange.

Most of our interviewees were original thinkers, but we learned more from their persons than from their ideas. We appreciated their openness in sharing their individual struggles to integrate their personal lives, clinical experience, and theoretical beliefs. The qualities of these persons that affected us most have to do with character. They include honesty and integrity, a commitment to learn from one's experience, a deep respect for another person, no matter how ill, and a fundamental kindness and generosity toward others.

LR: Having finished these interviews four years ago, completed my analysis two years ago, and graduated from PINE ten months ago, I am still in the throes of integrating these essential parts of my analytic identity. To some extent, I am stepping away from the analysts I knew in my training to examine who I am, to integrate my identity as an analyst with my practice as a general psychiatrist. I face a different professional world than they do, and I don't expect to have a full-time analytic practice in the future. Instead, I find myself wanting to bring my analytic training to non–mental-health settings in which listening with a third ear could be useful. I am grateful for the experience of my own analysis, for my formal analytic training at PINE, and for my informal education by the senior analysts we interviewed. Taken together, they have given me a profound appreciation of words, spoken and unspoken, which link our individual human experiences, as well as great respect for the way each of us makes sense of our lives.

Like Helen Keller's awakening at the well, when her outstretched hand put water and symbols together for the first time, my bringing together of my own preverbal feelings, images, and symbols during analysis helped me discover in myself and others a new universe in which I can now dwell. This was best represented to me in a dream I had before our first meeting with André Green, after I had read his book *On Private Madness*. Inside a room with a sliding glass door, I was looking through binoculars at fiery stars that were unnaturally close, within reach. André Green was outside, beckoning me to touch the stars, encouraging me to look closer at them myself, to put aside the binoculars.

My hope is that readers of this book will share our original excitement at hearing these senior analysts describe their personal travels into their own intuitive and theoretical worlds, historical journeys that can never be repeated by a younger generation.

SRR: A decade has passed since we began these interviews. I finished analysis, I teach at my institute, my children are grown. Though not yet old, I feel much closer in the life cycle to the analysts we interviewed than when we began, as though the years have added exponentially rather than arithmetically. Determining what to say in conclusion feels as challenging and unclear as deciding when to end an analysis. Rather than attempting a summation, I will assume the analyst's prerogative and offer a few associations of my own.

In trying to explain to people my great pleasure in preparing with Laurie for the interviews, I am repeatedly reminded of Oliver Sacks's experience treating a set of gifted, yet autistic twins, who themselves experienced tremendous joy in mentally computing and sharing extremely large prime numbers with each other. At first, I intended to explain my association simply by pointing out that in sharing their own and admiring each other's primes, the twins were sharing products of intense mental concentration that were a kind of private, though not secret, communication. The analogy, so I thought, was simply to Laurie's and my questions, which we developed independently after hours of intense scrutiny of each author's work and through which we revealed a great deal of our mental processes and personal interests to each other. We discovered a shared gratification in the somewhat obsessive mastery of each interviewee's writings. But, now, even more important parallels become evident. In writing about these twins, Sacks not only described their most unusual interaction and relationship, but his own participation in it. At first he was unable to grasp what they were sharing. His uncertainty was followed by the pleasure of recognition, as he realized the significance of their communication. Then, in relaying the story, Sacks confided to the reader his own earlier interest in prime numbers. As Sacks recounted, after grasping the meaning of the twins' conversation, he turned to his own book of prime numbers (not having the twins' native genius in computation) and was able, as a product of his skill, intuition, and creative effort, to join in their communication of primes.[1] Sacks was able to make this discovery

---

[1] I am grateful to Evelyn Schwaber for introducing me to this reading in her seminar on "Listening," where she included the reading to demonstrate the capacity for listening.

because he listened with great care and respect and, further, with the expectation that he could learn something from these unique patients. And he thereupon heard something wondrous.

I realize now that this vignette comes to mind for a second reason: witnessing and being inspired by Sacks's rare ability to listen with a truly open mind was similar to how I felt with certain of our interviewees as they described their work with patients. And still another similarity emerges: when Sacks shared the prime numbers, as well as his happiness in offering prime numbers to the twins, he moved, if only briefly, from a one-person to a two- and then a three-person field. And so with our project there was constant shifting from a one-person to a two-person and sometimes to a three-person field. What do I mean by the last? While in all the interviews important interpersonal dialogue took place that established a three-person field of sorts, in certain interviews there was sustained three-way experiencing of spontaneous, creative thinking originating in the moment, a three-way sharing of emotion, or both. A three-way experiencing transpired, for example, with Jim McLaughlin. Telling us about play in the psychoanalytic setting, he described "working with contrasts and boundaries. So you [the analyst] stretch those boundaries with what you choose to laugh at, cry with." He asked if we cried with patients, then told us a moving vignette about a time when he had. Within several moments, all three of us were spontaneously using word play: I spoke of play as creating building blocks of experience as a base, Laurie noted that with humor you have more of a mattress to fall down on; and McLaughlin agreed with her that we cushion our pain with humor.

Moving away from Sacks, I remember how after each interview Laurie and I would share our private experience of the meeting; we often felt warmed or moved by the interviewee. On the infrequent occasions when one or both of us felt upset after being confronted or ignored by one of the interviewees, the opportunity for affective discharge through humor was invaluable. Comparing impressions, we imagined together what it would be like to be in analysis with the interviewee. While our intellectual interests were quite distinct, our emotional reactions to our interviewees tended to be quite similar. I am convinced that this processing after each interview was an integral dynamic aspect of the way my total experience was internalized.

I think once again about our title, *The Inward Eye,* and how much more central that image is to me than when we first conceived of it. I now appreciate how, as M. Robert Gardner described, we analysts can see only from the lens of our own inner experience and can use only our own imagery, so often visual, to explain what we see. I think of Jacob

Arlow's conviction that unconscious fantasy is quasi-visual in nature and of his metaphor depicting how it works—that of two movie projectors, one revealing the world of inner fantasy, the other showing the contribution from external perceptions and reality working at one time; one placing its image on the obverse side of the screen, both going at the same time so that the two sets of images are superimposed. That brings to mind images of dreams, of the cinema, of the artist as spokesperson of culture, of talking with M. Robert Gardner about his painting and his visual images while analyzing.

I think of how much of my own memory is replayed visually and how my best reconstruction of this book project is as a kaleidoscope of vivid images, sometimes magical glimpses of a past world as seen through our interviewees' eyes—I'm sitting with Joyce McDougall as she described Freud's widow, Marthe Freud, opening a door, seeing a class of candidates with Anna, saying, "Humph, psychoanalysts!" I wonder what Marthe was like to live with, what Freud's life was really like. I think of sitting with Merton Gill as he recounted Leo Stone's depiction of the analyst of his day: "The classical analyst holds that if you pass your former analyst on the street you should have no more feeling than if you had passed a brass monkey." I think with pleasure of Merton then saying, "In the first place, if you pass a brass monkey walking down the street and have no feelings, what the hell is the matter with you? In the second place, the implicit remark that maybe your analyst was like a brass monkey should also not be ignored."

I think of how untenable that notion of the analytic relationship is to most of us today; of how hard it must be for younger practitioners even to believe it really existed in this way. I think with emotion of Leo Stone's special warmth and smile, which touched me so in meeting with him, and of how much good he did for our field in speaking out. And I keep seeing in my mind's eye this big brass monkey, a shiny, wondrous object. I would marvel at seeing it walking down the street. This leads me to think of the importance of the analyst's capacity to marvel, to witness, and to listen to the most unusual, the most outrageous, the most mundane concerns—and to do so with the deepest, most attentive respect, which is itself equivalent to a kind of belief.

I leave this project, finally, more knowledgeable of but less certain about psychoanalytic theory. I look at the body of psychoanalytic literature now less as gospel than as reflecting each individual contributor's highly subjective, carefully crafted, unique way of expressing what is most true and important for her or him, each with an imagery shaped by life experience. Relinquishing the notion of theory as empirical fact has only deepened my appreciation of the imagination and intellectual discipline required to generate clinical ideas. In this spirit, we direct the reader's attention to these interviews, which demonstrate the clear thinking and professional dedication of 16 eminent analysts of this past half century.

Laurie Raymond and Susan Rosbrow-Reich

REFERENCE

Sacks, Oliver (1987). The Twins. In: *The Man Who Mistook His Wife for a Hat and Other Clinical Tales*, New York: Harper Perennial, 1987, pp. 195–213.

The Inward Eye

TABLE OF CONTENTS

Arthur Valenstein

Arthur Valenstein, M.D. is a training analyst at the Psychoanalytic Institute of New England, East and Clinical Professor of Psychiatry Emeritus, Harvard Medical School. He is a consultant in psychiatry at Massachusetts General Hospital and an honorary psychiatrist at Beth Israel Hospital, and was formerly a faculty member of the Cambridge Hospital. Dr. Valenstein was Councilor-at-Large of the American Psychoanalytic Association and is a past Vice President of the Boston Psychoanalytic Society. He has served on the editorial board of the *Journal of the American Psychoanalytic Association* and has been a guest lecturer for many psychoanalytic societies. Dr. Valenstein has maintained an active involvement in psychoanalytic research. His major interests are the nature of the psychoanalytic and psychotherapeutic process and the developmental aspects of psychological functioning. Dr. Valenstein was interviewed June 17, 1988.

LR/SRR: We're interested in hearing about your life as an analyst, how you chose that path....

AV: Well, I'd have to go back 50 years to my beginning as a psychiatrist. I won't go further back to the implicit predilections that might have led me to be curious about people, but I know that they were there from early years. If I start from when I was a medical student, when I was far from sure that I would do psychiatry....

Actually, before I turned to medicine, my greatest enthusiasm was for hard science. I really wanted to be a physicist, but it wasn't timely. I didn't start in medicine. I started as an engineering student, and I enjoyed it very much. If it hadn't been for the Depression, I probably would have remained an engineer with strong interests in other directions. So I've always had one foot in hard science and one foot in the humanities, and fortunately I don't think I've fallen between the two. As in skiing, you've got two feet, but you ought to be able to stand on either just in case you hit a mogul. If you can shift your weight back and forth and keep your balance and your poise, you won't tumble—but it's good to be able to count on two feet though.

LR: When did you graduate from college?

AV: I entered Cornell in 1931. I started in the College of Engineering, but, as I said in answer to your first question, about halfway through engineering I transferred to Arts and Sciences and graduated with an A.B. in 1934. In fact, I had been keenly interested in physics since my high school years, and after my first year in engineering at Cornell I even took a summer course in modern experimental physics at Columbia, where I did some cloud chamber experiments to determine the charge on an electron. Had I followed this interest and concentrated on physics, perhaps I would have become a physicist, and in due course possibly a nuclear physicist. At that time, though—for those were the Depression years—it seemed impractical; nor did it seem plausible that completing my education as an electrical engineer would be economically viable. So I turned back toward an earlier interest in medicine, and transferred to the College of Arts and Sciences to complete the premedical requirements.

The curious thing is that I went to a medical school, also Cornell, where psychiatry was presented from a Meyerian, psychobiological direction but, nonetheless, significantly psychoanalytic in its orientation, especially when it came to the psychological development of the child—quite different from what seems to have come about now. Payne Whitney was the psychiatric unit of the New York Hospital. Phyllis Greenacre was in charge of the outpatient department, and Bettina Warburg, Louise Despert, Norvelle LaMar, Margaret Fries (who did an early innovative study of activity and passivity in newborns), Mabel Huschka, and other early analysts were there. Milton Senn and Benjamin Spock taught in the pediatric outpatient department. It was there and through them and others that the earliest interface between psychiatry and the developmental aspects of pediatrics originated.

As first-year medical students, we all made fun of the psychiatrists when they gave lectures. George Amsden was Chief of Psychiatry before Oscar Diethelm was brought to Payne Whitney from the Phipps Clinic, which was the citadel of Meyerian psychiatry. We used to call George Amsden "Radio Ralph" because he was quite deaf despite using the conspicuous hearing aid of those days. He was an early analyst who had previously been at Bloomingdale's in White Plains, now the Westchester Division of New York Hospital. I wish I had collected the history of some of these people from those days. I was curious...but it wasn't anything to be proud of then, to be curious about people and interested in psychiatry.

LR: Had many of them had had personal contact with Freud?

AV: I don't know. They were Americans who might have trained in Vienna or Berlin. They gave standard didactic lectures to the first-year class. As I look back, they presented a straightforward view of the libidinal sequences of the development of the infant and child, and the centrality of the oedipal situation in conflict formation. The prevailing response of the class was a mixture of interest, acceptance, and ridicule of the lecturers, making the most of their idiosyncrasies.

However, in my fourth year I did something quite unusual for those times: I took a one-month elective in psychiatry with George W. Henry, who also had been a pillar at Bloomingdale's and who did the psychiatric consultations throughout New York Hospital. He contributed to the history of psychiatry written by Gregory Zilboorg, who was a psychiatrist and psychoanalyst and who had graced the drama stage as well as holding political office in Russia during the brief Kerensky interval before the Bolsheviks took over, after which he left. Zilboorg was quite a character. You might appreciate how a dramatic or terpsichorean flare is conducive to becoming an analyst for some people. Analysis is a curious field, and one of its hazards is that it does appeal to people who are highly individualistic. But this is one of its gifts too, one of its assets, even though it also may be a handicap, depending. That goes back to Freud's associations with a number of people he favored, many of whom were very gifted but not easy, and sometimes quite egocentric, and a few more than neurotic.

Before I took this elective, I had tried to find out, What is this strange thing, psychoanalysis? I couldn't get an answer or even an informative reading about it. It's a funny story. In order to inform myself and decide whether there was anything to it, I decided that

I would read one book that was pro-psychoanalysis and one book that was negative about analysis, and see if I could come to a decision between them. The book that seemed to be the most concise and inclusive about analysis was *The Essentials of Psychoanalysis*, which later became Fenichel's textbook, *The Psychoanalytic Theory of Neurosis*. I scanned that, and it really made very little sense to me. Then by chance I picked up a journal in the medical library—God knows what the journal was—perhaps it would have been something akin to parapsychology by now. In it there was an article that purported to report the reminiscences of a man in analysis who told of his recollections when he was a germ cell, when he was a sperm, and when he was an ovum. Well, I looked at that and thought, If that's psychiatry, it's really for the birds. I'd do better to go into the ministry, it wouldn't be as far out.

And then the other book that I found was a simple diatribe against psychoanalysis, such as one can easily find even nowadays. It was as clear as a bell. I had decided by the end of my second year in medical school that psychiatry was really for "kooks," and I had no intention of going into it. Nonetheless my interest persisted and I did take this elective with George Henry, who was a serious, dour man and who was carrying out a heavily funded research project on homosexuality. And that opened a whole world to me that I had never known, especially the gay world, as it was called, and I learned something about it, even picking up some of its glossary of colloquial terms. Later George Henry and his research assistant published several books on homosexuality from a descriptive point of view.

Henry wrote several other books, a textbook on psychiatry and another book on psychopathology. I remember asking George Henry if I could attend the junior staff conference at Payne Whitney. The answer came back, No. With a sly smile on his face, Dr. Henry told me that Dr. Diethelm didn't think it would be right for a medical student to be at a conference at which he might be contradicted. Marianne Horney Eckhart was Chief Resident then. I didn't know her, but the teaching in the outpatient department was quite good. We were all assigned cases there during our third or fourth year.

Despite my ambivalence during medical school, I remained interested in psychiatry. I did an internship at the Cincinnati General Hospital, a rotating internship in medicine and surgery, and spent one month on the psychiatric service in the course of it. I then decided to take a psychiatric residency and by chance applied at the old Boston Psychopathic, and that's how I came to be in Boston. I never left except for one year in Neurology at Bellevue Hospital in New York with Foster Kennedy and my years in the military. Kennedy was another quite colorful man, a North Irish Orangeman of great sartorial splendor with a gift of eloquent, elegant speech that was out of this world. The stories about him and that neurological residency, which was a rich experience, are fascinating, but it takes us away from other reminiscences; except that we did have an analyst come around to consult on some of the neurological cases, a woman who had come from Vienna or Berlin. I can't remember her name at the moment.

During my first year at the Psychopathic, I already found the propositions of analysis engaging, even though the actual psychiatric orientation at the hospital was psychobiological and Meyerian, with a descriptive Kraepelinian approach to diagnosis. There was a rapid turnover of patients, and as residents we had a rich exposure to psychopathology. We were expected to work up the patients conscientiously and thoroughly, and to manage their hospital stay in a competent fashion, but there was very little about the treatment of the patient that had depth, other than for those whose conditions were clearly organic in origin. Mostly, the emphasis seemed to be on diagnostic classification and a psychobiological approach to their total life history. If one restored the possibility of *mens sana in corpore sano,* a sound mind in a sound body, then all might go well.

A few psychiatrists there had gone to Europe for analytic training under Commonwealth Fund grants—Ives Hendrick, Mo Kaufman, and several others. But by the time I arrived on the scene such grants were no longer available. What's more, professor and head of the Psychopathic C. McFee Campbell—who was a scholar of the Old World, not an entrepreneurial head of psychiatry, but a genuinely scholarly, yet contained and restrained proper Scotsman—had apparently reconsidered his acceptance of analysis and support for analytic training. I think Hans Sachs was still analyzing some psychiatrists under fellowship support. One of them was in charge of hospital admissions and some administrative matters. He was very conservative and an isolationist, and we used to argue vehemently about the war in Europe, which was going so badly for the allies at the time, and the Nazi threat to western civilization and the United States. His analysis, about which he seemed quite secretive, seemed to have been going for "n" years. He was about as rigid and as tight a New Englander as I had met, which was no advertisement for analysis.

But I later heard that Hans Sachs never said very much, that presumably he just sat there by the year and said very little. Although he was clearly a gifted man and an original contributor to psychoanalysis, perhaps something might have been lacking, which was not true of the "Professor" himself [Freud], who was surely anything but inactive as an analyst. This is not sufficiently realized because of the reification of the metaphor of the mirror and the aseptic field, which probably were not intended as exact advice, per se, for the practice of analysis or psychotherapy. They were technical metaphors but are often used to bash Freud and analysis, depending on whether one is pro or con.

But I remember that I became more in touch with analysts. I was Chief of Service during my second year of residency training in psychiatry, and one of the juniors on the service was Helen Tartakoff. After the *Anschluss* she had come back from Vienna to finish medical school in this country and by this time was fulfilling a requirement for a year of inpatient psychiatry. At the same time, she was doing control analyses to complete her candidacy at the Boston Psychoanalytic Institute. We became good friends. I wanted to attend some of the seminars at the Institute. I couldn't understand it when I was told that wouldn't be possible because I wasn't a candidate. It made no sense to me; it seemed nepotistic, utterly precious, with psychoanalysis turned back on itself. The Institute reminded me of a Masonic organization, and I had no intention of being analyzed.

It all changed for me once I was in the Army Air Force. All of a sudden psychiatrists came into their own, and it was the analysts in uniform who filled the void with a rationale and approach to treatment of emotionally disturbed and traumatically decompensated soldiers. Through my family I had long known a prominent internist and cardiologist who used to talk of the "shell-shocked" and those who suffered from "effort syndrome," or the "cardiac neuroses" of the First World War. Apparently they had no definitive treatment for such emotionally determined breakdowns. Similar traumatic syndromes occurring during the Second World War were termed "combat fatigue" and "flying fatigue," and under Roy Grinker and John Spiegel a pentothal abreactive method of treatment was innovated. Douglas Bond was with the 8th Air Force in England, and John Murray was in North Africa.

While in the Army Air Force I was stationed for over two years at the Air Transport Command replacement training center in New Mexico, where I was the only psychiatrist for most of the time. However, at my request another psychiatrist was finally sent to help. Elmer H.—he didn't like his given name and insisted on being called Jack—had trained at Chestnut Lodge in Washington. He clearly felt superior because he was a psychotherapist and clearly believed he knew how to treat those soldiers who might say, "Oh, I really want to be a soldier; I don't want out, but I just can't do it because of my aching back." "Back" was back home where mother lived. I had received no training in or exposure to the "art" of psychotherapy at Boston Psychopathic and felt rather inadequate under those circumstances. Jack H. wasn't particularly forthcoming, and I suffered from his air of superiority and patronization, that he knew it all, knew what he was doing. His approach was to put such soldiers into the hospital, where he induced prolonged, sleepy states, using very sizable amounts of barbiturates over a period of several days. Then, while they were in such chemically induced hypnoid sleepy states, wherein their defenses were down, he would make use of the marked regression to promote an abreactive uncovering, probably within the matrix of a provocative transference. His aim was for the soldiers to experience and acknowledge their anxiety and hostility consequent to their separation from home, and to the military experience and setting. He would confront such soldiers with their regressive wish to return to a mother who might have been a haven but also infantilizing.

I managed to be sent for a six-week course in intensive abreactive psychotherapy given by the Air Force at the Don Cesar Hospital, formerly a fashionable hotel near St. Petersburg, Florida. This course was designed for the training of flight surgeons and other medical officers who would be involved in the care of flyers who had decompensated as a result of "flying fatigue," as it was called. For the most part they suffered from traumatic neuroses—although some had been acutely psychotic—induced by the stress of extended combat flying. The treatment and the program of training had been developed by Roy Grinker with the collaboration of John Spiegel, and there were a number of analysts on the staff. It was an eye-opener for me, and it was obvious that I had to have analytic training if I was to stay in psychiatry.

Subsequently I was sent to the Pacific zone of operations, where I was to develop a standard operating procedure for the safe air evacuation of acutely disturbed soldiers, many of whom might have become psychotic and possibly highly agitated, and even violent, in the course of combat. This was in anticipation of the expected invasion of Kyushu, presumably scheduled for the fall of 1945, and in anticipation of a very large number of casualties. The dropping of the bomb and the surrender of the Japanese, however, made that campaign unnecessary.

I was returned to Fort Devens to be discharged from the army, and I immediately applied to the Boston Institute. My application interviews were with Helene Deutsch, Grete Bibring, and Erich Lindemann, while I was still in uniform, but knowing I'd be out of the Army in a month or two. I arranged for analysis just as I was beginning terminal leave. That was the trend at the time. There was suddenly a very substantial push to be psychoanalytically trained. Also, I wouldn't have stayed in psychiatry if I couldn't have found some treatment approach which made some sense and had coherence. Just classifying, and then warehousing and medicating patients seemed to me like—well, I could have been a higher quality inventory clerk in a large department store. But this devalues the treatment approach of hospitalized patients before the war beyond what was so, and also was helpful.

In retrospect, and from a psychoanalytic perspective, many of the treatment approaches and procedures make sense, like understanding how cold packs and continuous hot tubs, humanely and expertly done, were useful in sedating or managing the agitated or violent patient. But we didn't have the perspective to understand it then. The people in the field I really enjoyed were the mavericks; I always have, even though it might not seem so, because I maintain a healthy skepticism, but I do not necessarily join in their views or positions.

So I came into analysis because I had to. It seemed to me a frightfully expensive thing, and I had no idea that it would be remunerative. It just seemed excessive to have to pay for analysis even though the fees were a fraction of what they are now, but perhaps not when you consider inflation. I had to borrow money and take a job with the Veterans Administration to pay for it, but it seemed a necessity at that time. And that's the way my training began; it was fascinating. The spirit of excitement was indeed there. Analysis filled the void that I and others like me had known. It hadn't been filled from any other direction, and without analysis, psychiatry seemed very slim. At that time neuroscience and neuropsychiatric issues were not unfolding as they are now. Neurology was predominantly taxonomic, so it really became necessary to find some kind of Weltanschauung out of which one might build a psychiatric career.

The fact is, it became well paid. Before long I was being referred private patients to analyze. Even as a candidate I felt I should at least have had title to a cornerstone of 15 Commonwealth Avenue because of the money I contributed toward the buying of that building. It is pertinent because we had to remunerate the Institute with all of our supervised analysis fees. I was sending the Institute hundreds of dollars every month; the only amount one could keep out was the supervisory fee, all the rest went to the Institute, for all the cases. From the first and second cases you hoped to recover enough to pay your supervisor. If you didn't, you took it out of pocket. By the third and fourth cases, if you had any competence—some had more than others—you might have patients referred who couldn't be placed with more established senior people, so they would go to the promising senior candidates, and they would pay the full private patient fees. Usually they weren't told they were controls; it was considered that doing so would skew the transference and the analysis.

I did not tell my control cases that the analysis was Institute-sponsored or supervised, because there seemed no necessity for it. There was no Institute analysis committee. If you were referred a patient for analysis, you were the analyst. By the time I was a senior candidate, I was sending the Institute $300-400 each month, a considerable sum in those days. But, really, what counted was the satisfaction of the experience of doing analysis. And the seminars, some of them were marvelous. I took some of the theoretical courses two or three times; over and over, because each time my understanding deepened. I took Instinct Theory twice with Edward Bibring, and once with Ives Hendrick, and before long, I, too, was teaching. At least, that was my experience. There was much less feeling of being put upon. It did seem promising that one could practice as an analyst, and that it could be financially and ecologically stimulating and satisfying.

I don't think there was the resentment that often comes into the setting now. I cannot recall thinking of the training as if it were an initiation rite, as if it was subordinating one's maturity; nor that it was infantilizing, a feeling that became endemic and that caused trouble in Boston and in some other institutes. I may have been lucky, because I made friendships with some of the established analysts. It started with my friendship with Helen Tartakoff and some of the others, and early on I was accepted into the circle of some of the people I respected and began to work with them; so that was in itself quite rewarding.

SRR: That brings up a question we had about the difference between training then and now.

AV: In retrospect, it seems to me that the training analyses were more formalistic then; that the emphasis was maximally upon maintaining analytic neutrality in order to maintain ambiguity and not to sway the transference. As I look back, interpersonalization of the transference was to be avoided. This was stressed more by some training analysts than others. Probably it depended upon whose analysand you were. There were "easy" analysts and "hard" analysts, which I've always inveighed against; those who went more by the "rules," and those who were more conversant and responsive; although it wasn't so much as mutually exclusive a matter as it might seem.

Various essays depict it that way; for example, Leo Stone—who called the period of rule-regulated exactitude in the practice of analysis "neoclassic," in contrast to analysis as it was actually practiced by Freud and his early associates—whose actual practice was more flexible than Freud's essays on technique suggest. Eissler's seminal 1951 essay on the "standard" analysis and the introduction of parameters was written in response to Alexander's proposals for manipulations of the transference to facilitate curative emotional corrective experience.

Yet, turning to current trends, it seems to me that analytic technique in both training analyses and the supervision of analyses carried out by candidates as part of their training has been tilted toward an emphasis upon relational aspects and object relations theory to the detriment of conflict analysis. Analytic training nowadays may minimize, or even overlook, the fact that failure to satisfactorily resolve conflicts originating out of the oedipal phase of development may still be a major determinant of neurosis, requiring understanding of the technique of the analysis of conflict and competence in analyzing character within the context of a classical analysis. Optimally, current technique should allow for a balance between the analysis of preoedipal and oedipal aspects, and between relational and intrapsychic conflict features, depending upon the specificity of the neurosis, or more than neurosis.

SRR: Could you tell us what a formal analysis was like?

AV: Well, there have been jokes which have caricatured it. They're not altogether wrong. For example, Lillian Ross' "Vertical and Horizontal," of at least 25 years ago. But I think the issue was that in a standard analytic situation, meeting with a patient who had a good ego structure and in whom the regression in the service of the analysis was not itself iatrogenically pathogenic, the analyst would try to restrict himself and contain himself to essentially explanatory interpretations—the issue of doing other things, of introducing other technical measures when necessary, with which I happen to agree, doesn't necessarily induce untoward regression, or a kind of depersonalization, or other things that go on with borderlines.

Usually the patient can understand the necessity for ambiguity and gradually appreciate it as useful. In those circumstances, one doesn't have to go in for all kinds of gimmicks to foster a therapeutic alliance, such as beginning with what I call chit-chat so that the patient knows you are human. I think that suggests a kind of infantilization of the patient's capacity to manage an anxiety-producing situation. After all, an analytic situation is bound to be uncomfortable at first; it is difficult to talk to somebody about personal things uncensored and to a total stranger whom one has no reason to trust. I might say this even to a strong ego patient as an acknowledgment and clarification of how the analytic situation is first experienced, especially its implications for the emerging transference, but the primary intention in intervening this way is not to establish an alliance which otherwise might not be there.

The analytic work itself, if properly and sensitively done, enhances an initial trust and establishes an alliance toward the mutualization of a shared experience and project. Freud put it that analyst and analysand share a mutual love of truth, albeit that this is easier said than done, like so much in analysis and psychotherapy. There was a period with Elizabeth Zetzel, I think, in which relatively superficial talking in a vis-à-vis setting was considered an essential therapeutic measure so that the patient would have the experience of confirming that the analyst was a real person.

If a patient is actually in doubt that the analyst is a real person, and needs to have it reinforced by being told, "Sure, put your feet, shoes and all, on the couch," or, "If you need to go out, go out," then the analyst is into a different situation and has begun to tilt the transference prematurely and unnecessarily. To echo to some extent the patient's remarks, just to prove that I am an empathic listener, or that "I'm a better mother than your mother," is to play out the

"Chicago game" in a kind of artificial way. On the other hand, though, there are times when mutually known empathic resonance might be pivotal in the clinical situation. What is ultimately called for is understanding what the clinical situation is and who you are dealing with, as well as the ability to be flexible for specific clinical reasons, rather than on the basis of pop psychology or some fashionable trend.

As I mentioned earlier with respect to Eissler's essay on standard technique, the issue at that time—largely in response to Alexander's innovative but essentially radical proposals, which really continued from where Ferenczi left off—was that the introduction of parameters outside of or beyond the "set" of standard procedures would so deviate from standard analytic procedure and technique that the analytic process would be deleteriously affected or nullified. To an extent, the boundary between analysis and psychotherapy would be blurred and, consequently, an analysis might well become "schlampig," not just wild but sloppy. To some extent this is a valid theoretical and technical issue which bears upon the analytic procedure, but by no means does it suggest that the analyst in a standard or classical analysis is other than human. What's come to light, of course, is that Freud, as a practicing analyst, did not wear an English frock coat or go through a decontamination chamber. The cigar went with him into his consulting room, and so did his dog. I think it was with the introduction of ego psychology that a certain kind of analytic rigor or exactitude began to take hold, in order to define or to make explicit what the defenses were and to more thoroughly analyze them, as well as the transference.

But as I look back, in the days of my candidacy there were always those analysts whose particular characterological ways and predilections definitely influenced their way of carrying through an analysis. One senior training analyst I recall was quite the CEO—avuncular, dramatic, and confrontational, sometimes helpfully so. He was certainly a bit more hysteric rather than a bit more obsessional. Another highly revered analyst was an ultimate Buddha. His interventions and interpretations centered on evoking affects, an approach that has now found a more meaningful place in psychoanalytic technique than it did then.

To discuss it adequately would be a long, complicated matter, especially in light of the current priority accorded the theory of object relations and the importance of experience and reenactments in the transference. I must say that I better appreciate these issues now, and with more comfort than when I was groping toward them in 1955–1956, when I first became interested in the element of affect in analysis. Even then it seemed to me that the extent to which affect was involved in the analytic process was somehow not being appreciated, and I became quite interested in Ferenczi's proposals for an active technique. Perhaps it had much to do with the emphasis then being placed on the cognitively explicable and the cognitively interpretable features of the analytic material—everything should be truly verbal, so far as possible.

SRR: Were formal analyses more oedipally oriented?

AV: Yes, but that's not a matter of formal analysis. You can have a formal analysis now that might include the preoedipal, and as such, it might change how the issues are dealt with technically. However, it is true that the emphasis then was more upon oedipal features. Although early preoedipal issues were not being denied, they weren't centrally of interest. Even more so, that goes back to before ego analysis, but with ego analysis and with the analysis of the defenses, one was already involved in preoedipal aspects—for example, whether the defenses are predominantly archaic and indicative of early preoedipal developmental issues, rather than later evolved socially conditioned defenses such as identification, reaction formation, and intellectualization in a healthy adaptive way.

However, I don't think preoedipal aspects were clinically in the forefront, nor usually explicitly analyzed, except probably in England with the Kleinians and the object relationists who were about to make their entry on the psychoanalytic stage. Some of them went too far though; they went not only the distance, but the superdistance, and they flew off like Bugs Bunny over space, not looking down so as not to fall. And that's exactly where the problem is. So often schools of analysis, which have a contribution to make, fall into this position of *pars pro toto,* as Freud noted in his 1914 essay, "The Wolfman." Early deviationists, like Adler and Jung, and later Wilhelm Reich and Otto Rank, when they elaborated quite different clinical and theoretical positions, took off, as it were, to fly the whole distance on one wing.

In my opinion that includes the self psychology school of Kohut and his followers. Their ideas for revision or modification of psychoanalytic theory and practice are not usually integrated with what is still valid and heuristic from the past and the main line of psychoanalysis, nor offered with due proportion in that respect. In reaction, those like myself, who are from the tradition of "classical" analysis, albeit not rigid or doctrinaire, get our backs up in opposition.

As a matter of fact, a recent publication reported on a panel which addressed Hans Loewald's "On the Therapeutic Action of Psychoanalysis: A Classic Revisited." They praised Loewald because he had emphasized "the centrality of interaction and of object-relations,...a far cry from the idea of exact interpretation." But they also faulted him because he had tried to place it within the more traditional frame of analysis, as it was in 1962. Since he was really making a radical departure from traditional analysis, he should have declared himself a radical. It was implied that not doing so was something of a weakness, but I don't think so. Nonetheless, they felt he should be recognized and honored for his break with tradition, even though he apparently did not go the whole distance, or acknowledge that he was making a radical departure from accepted theory.

SRR: Having read your essay, "On Attachment to Pain and the Negative Therapeutic Reaction," we are interested in your thoughts about working with patients who have such limits on how far they are able to develop.

AV: I didn't look for such patients, but having found such a patient, or the patient having found me, I had to carry through as best I could. Then, if you stay with "more difficult" patients through the *Sturm and Drang* of it, you are likely to learn something. I can think of an instance when, shortly after I had graduated as an analyst and had opened a private office, my own analyst sent me a young man for analytic treatment. I was very grateful for the opportunity, but this young man came, just sat opposite me, and said hardly a word. He just glowered and I couldn't get anything out of him. He did come, however. The history was that he had been discharged from the Navy for schizophrenia, and no doubt he was schizoid. He was markedly obsessional and intensely compulsive, with disabling repeating rituals. He couldn't read more than a page without going back to start all over again. He lived in isolation, eating sweets and fast foods in binges, and I didn't know how to get going, to get any kind of therapy to move.

A gifted child therapist and colleague of mine, Kurt Rose, was working at Judge Baker, which was then on Joy street. I would see him walking on Commonwealth Avenue or in the Public Gardens with these children, who were nine, ten, thirteen, and he'd take them out for what was evidently a walking-talking therapy, and I even tried to do the same, to take my patient out for a walk. Finally, after a few weeks of this, I went back to my analyst and said, "I don't think I can treat this man, it's impossible to get anywhere, I didn't realize he was so sick." And he said, "Don't worry about getting anywhere, just see what you can understand." It was a great relief. I had been given permission not to have a success.

So I went back, and I did whatever I could. I tried to understand him at the same time that I was actively working with him. On one hand I'd say, "If we can't get anywhere, you'll have to go to a hospital," which pushed him because he neither wanted to go to a hospital nor did he want to be not so alienated from the world and his family. And then when we got working together, to communicate, that would threaten him, and he'd retreat into an "obstipated" silence and withdrawal. Over the 7–10 years that we worked together, though, we slowly achieved a result I would never have predicted.

Even though he remained a curious man with strongly obsessional trends, he started working effectively in his family's business and ultimately married and had children. It was an outcome I wouldn't have dreamed. It was the issue of understanding and a sustained relationship of trust and communication that proved pivotal. Such considerations are still to be borne in mind, because analysis can be long and tedious, and can become sinecures for both the patient and the analyst.

I am a member of a study group trying to study the "prolonged analysis," and we touch on such matters as the fact that the analyst may grow dependent on his very long-term patient just as the patient grows dependent upon him, and that patient and analyst may arrive at a mutuality which is no longer analysis. At that point one has to ask of oneself, What is going on? One is not entitled to maintain an extended analysis just because it is mutually comfortable or well-paid. Should you reach that point where everything negative is transference and everything positive is reality, then you've caught the analytic disease.

LR: How did your interest in preoedipal issues develop?

AV: I think it began early. I felt that in some ways—in my own experience as a candidate, in my own analysis, in the supervised analyses, and in the continuous case presentations—that something was missing. I came to appreciate the role of affect as more than a way of reaching understanding for purposes of interpretation; that is, that the abreaction was not just a relief, but a way of knowing what was true experientially, so that you could explain it. Even that, though, was not quite enough. I became interested in not only what is now called cognitive developmental psychology, but also in what might be termed "affect developmental psychology."

As early as 1955, I took a sabbatical in England and became a participant in a setting for child analysis which I have continued all these years. That took me further into my interest in affect, into the emotional set that is there from the word "go"; that the affect in the interplay between the mother and her infant, and then her young child couldn't be put to the side.

In retrospect, I can see that it took me toward the interactive experience with the object. I was about ready to travel on an object relations streetcar, even though I am not an object relationist per se, not in a "card-carrying" way. Implicitly, I was interested in object relations, but I didn't write of it as such for some time, because it would have become muddled in dogmatic controversy, which is really regrettable. When I went to England, I was already very stimulated by Ferenczi's essays on an active technique, because throughout my career as a psychoanalyst I have been interested in theories of "cure" and of technique, and the stalemating of analyses. Also, I had good teachers, who taught psychoanalysis from a historical perspective, both in its theoretical and in its technical dimensions. Some of these courses, in my opinion, have never been equalled. The Hungarian school, Ferenczi and his followers, like Balint, did not depart or become excluded from the mainstream of psychoanalysis, like Adler and Jung.

Jung became so caught up with mythology, that he was something of a religious; however, I wouldn't quite call him a mystic. The notion of an inchoate unconscious with its animae and its universality; the universal myths being handed down through Lamarckian evolution—it's an engaging romance, but it's no more true than Rider Haggard's *The Queen of Sheba*, which was wonderful reading. I was enthralled by such stories and would read such books under the desk in grammar school. As a child I wasn't interested in my classes, and often I was not paying attention. My teachers would sometimes call on me, and I might not answer as I was reading under the desk and was in another world. I was getting C's in my classwork because I was in the land of fantasy and inattentive.

As an analyst, people paid me to listen to their stories, both told and reenacted in their lives and in the transference—their experiences, or lack of them, or whatever. Perhaps it wasn't always fair, and perhaps I should have paid them, or at least the true storytellers, but just think what that would have done to the transference, not to mention the countertransference. It is probably from there that my interest in analysis began, for during a pivotal time of my childhood I became immersed in myths and stories; the Greek myths and Norse Gods, *The Adventures of Robin Hood*, *King Arthur and His Round Table*, imaginative stories of prehistoric man, seafarers before the mast, and the like.

LR: It seems to me that for you to have written the essay "Attachment to Painful Feelings," you had to have a certain kind of ear to hear the preoedipal material. It particularly struck me in the Schwaber book that your attention in the transference was to the preoedipal issues, you were talking about listening to those kinds of affects, and how they are expressed....

AV: Watching the experiential realm in reenactment, I am struck by the fact that if I go to the mimes, there is no spoken word. The richness of the tale is conveyed by the affect quality of voice and the expressive face of the tragedian; or the masks so characteristic of drama, or comedy, or tragedy; or in the theatre of the absurd, it is the improvisational spontaneity that seems so close to our work.

SRR: I noticed that at a 1983 meeting at PINE, reported in the *Psychoanalytic Quarterly,* you stated that an analysis hadn't gone as far as it might unless a patient's capacity for wordplay had developed. Is that the kind of level you're talking about? Interactional?

AV: Yes, interactional in a way, but that doesn't mean transactional as the prime intent or prime mover. The word is a pivot to the experiential realm and to the body and the visceral. Often it is the play on a word that counts, rather than its manifest meaning as cloak or cover. Much of the affect is likely to be bound into the variations and play upon the word. That is why poetry is an aesthetic road to the emotional and experiential realm in a most exquisite way, or poetic prose, or words without songs, or songs without words, or both together, depending upon the personal bent of the individual. If you have songs without words, the words must be there too, somewhere. And if you have words without songs, the songs must be there too. Have you ever heard Mendelssohn's "Songs Without Words," or Rachmaninov's "Vocalyse," or Villa-Lobos's song with cellos of his "Bachianas Brasileiras" suite?

When I listen to my patients, the songs and the words come back from all ages of my life. In consonance with a patient, as he speaks of his loneliness and longing, I may hear, "All alone by the telephone, and it never rings for me." With a patient who is searching for restoration of his self-esteem, I may think of that line from Schumann's "Widmung," "You are my better self." Some of these ballads are sentimental, some are not.

My interest grew because I felt that my interpretations were sometimes inadequate; that they didn't reach what was really going on; and that if I introduced an interpretation that seemed right, it might be outside the realm of what could be remembered, making it an artifact which was out of place and/or time. So it became incumbent on me to follow more appropriately, as I resonantly listened to each patient through the reenactments and the recapitulations in the living transference. It's a living transference, not a dead transference; the words to say it and to explain it run on parallel tracks. You can't always cross over, but it's therapeutically relevant—within the scope of analysis as a theory of therapy, and even what used to be called a theory of "cure"—to be ambient within these parallel tracks.

To articulate both the experiential and the explanatory lends coherence for the adult who is caught up in the recapitulation of his or her life as a child. An analyst who is sensitively aware of the transference cannot get out of it because it is largely through the transference as it unwinds, and unwinds, and unwinds, that an analysis takes place. Above all, it is through words and the perspective afforded through reenactment in the transference and extratransference that analyst and patient together work their way back and come to know that earlier life of the patient, or at least feel that you, the analyst, have come to know salient parts of that earlier life, and it is more than just narrative truth. The search is toward the genetic paradigms of conflict and developmental mishap, and the achievement of veritable insight regarding them.

Just the other day at the Child and Adolescent Service of a local hospital I heard the case presentation of a two-year, seven-month-old child, whose mother went off the trail into a tree while skiing. She was so badly injured that she was in a coma for four months. Finally, she emerged from the coma, aphasic and with the use of only one arm. She is now able now to understand and give some responses, and has begun to use a computer board to communicate.

Just lately she has asked to see her child, who has been with the father's parents ever since she went off on the skiing trip with a man other than the father of the child, with whom she was breaking up. The question is, How do you prepare this child to visit the mother in rehabilitation? The child was closely attached to her mother but hadn't seen her mother since this tragic interruption and interval.

A number of questions arose: When does a child develop a sense of the future, or an orientation regarding the past, present, and future? When is it possible for a child to comprehend death? When does a child gain some sense of permanence? When is prolonged separation not just traumatic abandonment, but emotionally tolerable and understandable? Certainly not at two and a half.

When we deal with patients, we have to bear in mind that we deal with them at every age they have gone through. We may discern developmental aspects in cross-section, as they vary and yet coexist in montage, much like a developmental CAT scan. At any one time in the psychoanalytic situation when an interpretation or any intervention (including silence) is made, it is implicitly addressable to all levels at the same time, although not with equal relevance to all developmental levels. Within and without the transference, all developmental levels are present, but in different hierarchical order and priority, depending upon factors both present and past, and where the analytic process is active at the time.

A patient, who at a particular moment may be caught up with feelings and memories, and with conflict within a particular developmental level of organization and conflict, may respond to an interpretation, "Well, you are right, but I feel angry at you; you don't understand me!" That is not where I am at right now. Although I may be in the content of my interpretation, I may be addressing a conflict which is not specific to the time frame my patient is at at that moment. More than just a matter of my listening, I am also alerted to what extent I am really tuned in and what effect I am having on that patient within the transference, as well as in reality. Such considerations never came up in this form during my training.

LR: Where have you found support for developing these ideas?

AV: I find it comfortable now to take up many aspects of object relations theory and practice, and even some of the Kleinian configurations as long as I don't have to buy the whole book. I'd rather pick and choose. As I recently told a colleague who is a disciple of Kohut and totally into self psychology, You know I'm not as completely closed to Kohut as it may appear, even though he turns me off for a variety of reasons, but I have to take it in my own way. Erikson, too, made a signal contribution to psychoanalysis in his elaboration of an inclusive psychosocial epigenetic schema of development. But to make a whole book, a *pars pro toto,* out of a technical innovation, or a chapter of psychoanalytic theory, or the substantial revision of a section of it without integrating it into the evolving book as a whole, is, to my thinking, the real hazard.

As a candidate and as a beginning analyst, I felt there had not been a sufficient integration of developmental aspects of the affective component in my own experience, and in my work with patients. Nor had it come up sufficiently in the course of my supervised experience. So I began to grope for it, and by 1955 I had become especially stimulated by Ferenczi's controversial essays on an active technique in instances of stalemated analysis. In 1962, I wrote an essay, "Affect, Emotional Re-living and Insight in the Psychoanalytic Situation," in which I tried to integrate these considerations. In it, I gave affect a more adequate place in the analytic process and situation, but not quite in the way I would do it now.

SRR: What is it like to live with so much transference, with so much reenactment?

AV: Notwithstanding the centrality of transference in the psychoanalytic process, I don't live with transference only. Transference is one room, as it were, that is always there, but I am not restricted to it. Using computers for purposes of analogy, the notion of parallel processing makes enormous sense, because in practice, while the patient's productions are heard and understood cognitively and emotionally, they are also evocative of associations and empathic currents of feeling in the analyst. While I am listening to the patient's communications in the present, I am also hearing the same communications with reference to his or her past.

All of these vectors are within the process simultaneously, even though I am not, nor could I be, equally attendant to each and all of them at the very same moment. But within a level of "free floating" awareness I can and do switch the searchlight of attention back and forth, here and there, depending upon the time, place, and relevance of the psychoanalytic material as it evolves. That also includes material within the transference, and, simultaneously, this same material outside of it, past and present. "Jack be nimble, Jack be quick," is the order for the analyst's jumping stick.

SRR: It reminds me of evenly hovering attention.

AV: Yes, not only the word associations, though, but also other symbolic transformations and displacements, and the various vectors which overdetermine the analytic material. As the time frame moves back and forth, past–present, present–future, that is, the anticipated future, all the elements—inclusive also of thought, feeling, action, word–thing, word–abstraction, word–concrete—of them are carried within the ambient time frame. There is a certain mobility of the analytic material, within and outside of the transference, and there is a constant shifting of it. If I am overwhelmed by any reenactment, I have to ask myself, Have I become overinvolved because that's my thing? I think that happened with Semrad who was totally into affect, even though he is deified for his limitless patience in eliciting and tolerating it in the treatment of psychotics. Or perhaps through the transference the patient may unconsciously inveigle the analyst into it because it's the only game in town for him, and then, again, is it just too much?

That's when I welcome more mobility of the analytic material. If a patient repeatedly and inveterately reacts in intensely emotional ways, "carrying on" as it were, then you are likely to be dealing with a person with borderline issues, especially if the affect is at an unstructured, unmodulated primal level. I used to meet with a supervisee who was carrying a heavy caseload of sick, borderline adolescents and young adults, and at one point I said, Maybe you want a practice like this, but you can accept just so many such patients before you burn out. Perhaps you should decide for yourself just how much of this you can undertake at any one time.

SRR: At a talk you gave several years ago at PINE, you said that if an analysis went beyond four years you would wonder, you would look very carefully—

AV: Well, I cut it too short by several years. It came up in a prolonged analysis study group. What I meant was not necessarily four years, or that there should be a set time for analysis. Historically, there is an interesting curve about the length of analysis, anyway, and there's also a geographical index. I think that both are bell curves. What the length of the usual, adequate, successful analysis should be depends on where you are. Why should it be seven years in one part and three and a half years in another part of New York City, or four years in Southern California? How did it happen to be a walk in the park for Ferenczi with Freud, and what does that mean? It is to some extent an expression of the changing scope of analysis, what's brought into the purview of the analytic experience.

Analysis started out to be a symptom treatment much like hypnosis. Analysis almost immediately became a conflict psychology and its earliest goal was symptom alleviation or dissolution. Character aspects were there, but they were really almost beyond the treatment until Wilhelm Reich came along and began to shatter character armor in his aggressive, possibly even persecutory approach. He was a gifted man, but very intrusive, both in his healthier period and in his later period, with his orgone mythology. With the notion that analysis is always character analysis, some say that the nosological question is, Has neurosis changed? Is it the "neurosis of our time," as Karen Horney said? Or, as some well-known analysts might say, is this the narcissistic age? They would coincide with Christopher Lasch, who wrote about that from a sociological point of view. Well, it depends upon what the therapeutic intention and ambition is.

The Kleinians probably would say, "Analysis is not complete until you reach far back into the depressive position and the paranoid position of the first year of life, to the split-object position, and the good and the bad breast, pathological envy, and so forth. You start with that, and you end with that, even if it may take you 'n' years to get back to that, because that's where the neurosis always begins. Neurosis is the converse of the psychosis, not of the perversion."

I think I constantly reflect upon this, but at a certain point I might ask, Where are we? Where are we likely to go? At what point am I continuing the analysis for reasons of my own? Is it time for the patient to interrupt, even if we haven't dotted every "I" or crossed every "t," or is there more to be gained which warrants continuing? Is there more to analyze which could be fruitful and mutative for change? I might silently query myself in such a fashion at four years, five years, six years, or beyond, but I surely want to ask myself these questions from time to time. I don't mean to suggest that analyses of four years are long enough. It often depends on external circumstances and pragmatic issues.

I once supervised an analysis wherein an academic had to move to another geographic area because he hadn't obtained tenure in this area. He didn't want to leave, nor did his analyst want to stop the analysis because more could have been done analytically. Yet he couldn't afford to remain here, as he might be without a job and at an academic dead end. That really accelerated certain aspects of the analysis, as if a date had been set. This is exactly what Otto Rank proposed as an innovation of what he finally called "will therapy"; that a date should be set, and set in force the battle of wills for autonomy, to deal with the birth trauma and emergence into the outer world with which every human being has to cope. And in due course they had better face that trauma and its aftermath; so the date is set, and the person has to mobilize his will and leave [the nest].

LR: What was your earlier involvement in analytic research?

AV: Well, there were some attempts when I was involved with the Bibrings and the Beth Israel Hospital. One analyst who had a great effect on me was Edward Bibring. As I look back, he was a theoretician of great distinction, a marvelous teacher. He was handicapped by having Parkinson's and died prematurely. I followed a great many of his interests as they happened to coincide with my own bent. He wanted me to write a book on ego psychology with him, but I wasn't yet ready to do that. It should have been his book, but he was quite an obsessional man and too involved with his own illness, and he could no longer do it. Nor had I relaxed enough myself, and I was too inexperienced as an analyst. Nonetheless, he wrote this marvelous essay on "Psychoanalysis and the Dynamic Psychotherapies" in 1954. It has been lost sight of now, but in my opinion it is still a very applicable essay.

I don't know of any other formulation and schema that sets forth a psychoanalytic frame of reference with working constructs with which it becomes possible to understand clinically and to succinctly specify what takes place according to a theory of psychotherapy and a theory of "cure." That was his interest. He was starting a research project at the Beth Israel Hospital on the nature of the therapeutic process when he ran out of steam. It would have been an enormous job, and perhaps it would have been impossible. Not long afterwards, I became involved in Grete Bibring's pregnancy study. It was a major research project, and I was very active in it.

LR: What was she looking at in particular?

AV: Pregnancy as a normal maturational experience, as a normative crisis towards the maturation of the girl/woman into womanhood. It was her intention to study normal pregnancy in presumably normal women, but our subjects proved to be more or less neurotic.

LR: These were women who weren't in treatment?

AV: No, they were selected from the obstetrical service—primigravidae who agreed to participate and who were successively chosen from the obstetrical clinic.

LR: Were they followed postpartum?

AV: They were followed postpartum for a period. The findings became so engrossing that our hope was to start a small nursery group in order to follow the children, but the research ran out of money and the research group disbanded. This was a project of thirty years ago, and was a heavily funded NIMH project. It was a time when one could do that sort of thing, an extensive longitudinal analytically oriented study, but it was interminable. The voluminous typescripts and other material are in the archives of The Henry A. Murray Research Center of Radcliffe College. I learned a lot from it, as did others, and finally I did write a few outcome articles....

SRR: Is there any kind of analytic research you would like to see undertaken today?

AV: I am still interested in the therapeutic process, and still doing something in that direction with small study groups of a few analysts, meeting now and again, one of them in New York that I participate in about once a month during the academic year, and another here with a few analysts with whom I have worked for some years.

LR: Could you tell us more about your time in England?

AV: I could never stay in London for extended periods, because I would have had to give up my practice. I went originally for four months, and, in 1962, my family actually moved there for a year. We took an apartment in Hampstead, and I joined them for three-month intervals on two occasions that year. In between I would come back, continuing my practice with these three-month interruptions.

It was manageable, but it didn't work out all that well. For one patient, it was unfortunate and she had to be hospitalized. To go for a continuous stay of a year or more I would have had to shut down my practice and give up earning anything. So I would visit the Hampstead Clinic for as long as I could, perhaps for a few weeks each year, extending into our summer holiday, and continue to be actively involved when I was there. I still go to the annual Scientific Colloquium at the Clinic, now called the Anna Freud Centre, every fall and take part in it.

LR: Did you have any contact with Winnicott?

AV: No, the only time I ever saw him is when he came here to give a paper.

LR: And at the Hampstead Clinic, it was largely Anna Freud?

AV: Yes, it was only Anna Freud and the clinic faculty, inclusive of some members of the B group of the British Institute who were quite separate from the Kleinians and even from the Middle group of the British Institute. The Middle group was largely the people who became the object relationists, taking conflict theory and particular aspects of metapsychology from the B group, who are the Freudian traditionalists, and from the Kleinians a considerable part of their theory about very early development and technical innovations in consequence of their theory; split objects, the good breast and the bad one, envy, and so forth, but without requiring of themselves all of one group or the other.

For a while, I couldn't quite understand what they represented, and I don't think they, themselves, knew. Nor do I think they knew that they were evolving predominantly as an object relations school. The Middle Group are now called the Independent Group, perhaps because that was their raison d'être—that they were independent of either of the established positions, either the A or the B group. It was a curious solution to settle the controversy confronting the British Society/Institute that way, to avoid an explicit organizational split.

LR: Where do you see the field of psychoanalysis going? Looking ahead, where do you think it will be in terms of people actually practicing?

AV: It's going in so many directions right now that it is difficult to know. The question in my mind is not where it's going, but whether a coherent and consistent Freudian psychoanalytic hub will remain from which the different directions can continue to emerge and develop, but without being emptied from within. It's a little bit like opening an umbrella—you can open the umbrella and you can stretch the umbrella, but at what point does the umbrella grow so thin and become so porous that it shelters nobody and nothing? And that`s the problem for analysis.

At the IPA Congress in Montreal, Wallerstein gave as his presidential address a paper titled "One Psychoanalysis or Many?" How many psychoanalyses can we have without a unifying theme, other than the fact that one might look at the same person clinically and then, using identical or similar terms for the most part but with different theories and concepts in mind, talk about clinical issues? We might come to a psychoanalytic babel, yet saying, in effect, that they are really not so far from each other. But if they are no longer able to communicate in a mutually meaningful way, we will have lost the psychoanalytic centrum, both historically and currently, and that is what I'm concerned about.

Perhaps that is why I am inclined to be cautious about innovations in psychoanalytic theory and practice. If that is conservative, then I believe in being conservative, but with an open mind and an open ear, and conserving for current use only what seems heuristic and historically valid from the past. I always remember the story of Charles Ives, whose father was a Civil War bandleader. As I understand it, all of his children were musically gifted, but he insisted that they go to proper musical conservatories and to have a traditional musical education. He said, "I don't worry about where you go afterwards, but I want you to know from where you came." And if we don't have the place from where we came with analysis more or less held in common and with sufficient consensus, analysis will be fragmented and probably atomized.

SRR: What are your thoughts about training analysis versus therapeutic analysis? Are they relatively the same or quite different?

AV: They're the same, except, paradoxically, they are different. The training analysis usually adds features and ambitions—not that the training analysis should be faulted on these accounts—which are not only human, but also extrinsic to the aim of analysis, per se, which may then qualify the freedom of the analysis. This is irrespective of whether it is a reporting or nonreporting institute setting. The trend nowadays is to make the training analysis an absolutely nonreported part of the educational curriculum, and to leave it entirely to the supervisors and seminar instructors to evaluate the progress of the candidate and his or her suitability to become a psychoanalyst. I, however, don't think they can do so adequately.

If you are analyzing a person who happens to be a computer scientist, or a musician, it isn't as if he has to compromise what he says in an analysis by reason of what he does in his computer work or in his music. But what if that person is going to analyze others with one set of values for analysis and yet have another set for himself or herself. To what extent does that coincide with what Freud called a mutual love of truth or honesty? If this isn't as consistent within oneself as it should be for one's patient, what kind of analyst will one be? Does the analyst then talk out of both sides of the mouth—one for oneself and the other for the patient?

A training analysis introduces that sort of complexity, and perhaps that issue amongst others, can be something of a burden. There is no doubt that the training analysis is more complicated, and it could happen that the candidate in training might very well think; well, this is what you say when you're sitting here, but I've heard stories that you've done such and such outside. Fair enough, fair enough; but how is that to be understood? Maybe it's true that one can remain in an artifactual, isolated compartment in the analysis, as if it were taking place in an anechoic chamber, and that outside of it things are different, but somewhere they have to connect. I think analysis suffered very greatly from that. On the other hand, analysis has also been enriched; that is the value of the training analysis, to learn what analysis is all about, firsthand, very personally.

I think I learned something about the meaningfulness of affect in my own analysis, and by the fact that it would have been well had I come to know it more thoroughly within the intricacies of the analysis. In consequence, I had to find my way further into it, however I could, inclusive of my work with patients and the nature of my interests outside of analysis. Perhaps that comes out of earlier times, out of one's childhood, too. Out of experiences wherein a child may feel that the "good mother" has failed in some salient way, he or she may yearn for and anticipate that someday he or she will find someone who really understands them. By chance, this "someone" may turn out to be the analyst, and lead to the glow of an idealizing transference, what Kohut called, "the grandiose transference."

The notion of a perfection of understanding within an ultra-sensitive empathy, however excessive this idealization of the empathic listener may be, sooner or later must leave room for that "unlust" or disenchantment which coincides with resistance to interpretation of the derivatives of warded off conflict and its unconscious paradigm sources. How else can one learn to know such matters except through the personal, that is, the training analysis?

LR: Has your involvement with PINE represented an attempt to create a hub, a desire to ensure the existence of a group of people keeping a standard for psychoanalysis?

AV: That's what was intended when it split, because beyond issues of personality and personal dissension, there was a genuine fear, and as I view it retrospectively, a justified apprehension that analysis in Boston, analysis as the core of the Society/Institute, would be lost in the hectic, antagonistic, "reformist," egalitarian thrust for change and psychoanalytic eclecticism. By analysis, I do not mean a dogma or a codified set of rules and observances, but a psychoanalysis which has a certain priority as a frame of reference, as a centrum within which candidates might be trained, from which they might go out, and to which they might return as a coherent discipline.

Looking back at the level of rhetoric of those days, and recalling some of those who were in the forefront of dispute, I think there was basis for that apprehension. Some of us felt quite strongly that analysis might very well be lost in a divisively eclectic outcome for the training situation. That was our concern, and our contention. Whether it has proven so, or to what extent, I'm not in a position to know, nor do I know. By now, I think it's for the candidates and faculty who are involved in the teaching, with more contact with things as they are now, to come to some impression, or conclusion.

LR: In our interviews with senior candidates and recent graduates, they expressed strong positive feelings about their analytic training. Some commented on the power of the unconscious. The feeling we had when talking to them was that they had seen enough of it to really believe that there was something to it, and they had very little question about that. It was a real thing, not just something one talked about.

AV: The unconscious is a real reservoir to dip into in searching toward the riddle of oneself, the riddle of life. It's also a creative source which is where it's the most fun. I made a site visit not long ago to a troubled institute, and sat in with a group of their candidates. The most positive thing about it was that they reflected exactly what you just said, which reassured me that the training situation there couldn't be all bad. Troubles there were aplenty, but at least a viable psychoanalytic education was palpable, because the seminar I observed was at a stimulating and scholarly level, and the candidates were really enthusiastic and felt that they were gaining something very worthwhile.

LR/SRR: Thank you very much.

SELECTED BIBLIOGRAPHY

Valenstein, A. F., Michaels, J. J., & Evje, M. (1953). Aspects of character in the neurotic veteran. *Journal of Nervous and Mental Disease,* Vol. 117, pp. 445–457.

Valenstein, A. F. (1958). The psychoanalytic concept of character (Panel, American Psychoanalytic Association, December, 1957). *Journal of the American Psychoanalytic Association,* Vol. 6, pp. 567–575.

Bibring, G. L., Dwyer, T. F., Huntington, D. S., & Valenstein, A. F. (1961). A study of the psychological processes in pregnancy and of the earliest mother-child relationships: 1. Some propositions and comments. 2. Methodological considerations. *The Psychoanalytic Study of the Child,* Vol. 16, pp. 9–72; Appendix B: A glossary of defenses, by A. F. Valenstein, pp. 62–71. New Haven, CT: Yale University Press.

Valenstein, A. F. (1962). The psycho-analytic situation: affects. emotional reliving, and insight in the psycho-analytic process. *International Journal of Psycho-Analysis,* Vol. 43, pp. 315–324.

Valenstein, A. F. (1964). Comment on "Silence in psychoanalysis." *International Journal of Psycho-Analysis*, Vol. 45, pp. 310–311.

Valenstein, A. F. (1965). On analytic goals and criteria for termination. *Bulletin of the Philadelphia Association for Psychoanalysis*, Vol.15, pp. 110–113.

Valenstein, A. F. (1968) Indications and contraindications of psychoanalytic treatment. *International Journal of Psycho-Analysis*, Vol. 49, p. 265.

Valenstein, A. F. (1968). Panel on psychoanalytic drive theory in relation to recent developments (reported by H. Dahl). *Journal of the American Psychoanalytic Association,* Vol. 16, pp. 613–637.

Heimann, P. & Valenstein, A. F. (1972). The psycho-analytic concept of aggression: an integrated summary. *International Journal of Psycho-Analysis,* Vol. 53, pp. 31–35.

Valenstein, A. F. (1973). On attachment to pain and the negative therapeutic reaction. *The Psychoanalytic Study of the Child*, Vol. 28, pp. 365–392. New Haven: Yale University Press.

Valenstein, A. F. (1974). On transference (Report of panel, International Psychoanalytic Association, July 23, 1973). *International Journal of Psycho-Analysis,* Vol. 55, pp. 311–321.

Valenstein, A. F. (1974). Toward a theory of affects (Panel, American Psychoanalytic Association, December, 1973, reported by P. Castelnuovo-Tedesco). *Journal of the American Psychoanalytic Association*, Vol. 22, pp. 612–625.

Bibring, G.L. & Valenstein, A. F. (1976). Psychological aspects of pregnancy. In: *Clinical Obstetrics and Gynecology*, Vol. 19, pp. 357–371. Hagerstown, MD: Harper and Row.

Valenstein, A. F. (1979). The concept of "classical" psychoanalysis. *Journal of the American Psychoanalytic Association,* Vol. 27 (Suppl.), pp. 113–136.

Valenstein, A. F. (1980). The transition from girlhood to womanhood: A unique shift in the self-image during pregnancy. In: *The Child in His Family: Preventive Child Psychiatry in an Age of Transition*, ed. E. J. Anthony & C. Chiland. New York: J. Wiley.

Valenstein, A. F. (1981). Insight as an embedded concept in the early historical phase of psychoanalysis. *The Psychoanalytic Study of the Child,* Vol. 36, pp. 307–315. New Haven, CT: Yale University Press.

Valenstein, A. F. (1981). Panel on the superego: Its early roots and the road from outer to inner conflict as seen in psychoanalysis (reported by Alex Holder). *Bulletin of the Hampstead Clinic*, Vol. 4, pp. 83–98.

Valenstein, A. F. (1984). Working through and resistance to change: Insight and the action system. *Journal of the American Psychoanalytic Association,* Vol. 32 (Suppl.), pp. 347–367.

Valenstein, A. F. (1985). A developmental approach to transference: Diagnostic and treatment considerations. In: *The Transference in Psychotherapy,* ed. E. Schwaber. New York: International Universities Press.

Valenstein, A. F. (1989). Pre-oedipal reconstructions in psychoanalysis. *International Journal of Psycho-Analysis*, Vol. 70, pp. 433–442.

Joseph and Anne-Marie Sandler

Anne-Marie Sandler received her degree in psychology in Switzerland as an assistant to Jean Piaget. She trained in child psychoanalysis at the Anna Freud Centre, formerly the Hampstead Clinic. She is a training and supervising analyst at the British Psychoanalytical Society as well as Director of the Anna Freud Centre. She has maintained an active involvement in clinical research throughout her career.

Joseph Sandler, M.D. is a training and supervising analyst in the British and Israel Psychoanalytical Societies and was formerly Sigmund Freud Professor of Psychoanalysis and Director of The Sigmund Freud Centre for Study and Research in Psychoanalysis at the University of London. He is a past Vice President of the International Psychoanalytical Association and served as Director of the Index Project of the Hampstead Child Therapy Clinic. Dr. Sandler was editor-in-chief of the *International Journal of Psycho-Analysis* and the *International Review of Psycho-Analysis*, which he founded.

The Sandlers were interviewed March 22, 1989.

SRR: We are interested in knowing what was really meaningful to each of you in developing a sense of yourself as an analyst.

JS: My training analyst worried that I did not seem terribly concerned about how things were going from a career viewpoint. I more or less coasted through the training. I took a big step when I went to work at Hampstead Clinic and started to work on the Index. My interest in analytic theory then increased enormously because we were fitting clinical material in the Index to theoretical concepts and trying new theoretical ideas. I had many years of that, and this gave direction to my career. Working with material from children was enormously useful. My wife was a big influence. She had come from Piaget to Hampstead, and my whole notion of the representational world was very much influenced by discussions with Anne-Marie.

I think my analytic orientation has altered over the years with my realization that the people I strongly disagreed with also had something to say. It was always a problem, of course, of how to make sense of what they were saying. I spent a lot of time whittling away at Kleinian theory and object relations theory, trying to pull what I thought was clinically relevant into my own frame of reference somehow. This has been a slow process, but it has led to an enlarged perspective. My teaching at universities outside the Institute was a good learning experience, too. I am hesitant because I have to think about the question you asked. I hadn't thought about it before. Anne-Marie?

AMS: I think my experience was rather different from yours. I had my first professional crisis when I was with Piaget. He offered me a university career. Although I very much enjoyed working with him, there was something missing so I took the plunge and went to London to train with Anna Freud, which I very much enjoyed. It represented a completely new vista for me. I was coming from Piaget's philosophy. The training I got from Anna Freud was very thorough and very systematic. It gave me a very good basic grounding in Freudian psychoanalysis. Then I got married. I found my time was taken up by having children, and for a while I did not do any analytic work. I did not feel I could be a mother and work at the same time; I was privileged in that I didn't need to work. When the children started school, it wasn't convenient to work after school with children. It seemed silly to have my own children and not see them when they came back from school because I was busy with other children. I felt the best thing would be to do the Institute of Psycho-analysis and become an adult analyst.

I enjoyed that enormously. It was a great eye opener for me because the Institute of Psycho-analysis in London is more oriented to clinical than theoretical issues. I had a pretty good basic theoretical background, so I could throw myself into the clinical work and try to understand what the Kleinian and the object relation theorists were talking about. In the beginning, it seemed they spoke a funny language. I got into a great but helpful muddle. I also had a second analysis with another analyst, which I found to be very helpful. My analyst was flexible, so I found I was able to relax more.

Then, of course, there was my husband. We helped each other a lot because my interest in theory tended to be secondary. My greatest interest was clinical work, so I could bring my clinical problem to Joe to discuss it. After discussing it, we could look at the technical side and the theoretical implications. Probably because of living in England and working with the British Society, I was constantly challenged by the viewpoints of my colleagues. I think my analytic technique has been greatly influenced over the years by my constant opportunity to discuss both analytic problems and matters of analytic interest with my colleagues. I very much liked and enjoyed the training with Anna Freud, but that training had a bit of a high school feeling to it. It was a systematic program without much space for individuality. This suited me very well because I was still very young and green. It gave me the basis I needed, and I am immensely grateful.

At the Institute it was a different kettle of fish because one was constantly confronted with both students and teachers who challenged you with completely different ideas. To be a simple, good, conscientious candidate, which was very suitable for Anna Freud, was not enough. I enjoyed my training with the British Society very much. I was ready for it and my children were old enough. I had had years of analysis. I don't know how it is for people who come quite green to the Institute. It must be overwhelming. I was extremely lucky and in a way got the best of both worlds.

JS: It was different for me because I started my analysis at 21 and came to the Institute at 22 and then had three years there. Coming from South Africa I was full of *chutzpah.* Somehow, I breezed through the training. I didn't go to Hampstead as a student, and even after I started work at the Hampstead Clinic there were times when I did not see eye-to-eye with Anna Freud. She was marvelous in many ways, but in other ways she could be rigid, and we disagreed in a friendly way.

AMS: But what was so impressive was that Joe got on immensely well with Anna Freud for two reasons. He knew his Freud inside out, so

Anna Freud admired him for that; and then he was a marvelous teacher. With those two assets he could sometime be a naughty boy.

LR: That was something I was curious about. There's a quality in your essays of stepping out of just one viewpoint and asking, "Why does this happen?" or "Let's look at it this way." I am curious about that. Is that characteristic of either of you, that you are free to take a perspective and don't feel bound to one ideology, or is it partly a function of your being in an environment in which you are constantly being challenged to define your terms and ideas in relation to others?

JS: It was and is partly the environment, but also we were never dependent on being followers for our living. We always had enough patients. Nor had we any wish to start a "school."

SRR: I noticed that two of your recent essays—yours, Mrs. Sandler, "Aspects of the Analysis of a Neurotic Patient," and your jointly written essay, "The Past Unconscious, The Present Unconscious and the Vicissitudes of Guilt," well-complemented each other. The case study served to illustrate the ideas in the theoretical essay so clearly. I imagine that being able to share ideas and work back and forth is very catalyzing.

AMS: The real original mind here is my husband's. He has the capacity to turn ideas upside down and to look at them sideways. Our close cooperation is more recent. When I had the children I was not ready to spend a lot of time writing essays. But my husband was creative all through that period.

LR: When during your development as analysts did each of you begin to write? What was it like to go from clinical work and clinical discussions to actually deciding to put something on paper, to formulate? For each of you, where did that come in your career, what influenced you, how did it begin for you?

JS: I began writing as a student in student newspapers. I also wrote a lot of statistical, psychometric things as a psychologist. My first essay in a scientific journal appeared in 1949. As a candidate, I was at both medical school and the Tavistock Clinic. In the early 50s, I wrote, with collaborators, a number of essays using a very psychoanalytically based questionnaire. That was very interesting. The first analytic essay was one that I gave in 1959. It was an essay on Safety at an I.P.A. Congress in Copenhagen. It was important to me, even though I was not then aware of its importance.

My first reported case was one I was treating just about the same time. It was given first at a conference on psychosomatic research and was published, together with the article on safety, in *From Safety to Superego.* That case, which was in fact my first control case, impressed me greatly because it brought home the importance of countertransference. In fact, a lot of the things we talk about now—the internal object relationship being externalized and the effect of countertransference—were all in that essay.

Then I wrote an essay for full membership on a very interesting man. He was a flier and I saw him for six days one week. Then he would fly to New York for the next week, and I would see him six days the following week. It continued on like that. It turned out that he slept in his mother's bed when she threw the father out. Then when the father came back, he was sent back to his room. Then the father was thrown out again, and he went back to his mother's bed. And all of this was repeated in his career. He got promoted when this material was worked through and didn't have to travel in the same way.

LR: What was your motivation to write? Was it sharing that experience with others? Was it your working out your own ideas?

JS: One gets pleasure from writing, all sorts of narcissistic pleasure, but I also think I had something to say.

SRR: I want to ask you about an essay you wrote a number of years ago with Walter Joffe, "Notes on Pain, Depression, and Individuation," in which you conceived of the object as a means to a feeling state of the self. I find that formulation helpful and wonder how you came to develop that idea?

JS: For a while I worked with Joffe and wrote a lot with him. The whole situation about depression in childhood was a controversial one, because at the Tavistock Clinic, which was just around the corner from the Hampstead Clinic, all the children were diagnosed depressed, but at Hampstead no child was ever diagnosed as depressed. We thought there was something wrong with this. We looked at the material in our Indexed cases and found that very often children were called depressed, but a diagnosis of depression was never made. We then looked at what the characteristics of depression were.

The first essay, published in the *International Journal* in 1965, was a shorter version of the one that was in the "Study of the Child." Things develop in my thinking as I work on an essay. The whole question of object relationships, which was never satisfactorily encompassed in classical Freudian theory, had certainly preoccupied me for a very long time. And then things seemed to fit together as we worked on the essay. In fact, most of the ideas in the paper developed during the production. This has been particularly useful because I work so much with collaborators. I do like to work with someone else and to have the interchange while I am sitting at the typewriter; now, of course, it's the word processor. Working with Anne-Marie has been very helpful to me.

AMS: But the way you work on your papers is very interesting. It starts with a little uneasiness about something. And it preoccupies you. Then you have an idea and bounce it off whomever you are working with. Then there's a lot of talk and a lot of argument. You also become quite withdrawn and preoccupied with what's on your mind.

JS: My family doesn't like it when I'm hatching an essay.

SRR: In class, we just discussed Ernst Kris' essay on the role of the preconscious in creativity, that is, looking at creativity as an intrapsychic process. You are describing an interactive process which also facilitates creative work.

JS: I thoroughly enjoy working in a group, and I've heard myself say things that have come out directly from the preconscious which gets very active when I'm talking. But I have to add that I find it harder to work on my own because I tend to postpone until I get to the point of anxiety because of a deadline and I feel pressured to write. So that's another factor. Getting back to your very first question, when Joffe died I was depressed and didn't write for two or three years. We had had a very close collaboration.

SRR: You have thought a great deal about the relationship between loss and individuation. Laurie and I wonder whether development of an analytic identity could be considered an ongoing process of individuation, since the work provides continuing opportunities for inner reworking stimulated by self-inquiry.

LR: Your more specific question was, "How does becoming an analyst stimulate one's psychic growth?" How have patients affected you or stimulated your thinking in ways that might possibly not have happened without your being analysts?

AMS: It is a very interesting question which certainly echos very much in me because I'm not a writer. By nature, I find writing very difficult, but I get very inspired by and interested in all my patients. I also feel that they are challenged to grow as I work with them. When I find myself in difficulty or at an impasse it really arouses a very deep preoccupation. I find myself writing either because I feel I have discovered something exciting for myself within the work with my patient, and I want to share it, or because I feel I am stuck and hope that writing my thoughts will help me get unstuck. Working with patients is a great stimulus to continue one's own analysis in a way which, if one weren't constantly confronted by someone else's conflicts, one would not otherwise do.

JS: Anne-Marie makes notes after her sessions; I rarely do. However, I have been very affected by certain patients. One in particular I remember. I had him on and off for about fifteen years. He had a tremendous borderline-narcissistic problem. I think that my technique has improved enormously following the struggle to deal with this patient. I think one gets more tolerant of people—at least I found that—and also more ready to see through one's own rationalizations. So I think that the process of self-analysis, which, of course, only occurs on and off and also goes on preconsciously, does help one outside the analytic setting.

AMS: When one finds oneself stuck over and over again in the same way, one is bound to see that there must be some kind of blind spot. It is a great help then to be able to talk with oneself and write about it.

LR: You mentioned that you found teaching nonanalysts very enriching. Over the course of your analytic careers, how you think contact with nonanalysts may have provided you with another valuable perspective?

JS: I didn't find going to medical school worthwhile. I was coerced into doing it, and I have never practiced medicine. But my experience in teaching psychologists who are nonanalysts has been enormously helpful. Also, in teaching at the Maudsley and Middlesex Hospital, when I was senior lecturer in general psychiatry, made me much more aware of the limitations of analysis. I became very preoccupied with how analysis works, with the relationship between psychic change and development, and with change which occurs outside analysis. People do have structural changes without having analysis. The whole issue of the distinction between psychoanalysis and psychotherapy has preoccupied me quite a lot lately.

I remember the old days when I suggested that certain patients really needed medication as well as analysis. This met with a lot of opposition in the analytic society, but I will never forget my experience with an obsessional patient who really could not work in analysis until his physician prescribed a very small dose of librium. Then the analysis took off. Since then I've had patients with manic tendencies who have been on lithium. That's been very useful. I think now it is generally accepted that patients can be on antidepressants and still be analyzed. But in the old days it was strictly taboo.

AMS: To return to the question of writing: One thing which surprises me is that I have never lost my amazement at what the patient is doing and that analysis really works. I find that in every way and in every patient I get a kind of amazement and delight. If it's that interesting, I want to write it down and not forget it. In particular, the moment within the session when I give an interpretation that really works is so nice that I have to write it down.

LR: I am interested in your concept of self-dialogue and the developmental process of learning how to talk to oneself, not just to others, which is in your joint essay on object relations and affects. How would you conceptualize self-dialogue for analysts? Do you see any usefulness in that concept in terms of one's development and identity as an analyst?

JS: I don't think we took it much further at the time than simply postulating the self as an object to oneself.

LR: What are your own thoughts about how you talk to yourselves as you listen to patients and think about them?

AMS: Over time I have developed a much greater awareness that very active work occurs in myself as I listen to patients. I am very active in conversations with myself until I am more or less clear where the difference is and until I conceptualize where we are stuck. Then, having grasped what the problem is, there is further internal discussion about the right words and sentences, considering from which angle could I actually address the problem without humiliating the patient or without increasing the resistance. Sometimes I will have considerable internal dialogue over days before feeling confident enough to verbalize something.

JS: It is a very difficult question you ask because so much of it goes on preconsciously.

AMS: But there is a time when it's just past the threshold, when one realizes that there is a very important process going on in one's mind.

LR: Do you each have a particular mode of listening to a patient; for example, visual or aural? Does that mode vary over time with the same patient or between different patients?

AMS: I think I shall slightly evade your question, but my tendency is to struggle with the feelings as if I am living something. I mean I'm in the process of living out something with my patient in the here and now. He confuses me, he irritates me, he makes me feel sad—whatever it may be. At the same time, I have the feeling that it doesn't make sense, that I don't know where I am. In my dialogue, I try to place it historically. I try to see it as imaginatively as I can. Where would it fit? How does it fit with what I've heard? With what I know of this man? How do I imagine it to have been when he was a little boy or with another patient when she was an adolescent girl? All this goes on, probably in different modalities, until something seems intuitively right. It's word, it's image, it's an attempt to fit what seems to me to be a plausible experience. Then I take it back. I try something else in my mind. I'm not very auditory and I don't play very much with words, maybe not enough. What would you do?

JS: When I think theoretically and have to write something, I am very visual. When I teach I like to use a blackboard to illustrate things. But with a patient I am a little more passive than Anne-Marie in the sense that I will let my mind go anywhere, and I can be thinking of all sorts of things, but then I catch myself as I resonate with something in the patient. I really don't think this free-floating attention is "evenly suspended attention." I think this term is very misleading. One ought to be able to think of one's shopping list or of things one has to do. Then suddenly one will ask, "What am I doing? What am I thinking about?," and then one may get a clue as to what is going on in the patient.

SRR: You have written extensively about the process of identification. In your essay on the vicissitudes of guilt, you discussed the usefulness of the patient identifying with the analyst's tolerance of the "silly" parts of the self. Do you consider the process of identification to be an integral part of an analysis? Following that perspective, do you consider therapeutic analysis and training analysis to be basically similar or significantly different?

JS: I don't know about the differences between ordinary analysis and training analysis, but I think it is not so great if one approaches it from the viewpoint of conflict and sees resistances as due to conflict—conflict not simply between, for example, the superego and the id, but between something that was once syntonic and some force which is opposing it, rendering it dystonic. What might be defended against in the present is a tendency to use a particular defense or think in a particular way, something that involves a lot of ego. That's the child within. Clinically, I think we both share the view that the conflicts we see in our patients are conflicts between tendencies and ways of functioning that were acceptable at one time but have become unacceptable because of some further developmental layer. The analytic work is to identify that which is being warded off, particularly if it is in the transference, and to interpret in such a way that you're showing respect for it just as much as respecting the defending part. And that's the analyst's tolerance—so the style of interpreting plays a very big part in it. Certainly, I think that the identification with the analyst's tolerance, with the ridiculous, with the childish, with the "silly," is a very important part of the patient's ability to tolerate that aspect of themselves, and to accept that they have perverse tendencies, and that they're childish in some ways, but that this acceptance doesn't mean acting on it.

This is rather different from what I was taught—that the aim was to sublimate that which was warded off. Certainly, Anna Freud held that view because she was thinking in terms of drive energies—that one should get to the point where one can sublimate the impulses which are bringing about conflict now. I would say no. Sublimation is another problem. The important thing is that people should be able to tolerate their murderous impulses, and I think that comes about through identification with the analyst. Obviously, it is not the only factor, but it is a very important one.

SRR: In class, we discussed the fact that termination is a different process in training analysis than in therapeutic analysis, since former analysands continue in the same community. What are your thoughts about how individuation occurs in the course of training analyses?

JS: If you identify in order to solve a conflict, then you are a little bit at risk, but there's no way around the tendency to identify with someone who, in a sense, has been teaching you, and you've been modeling your thinking on the way that person thinks. It's very natural to identify. Also it's natural to identify with those aspects when one stops analysis because there's a loss and it's a way of dealing with the loss. We do see from colleagues where the hostility, the ambivalence has not been taken up sufficiently, a dealing with the conflict by idealization and overidentification. It's very, very shaky afterwards, so such analysts become aggressively defensive and attack any who criticize their group. We see this quite a lot in London, so obviously it is very important. There was a game in our Society—people still play it—of guessing who a person was in analysis with or in supervision with when they spoke at meetings. Sometimes the identifications were caricatures. That's okay as long as it's only temporary.

AMS: I think you point to something important and perhaps more noticeable in our English system. Because we have this group system, it is relatively easy to displace one's hostilities away from one's analyst onto other groups. We sometimes get a certain splitting in which we think, "My group is all good, but the others are all bad," and this goes with an idealization. The danger is that if you are left with a strong identification with the aggressor because you have not been able to cope with your hostility, you are stuck in having to ape someone toward whom you feel ambivalent and have not worked through. Then, because you remain in the same milieu, the further working through is difficult...because too much is at stake; you have to get on with your peers, with your past analyst. In England, we have a fair amount of young colleagues who go through a second analysis, which is sometimes very helpful. I had two analyses, but that was because I did two trainings. I found it very helpful to have had a chance of a second analysis.

LR: One concept I want to ask about is actualization or reenactment of internal object relations within the analytic dyad. When you are observing that, what thoughts do you have about the technical interventions with the patient? Do you try to reconstruct it in terms of connecting it to the past? Do you keep it in the here and now? To what extent do you use a developmental framework? Do you use language that is attuned to the developmental level of the role they are enacting? You said you might visualize this patient as a small boy. Would you use different language with him and not directly address what he's enacting?

JS: You asked several questions. The actualization is simply trying to make the unconscious wish satisfied through turning it to reality. It oftentimes involves trying to push someone else into a role which the analyst experienced in the countertransference. Not that all countertransference is that, of course. How would one address it? My view is that you would go first for what's happening now and point to the conflict over what's happening, not to the child within because we are dealing with the adult version of the child within. So you would not want to go to the child, who, say, wants to kill off the oedipal father, but you'd want to point out, for example, that "You're having a problem because, while on the one hand you want to protect me, on the other hand you also feel murderous towards me because yesterday so and so...," or, "I think you're finding it very difficult because you're really cross with me and it's not easy to let yourself feel this." So it would be the present-day version one would go for.

We can differentiate between construction and reconstruction in the sense that people have an inner world and one can talk of current internal object relationships. This would be construction. One tries to construct the patterns of the way the patient is functioning; but only when resistance is lower following a piece of analytic work does one do construction, and then reconstruction in which one tries to tie it in with the past. I believe that the only time one should go directly to interpreting the past is when the patient is in a current conflict and the only way to approach the conflict is by way of the past. Then the aim is to look at the past to reflect on the present. I was very impressed by an incident in my own second analysis. My analyst was a very old lady who had been ill. I was having difficulty in associating and she said, "I know you love me, Joseph, but at the moment you could kill me." Then she laughed. I was relieved because it was absolutely true. Now the question of the childhood connection would be something to be explored later.

SRR: But in a way she treated you a little bit as a child by using your first name.

JS: She was so very much older than I. She had been my first supervisor. She was quite remarkable.

AMS: Your question is interesting because I think that what was important in this example was not that she treated my husband as a child, but that in her mind she could be totally aware of the emotions and address them without any worry whether it was adultlike or childlike.

JS: I think the very dry analysts who simply interpret do not get as good results as the ones who show feeling and affective recognition of the patient's feelings. In the interpretation, my analyst could recognize the affectionate side of my feelings as well, and I think that was tremendously important. If one does otherwise, one simply mobilizes more defenses.

AMS: Otherwise, the patient may feel accused and guilty.

SRR: I was impressed in your writing with your sensitivity to patients' experience of shame without pathologizing it.

LR: That was actually another question we talked about. When teaching analytic candidates, how do you help them be more attuned to levels of unconscious communication? Is it possible to teach such attunement? Does it seem as if some people have it and some don't?

JS: I think it's hard to teach in a class, but to some extent one can teach it. As you say, some people are gifted, and some are not. The best place for teaching is in supervision because one picks up in the material something that is going on which the candidate may not have seen. Then, of course, it's very dramatic when one can show the candidate in the material of the very next session the proof of it. So supervision is tremendously important.

AMS: What is also important is to show how the whole process involves a constant going forward even if you have given a good interpretation. It is important to listen to what comes just afterwards and not just sit back and say, Ah, I've done it now. I was just thinking about the interpretations that my husband recalled that had such warmth. I have a patient who is absolutely terrified of too great a closeness. If I had given such an interpretation to him, even if it were correct, he would be terrified because he would feel himself seduced. Thus, taking his sensitivities into account, the same conflict has to be expressed differently.

JS: If you ever work with children, it becomes clear that this plays an enormous role because one might say to a child, I knew a little boy once who and so on, and not go directly to what is going on in the child. The child understands at some level and connects it up. One has to gauge the distance for the patient. Child analytic experience is very valuable for dealing with adults; however, our experience has been that people trained first with children have to unlearn a lot when they start working with adults. What I mean, is, for example, that the tendency to give what Anna Freud called "developmental help"—which is not interpretative—might be too great.

SRR: In Europe, candidates come from a broader spectrum of backgrounds than in America. What are your thoughts about how these different backgrounds contribute to the field of psychoanalysis.

JS: I think having candidates from different backgrounds is very valuable for the analytic profession, particularly if there is interaction between the candidates in the training. Medical school in England, where no bachelor's degree is required beforehand, is essentially a technical college. I think that many doctors are very well educated, but one can see the difference when one brings in people from other disciplines—psychologists, anthropologists, sociologists, and historians. Sometimes, of course, if they were not medical or clinical psychologists before, problems arise when they start their clinical work; but the interesting thing is that there's also an advantage in not having been contaminated by psychotherapy.

SRR: Could you put that into words?

JS: Well, if you have been doing psychotherapy in a hospital and you have learned certain techniques and developed a certain therapeutic style, the switch to doing analysis is not easy. One wants to use one's usual psychotherapeutic technique. I have a candidate who has never treated patients psychotherapeutically. She was neither a physician nor a clinical psychologist, but she's got her first case now. She was quivering in her boots, but she's becoming a good analyst because this is all new for her.

SRR: Many of the European analysts came from different backgrounds.

JS: I think Kris was the greatest of these psychologists. His writings are terrific, really, and he was an art expert. He was the curator of the art museum in Vienna.

SRR: In the American Psychoanalytic Association Newsletter, you have written about the gap between theory and practice. In classes, we have had many discussions about the impediments, the inhibitions analysts feel towards tackling and exploring that gap. Do you have any thoughts about how training might encourage people to undertake that kind of work.

JS: I think this is a very important issue because we tend to have two streams of teaching—the clinical and the theoretical—so on one hand you have your practical school and on the other a yeshiva. The two very often don't integrate enough. There should be more courses on integration of theory and clinical material. It is quite a good idea to ask candidates to put what they've reported clinically into theoretical terms and to discuss the necessary theory as opposed to all the metapsychological frills. George Klein was really on the right track when he spoke of having a radical theorectomy in training. However, I think our metapsychology has gotten out of hand.

SRR: That was what you did with the Hampstead Index, at least what I've read in your epilogue to the book, in terms of getting the therapists to really have to conceptualize and look dynamically at what was going on in their work week by week. That really struck me because it's different from the way we learned.

JS: It is a tremendous learning experience.

AMS: What was also good was that the indexing was done afterwards. The candidates were expected to write a page every week about what had gone on. After a year, the task of indexing occurs. The indexing did not interfere with the flow of the work because it would be difficult to have to work clinically with the patient and at the same time put material into conceptual terms.

LR: That was one of my questions. In your essays, you mention the need for more research in different areas. Who do you think can best do that research? What about the potential conflict of trying to be a participant-observer and still maintain an empathic connection with the patient? We have seen in the literature all sorts of models—people who try to be a researcher-analyst right in the session, or people who aren't analysts, who try to look at what analysts have done. What are your thoughts about how research can be done in analytic work and how different models work?

JS: Lately, I've been pursuing a line of research which I think is very analytic. We regard the analyst as an instrument that is put into the analytic situation and preconsciously forms models of what is going on. Then we, as it were, withdraw the analytic probe and try to extract the implicit models from the analyst. They are often very different from the "official" theories.

For instance, in Frankfurt, at the Sigmund Freud Institute where I had a research group, we did a study on trauma. It was very clear from the interviews with analysts that the concept of trauma actually being used was not at all like the one usually taught, but that the trauma tended to be regarded as a sort of foreign body implanted in the person which had to be exorcized as an ongoing thing having an influence. That is quite a different view from saying that the trauma is an overwhelming of the ego by excitation. I think the same is true for many concepts. I think this is a very profitable line of research. I have a number of Ph.D. students using this technique. One is working on transference and finding out analysts' concepts of transference, which are quite different from the book.

AMS: The method is very ingenious. Joe first asks the analyst to talk of trauma. We, of course, would all rattle off definitions we know. Then Joe asks, "Can you think of two or three cases where a trauma has occurred?" Each analyst has a chance to change gear and go into clinical material and give examples. Then Joe asks for similarities and differences between the cases. You get a much freer conversation, and the subject realizes that the beautifully conceived definition just does not fit.

JS: One thing to do is to find the statements people make about, for example, transference, and then create a set of questions or statements for a semistructured interview in which you say, "Some people think this and other analysts think that. What are your feelings about it?" It gives license to the person to talk. What we have then are a set of questions that the interviewer has to answer on the basis of the material elicited. They are not seen by the subject. And the interviewer would go on, perhaps pointing to contradictions, asking further questions, and giving further examples. An example might be given to the subject, who is then asked, "Would you regard this as transference?" For example, a patient comes in at the very first session and is hesitant about speaking because of embarrassment at revealing intimate details to a stranger. The analyst interprets this. Some people would say this is transference interpretation. Some would not. We can ask, Where do you stand? It's fascinating. After a while the internal textbook model really gets put to one side and one gets a picture of people's views of transference. It is very clear now that for many people it includes all the externalizations and all the anxieties about treatment, or anything in the area of relationships.

LR: You talked about how hard it is to reflect on how we function as therapists/analysts in terms of the preconscious. It seems as if your research directly taps into the preconscious type of listening and thinking.

JS: And the other thing is that the preconscious models are part-models, so they don't have to be integrated one with the other. In a way, preconscious theories form a more flexible system. We have to be plausible when we go public.

LR: Is the ability to make use of preconscious information in responding to students an important aspect of a good teacher or supervisor? If so, how would you get them to define or eventually teach that capacity?

JS: I think it is very difficult. An affective experience which leaves its mark, is if the teacher can resonate the things which the candidates hesitate to say in public and get those things into the open.

SRR: One final question. From your interviewing, do you have a sense that most analysts continue to theorize about what they are doing in their work after their training, or do they tend to leave theory behind?

JS: My feeling is that it depends on the person entirely. I think most people leave it behind.

LR/SRR: Thank you both for sharing so much of yourselves with us.

SELECTED BIBLIOGRAPHY

Sandler, A-M. (1963). Aspects of passivity and ego development in the blind infant. *The Psychoanalytic Study of the Child*, Vol. 18, pp. 343–360. New Haven, CT: Yale University Press.

Sandler, A-M. (1975). Comments on the significance of Piaget's work for psychoanalysis. *International Review of Psychoanalysis*, Vol. 2, pp. 365–377.

Sandler, A-M. (1982). Selection and function of the training analyst in Europe. *International Review of Psychoanalysis*, Vol. 9, pp. 386–398.

Sandler, A-M. (1984). Problems of development and adaptation in an elderly patient. *The Psychoanalytic Study of the Child,* Vol. 39, pp. 471–489. New Haven, CT: Yale University Press.

Sandler, A-M. (1988). Aspects of the analysis of a neurotic patient. *International Journal of Psycho-Analysis,* Vol. 69, pp. 317–326.

Sandler, J. (1959). The body as phallus: A patient's fear of erection. *International Journal of Psycho-Analysis,* Vol. 40, pp. 191–198.

Sandler, J. (1960). The background of safety. *International Journal of Psycho-Analysis*, Vol. 41, pp. 352–365.

Sandler, J. (1960). On the concept of the superego. *The Psychoanalytic Study of the Child*, Vol. 15, pp. 128–162. New Haven, CT: Yale University Press.

Sandler, J. (1962). The Hampstead Index as an instrument of psychoanalytic research. *International Journal of Psycho-Analysis*, Vol. 43, pp. 287–291.

Sandler, J. & Rosenblattt, B. (1962). The concept of the representational world. *The Psychoanalytic Study of the Child,* Vol. 17, pp. 128–145. New Haven, CT: Yale University Press.

Joffe, W. G. & Sandler, J. (1965). Notes on pain, depression, and individuation. *The Psychoanalytic Study of the Child*, Vol. 20, pp. 394–424. New Haven, CT: Yale University Press.

Joffe, W. G. & Sandler, J. (1967). On some conceptual problems involved in the consideration of disorders of narcissism. *Journal of Child Psychotherapy,* Vol. 2, pp. 56–66.

Joffe, W. G. & Sandler, J. (1967). On the concept of pain, with special reference to depression and psychogenic pain. *Journal of Psychosomatic Research,* Vol. 11, p. 69.

Joffe, W. G. & Sandler, J. (1968). Comments on the psychoanalytic psychology of adaptation, with special reference to the role of affects and the representational world. *International Journal of Psycho-Analysis*, Vol. 49, pp. 445–454.

Sandler, J. & Joffe, W. G. (1969). Towards a basic psychoanalytic model. *International Journal of Psycho-Analysis,* Vol. 50, pp. 79–90.

Sandler, J., Dare, C., & Holder, A. (1973). *The Patient and the Analyst.* New York: International Universities Press.

Sandler, J. (1976). Dreams, unconscious fantasies, and "identity of perception." *International Review of Psychoanalysis*, Vol. 3, pp. 33–42.

Sandler, J. (1976). Countertransference and role-responsiveness. *International Review of Psychoanalysis*, Vol. 3, pp. 43-47.

Sandler, J. & Sandler, A-M. (1978). On the development of object relationships and affects. *International Journal of Psycho-Analysis,* Vol. 59, pp. 285–296.

Sandler, J. (1981). Character traits and object relationships. *Psychoanalytic Quarterly*, Vol. 50, pp. 694–708.

Sandler, J. (1983) Psychoanalytic concepts and psychoanalytic practice, *International Journal of Psycho-Analysis*, Vol. 64, pp. 35–45.

Sandler, J. & Sandler, A-M. (1983). The "second censorship," the "three box model," and some technical implications. *International Journal of Psycho-Analysis*, Vol. 64, pp. 413–425.

Sandler, J. & Freud, A. (1983). Discussion in the Hampstead Index of *The Ego and the Mechanisms of Defense*. *Journal of the American Psychoanalytic Association,* Vol. 31, Suppl., pp. 19–146.

Sandler, J. & Sandler, A-M. (1984). The past unconscious, the present unconscious, and interpretation of the transference. *Psychoanalytic Inquiry*, Vol. 4, pp. 367–400.

Sandler, J. & Freud, A. (1985). *The Analysis of Defense: The Ego and the Mechanisms of Defense Revisited.* New York: International Universities Press.

Sandler, J. & Sandler, A-M. (1987). The past unconscious, the present unconscious, and the vicissitudes of guilt. *International Journal of Psycho-Analysis,* Vol. 68, pp. 331–341.

Sandler, J. (1987). *From Safety to Superego.* New York: Guilford Press.

Sandler, J., ed. (1987). *Projection, Identification, Projective Identification.* Madison, CT: International Universities Press.

Sandler, J. (1988). Psychoanalytic Technique and "Analysis Terminable and Interminable." *International Journal of Psycho-Analysis*, Vol. 69, pp. 335–345.

Jacob Arlow

Jacob Arlow, M.D. graduated from New York University School of Medicine. He is Professor Emeritus at Albert Einstein College of Medicine and a training analyst at the New York Psychoanalytic Institute. He occupied the Freud Chair at Hebrew University and is a past President of the New York Psychoanalytic Institute and the American Psychoanalytic Association, as well as former Treasurer and Vice President of the International Psychoanalytic Association. Dr. Arlow has been Chairman of the Board of Professional Standards and Chairman of the Committee on Psychoanalytic Education of the American Psychoanalytic Association. He is a recipient of the Heinz Hartmann Award of the New York Psychoanalytic Institute, the Henry Loughlin Award, and the Mary S. Sigourney Award of the American Psychoanalytic Association. He has been on the editorial board of *Psyche* and was formerly editor-in-chief of *Psychoanalytic Quarterly*. Dr. Arlow was interviewed November 10, 1990.

SRR: You have stated that the really significant part of the analytic situation is the concentration of attention on the process of introspection; that is, the creation of a set of conditions that minimize the contribution of the external world and enhance the emergence of the derivatives of the inner world, the world of fantasy thinking. That world of fantasy, examining and elucidating it, has been at the center of your work for many decades. How did you develop that focus? What experiences were central to your developing that perspective?

JA: I think most of my formulations derive from an attempt to understand the patient's productions in the course of the analytic situation. In this respect, I was greatly influenced by my first supervisor, Dr. Sally Bonnett. It was from her that I learned that one has to listen to what the patient says, paying attention to the sequence in which the material appears, and to correlate the patient's responses with what the analyst has said. For this reason, I don't like the term interpretation; I prefer intervention.

Analysis is a talking cure, and it represents, in a special way, an extension of ordinary conversation and the manner in which meaning is extracted from such communication. The difference is, of course, that I expect complete candor from my patient. I ask him not to censor his thoughts or to withhold any other representations that come to his mind. In effect, what I am doing is getting a sampling of the free range of his thinking, uninterrupted and uninfluenced, as far as possible, by external circumstances. However, I do not let the patient continue in this vein for a long time. From time to time I interrupt him and, by what I say, cause the patient to change his stance from being merely a reporter of what presents itself to his consciousness to one who reflects upon what he has been saying and thinking.

In this connection, I was influenced by the very seminal essay by Richard Sterba, "The Split of the Ego in the Psychoanalytic Process." It was Sterba who pointed out exactly what we do in treatment, how we change the stance that the patient adopts by forcing him, through our interventions, to assume a role similar to that which we have adopted for him and toward him. We cause the patient to reflect upon his productions in the same manner as we have been reflecting upon his productions. But I think I took Sterba's ideas further by examining more closely the experience of the analyst.

While the analyst is listening passively to his patient, the representations in his conscious thinking are the patient's productions. At that point, the analyst has become identified with the patient, but every once in a while some reflections, some ideas, some conclusions intrude upon this passive experience of the analyst's listening. This introspective aspect of the analyst's experience constitutes a break in his function of passive listening, and it is the point where the analyst can see a connection or some possibility of meaning that has been stimulated in him, that has been evoked in him by what the patient has been saying.

In many respects, the form of the patient's productions, the mode of presentation, resembles the creative process. The same elements that combine to make art, poetry, and literature, are organized in a way to create a mood, a mental set. The patient's productions, so organized, ultimately lead to the evocation of a fantasy or a derivative of some fantasy in the analyst. Concerning these ideas, I was influenced by the writings of Freud and particularly by their extension by Hans Sachs in *The Creative Unconscious,* especially the concept of unconscious fantasies shared in common. Finally, there was the essay by Dr. Beres, in which he compared the psychoanalytic situation with the creative process.

SRR: At what point in your experience as an analyst did you develop your conceptualization of the analyst's inner experience? Were you already out of training?

JA: It came to me after many years of experience; perhaps 20 years of listening to patients. Only then did I begin to realize that, unless the analyst's attention is diverted by some physical pain he is experiencing or by some overwhelming realistic difficulty in his life, everything that the analyst thinks and feels in the course of listening to his patient is some commentary on the patient's material.

In the essay I wrote with Dr. Beres on empathy and the psychoanalytic situation, I included a daydream I had while the patient was reporting a dream to me. The content of my daydream and the wish of his dream were identical. This was a striking illustration of the experience. However, I had become aware of this interaction many years before. Accordingly, I now pay much more attention to the results of the introspective process and how it presents possible interpretations or indicators of interpretation to consciousness.

SRR: We want to ask more about your training and development as an analyst. Today, even as beginning candidates, we are taught to recognize and appreciate the inner processes of the analyst. How different was your training before those ideas were formulated?

JA: It's hard for me to think back to see how the inner processes of the analyst were introduced into my training. Certainly, they were not part of the organized, formal curriculum. There is a great deal that I would like to say about the curriculum, which we may reserve for another occasion. However, the next issue of *The American Psychoanalyst* will have an address that I gave to the graduating class of the San Francisco Institute. I don't want to give away the entire structure of the address because it's a fun piece. In it I gave some of my criticisms of the curriculum. However, returning to the inner experience of the analyst, no such ideas that I can recall were presented as part of the formal curriculum. I am not sure to what extent it was discussed in my supervisory experience, but it is something that I began to appreciate after that time.

SRR: Were there other particular people and experiences that influenced your perspective?

JA: When I came into training, we had the benefit of the outstanding European analysts who came to the United States to escape the Nazis. My class had the privilege of getting to know these analysts and to be able to talk with them straightforwardly about analytic problems. In addition, I would say that one of the principal experiences that determined the kind of analyst I became was probably the continuous study group with Drs. Brenner, Beres, and Wangh.

For a period of at least 20 years, we met every Thursday. We decided to get together because we realized when we finished our formal training at the Institute that we really knew very little. Fortunately for us, at that time Fenichel's textbook of psychoanalysis came out. For two years, once a week, we took one chapter and discussed it. We went through the book chapter by chapter. In the course of our seminars, we had occasion to challenge some of the things that were written, or one or another of us would ask the rest of the group for an explanation of some theory or idea which he felt didn't quite fit. From time to time, we would offer clinical material that would either illustrate something that was said in the book or refute it. This experience eventuated in the first essays each of us had occasion to write.

After finishing with Fenichel's book, we expanded our experience by inviting some of the leading people in the field to meet with us and discuss their work. What we would do, for example, would be to study Lewin's work; then we would invite him to come to talk to us. We took our guests to dinner after which we retired to the home of one of our group, where we would ply him with questions. In this manner, we interviewed Edith Jacobson, Charles Fisher, and others. We had several such meetings over the years with Hartmann, Kris, and Loewenstein. As you can see, we were really in a most fortunate situation.

LR: You demonstrate a rigorous scientific approach in your writing by detailing for the reader how you use the specific data of your patients' dreams, associative processes, and fantasies to reach your conclusions. You often make reference to Waelder's principles of clinical generalization, and you avoid excessive metapsychological abstractions. When in your development did you develop this respect for scientific rigor?

JA: Well, it seems we have developed a good group process among us because, if you hadn't stopped me, the next thing I was going to talk about was exactly that issue. This is what happened in our group. One of us would have some idea for an essay or some critique of theory or practice. He would present it to the rest of us. I can assure you that the criticism we received was exacting and thoroughgoing. I think it was there that all of us developed this particular discipline of presenting clinical material so that it made sense, so that it was consistent.

Whether we all attained the same level of objectivity I cannot say. If it is something specific in my work, I really am not sure how it developed, except for one thing. I have always been interested in writing and the criteria that I use in writing anything, especially analytic essays, is to take the position of the audience, not of the writer. As I write, I follow the principle that if I cannot make it clear enough for someone else to understand, then I haven't thoroughly mastered what I am trying to work out myself.

LR: So it's really a kind of empathy with the learner.

JA: Of course, there is another very important experience that I have omitted—the Kris study group. It was a postgraduate seminar and the experience there pertains exactly to the point you are interested in. After we were finished with our regular three or four years of courses at the Institute, even after graduation, if one wanted, one could attend a continuing seminar conducted by Ernst Kris. These seminars became very popular. Dr. Kris asked Dr. Brenner and myself to assist him in conducting the seminars. After a while, the membership got so large that we split the seminar into three groups and then into four groups. Dr. Brenner and I took the second and third groups, and Dr. Loewenstein took the fourth group.

The spirit that pervaded those seminars was to examine certain propositions by bringing them into contact with precise clinical material. We then evaluated the situation. Does the clinical material establish or does it refute the particular hypothesis? This training in analysis of clinical data and hypotheses certainly enhanced my rigorous approach to analytic theory and practice. Of course, not all of us work the same way, nor does it mean that all of the students or participants in the study group were equally appreciative of the same criteria for interpretation. Nonetheless, this was an outstanding aspect of the experience. When Kris died in 1956, I think Dr. Waldhorn led one of the groups, and later Dr. Calder did the same. After a while the groups began to contract. Now there is only one group, which Dr. Brenner is still leading.

LR: So it has continued to this day?

JA: The study group continues to this day, although much smaller than it had been. I guess the enthusiasm for a teacher like Kris or any other teacher is hard to carry for many years. But let us return to the point which you raised. Dr. Kris had a wonderful way of teaching. In a very genial way, he elicited the creative, exploratory, and conjectural thinking of the group members. Some of the ideas that were proffered were way out, but Kris always managed to discuss the issues in such a way that everybody's contribution seemed to have the quality of positive accretion to what we were talking about.

I remember distinctly saying to him after one of the meetings, How could you have said this and this about so-and-so's ideas? "Well," he said, "you have to make them feel that they have something to say." It was a very good lesson for me in how to teach. I mention this as an example of some unwillingness on my part to compromise with far-out ideas. I feel that Kris was much more open to such notions.

I like to get the evidence. For that reason, I don't like to discuss cases as such. However, if you give me process notes of two or three or four sessions in sequence—even if you give me only the minimum amount of introductory background material—I feel much more comfortable. For me that is the testing ground of any hypothesis or interpretation. Otherwise, anybody's theory is as good as anybody else's, which means that no theory is any good.

SRR: You described fantasy as having a quasivisual nature. How did you come upon that idea? Is it considered radical?

JA: I came to that notion from my clinical experience. In my essay on "Disturbances of the Sense of Time with Special Reference to Timelessness," I referred to one of my very first patients, who suffered from an hallucinatory form of hysteria. On one occasion, she walked a considerable distance along one of New York's busiest shopping streets, completely immersed in her fantasies, which she was experiencing visually. I connected my thoughts about this patient with my observations on the connection between masturbation fantasies and symptom formation. I recalled how frequently masturbation fantasies are experienced in visual terms. It occurred to me that the wish representations of the unconscious portion of the mind are easily translatable into visual terms and, in fact, have a constant potential for such easy translation.

Sometime later, on a Thanksgiving Day, Dr. Brenner and his children were visiting at our home. He had brought some movies, and since we did not have a standard motion picture screen, he projected the film onto a rather large window shade we had covering the picture window in our living room. I had occasion about that time to walk out of the house to take care of some item, and I noted that the image being projected from inside the room on one side of the screen could be observed from the outside on the opposite side of the screen. It occurred to me that an amusing effect could be achieved if at the same time another projector was placing its image on the obverse side of the screen. The two sets of images would be superimposed. It then occurred to me that this is an interesting metaphor for expressing the relationship between persistent unconscious fantasy, that is, the contribution from the "inner projector" and the contribution from external perception and reality—the "external projector." I realized that this was a very mechanical metaphor, not sufficiently dynamic for the rich interplay between fantasy and perception, but it crystallized in my mind the idea that unconscious fantasy activity is quasivisual in nature.

I was further influenced by Lewin's "The Image and the Past," in which he spoke of mental contents as comparable to images cast on the inner wall of the mind or skull. This led me to the visual thinking that takes place in the analyst's mind as he listens to his patient's dreams. The analyst tends to recast the images that the patient presents to him in terms of his own recalled stores of images. Gradually there is a match of the patient's images and the analyst's, much as I describe at the end of my essay, "Fantasy, Memory, and Reality Testing."

One other element was influential and that was Freud's observation about the very rapid translation of an experience during sleep and its incorporation into the dream which the experience stimulates; in other words, there are preformed fantasies that require only some external stimulus to bring them into a concrete visual experience.

SRR: You think that most people imagine in visual terms?

JA: By saying that fantasy thinking has a quasivisual quality, what I was trying to bring to the fore is the very specific, concrete nature in which fantasy thinking gets transmitted through its derivatives into our conscious presentations. In this respect, of course, my thoughts might be similar to Kubie's ideas about psychosis. Kubie said psychosis is a waking dream. The psychotic orients himself towards the external world of perception, the same as he does towards his inner world. It is as if he were dreaming all the time. Well, there is something of that quality about the persistent unconscious fantasy wishes we have.

The difficulty arises in part because of the way analysis evolved. With the early ideas of the "Three Contributions to the Theory of Sex" and of the stages of libidinal development in the context of Freud's mechanistic, quantitative way of thinking about the drives, the drive idea became a very abstract one, and people began to think of it in terms similar, as Freud said, to an electrical charge—something that could be increased or decreased, put on the surface of an idea, taken away from something, and so forth. This, of course, is an abstract, metapsychological way of thinking of the drives, but the drive is just a conceptualization, an abstraction that we make from the clinical data. In the clinical data, the drive representations are concretely expressed. They can be transformed into visual images.

What I like to do as an exercise in teaching sessions is to review an analytic session by putting the essential productions on the blackboard. Then I ask the group, What is the nature of the drive in this material, and how do you know? After a while, I ask them to underline every verb. They get to see what the patient has been saying, "I want to, I'd like to, and so forth." They follow the verbs that follow the "I want to" or "I'd like to." During the course of this exercise it is possible to demonstrate the interchangeability of the object and the drive. In the same way, I ask the group to underline every noun. We can examine the common features of the objects of the driving verb and abstract the nature of the drive.

It was on the basis of this approach that I emphasize in "The Genesis of Interpretation," how the criteria for interpretation are similarity, repetition, context, contiguity, the convergence of the similarities, and the repetitions, together with the figures of speech, into a coherent idea. This guides us to the nature of the unconscious fantasy of which the clinical material in the session constitutes derivative representations. In this way we can approach the problem of interpretation. By the way, you do know that there are people who fantasize visually.

LR/SRR: Yes.

LR: With regard to visual thinking, in your essay, "Fantasy, Memory, and Reality Testing," you quote Freud, "The closer a thought or fantasy is to pleasure-dominated unconscious instinctual tendencies, the greater the possibility it will be represented mentally in a visual form." Can you say from your clinical experience whether different instinctual roots to wishes that form fantasies are represented by particular sensory configurations in those fantasies; for example, sexual wishes having more visual representation, aggressive wishes having more somatic representation, and so forth?

JA: If you follow the quote I use from Freud, you will catch what I had in mind. Essentially I was paraphrasing what Freud said in "The Interpretation of Dreams." His idea was that powerful wishes that cannot be expressed in waking thought, or, as we say today, because of internal conflicts, can find representation in a fleeting thought, sometimes in a visual fantasy, and, at night, in dreams. It is a characteristic of the human mind that certain wishes and thoughts, when powerful enough, will find representation in dreams, and visual fantasy is sort of a midway station between dreaming and waking thinking—that is, thinking in words.

LR: Do you think there are differences between individuals in their style of perception, so that one person may have more auditory elements in his or her dreams and another more visual elements? Or do you think the form that sensory perceptions take in fantasies are more related to the instinctual elements being expressed?

JA: There is no question that there are styles of perception and visualization that differ from individual to individual. Certain aspects of the experience are influenced by interaction with others and by identifications, but part of the capacity must be inborn. Thus, there is no question that there are people—those who are artistically gifted in the graphic arts—who have an inborn capacity to visualize their thinking or to think in terms of pictures, sometimes in a way that is really uncanny.

Recently, I saw a videotape of Picasso painting. Someone just took a camera and stood by Picasso while he painted. What struck me was that Picasso looked at a blank canvas and drew a line on one part it; then he drew a line far removed, somewhere else on the canvas, totally unconnected.... Then he drew some lines somewhere in the middle. Before you knew it, he had the intermediary lines on the canvas, and there was a specific form—a person, an animal, whatever. I was struck that as he looked at the blank canvas, in his mind he saw exactly what he was going to draw. More than that, of course, he could get his hands to do exactly what he had in his mind.

In the same way I am struck by—in fact, I am in awe—of composers who think in sound and who visualize sound patterns. I refer here to gifted people, but there is no question that all of us think in modalities other than verbal ones. This concept grew on me gradually. In my 1961 essay "Ego Psychology and the Study of Mythology," I thought of the persistent unconscious fantasies and their derivative manifestations that developed over a period of time and tried to make some analogy that would permit me to express my concept in concrete terms. At that point I thought of a series of transparencies through which a strong light may pass so that a final composite image would appear on a screen. The final image would have traces of all or most of the intermediate representations of the unconscious fantasy, very much like a dream may contain visual representations of derivatives of the identical wish from different times of the individual's life.

Later, I thought in terms of two projectors casting simultaneous images on opposite sides of a screen—one projector representing the contribution of perception, the other one representing the contribution of persistent unconscious fantasy. Of course, this is far from a satisfactory construct. It is too static, not sufficiently dynamic. To borrow an element, however, from that kind of thinking, I would say that all the time we are awake, and some of the time we are asleep, it is as if we were unconsciously watching an inner, continually unfolding cinematic representation of our unconscious fantasies.

This is, of course, a very mechanical and incomplete metaphor for what I have in mind, but it may be more comprehensible if we think in terms of the visual hallucinations of psychotic patients. They "see" visual representations of the derivative expression of some unconscious fantasy. It is not just a question of the type of drive representation that is involved, nor is it simply a question of neurophysiological circuits in the brain. Inborn tendencies, learning, and specific experiences have to be taken into account.

SRR: That brings to mind your ideas concerning the giftedness or creativity of the analyst. In "The Genesis of Interpretation," you described the way in which the analyst perceives both the nonverbal and the verbal modes of the analysand's communication, sometimes subliminally, and how these communications are received by the analyst and elaborated and conceptualized unconsciously. You observed that there is something intensely aesthetic and creative about this mode of functioning.

We're interested in your thoughts about this kind of giftedness. Can it be developed? Can it be taught? How does one conceive of the ongoing psychic functioning of the analyst? Can the analyst's work be compared to that of a painter or sculptor? For each, the work can provide continuous opportunity for using processes of imagination and synthesis, enabling ongoing reworking of one's own fantasy life.

JA: The work of the analyst, I would say, is closer to that of the literary artist than to that of the plastic artist or musician. Like the creative writer, the analyst is influenced by the evocative power of the experience with other people. The analyst, very much like the literary artist, is sensitive to the unarticulated, but nonetheless communicated, aspirations, hopes, disappointments, and pain of the people about him. Neither the creative writer nor the analyst necessarily has to be aware at the moment of how these experiences have influenced him. They work upon him quietly and come out in the course of his creative or therapeutic work.

It was in this connection that Beres quoted Coleridge to the effect that artistic creativity is the result of powerful emotions recollected in tranquillity. Put another way, in the analytic context, there is a constant creative interchange between the patient and the analyst. Both are changed in the course of the experience. A little bit of every patient remains forever with the analyst, and a great deal of the analyst remains forever with the patient. It is very much the same as the interaction between the audience and the playwright, as well as the interaction between the person who stimulated the writer and the writer.

SRR: In discussing another aspect of the analyst's creativity, you state: "In my view, metaphor is an inherent quality of language in general and how the human mind integrates the experience of the individual." You note that a measure of the analyst's empathic capacities lies in his ability to be influenced by the form, sequence, and content and patterning of the patient's material, so that the analyst may be stimulated by the hidden message in the patient's associations, sometimes even before the analyst is aware of the unconscious fantasy. We are very interested in that process of how the analyst becomes stimulated. Again, can you teach it? Can you deepen that capacity for stimulation? If so, how?

JA: I'm not sure that I know the answer to the last question. But first, let me expand on one of the ideas you quoted, which might help round out the picture. I feel that the processing of information by the individual from earliest childhood is based upon sorting out of sensory impressions, according to two fundamental sets of criteria. First, the individual asks, "Is this sensation that I am experiencing familiar or unfamiliar?" An attempt is always made to see where the new experience fits in the stored memories of previous experiences, with the organization of previous memory traces. The other criterion for processing perceptual experience is, "Is the sensation pleasant or unpleasant?" As a result of this tendency to process according to these two fundamental criteria, memory systems are built. They are much more complicated than any computer can simulate.

On the basis of these memory systems, what is familiar or suggestibly familiar can easily pass over and be brought into context with something which is already known and already familiar. Thus, it becomes easy for one element to be substituted for another. This is what makes simile and metaphor, and is the basis, I believe, of all figures of speech that become an inherent way of how the human being experiences the world about him and the people in it. Speech, or thought in general, is inherently metaphoric. The mind stores and processes information in keeping with these principles. Our memories and thought processes are governed by associations, often using connections that are amazingly ingenious. Many analytic sessions, perhaps most sessions, are like works of art. They begin with an opening theme, and in the course of the patient's productions, the theme is subjected to innumerable variations and permutations. After the theme or the opening coda has been elaborated and repeated, very often, like in a good work of art, there is a closing summary, a finale that repeats the theme.

This is the aesthetic process that the analyst has to learn to appreciate and to recognize in keeping with the criteria of context, contiguity, repetition, similarity and opposite, and convergence—the various criteria which I have suggested pertain to interpretation. This is the sort of aesthetic sensibility that I had in mind. Now, as to the question you ask, "Is this something that can be taught or developed?"; although I have thought about it a great deal, I am not sure if it can be taught or developed.

SRR: You need to study the individual.

JA: Yes, that is true.

LR: In your essay, "Fantasy, Memory, and Reality Testing," you state: "Each version of fantasy corresponds to a different psychic moment, a particular time in a person's life when the ego integrated the demands of the instinctual wishes in keeping with its growing adaptive and defensive responsibilities." How do you think an individual unconsciously selects particular fantasies to express his or her intrapsychic conflicts?

JA: The part of the question that I can answer does not present too big a problem. There are experiential factors, the relationship with other people, the things that happen to one, where one fits into world history, one's background, what one has been taught, and so forth, all of which help shape how the individual organizes his fantasy life. This, of course, is only a small part of a more important issue, that has never been adequately resolved in analysis. It has been epitomized as the problem of a choice of symptom. How do people organize a certain fantasy in response to their conflicts? Why do they attempt to resolve these conflicts in terms of specific symptoms or character traits? I don't think we have adequately resolved that question. One attempt was made by Martin Wangh in his essay on the genesis of a phobia. It is the only essay I recall where someone tried to decide on the basis of how the analytic data illuminated the individual's experience, whether a particular symptom did develop.

Concerning the idea of different psychic moments, I'll illustrate my thoughts by referring once again to dreams. Dreams usually deal with one or two conflicting wishes and with different ways of how to resolve those conflicts. In the associations, you will find that some of the thoughts point to how the conflict was experienced when the patient was, let us say, eight years old. He will also remember something from his adolescence, an association from the day before, something pertaining to the transference, and so forth, so that the dream is, in a certain sense, a record of the individual's history. This is what I had in mind when I tried to use the image of several transparencies, one put behind the other and then having a light shine through them onto a screen. The resulting picture (which is the dream) will have some representations from each of the several transparencies through which the light has passed.

LR: In your essay "Fantasy, Memory, and Reality Testing," you state that fantasies developmentally serve as solutions to intrapsychic conflicts at different psychic moments, as evolving compromise formations. You note, however, that there are traumas that can overwhelm a person's adaptive capacities. Does it follow that trauma can create discontinuities in an individual's fantasy life over time? How do you think fantasy formation is affected by a holocaust-type situation or by overwhelming emotional trauma in early childhood?

JA: Once again it becomes a question of the relative distribution of forces. Much depends upon the ego's capacities, the ego strength that the individual had available when he experienced overwhelming external traumatization. There is an essay by Anna Ornstein on the holocaust based on her own experience. The effects of external trauma, she states, are not entirely in direct proportion to the nature or the intensity of the experience. Different people react to the same external injury in different ways.

In my essay, "Conflict, Trauma, and Deficit," I pursue some of those issues. One must bear in mind that the psychoanalytic concept of trauma is a retrospective one. Dr. Brenner has pointed out that whether an external event proves to be traumatic psychologically is identical with the concept of trauma in the physical sense. For example, several individuals exposed to the same bacteria will not all get ill. Much will depend upon their inner constitution, their immune system, their state of health at the time, whether they were fatigued, and so on. In the case of psychological trauma, we should add that noxious external events can prove very damaging precisely when they coincide with or evoke the fears connected with the preexistent, persistent unconscious fantasies and conflicts.

LR: In your paper on psychic reality, you gave an example where an adult may see an amoeba, but a child might see it as a dragon. You were talking about how a child's misperceptions may enter into the structure of unconscious fantasy. I wondered about the complement to that. When do you feel fantasy developmentally starts to affect perception? How early in the process of a child's development?

JA: I think I answered that question when I spoke about how information is processed. Sensory impressions are grouped according to whether they are pleasant or unpleasant, familiar or unfamiliar. What the individual would like is repetition of remembered experiences of pleasure. This is what Freud had in mind when he discussed the pleasure principle and the quest for an identity of perception. As a result of this principle, individuals tend to foist upon new sensations their hopes, their aspirations for realizing their unfulfilled wishes. Accordingly, what happens is that each individual has a set of characteristic or idiosyncratic fantasies that serve to create a mental set, on the basis of which the individual tends to selectively perceive, apperceive, interpret, respond to, and remember certain kinds of experiences. The dividing line between memory and hope is not very sharp. Often it is a question of timing. Memory, we know, is self-serving. It is related to ideas, to wishes of the past, and to anticipations for the future.

SRR: In writing about training, you stated, "Psychoanalysis serves as the family romance of the psychoanalyst." Do you think of training analysis as distinctly different from or as relatively similar to therapeutic analysis? Given the impact of the institute structure on training analysis, do you think of issues concerning separation, individuation?

JA: When you say separation, that's one thing. When you couple it with individuation, that's something else.

SRR: Right.

JA: When you first said separation, I thought about separation of the individual from his analyst or the individual from his institute; but when you couple it with individuation, you prejudge the situation in terms of a specific paradigm. You begin to talk of Mahler's concepts....

SRR: No, about mourning....I'm thinking about individuation separately, about how....

JA: And the next thing you introduce is mourning, and that is part of a similar paradigm.

SRR: Yes, but isn't that part of the resolution of analysis?

JA: Since different people have different problems, different analyses get resolved in different ways. Every analysis does not necessarily terminate in a process of mourning, nor do all separations necessarily mean loss of nurture, and so on.

SRR: We're interested in the "and so on."

JA: This is an issue that has concerned me for a long time. The language one uses indicates the kind of paradigm one has in mind. Separation, individuation, and mourning, are all part of a certain paradigm concerning analysis representing a recapitulation of the early mother-child relationship. That may be so, but not necessarily. In analysis, we observe the characteristic way in which the individual's mind functions. Different people are concerned with different themes and different conflicts. To be sure, there are certain basic problems that we all face. But they do not present all individuals with the same degree of intensity of conflict and challenge of problem-solving.

Let us consider, for example, the question of the end of an analysis, or let us make the issue simpler by considering the end of the analytic season. Summertime is coming and the analyst is due to go on vacation. The patient and the analyst are going to separate physically and the patient feels anxious. On the basis of this amount of material we don't know why the patient is anxious. There will be a physical separation, but we don't know why this makes the patient anxious. The patient may feel frightened because he or she feels they can't get along without you, as if to say, "I'm a hopeless, helpless babe, and if you're not there to nurture me, to hold me, to support me, I will die." That is one possibility.

It also happens that the patient may become anxious because he does not know whether you will return. Perhaps while you are away, something will happen to you, and you will die. Such a patient requires your presence to be free of the anxiety generated by the notion that his hostile wishes in the transference may cause your death. Described by Helene Deutsch, this mechanism is known as the mechanism of the protector under protection. The patient has to be assured that the analyst is well in order to prove to himself that his death wishes toward the analyst have not come true.

Or, finally, the patient may have a feeling that he might lose control of his impulses while you are away and he is not reporting his thoughts and wishes. He may practice some perverse sexual acts; he may resort to masturbation; he may lapse back into alcoholism. These are just three possibilities. One should not force the first paradigm onto the material only on the basis of the objective reality of physical separation. It's the fantasy wish and the conflict evoked by separation that we analyze. Something similar happens at the end of an analysis.

SRR: So you might not make very much distinction between training analyses and therapeutic analyses?

JA: Both should be conducted in the same way, with the same approach to the analysis of the material. Of course, there is the problem of the guarantee of confidentiality. Nonreporting is an essential aspect of the training analysis situation. However, while training analysis and therapeutic analysis should be carried out in the same manner technically, there are certain distinct hazards of the training analysis. The analysand will see the analyst, will read his works. The fantasies and wishes evoked by these experiences have to be analyzed. They should not be lost. There are certain built-in difficulties in the training analysis which are hard to overcome, among them the relationship to the institute and the problem of displaced transference. Freud said that after a while it is a good idea to get a second analysis, perhaps even a third. In the early days, this was easier. In my little study group, each one of us had at least two analyses.

SRR: Would you keep the structure basically as it is? Do you think there's anything that could be done structurally that would...?

JA: ...about the training analysis? I would emphasize the guarantee of confidentiality. For another, I would suggest paying more attention to certain aspects of training analysis that are often overlooked, as, for example, the relationship to the institute, the institutionalized idealization of Freud. The institutionalized deification of Freud is a persistent transference problem. These are among several of the factors that I've already pointed out as hazards of the training analysis.

SRR: A number of your essays demonstrate your knowledge of mythology and religion. We wonder about the analyst's own religious development. How does one's own experience with religion influence who one becomes as an analyst, in particular, one's perception of the world?

JA: Undoubtedly influenced by Freud's militant opposition to religion, for many years analysts regarded religious interest or observance as a form of neurotic behavior. In a discussion of some problems of psychoanalytic education and conflicts within training institutes, I noted that, as a rule, analysts are middle-class, liberal intellectuals, who express a spirit of individuality and freedom from narrow group identification. For many, psychoanalysis becomes a derivative expression of their family romance. In the training analyst, or in psychoanalysis, they find a superior set of parent substitutes and a rational belief superseding the religious instruction they had received.

In my farewell address to the Board on Professional Standards, I tried to point out how these elements contributed to some of the dissensions and group conflicts characteristic of the history of many institutes. As far as the development of the individual analyst is concerned, the issue of one's earlier religious experience is something that should be confronted in every analysis. Religion, after all, is one of the socializing, institutionalizing experiences leading to acculturation. How the particular individual or future analyst orients himself to the implicit conscious and unconscious themes of the religious training correlates very closely with the nature of the individual's persistent unconscious conflicts.

For many individuals, religion affords a transitional experience in resolving persistent unconscious conflicts, particularly oedipal ones. In this respect, both religion and mythology are closely related. Not only are many religions founded on organizing myths, but both religion and mythology suggest ideal types of character formation represented by certain heroes with whom the individual is influenced to identify. The specific ways in which the future analyst responds to the issues posed by religious identification ultimately influences choice of profession, character structure, and one's outlook on the issues of the day. Of course, religious experience is only one of many sets of experiences which influence the individual, but its significance has been underestimated by many analysts.

SRR: Your writings demonstrate a close attention to the influence of society on the individual in the analytic setting and in the larger world. I was reflecting on your papers on the role of the prophet…

JA: I have always had a strong liking for history.

LR: …and for language. Your whole sense of how we use speech and words and metaphor and how that connects from the earliest levels of development on up, the different ways of communicating.…

JA: I have already pointed out the basic principles that govern my approach to how the mind works. Because of the way that the human mind processes information, we become metaphorical thinkers, and that is why I chose to quote Robert Frost at the conclusion of my paper on metaphor. Frost said that even science is a kind of metaphor because of the fundamental characteristic of trying to express what is new and unknown in terms of what is known and familiar. When we come upon something unfamiliar, we try to fit it in, we try to correlate it, we try to sort it out in terms of what is familiar to us.

LR: That directly leads into a question about surprise. You said in your essay, "Affects and the Psychoanalytic Situation," "the analyst can expect to be surprised regularly by the patient's patterns of affectivity." You also state that "there's no absolute model against which patterns of affectivity may be judged." Could you say more about the element of surprise in the analyst's experience with the patient; how to use surprise, explore it; how the analyst judges the patient;...and how you deal with these issues in supervision?

JA: I think that the experience of surprise represents a critical point in the analyst's understanding of his patients. It represents the point where his own inner resistances to what the patient has been trying to say have been overcome. Suddenly he realizes that he has entered a new phase of insight or has seen something which he had been fending off. In a way, it's analogous to what Freud said about certain jokes.

A sudden release of tension is what gives us the feeling of humor. So surprise represents a shift in the balance of defenses in the compromise formation in the analyst's mind. It reveals that something has finally come through to the analyst, something which he'd been having difficulty with theretofore. Now, there was a second part of the question....

LR: The second part was the issue of judging patterns of affectivity. You make an appeal to the reader to not too quickly judge how a person affectively deals with certain situations.

JA: I think I answered that question before in one of my essays where I discussed the issue of moods.

LR/SRR: Yes.

JA: What I had in mind was that the pattern of affectivity has to be seen as a derivative manifestation of some unconscious fantasy and that the mood or the affectivity is consistent with what is going on in the patient's mind at that time, although he may not be aware of its origin. Under such circumstances the patient might try to rationalize his affectivity. A pattern of affectivity is a manifest phenomenon, and one cannot interpret it, one cannot understand it exclusively on the basis of its manifest appearance. In the course of treatment, one should try to understand patterns of affectivity in the context in which they appear, and then try to seek out the evidence indicating the relationship of the affectivity to unconscious processes.

Often enough the patient will say, "I was depressed all day. I have no idea why I was depressed." I gave an example of such a situation in my essay, "The Revenge Motive in the Primal Scene." The patient said, "There was a fire downtown. Some firemen lost their lives. I felt terrible." One should note that such things had happened in the patient's experience before. There had been other catastrophes, but it was only when we got material connecting the mood to the primal scene trauma that we could understand why the patient was depressed. A fire had been part of the general gestalt of the events during which the primal scene trauma had occurred. In fact, in a certain sense one could say that this patient was "latently" depressed all his life. All he needed was something to reevoke the primal scene trauma, some fragment of the experience to evoke the mood appropriate for the memory of the event.

SRR: In your essay on supervision, you illustrated a case in which you pointed out to the supervisee....

JA: ...he was identified with the patient.

SRR: What are your thoughts as to why, at a certain point in time, the analyst's countertransference would lead him or her to enact rather than respond in another way?

JA: What do you mean by enact?

SRR: In this situation to identify with through action, to demonstrate something through behavior rather than through verbalization.

LR: ...like in the cigarette example....

JA: I understand. What was happening to that analyst whom I was supervising...my guess would be that the patient's material exacerbated in him a warded-off fantasy wish of the same type that the patient was talking about.

SRR: Do you think, though, that sometimes the warding off might go by just somehow missing the boat? I guess what I'm wondering is why would actions....

JA: If you miss the boat—that's a metaphor. If it really means what that metaphor usually means, that you didn't see it at all....

SRR: That's the worst type of warding off.

JA: Sometimes it takes a little time for these concepts to sink in during supervision. Let us examine the situation of the "blind spot." I think it is a rare occasion when the analyst does not appreciate at all what the patient is saying. If one studies the record of the patient's productions carefully, and the analyst's response, one can observe how frequently the analyst intervenes at certain points to distract the patient from pursuing a certain subject. In those cases, the analyst is unconsciously acting to protect himself from some kind of conflict that the patient's material evokes in him.

If one observes carefully, usually one can recognize how the analyst's interventions correspond precisely to the defenses that the patient assumes. The analyst intervenes for the sake of his own equilibrium. He doesn't want the patient's material to bring out in him the sort of conflicts that he is trying to bring out in the patient. This is something that all of us tend to do until we finally catch ourselves.

LR: You have written several essays on phenomena like déjà vu, the sense of time,...the close connection between one's sense of self and the sense of time. You state that during intrapsychic conflict one may experience alterations in time, or space, or depersonalization. How does trauma similarly or differently alter one's sense of time, or space, and/or create states of depersonalization?

JA: How I understand states of depersonalization?

LR: Thinking of trauma as playing a role in states of depersonalization.

JA: Well, it depends upon the kind of trauma you have in mind. Depersonalization is very common in situations of realistic danger. People in cars that are turning over, as once happened to me, or in airplanes going down very frequently become depersonalized. The defensive response is, "This is not happening to me. I am just observing it." The same sort of thing may happen when a powerful fantasy of a traumatic nature threatens to emerge. The individual dissociates himself from the urge by a process of splitting in two. He identifies himself with the observing self, not with the experiencing self.

LR: You described one woman who had a split sense of self, and it appeared related to a memory of her having been teased in a group of people and as a child....

JA: "It's not happening to me." The humiliation in that case was overwhelming.

LR: Right. The repudiated self and the observing self. You also were talking about déjà vu as a phenomenon that you could see in epilepsy, for example, temporal lobe epilepsy, but you point out that there can be psychodynamic etiologies to the phenomenon. You raised the question of déjà vu being a symptom with several different etiologies.

JA: Well, not really. What we are dealing with are two different ways of looking at the same phenomenon. There are two realms of discourse here. There are individuals who are subject to déjà vu experiences and do have organic changes in the brain or demonstrable physiological disturbances of electrical activity in the brain. Our psychoanalytic method permits us only to understand those déjà vu phenomena that come under our purview during treatment. What are the concomitant electrophysiological changes that occur in our patients' brains when they have these déjà vu attacks? We do not know; we do not have the data. But we do have the data of the psychological significance of these attacks for our patients.

What is the status in those patients who have neurological disease, brain tumors, and so on? Certainly the altered electrical physiology must change the patient's mentation, leading as it does to déjà vu. The psychological significance of such experiences will have to be understood in psychological terms. These are questions that remain for the future, but we are talking about two different levels of experience, two different ways of examining the same kind of external, consciously reported phenomena. The kind of investigative tool one uses in any science dictates the nature of the results that one is going to get.

LR: It's very interesting to hear that there may be a dynamic dimension of experience for a phenomenon which has mainly been characterized as biological.

JA: It's not a question of either/or. They are two different instrumentalities of interpretation. There's an old, old essay, I forget by whom, and it's on the psychopathology of dementia praecox....

LR: Yes, I think you mention it in your papers....

JA: I was referring to patients with delusions of grandeur and other symptoms. For the longest time, the brains of schizophrenics were examined with procedures available in earlier periods, and nothing was found. Today, brains are being examined in many different ways and certain changes consistent with schizophrenia have been described. What are the implications of these findings as far as the nature of the patient's mental processes or the content of the delusions? At present we do not know.

SRR/LR: Thank you for discussing so much of your work with us.

SELECTED BIBLIOGRAPHY

Arlow, J. A. (1951). The consecration of the prophet. *Psychoanalytic Quarterly,* Vol. 20, pp. 374–397.

Arlow, J. A. (1951). Psychoanalytic study of religious initiation rite: Bar Mitzvah. *The Psychoanalytic Study of the Child,* Vol. 6, pp. 353–374. New York: International Universities Press.

Arlow, J. A. (1953). Masturbation and symptom formation. *Journal of the American Psychoanalytic Association*, Vol. 1, pp. 45–58.

Arlow, J. A. (1955). Notes on oral symbolism. *Psychoanalytic Quarterly,* Vol. 24, pp. 63–74.

Arlow, J. A. (1957). On smugness. *International Journal of Psycho-Analysis,* Vol. 38, pp. 1–8.

Arlow, J. A. (1959). The structure of the déjà-vu experience. *Journal of the American Psychoanalytic Association,* Vol. 7, pp. 611–631.

Arlow, J. A. (1960). Fantasy systems in twins. *Psychoanalytic Quarterly*, Vol. 29, pp. 175–199.

Arlow, J. A. (1961). Silence and the theory of technique. *Journal of the American Psychoanalytic Association,* Vol. 9, pp. 44–55.

Arlow, J. A. (1961). Ego psychology and the study of mythology. *Journal of the American Psychoanalytic Association,* Vol. 9, pp. 371–393.

Arlow, J. A. (1963). Conflict, regression, and symptom formation. *International Journal of Psycho-Analysis*, Vol. 44, pp. 12–22.

Arlow, J. A. (1963). The supervisory situation. *Journal of the American Psychoanalytic Association,* Vol. 11, pp. 576–594.

Arlow, J. A. (1964). Symptom formation and character formation. *International Journal of Psycho-Analysis*, Vol. 45, pp. 167–170.

Arlow, J. A. & Brenner, C. (1964). *Psychoanalytic Concepts and the Structural Theory*. New York: International Universities Press.

Arlow, J. A. & Brenner, C. (1969). The psychopathology of the psychoses: A proposed revision. *International Journal of Psycho-Analysis,* Vol. 50, pp. 5–14.

Arlow, J. A. (1972). Ten years of COPE: Perspectives in psychoanalytic education. *Journal of the American Psychoanalytic Association*, Vol. 20, pp. 556–566.

Arlow, J. A. (1972). The only child. *Psychoanalytic Quarterly*, Vol. 41, pp. 507–536.

Arlow, J. A. (1973). The examined life: In tribute to Bertram D. Lewin (1896–1971). *International Journal of Psycho-Analysis*, Vol. 54, pp. 103–109.

Arlow, J. A. (1973). Perspectives on aggression in human adaptation. *Psychoanalytic Quarterly*, Vol. 42, pp. 178–184.

Beres, D. & Arlow, J. A. (1974). Fantasy and identification in empathy. *Psychoanalytic Quarterly,* Vol. 43, pp. 26–50.

Arlow, J. A. (1975). The structural hypothesis—theoretical considerations. *Psychoanalytic Quarterly,* Vol. 44, pp. 509–525.

Arlow, J. A. (1976). Communication and character: A clinical study of a man raised by deaf-mute parents. *The Psychoanalytic Study of the Child,* Vol. 31, pp. 139–163. New Haven, CT: Yale University Press.

Arlow, J. A. (1977). Affects and the psychoanalytic situation. *International Journal of Psycho-Analysis*, Vol. 58, pp. 157–170.

Arlow, J. A. (1978). Pyromania and the primal scene: A psychoanalytic comment on the work of Yukio Mishima. *Psychoanalytic Quarterly,* Vol. 47, pp. 24–51.

Arlow, J. A. (1979). The genesis of interpretation. *Journal of the American Psychoanalytic Association,* Vol. 27 (Suppl.) pp. 193–206.

Arlow, J. A. (1979). Metaphor and the psychoanalytic situation. *Psychoanalytic Quarterly*, Vol. 48, pp. 363–385.

Arlow, J. A. (1980). Object concept and object choice. *Psychoanalytic Quarterly,* Vol. 49, pp. 109–133.

Arlow, J. A. (1982). Problems of the superego concept. *The Psychoanalytic Study of the Child,* Vol. 37, pp. 229–244. New Haven, CT: Yale University Press.

Arlow, J. A. (1984). Disturbances of the sense of time with special reference to the experience of timelessness. *Psychoanalytic Quarterly,* Vol. 53, pp. 113–137.

Arlow, J. A. (1985). The concept of psychic reality and related problems. *Journal of the American Psychoanalytic Association,* Vol. 33, pp. 521–535.

Arlow, J. A. (1985). Some technical problems of countertransference. *Psychoanalytic Quarterly,* Vol. 54, pp. 164–174.

Arlow, J. A. (1986). Psychoanalysis and time. *Journal of the American Psychoanalytic Association,* Vol. 34, pp. 507–528.

Arlow, J. A. (1986). The poet as prophet: A psychoanalytic perspective. *Psychoanalytic Quarterly*, Vol. 55, pp. 53–68.

Arlow, J. A. (1987). The dynamics of interpretation. *Psychoanalytic Quarterly*, Vol. 56, pp. 68–87.

Arlow, J. A. (1987). Trauma, play, and perversion. *The Psychoanalytic Study of the Child*, Vol. 42, pp. 31–44. New Haven, CT: Yale University Press.

Arlow, J. A. (1988). Leo Rangell: An appreciation. *Psychoanalytic Quarterly,* Vol. 57, pp. 297–312.

Arlow, J. A. & Brenner, C. (1988). The future of psychoanalysis. *Psychoanalytic Quarterly,* Vol. 57, pp. 1–14.

André Green

André Green was chief of the Clinic of Mental Diseases at the Paris Faculty and Director of the Paris Psychoanalytical Institute. He has occupied the Freud Memorial Chair at University College, London, and is a faculty member and training analyst at the Paris Psychoanalytical Society. He is a past President of the Paris Psychoanalytical Society, as well as a former Vice President of the International Psychoanalytical Association. He has been an editor of the *International Journal of Psycho-Analysis, International Review of Psychoanalysis,* and *Nouvelle Revue of Psychoanalyse.* Dr. Green remains dedicated to the practice of psychoanalysis and specializes in the treatment of difficult cases. He was interviewed April 8, 1990, and April 27, 1992.

SRR: We begin by asking you about the notion of private madness. In discussing passion, you described how inevitably "all the vicissitudes of Eros are tainted with a potential madness." You stated that even in the most ordinary of analyses, there has to be a moment of madness: "...There comes a time when the feeling arises in the analyst's countertransference that he is at grips with mad mental functioning." Can there be an analysis without this moment, or an analyst who hasn't experienced it?

AG: First, I have to say how I got to madness. It is a very old story, and I wasn't aware of it myself. I realized that, as we say in French, "apres coup," because when I think now of what could have been the sources of it—besides my own personal history, which is no matter for the interview—I think it started with my doctoral thesis at the end of my training in psychiatry. One of my professors had just told me, it was in 1954 or 1955, "You know, you should see what is going on with the parents of the schizophrenics." He said that his wife had been taking phone calls for appointments for him for his private practice and that when she had some people on the phone, she could tell—and she was not a psychiatrist or psychologist—that the patient was probably a schizophrenic. That was her intuition just from the way the parents talked to her and the way they seemed quite bizarre. That was the sole indication for my research in the beginning. I didn't know anything about it, and at that time in France nothing had been published on the mothers of schizophrenics.

I started by studying what was a significant amount of literature, which I hadn't known at the time, and then thinking on the subject. At the end of my doctoral thesis, I described something which was at the time rather new. I described what I called a "psychotic character." People all knew character neurosis or neurotic character. There had been a lot of discussion about the differences between the two, and finally I wanted to describe "psychotic characters." I had in mind some people, who, I would say today, have private madnesses. Instead of it being a discovery from analysis, it was a discovery of someone who cares for mental patients and who comes across the parents of some of them. We wouldn't use that term for the parents of the manic-depressive patients. We would especially apply it to the parents of schizophrenics. So it was, to some extent, a private madness, because I felt this madness was located and restricted to family relationships or to the relationship with the ill child. That was the starting point for what I have worked on since, on a different ground, of course, with other means of investigation, and with the instrumental concepts of psychoanalysis from the perspective of analytic treatment.

I don't want to spend much time on that because that's prehistory; at the time I wasn't even yet in analytic training. It is difficult for me to date exactly the time the problem of private madness became important to me. I can say it could be in the late 60s or beginning of the 70s. But it was during the period after my training was finished. On one hand, I had been a follower of Lacan since 1961. On the other hand, at the same time I was very interested in British psychoanalysis.

My first contact with British psychoanalysis dates from 1961. It was in the summer of 1961 at the Pre-Congress in London, which was organized by the British Society before the Edinburgh Congress of the IPA in 1961, when I first met some British psychoanalysts. It was there I met Winnicott, Rosenfeld, and John Klauber. I had personal contact with them. I attended seminars they gave, and this was an absolute revelation to me. Lacan, in a different way, was also a revelation to me, but he was part of my French background, and I could easily find my way in what was going on there. As for the British, it was not that I did not know them—I went to these psychoanalysts because I had already heard about them and had read their work—but I was not well-acquainted with them.

French psychoanalysts read a lot. They are not as chauvinistic as they seem, because they know more about foreign literature than the analysts from other countries used to know about how things went in France. It has changed. Now, some people are interested in the work of Chasseguet, Joyce McDougall, myself, or others, but this is quite recent. You had to wait until the 1980s before that could happen, but now we are speaking of the 1960s when French psychoanalysts were despised. They were despised because of that split we had in France and because when French psychoanalysts tried to say something it was considered as rationalizing, or overintellectualization, or oversophistication—well, all sorts of scornful criticisms that you may find to reject a contribution, which tried to raise the problem to the level of thought. At the time it was not in the spirit of the IPA.

It is true that the International at the time was dominated by American power. It was Hartmann's period, and Hartmann behaved like an autocrat. He had a tremendous reputation among the American scientists. While in Europe some British quoted him, in France nobody paid attention to what he wrote. It is not that we did not read it. We read his work, and found it nonpsychoanalytical and not at all interesting. We were in a very difficult position because Loewenstein had worked in France, and he was associated with Hartmann's work, and we had to distinguish between Hartmann's ideas and the contributions of Loewenstein and Kris.

I think that these three people are in fact very different. Kris is very different from Hartmann; Hartmann is very different from Loewenstein. Loewenstein was the clinician, and with the clinician we could talk. I remember being in New York in 1963 or 1964, visiting him, and having a very interesting discussion with him.

But as I was saying, the International was dominated by the Americans, and I'll say that the debate was mainly between the American and the English schools. That's why the British organized a pre-Congress. It was because they wanted the Americans, who were coming to the Congress to see how they were working, to come a little bit earlier and to see how those in Europe, particularly in London, practiced and with what concepts. Of course, this was the pursuit of the war between the Kleinians and the followers of Anna Freud. Heinz Hartmann came with others to support Anna Freud against the Kleinians. But whatever the Kleinians were, the International was dominated by these two main currents. The majority of the French were not at all interested in what the Americans were saying or writing—except for people like Fenichel or Nunberg and also Alexander—but they were very interested in what the British were saying even though they had reason to avoid them, since British psychoanalysis was empiricist. The French have a philosophical background and like something more intellectually structured, and so they had every reason to be reticent. But I would say the genius of some people transcended the differences in countries. To meet someone like Winnicott, to read Winnicott, or Bion, or other very clinically talented people, of which there are so many in the British Society, was very stimulating.

SRR: Would you say that your ideas of madness evolved?

AG: Yes, I have to say that. I have to say that because I think before meeting the British I had a slight idea of what was a borderline patient. I had already written an essay with Pierre Male, one of our best men in adolescent psychiatry, who was not known abroad, but who had considerable influence in France. He was a specialist of adolescents, probably the best one, and I had written an essay with him on the preschizophrenic states. But he was more of a psychiatrist and psychotherapist than a true analyst. When you have someone like Winnicott—I think that even he wasn't an orthodox analyst—it was so evidently analysis. I still remember; I can still see Winnicott, because the first Congress I ever attended was in 1957, in Paris. In those days, Congresses were not as large as they are now and candidates were used for help. I was one of those candidates, and, of course, it allowed me to attend the Congress. I still remember Winnicott's contribution, which was to distinguish between what is most deep and what is the earliest—the difference between the earlier and the deeper. When I listened to that I said, Well, here is someone obviously. It was at that Congress that I also met—I mean I could be a spectator at their performances—Melanie Klein and Anna Freud. I also remember Bion and Margaret Little.

It's interesting because I was a young candidate, so I had no prejudice about who was who, who was important, and who was not—except for the people I knew who were on the dais. I did not know who Winnicott really was, and I was very strongly impressed. So to some extent, I knew where I was going in 1961. I went to the seminar with Winnicott. He was studying the squiggle at that time, and from that time, from 1961 to nearly 1972, I did a lot of reading and thinking, but I had no real personal relationships with the British psychoanalysts. My relationship with the British started in 1972, because from that time I had regular contacts with them through Masud Khan. I had been appointed to the *Nouvelle Revue de Psychoanalyse*, founded by Pontalis. He asked me to become a member of the editorial board. There I met Masud Khan. Also, I went to London frequently. I did not often meet Winnicott because he died, I believe, in 1972, but I had more personal contacts with many British analysts—Rosenfeld, Hanna Segal, John Klauber, the Sandlers, and Enid Balint. I had other opportunities to meet with them in the subsequent years during Franco-British meetings between psychoanalysts. I also participated in the first European group of CAPS.

SRR: I'm not quite sure how to put this question, but being exposed to so many different ways of working and being so attuned to the idea of madness, I wonder, you must have quite a sense of how it affects the work, the actual....

AG: Yes, but I'm coming to that progressively, because all that I'm saying here is the history of the thing. And you know it came not only progressively, but really like concentric circles. I mean, it started by knowing the people and reading their work and then having that experience in my own experience, and then having my own conception that I created by myself, but borrowing things that I had already learned from them. So it is not until, I would say, the 1975 essay, that I really became aware of the importance of madness in my experience. I realized things which were not very easy to grasp in the French context, because the French context, dominated by Lacan, but not only him, is very classically Freudian, which means that the clinical model would still be the model of neurosis, and still be the model of the transference neurosis with the psychoneurosis as reference. There came a time when I realized it didn't work. I'm not so much an analyst who looks for recipes or asks for a trick to solve transference block situations. It was a fact that what I found in my readings of Freud and what I thought about my patients did not coincide. So something else had to be discovered, something else created. I found part of it in Winnicott. And then there's another date coming, 1976. I was invited by the Menninger Foundation to the Borderline Personality Symposium, where I met Bion and that's when a friendship started.

I can even tell you an anecdote which will amuse the American reader. My first or second day in Topeka the organizers had planned workshops with informal discussions in which they grouped the main participants of the symposium. So they decided they would have one workshop with Margaret Mahler, Bion, and myself. When Margaret Mahler saw that, she got so frightened that she went to the organizers and said, "I don't want to be with these two fellows. Please put me anywhere else but not with them." And that's what really happened. Thus, we enjoyed the company of Otto Kernberg, who wasn't afraid of these great monsters. He could handle them. This anecdote is very symbolic because I later met Margaret Mahler at a private party. She did not know who I was. I knew who she was, of course, and we started a private discussion. I make no compromise, whether Margaret Mahler or not, I say what I think. We started talking, and I said that I did not believe at all in her work. I thought her work was of considerable importance for psychology, but as far as psychoanalysis was concerned, I didn't find anything useful or inspiring in it. So I started arguing, "My main criticism is that what you observe is what you can observe from the outside, but from the intrapsychic point of view you cannot say anything. It is not your fault. It's not because you work badly, it's because it is impossible. That's all," and finally we parted. And as I told you, I met Bion, and it was the beginning of a friendship which lasted until he died.

One year after, there was a party at the Abelins' in New York. I was a friend of the Abelins because I had met them in 1969 at a symposium in Montreal. And here she was, Margaret Mahler, again, because Ernest Abelin used to work with her. We sat in a corner and talked. She asked, "So you still don't believe in my work?" I confirmed, and how surprised I was because she said, "You're right." "How come?" "You're right. Of what goes on intrapsychically we cannot say anything. It is true. But there are other useful aspects." I said, "If you can admit that, we can agree." I can toast Margaret Mahler if you wish, but I cannot admit the accuracy of her work for the advancement of psychoanalysis. It has nothing to do with the intrapsychic world or with the mixing and the linking of the intrapsychic and the interpersonal. It is one of the things that amaze me, that the genetic viewpoint has become so important here and that the main references have become Margaret Mahler and Piaget. For a European like me, thinking that he has spent years and years in his country in France to fight Piaget's influence because it was so contrary to psychoanalysis, there is so much against it. It was extraordinary that we got Piaget out the door, only to see him come back by the American window. We French were quite puzzled by this.

To me, this is a great danger. When I hear people say that psychoanalysis is a self-validating discipline, I recognize that from a scientific viewpoint this may be a problem that we have to resolve. But it is not enough for me, and I will not accept that the "validation" will come from a distortion of psychoanalysis in the first instance. The answer to this important problem requires that we find appropriate answers, which could be out of the criteria of present science.

SRR: It reminds me of your saying that what has changed is the analyst's eye in observing.

AG: I think that the real progress in psychoanalysis always came from people who devoted their time to psychoanalysis—even if it is Melanie Klein. I do not agree with two-thirds of what she said, but she obviously had some genius. I am much more in agreement with the way Bion thinks or Winnicott, and it's not a matter for me of having classical or orthodox analysis or not. It's just a matter of analytic thought, analytic knowledge, analytic experience with the type of patients that you meet in the analytic space. And what are the consequences for a theory of the mind?

That's why I came to that experience which you are talking about and to the necessity of changing, for instance, the basic model. The basic model of neurosis does not fit with what we are doing. So in 1975 I wrote that essay in which I propose another model based on the analyses of borderline patients. But now we come to a different conclusion. In the first instance, it was a matter of changing the model and opposing two models—the neurotic, the model of neurosis, and the borderline model. I next came to the idea of how to make them communicate, not reducing one to the other; not saying that the neurosis is a defense against psychosis or borderline, which is so commonly said; or not to say that, as other people have said, that the borderlines were only a different type of neurosis, but were still the same. No, by trying to find what is common to both and how things correspond. For instance, if you have castration anxiety in neurosis, then you have separation anxiety with borderline, and it's not easy to articulate other than to say that the second comes later than the first, which to me does not resolve anything.

Because it needs a lot of thinking to understand the meaning of separation anxiety—the meaning of, not the facts that people observe, the meaning for the mind, and the meaning in respect to the structure. Neither Margaret Mahler nor Daniel Stern can give me interesting clues to go forward, to gain the necessary changes in analysis. I think this is what we have to fight for, because the training in "psy"—whether you call it "-chiatry," or "-chology," or anything else—is a huge training. And it's such a wide body of knowledge that it can deserve ten years study, because what you have in the end are people who are overspecialized and sometimes ignorant. Today it is not infrequent to find people who have no cultural background. They barely have heard of Dostoevsky. For instance, you have to go to people of my generation to still find people who have a literary background. But it's not because they're lazy.

SRR: Even in France?

AG: I suppose even in France....It's because of competition. The students spend all their time preparing for scholarships or passing their exams. The programs are so heavy that they don't have time to do something else, and this is one of the factors. There may be others, but this is what I see. The true quarrel behind it is who has the power, the M.D.'s or the psychologists....The real questions, not the real power, the real things that matter are, What is the specificity of the human mind? What is the best way to approach it? What trust can we have in scientific methods to know what the "psychic" is?

The neurosciences—you cannot neglect them, you cannot discard them, you cannot say this is none of our business and get rid of what they say. You have to know what they're talking about to respond to them, to be able to say to them, What you're talking about is not the mind, and this is why, for such and such a reason. We can see by all these remarks how psychoanalysis is unduly threatened. It can be threatened and it is threatened through mass treatment, drug treatment, the neurosciences, all types of new techniques—behavior therapy, or primal scream, or whatever you want, you can have a new one everyday—and it lasts for some time, but it drives the people who are interested in psychoanalysis to go elsewhere. But it is also because psychoanalysts are careless.

Psychoanalysis must be made aware that something needs to be done, in terms not only of popularity, but in terms of improving the training, in terms of the quality of the clinical experience and by broadening the scope of theoretical knowledge that an analyst should possess. I think these are matters of real interest because, it is not true to say that Freud's theory is easy to understand or to assimilate. Freud's theory, when you study it very carefully, is very difficult. Its simplicity is surface. After my lecture, one of your colleagues came to me and thanked me for having come and for the lecture, and he said, "Unfortunately, the way Freud is presented is so strangulated and narrow that he seems so easily old-fashioned." That person was happy to hear me speak of Freud differently and show that he is still a useful thinker—not one to whom you must adhere to what he said, like the Talmud, but as one who is still capable of making us think, and of using his knowledge as a body of reflection from which we can still think about the work we are doing today. Even if we have to change parts of the theory, we are far from having finished with him.

It is not very astute to defend the idea that thanks to some new theories, we can leave Freud's work in the libraries and have the dust accumulate on the volumes, that there is no need to open them again because we have new things which are much more interesting—far more interesting, like the psychology of the self or preoedipal relationships. When I hear that, I laugh loudly. There are some strange things occurring, such as the rediscovery of narcissism in the United States.

Heinz Kohut gave great gifts to the Americans to rediscover narcissism. But why did they forget narcissism? This is the question. If you look at French psychoanalytic literature, starting after the second World War, narcissism has always been present. I can quote, apart from myself, two other authors who never forgot the word narcissism—Lacan and Grunberger. There are others, and you find a continuous thread which is not interrupted. So what's the point in rediscovering narcissism? But to some extent it couldn't be otherwise, because Kohut is what comes after ego psychology. Kohut is the heir of Hartmann. His work is the continuation of Hartmann, although in a different scope and in a different approach, but it is a kind of reparation to the harm made to the ego through the oversimplifications of ego psychology.

Today, I think the danger is psychology. Thinking that the danger is psychology does not mean that doctors are better because doctors themselves turn to psychology. Kohut was a doctor; he invented the psychology of the self. Hartmann was a doctor; he invented ego psychology. Peirce said, "The psychical is not the psychological," and he was more Freudian than many psychoanalysts in saying that. So that's why at the point of my lecture I said, Freud said, "Psychology is a natural science." Psychoanalysis is a part of psychology, but what psychology? What Freud is alluding to is "metapsychology"...something which is quite different....

You can see from this all the discussion which arises about the question of the drives. The drives are now old-fashioned because they are not taken as a metaphorical concept. They are taken at face value. They are taken as if we are speaking of biology. Freud never said that the drives were of a biological nature. He said—it's what I recalled this morning—this "kind of primary mental activity," which is quite different, and which is something he puts forward because nobody else accounts for it. You can change the names, if you wish, I don't mind, but you can't change the spirit. If you want to call it otherwise—never mind, why not? I can use another term. I can adjust myself to that situation, but you cannot give up what he tries to convey through the term. I thought, while reading some essays recently, that it was like describing psychic phenomenon—using psychological explanations in terms of secondary benefits.

Why doesn't the child want to go to school anymore? Because he wants to stay at home with Mommy. This is very close to secondary benefit. The psychological explanation is an explanation in terms of secondary benefit. Why does that hysteric woman have a fit in the middle of the audience? She feels nobody pays attention to her. For that type of explanation, you don't need to be a psychoanalyst. Your concierge—but you have no concierge in America—can give you that explanation as well.

SRR: Do you think there's an impact on the analyses that people are having?

AG: Yes. You know, I was a follower of Lacan and then I parted from Lacan, but some of the things that Lacan said seem to me quite exact. Lacan was afraid of a new era starting, the era of the "homo psychologicus." I think that era has happened in terms of psychological explanations for everything. From my view, psychological explanations are only rationalizations. Here is a very simple example of what I'm talking about. Nine out of ten films resort to psychological explanations, psychosociological explanations. One of the ten escapes them because what it says, without knowing it is saying it, is not psychology. And they are the only ones who will escape forgetfulness.

LR: I have a theoretical question. When you were addressing the issue of separation anxiety, you asked, "What is the meaning of separation anxiety?" In one of your essays in your book, *On Private Madness*, you talked of two objects which separate....

AG: Yes, this is the borderline concept.

LR: Yes, that they maintain parts of the other.

AG: Yes.

LR: And also in several places you talked about the quality of affects, not just the quantity.

AG: Yes.

LR: In thinking of the possible formative aspects of the borderline experience, are you suggesting that there is something about the pace at which a separation occurs between the mother and child that later contributes to the form of the affect that they might have in response to future separations?

AG: Yes, absolutely.

LR: I wanted to make sure I understood that.

AG: You understood.

LR: Your idea very nicely captures not only the quality of the affect, but also the issues of wholeness and fragmentation. In terms of object representation, if there is a very abrupt separation without any ability to contain it or process it, there might be a resulting wish on the part of the participants, an intense wish to reattach because of their psychic sense of incompleteness.

AG: Rebinding.

LR: Yes. I thought what was useful about your theory and your idea of the pieces of the "one in the other" is that they help put together the part-object representations with the quality of the "traumatic affect" in the borderline state. In the theories that I have read before, maybe it was there, but I didn't see it as clearly. Your conceptualization was very helpful for me.

AG: Well, you quite grasped what I meant. You see these are not preconceptions. For instance, when I thought of this binding, unbinding, rebinding, it wasn't a preconception of mine—it's something which I experience when thinking about my patients and about our prejudice. We think that we get in touch with things and experience in a state in which they are already bound, so we consider this as a primary state. But we are not aware that what we take as the primary "bound" is in fact a "rebound." So you have to have a dialectical thought in which you have to imagine that something can be at the same time "bound" from a certain perspective and "rebound" from another. From one angle you can see it as "bound," as a given whole. But from another angle, you consider it as "rebound." In other words, you can consider the term as being one or three.

SRR: It makes me think of transitional space in Winnicott's sense.

AG: You see, I seem to talk of things which are very abstract, but let us take a session. The patient starts talking, so what he gives you is primary material up to a certain point. While you think about what he is saying, you note that one of the things he says is related to something he said in the previous session. So it is not "bound," it is "rebound." It is what has come after the separation between the last session and the new session. And the new totality which is brought forward and offered to the analyst is something new. The patient is not aware that he is repeating something, but you have to be. So you see, people think that we are dealing with very abstract matters. No, it is just interpretation of the material which comes, which is given in the relationship to the analyst, and that's all.

SRR: Dr. Green, we were both very moved by your essay, "The Dead Mother." Reflecting on your ideas about countertransference and your belief that we need a more comprehensive theory to understand it, what can you tell us about the countertransference evoked in working with the kinds of patients you described in that essay? How does the treatment develop and progress?

AG: Again I would say that I have no recipe to offer. What I can say is that countertransference is much more loaded than in neurotic patients. In neurotic patients, you sit and wait as the process develops, and from time-to-time you make one or two remarks, link up different things, and that's all. You can't do that with a borderline patient. You have to be there, and you have to be there all the time, listening very carefully. No free-floating. In terms of countertransference, there are moments during the experience with such patients when you experience a private madness. If you want to understand them, you have to put yourself in some sort of madness. You have to be able to think in terms of paradoxes and in terms of things which seem illogical or irrational—not irrational in terms of superstition, but irrational in terms that you have to find other ways of reasoning. Once I gave an interpretation to a very anxious patient. He came to me for a third analysis—he was a depressed psychoanalyst. I gave an interpretation to him. He replied to that interpretation, "You're mad. I have an analyst who is mad." I was really happy hearing that because I thought that if he projected the madness to me, it was because I had touched upon something which was really important.

I have an example here about another patient, who comes to me for a third analysis, but she is in a face-to-face relationship. Let me illustrate the bizarre features we confronted. She would say, "You know, when I look myself at the mirror, I do not see anyone." As she is not totally psychotic, she says, "Of course, I see something, but I do not recognize myself." For me this is a case of negative hallucination to which I attribute enormous importance in analytic work with this patient. "But," she adds, "if my image in a mirror is reflected in a second mirror, then I can recognize myself." Such a sentence deserves an enormous amount of interpretation, which I cannot give here, but you will not be surprised to learn that she was very strongly opposed to her mother, though tied to her in a fusional way from which she never recovered. She really never accepted separation. She did have a good relationship with her father.

LR: ...the second mirror?

AG: She couldn't be seen by the mother or recognize herself in the look of her mother (Winnicott), but if the father was looking through the mother, then she could recognize herself. What kind of psychology can you do with these people? Are you really going to talk only about separation anxiety? Separation anxiety is obvious. It is also mysteriously obvious. Each time we have an interruption, it's terrible for her. She comes, she's torn to pieces, she cries, and I have the whole range of emotions about that; but where does it lead me? She's angry; she wants to destroy me. Of course, this has been said many, many times. For the first time, at Easter she took the initiative of the separation. She went to a Congress and instead of coming back immediately to have sessions before the holiday, she decided to spend a few days in Italy by herself, which was quite new. So, when I read the psychological explanations of that state, I am afraid that my colleagues are satisfying themselves with fairy tales.

LR: One thing I'm curious about.... You talk about your own attunement to the preconscious, in terms of being able to lend meaning to the absence of meaning for the patient.

AG: Yes, yes.

LR: ...and I'm curious in your own work whether you notice any patterns, whether patterns are specific to a particular patient or to a specific phase in the analysis, in terms of whether you get more visual imagery, more auditory cues, somatic feelings....

AG: It is a very interesting question because without knowing, you put your finger on one of the specifics of French analysis. This is where I also need to clarify a possible misunderstanding. I am known abroad as one of the French people who is interested in object relations. In fact, I am not especially interested in object relations. I have many reservations about object relations. For me, Winnicott is Winnicott by himself, and I don't consider that everything Winnicott says is all right with me. There are enormous issues which are lacking in Winnicott's theory, for instance the importance of sexuality to which I continue to adhere. I have no special links to the object relations approach.

I do not think that being interested in the work of Winnicott or of Bion means that I am object relations-oriented. This is a label, which is, I would say, fitting with modern labeling. I have heard that in some institutes you have different tracks and one is named the object relations track. For me, it is inconceivable that one could be trained in the object relations track without knowing the other possibilities. But one of the specifics of French psychoanalysis is what we call mental functioning.

You alluded to mental functioning when you said, "If you are very much concerned with the preconscious, do you have patterns of visual imagery, or auditory, or so on?" I have put it into other words, some of which you heard this morning. Many of the French analysts are very concerned about the quality of mental functioning; we examine, for example, the particular ways the patient might elaborate upon interpretations. We pay enormous attention to the patient's response to the analyst's interpretation and what comes after. In this meeting, I heard a commentary on a presentation based exclusively on the analysis of dreams through their manifest content. This is the answer to what you say. A patient tells you a dream. You interpret the dream in a paricular way. You decide whether you are going to interpret this part of the dream, or this aspect of it, or this other aspect.

Anyhow, thanks to Lacan, we are very attentive. We pay enormous attention to the words of the patient, to what the patient actually says. You know, in terms of what he means; you cannot change his words and use other words in place of what he says. It's really that the words which are used are important in themselves, and the idioms and the expressions and the associations that the words suggest, and what comes after the interpretation. A Lacanian would only interpret in terms of linguistics. I will not interpret only in terms of linguistics, but I would never forget that the words were such and such. It can play a role in what is communicated, and it depends on what level the patient communicates. The words are important also to see what other type of material they are connected to.

For example, if you have a very regressed patient, the communication is much easier when acting out as a way of remembering or communicating with the analyst; or an affective communicative with or without representations and representations of a different nature. The interplay between these forms of mental activity plays an enormous role in our appraisal of mental function. The current trend in France is the Psychosomatic School under Pierre Marty, which pays close attention to that interplay because they believe that in the diseases involving psychosomatic conditions—the heavy ones, ulcerative colitis, and so forth—it is essential that mental functioning be investigated through an appraisal of the system preconscious and its permeability. There are different features, asthma, for example, which they consider as in between hysteria and psychosomatic. They pay enormous attention to the mental functioning of the patient and to the patient's capacity to elaborate while fantasizing. Their findings are debatable, but they are interesting. Psychosomatic patients have an enormous difficulty elaborating. They will tell you something that happened during the day or in a dream, and then when you say, "Well, please continue...", they reply, "That's all....That's all." But all this is controversial.

The mental functioning, *le fonctionnement mental*, is overall important, and to me this is one thing British psychoanalysis lacks because of object relationship theory. When you adopt a perspective of object relationship—no matter if it is a dream, a fantasy, a verbal communication, or an acting out—you always translate it in terms of object relationship, that is, what the ego does with the object, and how the patient deals with it in nonspecific terms, regardless of the functional value of the channels of expression of meaning to which Freud used to pay the greatest interest. What does the ego do from the perspective of object relationships? It introjects, it projects, it splits off. But what about the problem of the mental quality or the type of processes which are involved—primary, secondary, tertiary, even? And so, I think that the two perspectives are complementary.

SRR: We have one other question. You talked about the intersubjective exchange of the unconscious that transpires between the analyst and the patient.

AG: Yes.

SRR: Could say something more about that?

AG: The intersubjective exchange?

SRR: Yes.

AG: I wonder how that would be translated in French. Yes, we've nearly come to the end. I think that psychoanalysis—because of the progress we have made with borderline patients and the experience we have accumulated in working with them and in working with neurotics, or even psychotics, or children, and so on—has been caught in a kind of quarrel or opposition, as I said this morning, between the internal and the external in terms of objects. In fact, I think that if we try to gather this experience and try to draw some conclusions, we will find that psychoanalysis is the combination of two perspectives—intrapsychic and intersubjective. Intrapsychic needs no comment. You know what I mean. Intersubjective is important because intersubjective is not interpersonal, and it is not interaction nor interactive. Interactive is a very, very inappropriate term because it is about actions.

In the analytic situation, what you are alluding to by your question is the intersubjective aspect. What does an intersubjective aspect mean? It means that two subjects relate, and if you remember what I said this morning, I said that there is a subject only for another subject. In that formulation, it means that the importance of intersubjectivity lies in intentionality. What is this for? You can draw a parallel with what Sartre says, "En soi, pour soi, pour autrui"—"In itself, for oneself, for someone else." The intrapsychic is for oneself. The intersubjective is for someone else; it means, "What do you want from me?" I'm not addressing the whole person. I am not addressing the personality. I am not addressing some global entities, but I am addressing some very specific thing which is, "What are you interested in from me? What do you expect from me?"

This, of course, is very close to what Lacan described in terms of desire—desire for the other, desire of the other, desire of desire of the other. I think that this dimension is quite important because it makes two subjects communicate—not only two people, not only two bodies, but two subjects. And the fact that it is two subjects changes the thing, because it gives it a specific human condition, because only a human being can be a subject.

It doesn't mean that we do not depend on an animal part of us. This is the intrapsychic problem—the relationship of the id to the ego and the superego—but now what occurs, and is interesting, is that as a consequence of making an intersubjective relationship each of the two subjects will have to also relate through their intrapsychic dimension. What do you want from me? You will not be able to pose the question unless you can consider your own intrapsychic world, your previous history, the organization of your thoughts, desires, deeds, volition, and so on; the same applies to myself. And while you are addressing your intrapsychic world to relate intersubjectively, your response will have an indirect and unknown effect not only on the other's subjectivity, but also—although in a manner totally unknown—on his own intrapsychic world, inducing other intersubjective effects and so on.... So you see, seen this way psychoanalysis really is interesting.

SRR: As you know, this project evolved from our desire to study the development of the analyst. From that perspective, I've been particularly interested in your description of the analyst as carrying something of the inner person of his or her own analyst. I'm trying to formulate what you've just been saying in terms of the analyst's psyche.

AG: I didn't feel so much like commenting on what you said about the analyst of the analyst because I thought that we were in agreement. But if you want me to expand on this point, I can tell you, for example, that in France some people now are very much interested in what they call "intergenerational transmission." It means that there is a kind of circulation of meaning about what is conveyed, unconsciously, what is not spelled out, what is unspoken and nevertheless handed over, and how something of the contents of what is unspoken is transmitted from one generation to another. Of course, this is not a mystical hypothesis. This is only a way of saying that when you do not verbalize plainly or explicitly something, it finds other ways to reach its target. Not as such, of course, but in some distorted and disguised way, and the reference is there. This is an extension of what you were alluding to in reminding me of statements about the analyst of the analyst.

The analyst's analyst is present for a long time in his analysis of a patient. It is only a way of insisting on the different types of transmission, and insisting on the fact that it is impossible to restrict it to some kind of realistic assessment, like when we refer to simplistic statements such as, "Here we have two people. We have a dual relationship, and it's like that because at the beginning of life it's the same. Analysis is a reproduction of the mother-infant relationship." These statements forget the fact that to have a mother-child relationship a father is necessarily around. Not present from the start—absent—but affective on the mother's mind.

Let me tell you something. There was a meeting in Vienna two years ago in which four people were each asked to give an essay on the topic "What is an Object?" The four people who gave the essays were Joe Sandler, Hannah Segal, James Innes-Smith, and myself. We all gave essays on "What is an Object?" These meetings of the European Federation are closed meetings, and not more than fifty people come to them from all over Europe. The discussion is supposed to occur at the highest possible level. After the meeting in Vienna, it was decided, because the organizers felt the discussion was perhaps too abstract, to return to clinical material. They decided that in Helsinki two people would present a clinical essay. The first one was French and the second was one of the British Society.

My British colleague's essay represented the postmodern Kleinians' position. I heard him say that it was quite irrelevant to pay attention to what is usually considered important in the material, which means the way it relates to the history of the patient, what he talks about, his present fantasies, the reference he makes to people with which he is involved, and the questions that an analyst may ask himself about the patient's fantasies. The only thing that the analyst had to bother with was the element of "presence," which is the atmosphere the patient alone created in the session. This was supposed to represent the bottom of mental universe. So you see the return of "presence." For two days, people only talked of the way they understood that mother-infant relationship, and so on. The whole thing was about the task of the analyst to discover the "true internal objects." But for two days the discussion about the true internal objects was only about the mother. So, in the end I asked, "Could the father be an internal object?" Everybody was panicked. And what could they say? They said, "Of course, the father can be an internal object." I asked, "Then, why for two days haven't you even mentioned his existence." The only answer from the presenter was, "If I had done so I would have had to present a longer essay."

SRR: This next question also takes us back to the early mother-child relationship. You have described how language itself becomes instinctualized in the process of psychoanalysis.

AG: "Instinctualized" is a strong word, but I'll explain it to you.

SRR: I'll give you the quotation: "It is important to note that the patient is not allowed to act but is asked to say everything which comes to his mind by means of language. This entails that analytic treatment necessarily leads to an 'instinctualization of language.' This results in language no longer being used for communication as in everyday life. Talking to the analyst involves entering into a very close relationship with him, which is both loving and destructive. There's no equivalent to this in everyday life because besides language there are other means of communication such as gestures, actions, and face-to-face relations, which vary with the reactions of the recipient." I am very interested in what you have written about writing and the need to write. Do you see links between this instinctualization of language and writing?

Also, does language remain more instinctualized for the analysand who writes, or instinctualized in a different way? Have you considered whether writers outside of the sphere of psychoanalysis have a more instinctual relationship to language and words?

AG: Yes, it is a very important question. I wrote that in 1975. I suppose it's from the 1975 essay. I then wrote an extensive essay on language and found a better expression, though it doesn't contradict this one. That explains my reaction when I said that I find it was maybe too strong a word. I used an expression and even created a new word for the circumstance. I should say it in French, "la parole analytique desendeuille le langage," which translated is, "analytic speech 'unmourns' language."

SRR: I had wanted to include a quotation of yours on mourning to illustrate that point.

AG: Many people have shown, and most of them were Kleinians, that language is associated with the depressive position. Lacanian theory states it in other ways. But there has been some sort of agreement that when language is acquired, something happens which is philosophically called—I think, in Hegel's philosophy—"the murder of the thing." The relationship to the thing is not direct any more as it is through the senses. With the word, the thing is at the same time present and absent. And this can also be conceived in psychoanalytic terms, it has something to do with the "present" position. Naming something instead of touching it, smelling it, experiencing it through the senses creates some mourning of a previous relationship, which is based essentially on immediate contact. It's more than distance.

Here we meet Freud's hypothesis that the reality principle can only establish itself when the objects which once afforded satisfaction have been lost. This sentence is really one of the most beautiful metaphors of Freud, and people simply do not understand what he says. They have to give it a more handy equivalent, but it's really very important that Freud thinks that something has been lost forever once you establish the reality principle, because it means that you will never refind again that supposed state of bliss in which needs were directly and immediately satisfied. Of course, this is not a realistic way of stating things, because one can say that it is a retrospective fantasy of what has been—the feeling of loss is experienced, but what was before the loss is probably retrospectively idealized.

With language you can give an unmatchable view of psychic reality, as in my quotation of Wordsworth yesterday. In the conditions of the analytic setting, there is a reactivation, a reenactment of all the unsatisfied needs, which spread even to verbalization. This is what I mean by the reinstinctualization of language. It doesn't mean that words become instincts. It tries to account for the fact that the same sentence in a session and out of the session are quite different, because of the nature of the relationship—because of what you put in the relationship; because of all you expect from the relationship; because of what is prohibited by the relationship. This is why I said that analytic speech unmourns language.

SRR: Could you tell us something about those links or those processes in terms of the analyst's writing?

AG: There's an essay on the unbinding process at the end of *On Private Madness*, and I just published a book of collected essays called, *La Deliaison* (*The Unbinding Process*). I talked yesterday with Bennett Simon, and we wondered if that was really the right word for it because binding and unbinding are classical Freudian theory terms. What I mean here is something like tying and untying. But we can keep binding. In that essay on psychoanalytic criticism, I try to analyze what psychoanalytic reading is.

The question of the writing process has something to do with the function of speech in analysis, but differently. I think Derrida's contribution is quite interesting. Derrida's major essay, "The Scene of Writing," was first given at my seminar in Paris. He had a very important idea. He reminds us that writing is usually considered a secondary function of speech. He reversed it, and said that it was speech that was a secondary function to writing. It is not important to discuss what is primary and what is secondary except if you think of the underlying thoughts. What Derrida meant, I think, was that the concept of trace was essential. Of course, this goes in the same direction as do psychoanalysts when they speak of memory traces, at least those of them who still think in those terms. We can see speech in the session as an actualization of these memory traces, at least in part. Derrida also recalled that Freud had said that writing was an address to the absent. It's of major importance. We can understand what is behind your question because there is also the same reactivation of the needs and of all the unanswered demands which are expressed through writing, also related to the relationship in the clinical situation.

But there are different uses of writing. Writing is a very extensive activity; analytic speech is very specialized. As I said yesterday, if you consider writing, when you come to poetics, then you can find some common mechanisms between the organization of psychoanalytic speech and poetics, especially in the treatment of affect. One can agree with what you say about writing, but it all depends upon the uses of writing. Consider analytic writing. I have written an untranslated essay, "Transcription of Unknown Origin," on analytic writing. We're having a conference in London organized by the IPA in November on Applied Psychoanalysis to Literature. Hannah Segal and I will present papers.

SRR: This quotation is from "The Double and the Absent": "…It would in any case seem that what is important in analysis is not that the analyst succeed at any price in reconstructing a puzzle, but that his interpretations help the patient free himself from the alienating burden he bears and, if possible, help him to utilize his energies in more productive ways." Thus, analysis should lead to the "sharing of a truth supposed possible" between the analyst and the analysand, "acknowledgment of which aids in their mutual emancipation." You continue later: "Moreover, since psychoanalytic interpretation involves the process of deformation of the subject's conscious intention"—and I excerpt—"…we must recognize the fact that if someone is to be helped here, it is certainly not the author, who could not care less, but the analyst-interpreter, who helps himself through seeking to comprehend the emotions the text awakens in him. Thus, the patient, the potential analysand, is not the author, as everyone believes and fears, but the analyst himself." Here you address the extreme subjectivity of the analytic process for both involved.

The following quotation, though quite different, was evoked for me when reading the passages just cited. In "Potential Space in Analysis," you state: "…There is urgent and growing need for another system of reference which gives pride of place to the countertransference and clarifies its elaborative potentialities." Could you say more about this? I know we've been discussing it already, but….

AG: What more do you need?

SRR: Since this discussion is intended for the reader as well, we'd like more of your perspective on the entire topic of countertransference.

AG: Yes, I wrote these lines long ago; I think it was in 1973. The major statement which survived from it was the following: "The analyst is the analysand of the text." I didn't mean so much that I was talking of countertransference as it is now spoken of. What I want to say is that the power of the text, which is itself an elaborated construct with no definite purpose except to move the reader, or to please the reader, or to be admired by the reader, or to be liked by the reader, is that it triggers a process of elaboration which has as an effect to create some correspondence between the process of consumption of the work of art and the process of the creation of the work of art, bringing these two aspects as close as possible to each other, but always preserving a gap, which can never be filled.

It helps to relate, when you read something, what you are experiencing and the experience of the person who has written what you read. Of course, between these two there is the enormous problem of style and fabrication of literature. Sometimes you succeed in clarifying some of the features which have an effect on the reader. I think that it relates to what Winnicott has said about transitional space. This is really a major discovery. There are connections between the text you quoted and what Laurie was quoting about the "maybe." It is also about what Winnicott has said on the location of the cultural experience. I think that there is a lot of work to do on what kinds of objects are the cultural objects, how we use them, and what function they have for us. All this is in the question about the function of applied psychoanalysis.

There is a transitional area, but one must know that the work of art as a transitional object can lead to what I call the "transference of existence," which means only that for an artist the preservation of his work is more important than the preservation of his life. His true existence is his work, not his life, and he is quite ready to sacrifice his life for his work. This is one example of what I mentioned yesterday about passion and faith.

SRR: Like a mother with a child.

AG: Like a mother with a child, and like Moses with God.

SRR: Like Freud looking at the Michelangelo.

AG: Yes.

SRR: You have discussed the need that some analysts have to write as well as to analyze. Might the analyst also need to experience certain kinds of affect states. For example, for some analysts might one aspect of the need to analyze also be a need to reexperience a certain quality of transitional object-relatedness?

AG: I think we have to return to some fundamental problems. First, we have to consider that in this century, more so than in the previous twenty-five centuries, the reflection on language has come to the fore. We think of Wittgenstein, the philosophy of language, and all of the works of modern linguists. Thus, the concern about what we are really communicating to each other when we use words comes to the forefront. How can analysts escape that when their work implies a major use of language. Language is not the only tool, whatever may be said about empathic communication and so on, that exists. But the main difference between us and other approaches to psychology, which usually are about behavior, is our use of language. And from there, we are driven to consider what is the relationship between the world of language and the world of psychic reality, and analysis is at the center of this problem.

To write is really to try to reach a production of meaning—less than *communication* than *production* of meaning. It also has a communication function, but I do not emphasize the communication aspect because it's so generally mentioned, and it seems to go without saying, though the problem is more complex than it seems. But the production of meaning is something underestimated. To talk is to produce meaning. There are many very interesting works about the relationship between language and thought or language and psychic activity. When an analyst writes, it's really a double process of communication, because first it's a tremendous effort to transform into words all that he has experienced in the widest sense during his analytical practice and also outside his analytical practice with his analytical mind. Then it is the need to find an echo in others behind all the secondary gratifications—to be recognized, to be praised, to be celebrated. There is the hope that someone will stand and say, "What I experience, you have put it into words. Having it spelled out helps me." And once this has been established, I would say a memory trace has been created, which gives life to something which may have been but which would have vanished without anyone noticing that it had ever existed.

LR: In the workshop you gave, you made the comment, "We should be ashamed of how we write about time and space compared to what we know of it." It reminded me of your own descriptions of space and time in relation to the negative therapeutic reaction in your essay, "Negation and Contradiction":

> "The work of the mirror, a product of the logic of opposites, which operates in the analytic setting, is undermined by the realization of this deficiency (negative hallucination). It is as though, in these analytic situations, the nonemergence of a living, present object were due to the fact that the interval between the loss of the bad object and its replacement by a good object had been experienced and considered as a fatal desert. Thus, space and time—for it is really a matter of a period of time that was experienced as interminable—are linked.... Whence comes the idea of a 'dead time' as the suspension of all affective and perceptive experience. The subject does not think he can survive this dead time. Consequently, the analyst becomes the object of the negative therapeutic reaction because he is the only reliable object, the

only one that survives these destructive periods of which he is the no-object. Any other object would run the risk of never reappearing at the other end of the dead time or of never lasting long enough to be experienced as present. Whence the importance for the patient to assure himself at every session that he has perceived the analyst."

Could you share any further thoughts about space and time in the analytic setting?

AG: You're right to emphasize that point. I recently wrote two essays on time. I think that you could dig into these papers and find some answers to your questions. But you've now raised an important point, because the interesting thing about this interview is for me to see how you link some ideas on which I have written in different contexts. I didn't think of the way you have been linking them; I'm thinking of links in different ways.

Freud made a momentous step, which has not been noticed quite enough, when he wrote "Beyond the Pleasure Principle." At the end of the essay, he comes, for the first time in his life, to question the pleasure principle as a principle that is really there from the start. And he comes to the idea that there are some other psychic events which are supposed to happen before. We are speaking of hypotheses, we are not speaking of real development, even if Freud had the idea that it also happens in reality. He said that it was the binding process, the possibility of assembling things together. His language becomes quite vague, because it is obvious that he is not speaking of representation—he is trying to speak of something which is more elementary than representation. He's probably speaking of instinctual impulses, if not drives. It is in that capacity to link and to establish some chain that he considers the starting point of psychic activity. In biology it is the same. When you explain the beginning of life, this is how it works.

What is the basis of the concept of time which will afford all the further variations. I mean developmental line, or deferred action, or repetition, or timelessness? Is it not the possibility of creating a chain of events, or linkage of meanings, or whatever? Once you have established some kind of stable connection, then you can play with it. You can cut it into pieces; you can take one piece, remove it, and link it with some other. I think it is absolutely essential for the basis of our conception of time. It is also essential when you are with the patient—the kind of patient I was talking about yesterday—who is so destructive and who can forget what was said a few minutes ago and say he has erased it. This operates like a matrix. It also has to do with the relationship—the object relationship—because it has to do with the establishment of what Winnicott calls basic trust.

It means that a certain number of things will not be questioned because you can trust your perceptions and your feelings which are validated by the object. It is on this basis that we're going to do all sorts of things, and even destroy everything if we need to. The relationship will survive anyway. This accounts for the fact that up to the point where the patient comes to his session, there is always the idea that something else could happen. It may never happen, but the idea is still there that it could happen. You have to ask yourself, Why is the patient coming? There's no simple answer.

LR: As you are talking, I'm remembering your having emphasized in your writing Winnicott's distinction between destructiveness and aggressiveness.

AG: Well, I'm saying in other terms what Winnicott wrote about the use of an object.

LR: But you're highlighting that distinction.

AG: Yes, because I really believe that sometimes the conceptual use of the object is something which is absolutely indispensable and is absolutely necessary for the analyst, but it is not self-sufficient for theory.

SRR: One last question. In your essay, "Aggression, Femininity, Paranoia, and Reality," you describe the girl's difficulty in transferring her love to her father as caused by the mourning implied, the giving up of the erotic cathexes to the mother, "the first seducer." You emphasize the necessity for the girl to transfer her aggressive cathexes as well as her erotic ones, and describe this displacement onto the father as "indispensable if the final post-pubertal displacements are to take place and thus permit cathexes of a nonparental, masculine figure."

You observed that if these dynamics do not transpire, the husband can easily become a mother-substitute. You then state: "These remarks may lead to the reconsideration of the existence or absence of specific feminine guilt mechanisms in women. Educational features will, of course, interfere with these mechanisms, but it will be worth exploring whether a specific structure may be found owing to the peculiarities of the development and transformations of aggressive drives in women and their narcissistic links."

I know we have almost no time, but I want to know if you have thought further about this problem.

AG: Yes, I have thought about it and have written an essay for one of my colleagues, who gave a stimulating essay on the relationship between womanhood and motherhood. I'm afraid the time is too short for a detailed discussion, but I still think that the issue is important because from that perspective there is a difference between the sexes. There is no similar distinction between manhood and fatherhood. Aggression in men is not only culturally different from aggression in women, but there is a difference in the nature of aggression in each sex. I am unable to say if women are less aggressive, but surely the outward expression of their aggressiveness is not the same, the outcome doesn't happen so easily. That it is culturally bound is evident, but I'm not sure that it is only culturally bound. One difference may lie in the fact that women bear children.

This is a very short answer and a very schematic one, for which I have to excuse myself. But we really can say that Freud left us with two unsolved problems in theory. There are many, but these are really two basic and fundamental issues. One is the problem of the death instinct to which aggression is linked, and the other is his conception of femininity. I have to say that even if we are quite aware that his conceptions were incomplete or sometimes wrong, we are still in want of a good theory of femininity. It's interesting to see that even women have difficulty in stating this conception of their own problems.

SRR, LR: Thank you so much.

AG: Thank you.

SELECTED BIBLIOGRAPHY

Green, A. (1962). L'inconscient freudien psychanalyse francaise contemporaine. *Temps Modernes*, Vol. 18, pp. 363–379.

Green, A. (1966). L'object (a) de J. Lacan, sa logique et la theorie freudienne. *Cahiers L'analyse*, Vol. 3, pp. 15–37.

Green, A. (1967). La diachronie dans le freudisme. *Critique,* Vol. 238, pp. 359–385.

Green, A. (1967). Le narcissisme primaire: Structure ou etat. *L'Inconscient,* Vol. 1, pp. 127–157; Vol. 2, pp. 89–116.

Green, A. (1969). Le narcissisme moral. *Revue francaise Psychanalyse,* Vol. 33, pp. 341–374.

Green, A. (1969). La nosographie psychanalytique des psychoses. In: *Problems of Psychosis,* Vol. 1, ed. C. Laurin & P. Doucet. Amsterdam: Exerp. Med.

Green, A. (1970). L'affect. *Revue francaise Psychanalyse,* Vol. 34, pp. 883–1141.

Green, A. (1970). Repetition, difference, replication. *Revue francaise Psychanalyse,* Vol. 34, pp. 461–501.

Green, A. (1972). De l''esquisse' a 'L'Interpretation des Reves.' *Nouvelle Revue de Psychanalyse,* Vol. 5, pp. 155–180.

Green, A. (1972). Note sur les processus tertiaires. *Revue francaise Psychanalyse,* Vol. 36, pp. 407–410.

Green, A. (1972). Aggression, femininity, paranoia, and reality. *International Journal of Psycho-Analysis*, Vol. 53, pp. 205–211.

Green, A. (1973). *Le discours vivant, La conception psychanalytique de l'affect.* Paris: Presses Universitaires de France, 1992.

Green, A. (1973). On negative capability: A critical review of W.R. Bion's *Attention and Interpretation. International Journal of Psycho-Analysis,* Vol. 54, pp. 115–119.

Green, A. (1974). Surface analysis, deep analysis (The role of the preconscious in psychoanalytical technique). *International Review of Psycho-Analysis,* Vol. 1, pp. 415–423.

Green, A. (1975). The analyst, symbolization and absence in the analytic setting (On changes in analytic practice and analytic experience). *International Journal of Psycho-Analysis*, Vol. 56, pp. 1–22.

Green, A. (1975). Orestes and Oedipus. *International Review of Psycho-Analysis,* Vol. 2, pp. 355–364.

Green, A. (1977). Conceptions of affect. *International Journal of Psycho-Analysis,* Vol. 58, pp. 129–156.

Green, A. (1983). *Narcissisme de vie, Narcissisme de mort.* Paris: Minuit.

Green, A. (1984). Le langage dans la psychanalyse. In: *Langages*. Paris: Les Belles Lettres.

Green, A. (1986). *On Private Madness.* London: Hogarth Press.

Green, A. (1990). From the non-unifiable object to the objectalizing function. *Psychoanalysis in Europe, Bulletin of the European Federation of Psychoanalysis,* Vol. 35.

Green, A. (1990). Temps et memoire. *Nouvelle Revue de Psychanalyse,* Vol. 41, pp. 179–205.

Green, A. (1990). La rememoration: effect de memoire ou temporalite a l'ouevre. *Revue francaise Psychanalyse,* Vol. 54, pp. 947–972.

Green, A. (1991). Instincts in the late works of Freud. In: *On Freud's Analysis Terminable and Interminable.* J. Sandler. New Haven, CT: Yale University Press.

Green, A. (1992). *La deliaison.* Paris: Les Belles Lettres.

Green, A. (1993). *Le travail du negatif.* Paris: Minuit.

LEO STONE

Leo Stone, M.D. is a training analyst at the Columbia Institute and a past President of the New York Psychoanalytic Institute and the New York Psychoanalytic Society. He was Director of the New York Psychoanalytic Institute's Treatment Center and is a member of the faculty. He is the recipient of a *Journal of the American Psychoanalytic Association* Award, the Heinz Hartmann Award of the New York Psychoanalytic Institute, and the Mary S. Sigourney Award of the American Psychoanalytic Association. He has delivered the Freud Anniversary Lecture of the New York Psychoanalytic Institute, the Brill Memorial Lecture of the New York Psychoanalytic Society, and the Freud Anniversary Lecture of the Psychoanalytic Association of New York. Dr. Stone was interviewed February 2, 1991.

SRR: In this summer's issue of *Psychoanalytic Review,* there was a review of your workshop at the National Psychological Association for Psychoanalysis. At this workshop, you said that it would be preferable if the various psychoanalytic orientations now predominant in the United States could be understood to be contributing together to the body of psychoanalytic lore, rather than as competing bodies. You reminded the audience that your practice spanned earlier periods of schism, including the period involving Karen Horney and the neo-Freudians who broke with classical drive theory. You pointed out that valuable contributions that should have been integrated into the mainstream, for example, Sullivan's, were left to develop along separate lines. We are very interested in hearing your thoughts on the history of this and the other schisms that you observed, and their impact on theory and practice. We wondered if you think there is some link between people staying within their own schools and the sense of omniscience that has been described as developing in certain analysts.

LS: ...The omniscience?

SRR: Yes. We wondered if you thought there was a link between the history of schisms and the development of a sense of omniscience in certain analysts. Also, have you observed other factors that contribute to analysts remaining closely bound to one school and taking competitive positions toward different ways of thinking?

LS: ...A complicated order. I think in brief you've said what I think, because I do feel that there are contributing factors. Psychoanalysis is unlike other sciences in that it has so few grounds for demonstrable certainty and for absolute and convincing proofs. But I insist on regarding it as a science, at least in its direction and its effort. There are some things that are very hard to get around if people are at all open minded, like the significance of dreams and matters of that sort. But it's not like physics, you know. You could be bombed on the basis of a few formulae. So that leaves open the question of certainty. I think that gap tends to be filled by most people by religious faith and matters of that sort. They want it, they need it, and it serves millions and millions of people in that sense. And so it is with people of the scientific bent of mind. They disclaim any tendency of that sort, but it's there anyway. My observations have supported it.

One goes from that, especially since arguments and schisms very soon begin to appear. They're there from early on in psychoanalysis, things that we don't even regard as competing now, like Jungian analysis, Adlerian analysis, and Rankian analysis, and so forth. There's always been some tendency to deviation, and there are strong feelings connected to that. That tendency summons aggression, group loyalties, and the wish of individuals to feel they have the absolute truth. I think this is partly a defensive phenomenon because of the inevitable uncertainties, and partly a matter of group spirit and aggression. I mean, after all, what can be more peaceful than analytic practice, sitting down all day and listening to people talk and being completely neutral. So the fighting, I think, has some appeal in itself. It explains what happens in societies and institutes who are presumably of the same general commitment. They fight about various things—who'll be a training analyst, what will be the criteria for admission, and so forth. I think in all the schismatic groups—except for things that by common consent are crackpot or born of ignorance or inexperience—there is a germ of something that's worthwhile. There is something that could be a contribution if added to the general view of what goes on in the unconscious, how it's manifested in symptoms or behavior, how it may be approached technically, and so on. But as soon as it's met with by rejection, then the clamor for new grouping and new leadership asserts itself. Everybody wants to be a savior if possible. Those who are leaders begin to feel this all the more strongly if they are rejected. And so it becomes a two-sided thing, a fight begins, and something is lost to both sides.

I recently wrote a letter. A man associated with the official Horney journal, I think, wrote to ask my opinion about the original episode at the New York Institute, which led to Horney's resignation and to the resignation of several people in sympathy with her. They didn't even stay with her, like the Thompson-Sullivan group. They split off and founded their own institute. But they resigned in sympathy with Horney originally. This man asked if I could say something about it. The truth is that that was a bit early in my own analytic career. I wrote that, frankly, I couldn't remember whether I was just about to graduate or had just graduated when the episode occurred. But obviously, even if one was a student, or maybe all the more if one was a student, it was a very disturbing thing to everybody concerned..., that is, everyone with sensibilities...capable of being shaken by things like that. I felt that that was a very good example because the Horney group became sequestered, multiplying and elaborating their own ideas based on some of Horney's original premises and thoughts. But for a time, at least as I saw it, they were becoming increasingly idiosyncratic. Now, I don't know that that has continued. Sometimes they tend to circle back.

I think some of the groups that have separated are liable, when you meet them as individuals, to include more of the traditional analytic views in their thought and teaching than was the case originally, when the wounds were raw and the fight was recent. As a matter of fact, I was once asked to give an informal talk or to discuss a student case at the William Alanson White group. There was no particular trouble that arose from different orientations. They may have had some different emphases, which would be quite natural, but I think there was already some evidence of their beginning to return. That was about fifteen years ago. Assuming that the people who offer new ideas, or what were once called deviant ideas, are intelligent, responsible, serious, and capable of observations of their own and of interpreting them, then there is usually something worthwhile that becomes lost to the main body, and that ceases to develop as well in isolation, as it might have if they had remained, whoever it might be who is ultimately responsible for it.

SRR: Do you feel that candidates are more open to new ideas earlier in their training, or do you think that it's just a matter of the individual…?

LS: Well, there are some people who are chronically open to ideas, like the young people who vote for any new political idea, new sociology, or whatnot, and who naturally have a chronic quarrel with the establishment. I saw them even when I was a student, those who fight with every instructor. But omitting such people, I'm inclined to think otherwise. You see, the power of the transferences and the wish for certainty, the wish to have the true belief, to know what is the real answer to everything, and also to remain in the good graces of the powers that be, that cannot be ignored and is a very important thing whether conscious or not. I can remember that when I was graduating we had to write a brief essay as part of the process. For some reason that fell into disuse and was discontinued. I'm sorry about that. I thought it was an interesting thing to hear these essays of the newborn; they were sometimes quite good. But people would worry, "Was my essay orthodox enough? Will it pass? Did I give enough weight to the Oedipus complex as opposed to preoedipal things?," and so on. There was no doubt that this was felt. I'm inclined to think that's a little less so now. Maybe that's optimistic. I think there is somewhat greater openness, and students are less afraid to speak their minds, or at least to ask questions about things that are regarded as established. Previously, the tendency was to very great conformism.

LR: In your writing about psychoanalysis and the widening scope, you used a phrase, "arbitrary authoritarianism." Were you describing an environment in which people were more rigid about the way psychoanalysis was conducted?

LS: It is quite possible that what you suggest is true, because during my early training there were a few people who were conspicuous, and they were in control of the teaching; maybe not officially necessarily, but through their influence. And there was a great deal of that feeling, that this is the way it is. You might not be punished or threatened with hell's fire if you asked the wrong question, but sometimes they might not even answer it.

LR: This phrase came from your essay, "Psychoanalytic Situation: Excerpts," which is in your book, *Transference and Its Context.* This was the passage: "What I have in mind in stressing such matters is that there is an element in analytic technique, however strictly interpreted, which does inevitably and legitimately provide transference gratification and that there are in addition areas of option where the choice lies between arbitrary authoritarianism and the engagement of rational cooperation based on understanding. With the rarest of exceptions, the latter is the more desirable course."

LS: It is true that they were much more rigid and simplistic—simplistically rigid about certain of Freud's aphoristic teachings. That's true, but I don't think I thought of that as something that was built into the very idea of good analytic technique. I mean, for example, You don't answer questions. This has been carried to the point of absurdity by some people. I don't know whether true or not, but one person used to say that if he asked his analyst whether he was going to be there on Thursday, Thanksgiving, the analyst wouldn't answer. He would come there and find that he wasn't there. Now that I think is an absurdity, and the story may be apocryphal. But in general—"You don't answer questions," "You don't give the person any information about yourself under any conditions"—the fact is that none of those things are without exceptions, nor should they be without exceptions. It's true that the basic idea, the relative anonymity of the analyst, is important and probably necessary in the development of a valid transference neurosis. But if it goes to an extreme, it leads to complications which are more severe than an occasional reasonable response. It leads to legitimate anger, some legitimate sense of frustration, and to things that might be called negative transference, which may not have been. They might be just responses to undue rigidity in a place where it was not important to the technique, but was only important to the analyst's sense of being absolutely correct.

I went to an institute that was regarded as one of the strongly "orthodox" ones, so it may have been more evident in that atmosphere than in some others, although I think it was pretty generally prevalent. For example, let's say in my recent illness; it wasn't really an illness in the usual sense. It was a fracture of the femur superimposed on a bad hip. I saw the miscarriage of certain information through my well-meaning secretary, very part-time in the first place and very busy with things in her own life. She tried very hard to get in touch with every patient to tell them that I wouldn't be there the next week, that I had had an injury, but that I was not in any danger, that things would be all right, and that they would be further informed. Well, in some instances it was slight miscarriages. She told some people that she would be in touch with them later and then forgot to do it. These people were terribly and unnecessarily disturbed.

I mean, the answering service. I don't know how it is in Boston, but here the operators' responsiveness, and their intelligence, and even sometimes their goodwill varies greatly. You can tell that some of them are half asleep on the job. Occasionally, there's a very bright, responsive person, who takes it seriously, and you can almost tell that as soon as you hear the voice. Well, my patients would sometimes call the answering service and be told absurd things. One was told that I was here everyday seeing patients as usual, but I was still in the hospital. So one can see that the impact of no information or garbled information could be unnecessarily distressing. It wouldn't alter the person's fundamental neurosis, but it would unnecessarily give the person a hard time and would leave some effects, and take a while for it to be dissolved in its immediate impact. The part that simple reality plays in people's lives and continues to play, even when they're in analysis, is sometimes set aside.

I remember an American analyst, a woman who had trained abroad. She would talk about a given patient and say that the patient kept saying she couldn't afford an increase in fee. I'd say, "Well, it sometimes happens." And she would say, "Well, she should be able to get a better job and earn more money and continue with her analysis at a more reasonable fee." She felt that everything was up to the patient's wish to be analyzed. Well, of course, there are people who hide in poverty. Many years ago, I had a patient who, after a few years, told me that he had originally lied about his income. That, of course, does happen, but that's very unusual. He was very guilty, deeply apologetic, and accepted without question a reasonable increase in what had been an unnecessarily minimal fee. But this lady spoke as if this were a built-in natural phenomenon—that if you want analysis, you get it, and if you need money for it, you get the money for it or if you don't it's a part of your neurosis. I don't think one would hear that kind of thing now. You might very well hear, maybe even more among the younger people than older, that they can't take patients that don't meet a certain fee, which is in the minds of many of us quite high-handed for people who are just beginning their work, but I don't think they would have a ridiculous attitude of that kind.

LR: Who influenced you in your development as an analyst? How did you develop some of your own theoretical formulations?

SRR: Supervisors, people who influenced you,...

LS: Yes, well, of course, in a sense, all my teachers influenced me. I came from the Menninger Clinic. I spent three and a half years there, although I came from here originally. At that time, a kind of simplistic orthodoxy was very prevalent. I say simplistic because there were a few essential things like the Oedipus complex, and everything revolved around them. You know, it was before Anna Freud's book was circulated in English. It had appeared in German somewhere around the time that I was out there, but it didn't get wide reading among English-speaking people, about the importance of defense and the analysis of defense. Even that was regarded as kind of new.

My view of analysis was acquired out there. I don't mean it was uncritical, because I do think I always had a naturally critical mind. I knew there must be more to it than showing a man that he wanted to sleep with his mother when he was three years old or that he was afraid he would be killed or castrated by his father, and so on. There must be more than that. You know Freud's work on infantile sexuality, the contributions to the theory of sex. Anyway, they knew there was an oral phase, and an anal phase, and all those things, but they weren't seen so much in a developmental relationship to later phases. There was much less sense of continuity; for example, that how a person might have experienced things in the oral phase might influence his genitality later. There was very little of that.

When I came to New York, it was a much larger and more sophisticated group. Karl Menninger himself had gone to Alexander in Chicago to be analyzed, and I'm quite sure that he had some work later with Ruth Mack-Brunswick in the New York area. He was a very smart man. In fact, I've always said that I thought he was the most able psychiatrist I have ever known, so I really owe him a considerable debt in relation to clinical psychiatry. The orientation in analysis was of that simplistic type, but in New York it was a larger, more sophisticated group. There were people who had been analyzed by Freud and by Ferenczi and by others. And this included Americans. This was before the influx of the refugee analysts, who brought a great deal of freshness of outlook. It's a curious thing, you know. This may be a somewhat idiosyncratic view—but I feel there was truth in it—that the Europeans who came, the more experienced, sophisticated ones, were less rigid in their technical outlook than the Americans, who may have been trained by them, even in Vienna. Because there was something of that student attitude that carried over, and I am sure that the teachings at our own institute in that respect were stiffer than those in Vienna. I know that because I knew some of them very well. In fact, I had analysis with one of them.

It was a positive experience, and this was a person who was not regarded as a deviant. But they allowed much more room for ordinary human attitude. At any rate, it was a wider horizon, and then it began to include people who deviated strongly, like Karen Horney, Clara Thompson, and Sullivan. I think Sullivan, too, was a member of the New York Institute; not active in its politics, but I think he was a member. And he, with Thompson and many of the younger followers, resigned when Horney resigned. As I remember it, I was in this somewhat ambiguous position. I wasn't sitting on any of the major committees at that time when her teaching privileges were suspended. She immediately resigned, and those people resigned with her.

Of the people who influenced me most, I had some early contact with Clara Thompson. I definitely turned away from her basic orientation, many of her teaching principles, and certainly her attitudes toward analytic orthodoxy, which I thought were more orthodoxly critical than the orthodox affirmations were. I mean, she could say some things that would annoy the hell out of me, and which I thought were completely unjustified. Anyway, she was a smart woman. Some of the things that later appeared in some of the group attitudes, maybe also in Sullivan's interpersonal psychiatry, which were present in her attitudes, were useful because they kept a little closer to everyday human experience. They didn't as readily get off into word formulations instead of observations. So, in my contact with her, she had a certain influence plus and minus.

Of course, there were people like Bert Lewin, who was brilliant. I don't know if you've had any contact with him, or maybe with his writings, but he was literally brilliant. He had a mind that sparked. I think some of his ideas are still somewhat neglected, because people may get impatient with what they think is too much of a depth-reconstructive element in them. At any rate,

I am stimulated a great deal by his work intellectually…I don't know how much technically, but the ideas about oral psychology and dreams. Then the person who influenced me most, with whom I actually worked for a considerable period, was Ernst Kris, because he was a person of a very wide culture. As you know, he began as a student psychologist, a writer about art from an analytic viewpoint, and then he gradually became a critical analyst. He was a person who combined a definite adherence to traditional analysis in its broad framework with a certain human element that was palpable at all times and which was not regarded as a transgression. I mean, for example, if you had an operation, he might not think it would spoil the analysis if he wished you well. He simply hoped you were feeling better.

At one time, some people were afraid to say those things. That sounds ridiculous now. There used to be a joke about somebody jumping out of a window from an upper story, and as the person passed by the window, the patient on the couch started up and looked, and ejaculated something or other, and the analyst calmly asked for his associations. Ernst Kris was a considerable influence for me in that sense, with a broad, humanistic background of good analytic technique, and yet a perfectly reasonable human attitude toward his patients.

As for my own ideas that you were asking about, those I think were essentially mine. There were people, of course, who were writing along the same lines like Spitz, Phyllis Greenacre, and others, who were touching on the same subject matter. And later, shortly before he died, Greenson wrote several essays on the importance of the real relationship, the actuality of the relationship as opposed to the pure transference. So there were many people who were sympathetic to this sort of thing, and yet mine departed from theirs because it perhaps had a little more of an organic, biological underpinning.

I was influenced by everything that I read and that was going on that I thought was worthwhile and true, with particular emphasis on the fact that the principle of abstinence, while essentially sound in its origin, can be overdone to a degree where it has paradoxical effects. There was an analyst many years ago whom I took particular notice of because she was a woman whom I had met when I was hardly more than a boy, an adolescent. Then, I think, she was a few years older than I. I didn't see her for many years until I met her at someone's house. She wrote an essay called, "The Masochistic Factor in the Analytic Situation." Her name was

Esther Menaker. I thought very well of that essay, because I did think there was something of that sort in many analyses, in which people were pressed into a kind of conformity and a degree of abstinence of reasonable human responsiveness which led to deeper and deeper regression, and which led to negative or hostile transference. It might not be something of which the person is aware, because a good analysand would tend to conform, and what might occur unconsciously would be excluded from awareness.

I mean, the idea that this is a person whom I'm seeing every day, I've seen him or her for five years now, and I don't even know if he's married or she's married or anything. There is a lack there, if it gets beyond a certain degree.... That, of course, is a matter of judgment, no question about it. There are people who talk all about themselves to their analysands, and they might be profound in their belief in absolute abstinence. But the fact is that once in awhile an answer to a reasonable question—I think in my essays I mention a couple of examples—whether I know more about sailing or about golf—I never could see that that hurt anybody. As a matter of fact, it could even be productive, because it could produce more of a reaction to something that was tangibly and obviously human and real, instead of having to construct a whole person, as was the case with some analytic experiences.

SRR: It makes me think of your conceptualization of the mature transference. Perhaps it facilitates that.

LS: That's right. Now, I don't know about other people who influenced me. There were a lot of people whose work obviously influenced me as a student. I admired Wilhelm Reich's character analysis a great deal. Even though there are some exaggerated emphases in it, it was a brilliant new contribution. He went off the deep end later. There was a German analyst who used to write about resistance, who went to much greater extremes than Reich. I mean that he absolutely excluded any contact in analysis. Contact came only from the patient. By sheer exaggeration he was an important influence. How can you interpret a resistance if you don't have some inspection as to what's being resisted? I mean, it becomes reductio ad absurdum. Nevertheless, it was valuable and stimulating. Reich didn't go that far.

LR: You mention Kaiser in your essay; is that who it was?

LS: Yes, that's who it was. You see, some people might influence you who do not loom so tremendously large in the general analytic horizon.

LR: How did you develop your own interest in writing? How have your writing and people's reactions to your writing enriched your clinical work, helped you formulate things further, and so forth?

SRR: One thing I note is that you are very aware of the responses people have had to your writing.

LS: Especially negative.

LR/SRR: Really?

LS: Well, about writing, I assume you mean psychoanalytic writing. My interest in writing started much earlier.

LR: Can you tell us about that?

LS: Like many young people, I had dreams of being an author. At one time, I was interested in writing some poetry and so forth, so the interest in writing as such was always there. I don't think that this was much influenced manifestly by that tendency. Whatever I wrote in psychoanalysis was, as far as I know, stimulated by an interest in the subject matter. I thought I had an idea that was worthwhile, and so I ought to write about it.

And, now, as to people's responses to my writing. Some of the early things I wrote, like the one about psychotherapy, were almost too well received. It was as if, "Gee whiz, an analyst really writing about psychotherapy seriously?" Some of the hospitals, like Einstein, were at one time strongly oriented analytically, just as many of the large hospitals now are practically turning into psychopharmacological services in psychiatry. But I know they used to refer to that essay and give it to their students. That was very well received.

As to my essay about the "Widening Scope"—that's the way it's usually referred to—I must make a correction, which I have made about every two or three years. The title was not mine. Ernst Kris was chairman of the committee that arranged a meeting at Arden House when Anna Freud was visiting. As a matter of fact, she was there and discussed that essay. Originally, her discussion of it was much more favorable than in later years. Although she mentioned something of that note even then—that we have so much work to do with ordinary neuroses and can help them so much more, why should we involve ourselves with these people who can't form adequate transferences. But, on the whole, she was quite laudatory about the essay. But it was Kris who gave the title and suggested that I give the essay—that was the general subject, the "Widening Scope of Indications for Psychoanalysis," something like that. Well, at first it was very well received and regarded as a breath of fresh air, the idea you could treat sicker people. There were some modest rationales that I proposed for it, about diminishing the vacuum between the patient and analyst as necessary with those patients.

Later, there was some kind of reaction against it. It was regarded as something of an apostasy, although of a mildly revolutionary sort. I was not the first person who wrote about treating borderline patients. There was an old doctor, Adolf Stern, who was a teacher at the Institute when I was a student, who wrote one of the early essays of that kind. He didn't speak very much about the technique. He didn't go into it, the same way I did, but he certainly antedated my writing by quite a bit.

But people began to turn back. I think the reason they had this change of heart was that they began to find that it's hard to treat severe borderline patients, and you don't get the same results with them that you do with some young woman who has a phobia of eating in public, who has a relatively monosymptomatic thing but is otherwise well-oriented and healthy. You don't see many such patients anymore. I don't know where they are, maybe in some of the outpatient clinics. But Lord knows, the analytic institute clinics can't find them for their candidates. The point is that people began to find that this was very difficult, and that it is a strain to treat such patients. I mean, that the countertransferences that they tend to excite are much more troubling, and it takes a certain fortitude to sit it out while they are telling you all sorts of damning and terrible things about yourself, and to go through long periods of hostile transference. So this was disappointing. And then people began to speak of the "narrowing scope." This was often mentioned with my name attached to the opposite. Nevertheless, I think it still has its certain place of which I am not ashamed. If I were to write it now, I think I could do a better job, but I think it was still worth saying. And as I was saying, they can damn it all they want.

SRR: I very much appreciate what you said about the importance of particular personal traits in the analysand, such as courage or endurance for pain. It seems there has been relatively little emphasis on the importance of these kinds of attributes in the psychoanalytic literature.

LS: That is true. I thought I was quite bold to talk about such things to analysts. Who cares about courage and perseverance? The fact is that there are people who can tough it out through severe difficulties in analysis because they think it's worthwhile, and there are those who disappear at the first hint that this isn't all just talking free association. Anyway, that got a lot of attention.

Then, there was the essay on aggression, which was regarded as quite unorthodox because it challenged the dual instinct theory. For practical purposes, aggression has a life of its own in human beings and certainly is the strongest force that militates against the operation of loving and creative instincts. That's true, but its wellspring is another matter. I tried to argue that there is no evidence that aggression is biologically there, that it undergoes a certain development, and so forth. I still hold to that essential argument. I gave that as the Brill Lecture, and it was received in a friendly, general way. Nobody decided that it was a reversal, like the "narrowing scope," although I remember someone was quoted as saying, "How can you have depression without aggression?" I don't believe you have depression without aggression, and I don't think there was anything I said that would suggest otherwise. I am quite convinced of the power and importance of aggression.

Later, if you remember, I wrote a sort of sequel—which many people liked because it was imaginative, but more for that reason than others—about language and fire and aggression, trying to weave these things together anthropologically. I still think it's true, but as I say, many people liked it only because it was imaginative, just as many people liked that thing about the "principal obscene word in the English language." They liked it because they thought it was bawdy. All they remember is "fuck" and "suck," despite all my efforts to read into the various dictionaries of Indo-European languages or the historical part of it. But they do remember that with some kind of amused appreciation of it. Then, the review in the *International Journal* was well-received and had considerable influence, which surprised me. I was surprised, actually pleased, but a little puzzled, when Columbia had one session about returns to classics. That was one of the things they devoted an evening to, and I was there and discussed it. That very much surprised me.

At one time I was more active, going out of town and giving essays. For a few years I've avoided that now, and I haven't written much. I have very bad eyes, and reading and writing are difficult. Being old-fashioned, I am used to longhand. Maybe before I die I'll write one thing more. But anyway, I haven't done that. Wherever I would go out of town, people would mention this as if it were just a natural part of their curriculum. So I can say that that has had its influence. Now there have been several shorter things, like the thing about Merton Gill and his extreme emphasis on transference interpretation. I think Dr. Gill is a very bright and knowledgeable man; interesting, although very pugnacious at times. It was very funny once. We were both in Atlanta on a panel. He made some remark. And I said, "I'm sure Dr. Gill didn't mean his remarks personally." But he said, "I do." We get along very well. We meet, and we have some pleasant reminiscences. But I was not an admirer of that series of things, because I thought that they strained the patient's credulity and rationality, and transformed the world into a world of transference, which it certainly isn't. I mean, transference is powerful and important, but every time a taxi driver, for example, makes a nasty remark, it isn't because he represents the analyst. That kind of thing I object to.

SRR: We are very interested in your writings about training, the progress of students, what you describe as the "present and potential...."

LS: Oh, yes, "The Present State and Potentialities for the Future." Everybody's writing about that now.

SRR: We hope to hear your thoughts about training and training analysis. You have said that, "Any colleague of some experience knows that its (training analysis) distinction from therapy is essentially fictive. It is usually a prolonged therapeutic analysis in which the professional aspiration is a special and complicating condition. The training aspect is an incidental by-product." This is not something that was discussed in our training. We're interested in hearing more about what you think of as complicating conditions.

LS: Oh, the complicating conditions. Well, I certainly still believe that it's fictive, that the training analysis is really different. I always admired Ida Macalpine's essay. It's in the bibliography there on transference. Now, to me, it is rather poorly written, but she did have an essential idea, which was very important to me—that the transference is in part stimulated by a regressive response to the failure of reality in the analytic situation. Somewhere in the patient there is inevitably, "Who is this person? What is their relation to me? What is my real relation to them? It isn't just talking free association." In that failure of response, which is a part of classical analytic technique and which still holds its place within reasonable limits, the patient responds by creating a psychic reality, which is the transference. It's a regressive thing.

To my knowledge, she was the first person who ever said that flat-footedly. There were other things in the essay that I didn't admire so much. For example, I think she said that the training analysis is different from the ordinary analysis. But that was an idea that I had not seen elsewhere. It was taken over by a Frenchman, Lagache, because I know in one or two of his essays—I don't know whether he refers to her or not—he states the same idea. It certainly came after her essay, which was somewhere in the very late 40s, but I think more likely in the early 50s. I don't know why I got off on that....

SRR: ...the complicating conditions?

LS: The matter of the training analysis....Well, I'm firm in the belief that that's a fictive difference, that any real analysis is analysis. You can't change its character. Most people who seek analysis for training purposes have enough neurosis to justify it and really need it to be at their optimum for the work. Now what was the part that you especially....

SRR: The complicating factors of a training analysis versus a regular therapeutic analysis....

LS: Well, there is the fact that in the old days the analyst reported on the analytic patient. Today, there are very few institutes who still do it. To me, that undermined the whole basic structure of analysis. That one was being watched and judged and reported on to authority was to me an absolute disqualification. And also, the tendency to want to be more healthy and to appear more healthy, I don't mean to the point of faking, but just the entering symptom—"I don't want this person to think I'm crazy or that I have an ungovernable phobia." Those are impediments, there is no doubt about it. Then, of course, the work itself is taxing. One of the reasons I believe it's best for candidates to start their supervised work while they are in analysis is the linked countertransferences, which really only tend to come out with the actual work, when one is in the same kind of intimate relationship with the patient upside down from the other. And those make it hard. I think that's what makes the analyses of those who are going to practice analysis longer, and they should be.

SRR: What about the process of termination and the complication of institute relationships? It seems that in this aspect training analyses are quite different from therapeutic analyses.

LS: You're perfectly right. That, too, is another thing. That the person is destined to make in reality an identification that the ordinary therapeutic patient may dream about or may even manifestly wish. Every now and then there's an analytic patient who wants to become an analyst as a result of the analytic relationship. That, too, is another problem. And then the inevitable contacts with colleagues. Sometimes they try to avoid it, but not in all instances. We have some striking instances here in New York, where it has been the opposite of avoidance, where people have later worked with the analyst or analysand, and so on. But, in most instances, at least for a few years, there's an effort to avoid too much contact, but it's there at meetings, and in discussing essays, and so on. Yes, there's no doubt. Those are complications; they make it harder, and they have to be understood thoroughly.

SRR: In your writing you discuss doing a lot of reanalyses as well as working with many older patients. I have two separate questions. In analyzing older patients, do you find the transference neurosis to be significantly different? I'm thinking about analytic work with patients who have gone through many stages of life, far beyond adolescence; for example, having experienced their parents' deaths. I'm also interested in your thoughts about reanalysis in general, what it has meant for your patients to have had other analysts, and the impact of the internalizations from those earlier analyses.

LS: Those are rather interesting and complicated things. There's one part that's paradoxical. Two of my early patients, when I was still a relatively young man, were men who were considerably older than I. It amazed me, as part of the confirmation of certain important validities, that they both developed father transferences. I mean, they could look at me, and they knew that I was younger than they. That was the reality of which they were aware, but their dreams, and certain actings-out, and matters of that sort were unequivocally the behavior of sons with a father. So that can happen, no doubt about it.

On the other hand, the accidents and experiences of later life are also important. I'm seeing people through the deaths of parents and all kinds of special reactions, which of course are less frequent in younger people—not that they don't occur, but some have occurred long before people came into analysis. Those are interesting and special features. I don't believe that older people, just because they're older, are beyond analysis. They sometimes respond very warmly to it. And as I say, they can develop very strong transferences. You see, just the absence in their lives of things that younger people have sometimes facilitates things, there's a sort of craving for it.

Once I was interested in hypnosis, just in a clinical way. I never regarded it as a special matter of study, although I used to read the things by analysts who were at the same time interested in it. I used to do some of it, even trying it with psychotic patients when I was at Menninger's...and here, when I was on the neurological service at Montefiore, and then for a short time at Beth Israel. They used to call me, you know how little it takes to get a reputation for something. You hypnotize a few people, somebody has a favorable result, and then everybody wants your services, sometimes to their great disappointment. And sometimes it shows how absurd human expectation can be. I remember it was very sad. I was called to see an elderly internist, whose name I had known for years when I was a medical student, who was in his fatal final illness, because he had some disturbing symptom, uncontrollable hiccoughing, or something like that. Somebody insisted they must get me down there to stop it. I couldn't. The point that I am making is this. Sometimes I did hypnotize quite older people, people in the senile or immediate presenile period, very late sixties, seventies, and so on. Once I saw an elderly woman with a tic douloureux, trigeminal neuralgia with good results. I don't know what the actual etiology or pathology was, but she responded symptomatically. What struck me was how rapidly these people would go into a trance, these old people. I mean, it was just as if they were longing to be babes in arms again. So there are things that are kind of paradoxical in those situations.

I can't go into all the things you mention. But the repeat analyses are especially interesting because one of the things that struck me most was how little people remember of interpretive material. It amazes me. They have spent several years in analysis, and they hardly ever talk about that aspect of it. What they do mention are the habits of the analyst, the tones of voice, the question of whether he was considerate and reasonable, or whether he was very strict, or even said some harsh things that jolted them, or whatnot. It is really quite amazing. That's one thing that has struck me. Now you might say that in those who have had some favorable results, the interpretive process as such has been absorbed and become a part of the psychic structures. That would be the favorable way to look at it. But not too many people who have had favorable analyses are looking for reanalysis, so I think there may be some other reason for it. And that other reason, as far as I can see, is that the basic, affective relationship between the two as persons, what Greenson later emphasized, so dominated the actual responses that this other seemed unimportant to them. That may be a simplistic explanation. There may be something much more profound, or there may be multiple reasons. That would be a large subject in itself, and one would have to think about it and prepare one's thoughts.

LR: What is your view of how people grow psychically through analysis, repeated analyses, and life experience? What elements are important for growth to occur?

LS: That's a good question. If one puts aside the commonplaces of our work, with all that occurs when a person is freed of certain anxieties and fixations or certain impediments to the development of normal genitality, they go ahead. It's a matter of removing roadblocks. Usually there is required some favorable intervention from the world of reality. This is often ignored. Something good has to come along to enable a person to use this changed attitude. That is true. Just as misfortune can sometimes render futile a great deal of good analytic work. You know, one would have to think a lot about some of these things. That very simple idea has had great force in my own consciousness. You see, I'm pretty old. I don't know if you know how old I am, much older than you probably think. I'm well along in my eighties, eighty-six and one-half.

LR: You look a lot younger.

SRR: We would never know.

LS: ...even with the cane? Well, at any rate, I mention it only because of its relevance to what I was going to say. You see, I believe analysis is a continuous thing in the individual who is analyzed. Obviously, there is further analysis from the same analyst or with another analyst that's taking up something with a new dramatis personae, so to speak. But I do believe that the process once initiated is an ongoing one. I suppose ideally one thinks of a certain amount of self-analysis being initiated, which, with the regular analysis behind it, can be more useful than attempts to do without it. You know, Freud seemed to make use of it somehow. In any case, what I have observed in myself is that even in pretty advanced old age, I sometimes think of things that puzzled me long ago, that may have been touched on in analysis, but perhaps were not fully resolved, and I have even developed fresh insights.

To me it's quite startling. Examples are certain things about the basic things in life, about my mother and what posture she used to take. She was a very tiny person; her knees on the chair leaning over a table or a desk and reading a book; and fantasies that were associated with that suddenly began to achieve much wider meaning to me. It involved some things about my father, and so on. So that is one thing I believe—that there is a continuous process under favorable circumstances, and that a person can make use of it for many years.

SRR: That's so meaningful to hear.

LS: Because it almost startled me to find that something that had been a commonplace of my boyhood suddenly achieved a much richer meaning to me. That's the only thing I can think of as usual. The other things are ordinary. I mean, they're covered by some of the things that we take for granted. Do you have some ideas?

SRR: What you said about your mother made me think of the whole way you conceptualize the primordial transference, which actually feels quite modern to us, especially in terms of its enduring nature and its sustained ability to color our experience. You described how the residual relationship endures because of the pull of that transference.

LS: And even includes certain of the later phases of childhood; this would be the underlying thing in the incest complex, for example.

SRR: When you were discussing the mature transference as derived from the child's desire in the patient to continue to learn and develop, I wondered if you also included adolescence in that conceptualization. The mature transference impressed me as a developmental formulation, encompassing learning, that went well beyond....

LS: Well, I'm sure that adolescence does recapitulate certain things of childhood in a new context. It's interesting that you mention that about learning because I remember being at some pains to try to demonstrate that that was not just a maturational ego function but could actually be a transference…because I have seen a child pester a mother to sing certain things, to play certain games….

LR: That was a very striking observation. I remember it in your paper, your description of the drive quality of curiosity, the way a child implores others to be taught.

LS: That's right.

LR: When you were talking about your own self-analysis, I wondered if over time you noted any changes in your own associative processes as you listened to your patients?

LS: What I may associate with the patient may have nothing to do with the actual patient. There is inevitably a change. There is no question. You are simply at a different phase of your life, and your life is different. Your responses to people are definitely and inevitably different, so I would say that there is a change. There is ongoing development or, in some instances, regressive development as time goes on. And this surely does make a difference. Just to oversimplify, if a man in his eighties hears somebody talking about how he played four sets of tennis and then jumped in to swim for a half-mile to cool off, of course, the associations would be colored by that. You know, they'd be colored by nostalgia, maybe a little, we trust, well-governed envy, and so on. They're bound to change.

LR: That reminds me of the way you write about the analyst as a real person. You address the potential vulnerabilities of analysts during their lifetime of work, that they may not always have the same kind of energy to work with certain kinds of patients. That's something we don't hear discussed or acknowledged very often.

LS: It had to do with the question of the severe borderline patient. There probably is a certain peaking of energy for that type of work with different analysts.

LR: Your attunement to particular developmental issues within the analytic relationship in your writing impresses me. For example, you compare the analyst's interpretations in response to a patient's free associations with a mother's putting words to her infant's babbling. You also note the importance of separation anxiety as a powerful dynamic within the treatment relationship. In addition, you demonstrate a sensitivity to and appreciation for individuals who have survived by not abandoning their infantile longings.

More specifically, you refer to vulnerable patients in terms of "the thin layer of observing reality-testing ego and the thin thread of transference love and hope for love which enabled these patients to grow up in the first place and sustain the analytic situation." To what experiences or training of your own do you attribute your sensitivity to these particular developmental issues and experiences?

LS: You're not speaking of my own life? ...My professional...?

LR: Either your own life, if you feel free to talk about that, or your clinical experience. You have a uniquely profound appreciation for early developmental experiences.

LS: Well, about myself, that would be too complicated. I didn't have a very pathological childhood. I think, all in all, counting on averages, the existence of certain reasonable neurotic things, the atmosphere was pretty good and fulfilled some of these basic requirements quite well, with here and there an exception, naturally. But I think most of it was actually due to my own adult analytic observations. I did not have child training. When I was at Menninger's, as a matter of course we visited the Southard School, but some of the children there were organically impaired. It was very rare that any of them were susceptible to psychological treatment. That undoubtedly changed later, but I was there in the early 30s. That was a very long time ago.

From adult patients, I have done reconstructive thinking about the phenomenology. It was what I was saying about patients and their past analyses. They seemed to be more concerned, with the occasional exception, with simple, conscious human experiences than they were about the important things that were told them. About the matter of separation, I still think of that as the fundamental painful human experience, the one that is struggled with throughout the rest of life. There are various forms in the efforts to overcome it. Marriage is one of them, one of the institutionalized ones, and another is the struggle with the ending of an analysis. Sometimes, with some people in whom it's very acute, just the missing of two days of analysis or one day. Having observed that, I came to this feeling.

Of course, in my own experience I know when I went off to college, all of that was handled with denial to such an extreme degree that it is transparent to me in later years. Anyway, that is a matter of observation and of conviction about the observation. You know, somebody else may negate it altogether. Out of that I developed this whole business that goes on in the book. Now, what was the other thing you mentioned?

LR: There was your formulation of the babbling....

LS: Oh, yes. I remember that very well. Yes, I thought of that as the anlage of interpretation. The baby is trying to say something, trying to communicate, and the mother gives it words which sooner or later it begins to adopt and make its own. That is my own notion.

LR: You said that most patients don't remember interpretations, but they remember the human contact. Similarly, we don't remember the first time our mother interpreted to us what we were saying, but we remember the process of contact.

LS: With regard to the basic question of that relationship with the mother, I remember that at one time I was interested in boorishness. It's a funny thing to be interested in, but I had a patient who was a very intelligent man, capable in his way, but he was an utter boor, and I mean boor in its widest sense. He had a way of saying things that would be hurtful to another person without even knowing that it was so. That takes some doing. I thought of an example of it, but I think it can just as well be left out because it's personal.

This man's mother, as nearly as I can reconstruct their relationship, didn't have the slightest sensitivity to his feelings as he grew up—not the slightest. I could only see this poor fellow reproducing in his life what he must have experienced in some form with her. Now that doesn't have much to do with separation, but it has something to do with the question of verbal expression and how it is communicated, and how a child might learn to talk and to express himself from a mother with that quality. Of course, that neglects all the particular nuances that would make the person a boor, instead of something else. For that, I think you'd have to go through a whole analysis.

LR: Did he change over time in the process?

LS: I'm afraid not. Not in that respect. It was something so deep-rooted that while he changed in other respects, that quality persisted in him.

SRR: This is just an association before we move to another topic. I was thinking of what you said about patients not remembering what was spoken. My thought was that with the mother, the child learns to speak rather than remembering what the mother says, so that the proof of the analysis might be the patient's ability to be able to speak from the heart in a different way.

LS: I think you're quite right about that. The whole matter of interpreting the baby's babbling is done as colored by the mother's attitude toward the baby, whether it is something coercive from the very beginning, or loving, giving something to the child, and so on. I think it is a very fundamental phenomenon. Just as the question of the mother singing to the child; the lullabies and so on are so profoundly important.

LR: I want to ask you about another of your theoretical concepts, "deprivation in intimacy." I think that concept also reflects your attunement to the child primordial transference, but you demonstrate how it's different in treatment with the conditions of abstinence.

LS: Well, to me that is very important because it is one of the few things that rather sharply differentiated my ideas from those of my predecessors, most of whom were slightly older than I, like Phyllis Greenacre or Rene Spitz. I felt that the fundamental dynamic of the analytic situation lies in that deprivation in intimacy. However you look at it, it's an intimate relationship. Two people meet in a room alone, day after day, that's intimate. And at the same time, one of them gets no cognitive satisfaction about the other, very little emotional gratification, and certainly no primitive gratifications of any kind. I think that is the driving force that activates the primordial type of transference. The wish for reunion becomes exaggerated and intensified through that deprivation.

In a sense, I was somewhat influenced by Ida Macalpine. It has something to do with creating the transference as we know it clinically, to make this person into somebody who is meaningful and who might give rise to fantasies of gratification and so on. The idea that the negative aspect, the deprivation, drives the analysis is a little bit different from how Spitz, and Greenacre, and others emphasize the sense of intimacy and the mother-baby relationship in some of its positive aspects. Surely those positive aspects are there, and some people whose life histories have been very fortunate can experience them more readily than other people. Furthermore, the deprivation is not often felt as such. That is another thing I had to emphasize, that it is an unconsciously motivated response to the cognitive and affective deprivation.

A person doesn't think, "I'm getting madder and madder at you because you never tell me anything, because you never say anything nice." Some very naive patients might do that, but most don't. Instead they think, "This is the way it is. You have certain rules, and you follow them." But a process nevertheless goes on in the unconscious, which is quite different. So that's what I meant by that, and to me it was very important. I don't know how seriously other people take it.

SRR: We are very interested in what you have written about religion. You stated: "The diminution of attachment to the idea of God in terms of vivid personal imagery, even to diminished and unreliable secular equivalents, diminishes the facility of solution by displacement of residual basic transferences." Could you say more about that?

LS: Well, Freud, in relation to Pfister, who was a Swiss Protestant clergyman, said something which was unusual for him. He wrote a little appreciation of Pfister, a very thin volume or else an essay. You see, Pfister was one of the early people who appreciated Freud and his contribution. Freud said of Pfister something to this general effect, that it was something to be envied that Pfister could include his faith in God in his concept of what awaited the patient in the hereafter. I do think that belief in God is one of the permanent longings in human beings. They want someone who is all-caring, omnipotent, omniscient. I don't believe it's ever wholly given up. Some people find it in a political credo and others find it in psychoanalysis.

There's no doubt that there was a time when people thought that psychoanalysis was the solution to everything and that nothing else is important, except as you understand various aspects of it. I think that these beliefs have something to do with the unresolved residue of what I call the primordial transference. I don't admire my choice of words, but the idea was there, that this is something that remains highly sublimated and quite well integrated or reconciled with scientific beliefs in some people. They say that some astronomers and mathematical physicists become religious because they find that things can't always be explained scientifically. I think it was the reference to Pfister by Freud that struck me at one time, because Freud was not only a freethinker, but very much an atheist in the conventional sense that he believed that the belief in God was a mass community transference, and anyone can argue that.

I met a young Jesuit priest at Rudolf Loewenstein's home, who is one of several Jesuits in Montreal very much interested in psychoanalysis. He gave me a little essay, which I have somewhere among my old papers. I'm swamped with them and don't have room for them. But I valued this one because the Jesuits are interested in knowledge. They may interpret it a certain, special way, but they do go after it. And psychoanalysis was one form of knowledge that appealed to him and his group. They used to meet regularly, and he took up this question of religion and psychoanalysis. The essay was about three pages long. He said, "Yes, all that was undoubtedly true of those people." He further said, "And one of the goals of psychoanalysis was to free people of the transferential element, then they could come face to face with the true concept of God." That's very interesting. He stated it very simply and forthrightly, "Yes, of course that's true, but the transference is something to be dissolved. Then you would be able to feel what God really was." It was very interesting. He was a very nice young man. I never saw him again.

LR: You wrote a review of two essays on treating schizophrenics. What have been your own interests and experiences in treating psychotic and borderline patients?

LS: It was about Johnny Rosen and that Viennese nurse, Gertrude Schwing. I thought they were so different, and yet there was a common factor. They did something in their respective lives with the patient that enabled them to enter the psychosis. I don't know whether you remember it, but Rosen put himself in the psychosis. If the patient was afraid of the devil, Rosen would approach that fear directly, he would be the devil and reassure him. If the patient had a feeling that he had a terrible body odor—I don't know if he mentions it in that book—he would sniff between the patient's toes to assure him that there was nothing. He would thus get a relationship with the patient that was quite remarkable. Now, he ended up not so well. He had some trouble, I don't know whether it was medical, legal, or what. But he did have an idea, and for a while he got rather striking temporary results. Then he wrote a book in which he tried what he called "direct analysis," in which he would interpret things immediately and broadly. This showed some of the weaknesses in his thinking. The first part was, no question, the striking finding.

Now Schwing did the opposite. She took the maternal tack. She was just all mother. She made a distinction between "motherly love" and "motherliness." Do you recall that? Motherliness being the truly loving, considerate, all considerate, and all accepting relationship of the ideal mother to a child. Motherly love she regarded as like the animals, just some kind of fierce, possessive protectiveness, and so on. Well, the patients of Schwing, like those of Rosen, didn't hold their results very well, because it was under the spell of this relationship that they were well. I don't know whether Gertrude Schwing married or then had a baby, diminishing her interest in these patients, but there were immediate reactions to it. The whole thing caved in. She was quite honest about that; that this was the limitation; that she would have had to go on mothering them indefinitely.

In terms of my own experience, as time went on I got more and more involved in clinical analysis, which usually has to do with ambulatory, self-sustaining people, so I saw less and less of that sort of patient. A person like Kernberg has always been associated with hospitals, and he sees people where he can immediately invoke the protection of a hospital and its resources. I think he sees more severely ill patients than analysts who practice without that backing. At one time, I was very interested in it. When I was at Menninger's, for example, I had a lot to do with psychotic patients. And I did everything possible, which in some sense might have approximated the techniques that either Schwing and Rosen used, but not to the extreme, of course. I played the fiddle and there was one paranoid young man who played the violin. I had him come to my home, and we'd play duets. There's no doubt that this formed a very strong bond. He was very much attached to me, and he would listen to my critique of his paranoid notions. I can't remember how he ended up. He was in the sanitarium for maybe a year or so. He went home somewhat improved, but not free of this basic paranoid schizophrenia. I even tried to hypnotize some of them. As with the old persons, I was startled when one schizophrenic girl went into a deep trance. Another man, somewhere around midnight, called out to the nurses that they would have to call Dr. Stone to take him out of the hypnosis, because he wanted to go to sleep.

SRR: I hope they didn't call you.

LS: They called me. I told them to tell him, "Dr. Stone says that you can wake up now." But you know, they would sometimes respond to that kind of primitive relationship, just as some of the old people did. I did not reach any formulation of the kind that Schwing or Rosen did. In Chestnut Lodge, Frieda Fromm-Reichmann came close to doing some intermediate thing. She would get down on the floor with some patients and behave in a way that they found acceptable or responsive. The first thing, of course, is to penetrate that deep narcissistic regression that is a part of any psychosis, to call out something that makes a person want to risk a relationship with another human being. Sometimes I failed miserably in my naiveté.

I can remember the name of this patient, a young woman, who was one of those schizophrenics with marked physical vegetative changes, the skin of her face, and so on. I used to sit with her and lecture her on how to give out, to try to feel for other people, and so on. I was so disappointed when she would look at me with glassy eyes. She must have just wondered what this idiot was talking about, about this interest in other people. But I got over that. I knew that the approach had to be a little more subtle than that. But you penetrate sometimes without the person knowing it, or knowing it yourself.

We used to see quite a few people from Kansas farms. As places went out there, Menninger's was pretty expensive, even though this was during the Depression, and they were often slack on patients. I was there until 1936, which was pretty much the peak of the Depression. I went out there in late 1932, or something like that. Anyway, there would occasionally be these youngsters from prosperous farm families. I don't know what your places of origin are, but we used to think a few acres was a good-sized place. In Kansas, they spoke of sections, which is, I think, 640 acres. So it was a question of how many sections a person had. Some of these farmers were pretty well off, and they could send their sick youngsters to Menninger's. One was a young fellow who was practically mute. I didn't try with him any of that nonsense that I did with Ms. So-and-So. At least I was intelligent enough to see that I was talking sheer nonsense. She just looked at me. Well, anyway, with this fellow I just used to try to talk to him about life on the farm. He didn't talk, but I used to ask questions about it. I'd say that I had lived on a farm in the east for six years when I was a young fellow, and I was interested in those things, and maybe sometime he could tell me about his life. I tried to make contact with something in his life.

Well, he improved gradually. In other words, he said "Hello" to me when I came in and maybe even "See you tomorrow" or something like that. He once said one or two things about his brother, and he became more interested in his dress and started getting along with some of the other patients there, although still relatively mute. He left and went back to his farm home. He never addressed me by name, that was one of the important things. A few months later, I got one of those night calls from the supervising nurse in charge, and she said, "Dr. Stone, who do you think just came to the door of the sanitarium?" I said, "Who?" and she named this fellow. I forget his name. I remember the name of that young woman because I can still picture her staring at me when I told her about the need to love people. Anyway, I don't remember his name, but she said, "He came to the door and when we opened the door, he said, 'Call Dr. Stone. I have to come here and be here for a while.'" So you see, a relationship was going on and developing, simply on the basis of my being interested in him and wanting to talk with him, and so on. What happened later? I think after some few months he felt better and went away again. But I'll never forget that, specifically asking for me by name.

Well, I got more and more interested and involved in analysis, and the practice took shape accordingly. There were still some severe borderline patients. There were one or two whom I regarded as ambulatory schizophrenics, to use the term I think Zilboorg coined. Why ambulatory I don't know, because they nearly all could walk, but as far as he meant, maybe outside the sanitariums. I had a few of those patients, and I was very much interested in them. It's from working with them that I evolved some of these feelings about borderline patients, and the way the transference had to be handled, and the way that the "analytic vacuum," as I call it, had to be diminished to permit them to develop any contact with me.

I know one of the schizophrenics I mentioned was a young woman who had a pail with her vomitus in it, which was her mother, you see. She used to throw her purse down on the little coffee table in my office, with a clank. She announced that she wanted to kill me. Every time she would throw her purse down, I thought there was a revolver in it. It was just her cigarette case. She left considerably improved. She definitely had psychotic symptoms. There were people shining flashlights from the adjacent roof to annoy her, and she was afraid of the breasts of her employer. She was a secretary, apparently a skilled secretary, but her employer had rather large breasts, and these frightened her. She improved, but I never heard from her again. Sometimes I would surprisingly hear from people after some years. I don't know what became of her.

SRR: You said, "Psychoanalysis in its present form has a plenitude of untapped resources to offer as science, as therapy, and as the parent to other therapeutic methods. But it would be fundamentally wrong to assume that it cannot change or should not be changed, if adequate reasons for such change are developed." We're interested in what changes you hope to see or that you anticipate.

LS: Well, changes...I stated that the old model was quantitatively too severe to be realistic, too severe to be accompanied by the expectation of an optimal response of the patient. It's more quantitative than anything else. Perhaps the model should also be qualitatively altered for patients who are a little more sick. Even the matter of sitting up, the vis-à-vis contact, may be necessary for some patients, so that they can feel the reality as part of the governance of transference fantasies that may be too disturbing. I'm very much interested in the future of psychotherapy because at the very best, the number of people that can be treated with intensive psychoanalysis is very few. I do think that psychotherapy can be developed and researched more seriously than it has been, and experimented with more thoroughly. In many instances, a good, well-conducted psychoanalytically oriented psychotherapy can do as much as analysis can, and for some people it might be better.

Differential diagnosis and differential indications are very important, and those things can be developed further. I really think there is a future for psychoanalysis despite all the gloom, even if it includes knowingly and willingly giving over a certain part of its territory to psychotherapy. Some people simply cannot, in an economic sense, afford what it takes to provide a living for an analyst. It's a reality, it's a hard reality, but it is real. You can't have only people who are very well off, or whose commitment to the work is such that it's going to be professionally important to them to make sacrifices. There are just plain people with neuroses that can be very disturbing, and they can be helped by other means. I must admit I'm not very much taken with behavior therapy and matters of that sort. I think their application is very limited, but the derivatives of psychoanalysis can be really useful. They can be the clue to interpretive work.

LR: One of the things we appreciate in your work is your attention to different aspects of reality. You emphasize, for example, the importance of a patient actually experiencing his or her neurotic conflict within the transference.

LS: That's right.

LR: As you talk now, you attend to the real life situations of both patients and analysts, the reality factors that might make analysis difficult.

LS: I think it's very important. That's why I mentioned the lady whom I actually met out West. She died some years ago. I'm not criticizing her as a person; as a matter of fact she was a good friend. But she had been in Vienna, was analyzed there, and was steeped in the very literal conception of analysis of that time. When she said, "Why can't this patient go earn more money?" I thought, "Well, maybe she could, but many people can't."

LR: I had a somewhat strange question to ask about your writing style. You often use double negatives.

LS: Do I?

LR: I have written them down.

LS: It would be interesting.

LR: It struck me as a very unique style, and I was curious whether you were aware of it.

LS: No, but I'll tell you what my immediate association was. It will be even stranger to you. Years ago, I studied Persian. What I know of it now is negligible. But at that time, I was interested in the poets and read some in the original. Persian has double negatives as negatives. "Nah" would be "not" and would be nothing and to say "Nah Nich" just means doubly strong nothing.

LR: This is a sentence from your essay, "Psychoanalytic Situation": "In the former instances, I refer to the blanketing, one, which does not concern matters that impinge importantly on the central dynamics of the transference neurosis, and two, which is not invoked to avoid undesirable impedance of an important flow of free association at a given time in both its cognitive and its emotional significance."

LS: That's what I said?

LR: There are a lot of negatives here. I don't know if it's related to your Persian.

LS: In other words, blanketing of things which would not interfere with the transference…that you don't stop the patient's free association.

You know, my prose style has often been criticized, and paradoxically it sometimes happens a few people admire it.

SRR: It may go back to your poetic background.

LS: Well, I don't know if I'd call it my background, but it is true. For example, I always remember that I used to admire Sir Thomas Brown very much, "religio medici." When people would speak in these very long convoluted sentences, I would rather take them in. Maybe it was an influence, I don't know. But I recognize that sometimes there are sentences that are almost a paragraph long. And when I'm writing them, it just comes out that way. People tell me, even my own analysands say, "What convoluted sentences you write." On the other hand, this woman who wrote that book, the New Yorker,...

SRR: Janet Malcolm?

LS: Janet Malcolm, she admired the prose style.

SRR: This brings up one more question. I wonder about the effect of your writing on your patients.

LS: Well, they all react to it. There have been one or two who react to it by sheer avoidance, like some kind of forbidden oral gratification. On the other hand, some are very temperate about it, give reasonable critiques or appreciations of it, none though of my prose style.

SRR/LR: Well, thank you very much.

LS: I've enjoyed it myself.

SELECTED BIBLIOGRAPHY

Stone, L. (1938). Concerning the psychogenesis of somatic disease: Physiological and neurological correlations with the psychological theory. *International Journal of Psycho-Analysis*, Vol. 19, pp. 63–76.

Stone, L. (1947). Transference sleep in a neurosis with duodenal ulcer. *International Journal of Psycho-Analysis*, Vol. 28, pp. 18–32.

Stone, L. (1951). The psychoanalytic and psychotherapeutic situations. *Psychoanalytic Quarterly*, Vol. 20, pp. 215–236.

Stone, L. (1954). The widening scope of indications for psychoanalysis. *Journal of the American Psychoanalytic Association,* Vol. 2, pp. 567–594.

Stone, L. (1954). On the principal obscene word of the English language. *International Journal of Psycho-Analysis,* Vol. 35, pp. 30–56.

Stone, L. (1955). Two avenues of approach to the schizophrenic patient. *Journal of the American Psychoanalytic Association*, Vol. 3, pp. 126–148.

Stone, L. (1957). Review of Franz Alexander's *Psychoanalysis and Psychotherapy: Developments in Theory, Technique, and Training. Psychoanalytic Quarterly*, Vol. 26, pp. 397–405.

Stone, L. (1961). *The Psychoanalytic Situation: An Examination of Its Development and Essential Nature*. New York: International Universities Press.

Stone, L. (1967). The psychoanalytic situation and transference: Postscript to an earlier communication. *Journal of the American Psychoanalytic Association*, Vol. 15, pp. 3–58.

Stone, L. (1971). Reflections on the psychoanalytic concept of aggression. *Psychoanalytic Quarterly*, Vol. 40, pp. 195–244.

Stone, L. (1973). On resistance to the psychoanalytic process. *Psychoanalysis and Contemporary Science*, Vol. 2, pp. 42–76.

Stone, L. (1974). The assessment of students' progress. *The Annual of Psychoanalysis*, Vol. 2, pp. 308–322. New York: International Universities Press.

Stone, L. (1975). Some problems and potentialities of present-day psychoanalysis. *Psychoanalytic Quarterly,* Vol. 44, pp. 331–370.

Stone, L. (1979). Remarks on certain unique conditions of human aggression (the hand, speech, and the use of fire). *Journal of the American Psychoanalytic Association,* Vol. 27, pp. 27–63.

Stone, L. (1981). Notes on the noninterpretive elements in the psychoanalytic situation and process. *Journal of the American Psychoanalytic Association*, Vol. 29, pp. 89–118.

Stone, L. (1981). Some thoughts on the "here and now" in psychoanalytic technique and process. *Psychoanalytic Quarterly,* Vol. 50, pp. 709–733.

Stone, L. (1982). The influence of the practice and theory of psychotherapy on education in psychoanalysis. In: *Psychotherapy: Impact on Psychoanalytic Training*, ed. E. D. Joseph & R. S. Wallerstein. New York: International Universities Press, pp. 75–118.

Stone, L. (1984). *Transference and Its Context.* New York: Aronson.

Stone, L. (1986). Psychoanalytic observations on the pathology of depressive illness: Selected spheres of ambiguity or disagreement. *Journal of the American Psychoanalytic Association*, Vol. 34, pp. 329–362.

LEO AND ANITA RANGELL

Anita Rangell, a student of art history, developed an expertise in prints and drawings. She has been a docent and served on the Board of the Docent Council at the Los Angeles County Museum of Art. She also was a docent at the Hammer Museum of Art, now at U.C.L.A.

Throughout a half century of married life, Mrs. Rangell has been an active participant and partner to Dr. Rangell in his scientific, educational, and administrative work, and in his interpersonal relations and travels throughout the psychoanalytic world.

Leo Rangell, M.D. is Clinical Professor of Psychiatry at U.C.L.A. and the University of California, San Francisco, and honorary member of the Los Angeles Psychoanalytic Society and Institute, the Southern California Society and Institute, and the Peru Psychoanalytical Society. He is past President twice of the American Psychoanalytic Association and the International Psychoanalytical Association. He was twice recipient of the International Clinical Essay Prize of the British Institute for Psychoanalysis and has received the Heinz Hartmann Award of the New York Psychoanalytic Institute, the Mary S. Sigourney Award of the American Psychoanalytic Association, and awards from the Philadelphia Psychoanalytic Institute and the University of Chicago School of Medicine.

Dr. Rangell delivered the Freud Anniversary Lectures of the New York Psychoanalytic Institute and of the Downstate Psychoanalytic Institute, the Franz Alexander Lecture, the Robert Waelder Lecture, the Fenichel-Simmel Lecture, and many other Honorary Lectureships. He has been a Fellow at the Center for Advanced Study in the Behavioral Sciences at Stanford University and a Guggenheim Foundation Fellow. His Visiting Professorships include the John B. Turner Visiting Professorship of Psychiatry, Columbia University and an appointment as Visiting Scholar, Sigmund Freud Centre, Hebrew University. He has served on numerous editorial boards of books and journals.

The Rangells were interviewed May 9 and 11, 1991.

LR: First, my wife Anita has traveled with me throughout the analytic world for over fifty years, and has hardly missed a meeting I have been active in during that time. I think it would be appropriate and helpful, and hope you don't mind, to have her here with us for the interview.

SRR: Yes, of course. Welcome to both of you. We're going to start with your concept of "unconscious insight." You wrote: "The patient, whatever he does consciously with our interpretations, often carries it to greater completion, knowledge, and action unconsciously. This results in unconscious insight, which can be more than its preconscious–conscious articulation. The ultimate terror is still kept repressed, but is now inwardly known and can be used. Unconscious insight is consonant with Freud's unconscious ego or Arlow's unconscious fantasy, and a total complex system of unconscious cognition and even action."

Can you say more about this process of something being both repressed and known. As an analyst, how do you see or surmise when unconscious insight has occurred? I'd like to ask several questions. You take it wherever you want. First, is the patient aware or do you see awareness develop over time? Is there a difference psychically, or economically, or dynamically, in terms of insight that becomes conscious and that that doesn't? Also, does what stays unconscious have to do with earlier development or trauma?

LR: That's an important set of questions, which point immediately to my theoretical conceptualization that the unconscious is far from being just a cauldron of the id. Little by little, other things have come to be known as having their territory within the unconscious, which also expands the psychoanalytic process therapeutically and the understanding of the dynamics of normal action. For example, this fits with my concept of unconscious decision-making, which is also a cognitive process. A wide, complex psychic life takes place in the unconscious, not just id impulses. In fact, both sides of a conflict, and even the resolution of a conflict, I feel, take place in the unconscious. This is synchronous, by the way, with Loewald's idea that the unconscious can be partly rational and the conscious irrational. It's sort of a crisscrossing.

But the evidence for all of this unconscious insight and unconscious cognition, is the psychoanalytic situation. As we analyze our patients, we see again and again that they are revealing to us not just wishes and drives, but solutions which they don't admit. They don't know or acknowledge to themselves why they made certain vital decisions in their lives, why they chose their profession, why they chose their spouse, why a divorce, why they did something extreme which was a crossroads in their life. When all these are unrepressed and come to the surface as knowledge in the analytic process, you realize what a very complex life took place unconsciously. It includes affects and cognition; cognition as much as affects and drives.

Ed Joseph wrote an essay stating that decisions are made consciously, while the preparations for them are made unconsciously. That is counter to what I believe, which is that the entire process can lie repressed and has to be uncovered during the analytic process. Now, you asked, "Is there any difference between awareness that stays unconscious and that which does not stay unconscious?"

There is such a thing as the deepest resistances of the id, written about by Freud and by Leo Stone, which keep certain elements and experiences from consciousness. I think that the basic terror, not just anxiety, but terror, and basic loneliness, not just fear of separation, but fear of utter and permanent aloneness, can never be reached by conscious awareness. I have a patient now who has tremendous anxiety and indecision because of this basic infantile terror. I don't think analysis reaches beyond the third year or so, as far as conscious recovery is concerned, yet I feel that inputs in the analysis can reach and touch those layers beyond what can be known consciously. Many things that soothe the inner man, that soothe his infantile anxieties, which cannot come to the surface, nevertheless operate below the level at which we see it.

How do we know these effects? By the patient's comfort, or by his actions; he does things in life which indicate that he has acquired more peace and more decisiveness. I think much of the analytic process takes place at the preconscious level, and that dips down and reaches up, and that a patient doesn't even remember a lot of the things that take place. Sometimes the analyst doesn't remember what happened. I have patients who come back years later, and what I remember and what they remember are two different things. A patient is sometimes amazed at the little summary or reminder that I give him. He says, "I didn't know. I don't remember that." I say, "Well, I hardly do either, but I'm offering it." He can still deny it if he wants. But he doesn't. He usually accepts it, and it's very much a part of him. I mean, you picked something which points to an underappreciated area and yet to me an inescapable one. I don't know, about some of your questions that I didn't get into, like "How do you know the difference?," but we'll come to it, I'm sure.

SRR: The next quote is from "Insight to Change." "With the knowledge that is acquired, the ego is now confronted with the possibility of action, which presents an opportunity but also a responsibility. This moment of decision is part of a process, as much unconscious as preconscious-conscious....But while expansions of insight and reduction of anxiety are major steps, they are only waystations toward the goal. Results then depend on actions, which were tested and interrupted during the formation of the neurosis, now being completed." Is it the ability to act, in the way you are conceiving of it, that allows for the resolution of the analysis or…

LR: …or the absence of it, its failure. The positive ability to do that speaks for the completion....I wonder, percentage-wise, how often that happens. I think a lot of analyses falter at that point of the execution of insight into the behavioral life of the patient. How did

I get to that? That idea germinated since the early 1960s. It's thirty years since germination of that idea of unconscious resolution of conflicts leading to an unconscious decision toward action, which then percolates up through the preconscious into the patient's conscious statement, "Oh, I'm going to do such and such; I'm going to...." In the early days, you asked, What will I be when I grow up? At this point in the analysis, the patient says, in effect, "I've grown up. Now I am a good husband. Now I'm not going to put up with any masochistic, self-destructive behavior anymore. I'm now going to assert myself. I now say to someone in an argument, 'I don't agree with that,' instead of being obsequious."

Now all that is prepared in the unconscious, is decided in the unconscious, and is executed into the conscious. The idea...you asked where did I get that idea? It began on a panel on intrapsychic conflict. It was the only time I worked with Heinz Hartmann directly. He was on that panel. Max Schur, Heinz Hartmann, Jack Arlow, myself, and others. Some of the discussion on that panel was elaborated into two essays, which were published in *The Psychoanalytic Study of the Child,* on intrapsychic conflict. One I called "The Scope of Intrapsychic Conflict"; the other was "Structural Problems in Intrapsychic Conflict." Both are included in *The Human Core*. In those essays, I started to describe what later became the intrapsychic process, namely thought as preliminary action expanded into a much wider and more complete process. After the signal of anxiety or safety is received by the ego, all the possibilities are traced, the different potentials for actions or other outcomes from which the patient unconsciously chooses. The rest does not happen without choosing. All analysts ignore the choosing. The patient, in part, chooses to be neurotic, or perverse, or normal. A perversion doesn't flow over him like a river. He chooses it. That's why we use the phrase choice of symptom. But we don't use the phrase choice of perversion. Why not? If there is choice of a symptom, there is of a perversion as well. A fetishist chose a fetish. A hysteric chose a paralysis of the arm. A normal character chose normalcy.

So all this, every phase on this intrapsychic sequence left a link for future development of another essay. That's why I have hundreds of them, because there were hundreds of links in the chain, and they were all unexplored and very important, every one of them. None of them could have been left out without jeopardizing the whole process. Now, thirty years later, you know each one of them has developed into something. Like one, from "Insight to

Change," is a very important node in this whole chain because it points to the fact that the patient, not the analyst, now has to go out to live the patient's life. Whose life is it anyway? It's the patient's life. And if he doesn't do anything with the analysis, he can thwart all your effort. If he does something with it, you're both happy.

SRR: Why do you think so many analyses fail at this point? Do you have any recommendations as to what the analyst could do at this point?

LR: There are two reasons. One is that the analyst and the patient didn't understand what the roles of each one were. Two, the reason for this transference-countertransference blurring, and nonresolution is that the analyst didn't resolve his countertransference of whose life is it anyway, his or the patient's? Look how much that affects the countertransference. He won't let the patient go, or he won't urge. He won't do what Freud did with the Wolfman, and say, "By July, you've got to do it or goodbye." I don't recommend that, but there should be some recognition of a kind of shifting to the patient of the responsibility of insight. Erikson wrote a book called "Insight and Responsibility." I changed that phrase to "the responsibility of insight." By the way, he got that title partly from Anita. Remember that, in Palo Alto?

AR: Well, he came for dinner. They were both at the Center for Advanced Study at Stanford. Erik Erikson said, "I don't know what to call my book." We talked about it, and finally that title came out.

LR: It came out, "Insight and Responsibility." I was intrigued by that, and in this essay, I realized that what I was talking about is the responsibility of insight, not insight and responsibility. Once insight is achieved, whose task is it now? What if a patient says, as some patients say, "Okay, so now I know. So what?" I say, "If you say so what, it's your choice. If you want to do nothing with it, just go home with insight with no benefit. But you have an opportunity and more than that a responsibility to put it into effect if you mean what you say."

Here is where we test a patient's superego as well. Because if his superego is such that he can have values, but not live by them, that's his choice, too. But if he has values, I say, "How come you're not living by your superego values?" That led into my Nixon and Watergate book. That whole thing about integrity.

LRAYMOND: My question actually follows very much on what you're saying. In your paper on action theory, you state, "The task is to achieve a balance, what psychoanalytic understanding might be able to contribute about unconscious assumptions of too much, and also too little responsibility. That is a tall order. But that is what analysis has always faced. What seems surprising is the block among psychoanalysts themselves, to extending knowledge of the workings of the unconscious into the full range of unconscious activity, evaluating, planning and executing action." How do you see this "block" being expressed by other analysts in your work with them?

LR: Well, there are several very important theoretical subjects in this question. Let's see if I can remember them. The first has to do with the too little and too much responsibility, which is due to the unexplored dichotomy between psychic determinism and will. Whatever comes about by psychic determinism, outside of ego control, the patient has little or no responsibility for, because it's not only automatic and unconscious, but, more importantly, it's outside of the control of his unconscious ego. Therefore, if he's impotent, he can't will himself to be potent. If he has preoedipal and pregenital pressures or requirements that prevent proper sexual function, you can't say to a patient, at the beginning, "Just do the right thing," because he's consumed with impulses out of his control.

Analysis, then, by making these things conscious, increases the patient's control. Now, while the forces were out of his control, he had little or no responsibility. But, as many neurotic patients do, he took excessive responsibility. He blamed himself for his parents' divorce, for example, because he had unconscious aggression which he didn't know about. A person who has too much self-blame because of psychic determinism outside of his control, during the analysis becomes one who dilutes the self-blame and his own sense of responsibility. He comes to see that he is less responsible for things that happen than he thought (a) because other people did a lot of things and (b) because what he did was out of his control. Analysis will lead a person like that to feel less responsible and therefore also less guilty. On the other hand, many times people project blame to other people for things they were inwardly responsible for; they absolve themselves of responsibility and feel no guilt. They feel they were mistreated. Maybe they were. Or maybe they were not mistreated, or brought on the mistreatment. So in that respect the analysis of that segment of their psychic disturbance would lead them to see—this is where unconscious action comes in—that they did more than they know they did. Therefore, they were responsible for setting up a chain of activities that reverberated back against their own self-interests. So in that segment, they acquire in analysis a greater sense of responsibility, where in the former instance they acquired less.

The balance of the two makes for a more normal acknowledgment and sense of responsibility, namely not too much, not too little but appropriate and optimal. I am responsible for what I did. After I was brought up by my parents, I then did things to make the world hate me or traumatize me. Therefore, I can also stop it. It gives the person a sense of power. As soon as he knows he's responsible, he can also stop. That's the first part of that question. The second part was....

Oh, you asked another thing in that first question. There was something that struck me....

LRAYMOND: Let's see. "The task is to achieve a balance." Then you say, "What seems surprising is the block among psychoanalysts...."

LR: Oh, yes, that's right. Now why is this so unique to me? Why am I pushing it? And why don't other people either also agree to it or pick it up quickly? Because there is a confusion and a resistance and an opposition to the little word "homunculus." Was that in...?

LRAYMOND: Yes, you talked about that.

LR: This has to do with who is or what is the agent of action. Is the agent the self, or is it the ego? In my view, it is the ego. That is the crowning achievement of the structural viewpoint—the ego integrates all the inputs of the inner and outer worlds, and then puts them into effect, bringing about all these actions. Some people react rather sarcastically to that. Brenner, for example, replied to Waelder, who said the same thing as I—that there is an inner planning agency—in a criticism which I don't agree with, and with a note of sarcasm, "It's as if there's a little man sitting on the psychic apparatus directing everything." Well, first of all, while there is that little something in there, it's not a little man. It's little, and it's something, but it's not the whole man because it's the ego. If it were the whole man, like a homunculus, then that homunc would have divided himself into ego, superego, and id, and then there would be a homunc in the homunc, and you'd go on forever that way.

In psychoanalysis, there are divisions and subdivisions in its theory to understand and explain things. A psychoanalysis of the whole without the component parts would be preanalytic and go back to pre-Freud. If you accept and proceed with Freud's theoretical path, in contrast to Kohut or object-relations theorists who are interpersonalists, and think in terms of the whole self or the whole object without component structures within each, and subdivide the person into his component parts, then you have to ask, What does this or that mean? Which mental structure or element deals with this function? Does the id do it? Does the superego do it? No, the superego contains the values; the id, the drives; the ego, it's the one. I'm the one. I am my ego.

By the way, I am all of these things together—I'm the id, the superego, and the ego—but its my ego that determines the executing branch of my character. How I look to the outside world depends a good deal on whether I have a strong ego or a weak ego. Why do we use these terms? We don't say weak id. We do, but it has a different meaning. Strong ego is an executive, the CEO of the internal apparatus. I wrote on the executive functions of the ego. That again is a term not used very much; only occasionally with different meanings than I have. But that executive function of the ego is the agent of action. Why is there a block against it? I said an opposition; there is also a confusion as much as an opposition, namely, they confuse homunculus with ego.

LRAYMOND: As an extension of that question, how do you help analytic candidates work with these ideas in supervision? How do you help them appreciate these critical ways of looking at the unconscious part of the ego?

LR: The clinical material always points to this. Every time you see a case, you have examples of interpretations that increase the patient's responsibility rather than decrease it. In the early days, people said that analysis made everyone think he was right about everything, and it absolved the whole sense of guilt. I think now that sometimes analysis should increase the sense of guilt, instead of only decrease it. This is seen in interpretations of the clinical material.

LRAYMOND: Do you run into resistance on the candidates' part to your understanding of the patient's responsibility?

LR: Well, not only resistance, but ignorance—not "knowing" these ideas—because they have the weight of the whole institute, which is very much now on a different tack, around self psychology, interest in borderlines, and "Where is the narcissism?" in this or that behavior. To me these deflect from this whole subject.

LRAYMOND: You comment on self psychology's impact on psychoanalysis in your action theory essay:

"There is another consequence for psychoanalysis of the shift from conflicts to deficits as underlying etiology. As a byproduct of this change in focus, the therapeutic process is now directed not at anxiety and its derivatives but at the self, which the person has become, a shift in effect from the analytic to the existential mode of treatment. Treatment is no longer for what the patient suffers, but for what he is.

"The new expectation is both wished for and feared by patients. On the one hand, it is welcomed and widely preferred to the tender exposure and touching of conflicts, accounting in part for its initial popularity. 'Who am I?' and 'What am I?' have become cliché summaries of symptoms. On the other hand, this avowed purpose of the new analysis meets head on a frequent fear expressed by patients, notably those with creative aspirations, that who they are will be changed rather than their neuroses."

In your experience, what are the possible consequences of and losses from the approach of "Who am I?," "What am I?"

LR: The loss is the failure to analyze intrapsychic conflicts. I mean that "Who am I?" comes to be explained on a superficial basis. For example, there is a book out on fictive personalities, by an analyst who was trained in Los Angeles more or less around the self psychology paradigm. The whole idea is which self am I? That's a good example of this. The analyst, who happens to be a very literary person, finds that in the literate group of patients he treats, one patient throughout his life becomes Huckleberry Finn, or a character of Shakespeare, for example, if he is indecisive, or a character from Studs Lonigan, that is, some kind of fictive personality with whom he identifies. It is mostly a total or global identification. The patient identifies with a total person. You can see the same thing in psychobiography. I think of a certain psychobiography from afar, which, like the analysis of the fictive personality, becomes an analysis of a total self or a whole identification, rather than of partial and irregular attributes, as in more typical microscopic analyses.

In psychoanalysis, you find that a patient identified with the id of his father and the superego of his mother, and he's not all his father, or his mother, or his teacher, or his friend. He's a unique blend of all of them. Only a dynamic intrapsychic approach and the analysis of intrapsychic conflicts will expose the elements of the self into their component parts and show where this unique individual makes his own solutions to his own neurotic identifications, with a little of this one and a little of that one. It's a total different thing than existentialism, which shifts up to the total man, and which doesn't need either Freud or the whole further breakdown of psychoanalytic explanations. And that's a drawback of self psychology, or object relations psychology, nonstructural psychology, and analyses of total characteristics, rather than of internal, partial, splintered conflicts. Attending to all these is like writing a textbook because it involves many small, very detailed theoretical concepts.

LRAYMOND: What I'm impressed by is how readily available these various theoretical concepts are to you.

LR: These little answers will be different than anything in any one essay because they are mixtures of them all.

LRAYMOND: That's what we like about the process. My next question comes from your essay on the self. You note, "A clinical finding that links self psychology with all that has preceded it in psychoanalytic theory is the equation 'phallus equals self' a common finding in normalcy and pathology for any clinician working at the unconscious depths." And you mention having written an essay in 1953 about the interchangeability of the male and female genitals....

LR: Yes, I wrote a small essay on that subject.

LRAYMOND: You continue in the self essay: "The mechanism of the genitals symbolizing the whole applies clinically to both sexes. In historical psychoanalytic parlance, although now questioned and objected to, a mature character is referred to as a genital one."

LR: It was Karl Menninger who opposed, or rather made fun of that, of referring to a person as "a genital character."

LRAYMOND: Can you say more about how this "phallus equals self" and "genital interchangeability" is expressed by patients? I'm also curious how this concept relates to your ideas about castration anxiety versus separation anxiety.

LR: First, the phenomenology and then the explanation. Phenomenologically, some of it is obvious and overt, and some of it is subtle. It is even in the language. When a man or a woman says, in a certain way, "He touched me," she doesn't mean "he touched me," she means "he touched my vagina or my clitoris." And the man says the same thing, "She touched me." It's a coy way of saying the main part of me, where it counted. At that moment, "I didn't want her to touch my forehead." You know, "I am the phallus," or "I am the vagina." There you see the unconscious equation in the colloquial expression. Then you have things like someone walking along, an arrogant narcissistic person, of whom one might say, "He looks like a big prick." It's a common expression. He is a phallus, someone who walks around like an erect phallus.

An interesting thing theoretically about this is that often, in clinical material, in emphasizing the self, one denies preoedipal or oedipal phallic castration, partial component instincts, anal or oral, leading to the phallic. The exclusive use of the total self obliterates the parts. This operates in theoretical thinking and in concrete application to body parts. Again the parts are not the knee or the fingers, but the sensitive parts which are kept covered. People go on the beach naked except for a little bikini because the crucial little points of the body that have the most—here's another old word not used today, cathexis—that have the most cathexis are the tender, covered, personal areas. It's very interesting theoretically that all these hidden parts, which are so much made into a "no-no" in society and civilization, are the most essential parts anatomically and have their counterparts theoretically in the fact that the sexual drives are so denied by self psychologists.

There are theoreticians who say there are no drives, there are only affects. This is one of Kernberg's formulations that I disagree with. He replaces drives with affects. I do not agree with an obliteration of the drives. If you eliminate the drives, you might as well obliterate the ego. You need them both to counterpoint, to be in conflict with each other. So these are some phenomenologic and theoretical examples of the ubiquity of phallus equals self.

Theory follows the phenomenology. The obscuring of the anatomy has its counterpart in an obscuring of the concept and the theory. The conceptualization is total instead of making room also for parts. Now, the essay you referred to that showed a vivid example of this obliteration of differences with a metaphor that explained it, is of a patient who, in terms of castration, male-female, differences between the sexes, and castration anxiety, had a fantasy. This is what led me to that essay—that there is no difference between the male and the female. In the female, the phallus has been inverted like the finger of a balloon, which is pushed in, and it's kept that way so that it's a receptacle. And in a male, this balloon is pushed out, and it's a fingerlike projection. So it's really the same. It's just that the vaginal mucosa is the inverted skin of the penis, and the penis is the everted mucosa of the vagina. That led to the essay, the interchangeability of the phallus and female genital. I wrote that when I was a candidate. There were a number of essays then; it was a small essay, and I find it very useful even now, almost fifty years later.

SRR: You have stated that "corrective, affective experiences not only occur in analysis, they're necessary and routine." Could you say more about that?

LR: The analytic experience itself is a corrective experience. Meeting an analyst who acts the way an analyst does is the chance of a lifetime and a unique experience. But not because the analyst loves the patient, or reassures him, or puts his arm around him, but because he gives him an opportunity which is also unique—if analysts stick to that, of insight and of exposing his deepest secrets and learning how to live with them. The "corrective emotional experience" is used by a correctly operating analyst, and is a unique opportunity that the patient has the chance to experience and live and benefit from.

Unfortunately, the term corrective emotional experience was introduced as a corruption of that unique analytic attitude by providing the patient the opposite of what life provided him, which is impossible because an analyst can never assume so many faces. During the course of an eight-hour day, he'd have to love one, hate another, soothe one, irritate another, gratify one, deprive another, and he'd have to wear so many hats that it would be impossible, and it would be antitherapeutic because that's not the way. You can't counteract a lifetime of influence by an hour or a year of hours of opposite influences. But what you can use to influence the patient is this unique correct corrective analytic experience.

SRR: You also said that a "core process in psychoanalytic treatment is the patient's experience of an object relationship never before known in life."

LR: That's the attitude and relationship I just described, namely with one who is nongratifying, but also nonmoralizing and nonjudgmental. The patient has never experienced that because everyone else in his life has an opinion about him. Not that the analyst doesn't. But the analyst has it as a scientist, not as an antagonist or protagonist. Not as one who's going to gratify or supply needs, but who's going to supply understanding.

LRAYMOND: Your recent castration essay makes reference to that. You wrote, "The childhood etiologic figures of my patients have been all too alive and vivid. The need is to detoxify them in the present through whatever transference or extratransference paths are available. Transference is not the only mutative interpretation." Could you say more about your experience with the "extratransference paths?"

LR: Analysis sometimes grabs hold of a concept and concretizes it, making it immutable. Now such a course took place, to the disadvantage of analysis, as a result of Strachey's 1934 essay—which could have been a very good essay if it weren't so idealized and distorted—on transference being the only mutative interpretation. This became a byword for certain schools of analysis and almost for all of analysis. It was very Kleinian, but it was also accepted—perhaps this was its greatest danger—by all schools, to the exclusion of all other attempted mutative efforts on the part of the analyst to the patient. It led to the conclusion that only a transference interpretation, and therefore only a transference understanding, was the way of analysis.The result was that every association of the patient was too quickly deemed transference, rather than an event in the patient's life in the past or present which had to be respected as much as what was taking place in the analytic consulting room. In the early days, transferences were overlooked. Now they're overdone. They're tremendously overdone.

As an example, in Jerusalem, I was on a panel on the comparisons of clinical methods with relation to anxiety with a Kleinian analyst. We each presented clinical material. She presented a clinical hour in which the patient—roughly this is the way it was—comes in and reports that he had a violent argument with his wife last night. The analyst asked the patient, "Why were you angry at me?" I asked, "How do you know he was angry at you? He was angry at his wife." "Well," she said, "It was transference." I asked,

"Why?" She replied, "Everything is transference." Well, some things are, but some things are not. Extratransference material is the fact that this man had a wife, and he had an argument with her yesterday, and she might have provoked it, and he might have provoked it. My approach is, What did you say to cause the argument? What did she say or do to cause the argument? Maybe I'm in there too, but maybe not. I'm not in everything.

In a dialogue between Sandler and Anna Freud in a book discussing defense, Anna Freud takes this same position, saying that she cannot understand why some analysts always insert themselves. To me, it is like the joke in which someone says, "That's enough talking about me. What do you think of me?" Extra-analytic transference is also extremely important—that's the here and now, but not in this room. It may be in the patient's environment, in the wider present, though derived from the past. Strachey's idea about "mummified" persons in the past—which was Freud's—"That you cannot hang someone in effigy"—is such a regression and false direction. It is a cynicism to conclude that past figures, who we are trying to understand and see their influences, are nothing but mummies lying in the patient's words or space.

To imbue only the analyst with life is a reversal of the entire analytic exploration. Empirically, phenomenologically, and clinically, my patients' parents and past figures are too much alive. A patient will talk about his father who's been dead for ten years as if he's in this room affecting him again. And he's just as upset and just as nervous and starts to cry and sweat as if the father was alive. How can an analyst in good faith say that he's mummified? And why, even more than that, does a whole school take that up and applaud it. I think there is too much myth formation, cultism, and "follow the leader" in analysis. Incidentally, Strachey is not alive either. But he's far from mummified. That idea is glorified and vivified instead of mummified.

SRR: In a Congress, I'm not sure what year it was, you said, "In my opinion, empirically castration anxiety is not much less in a girl than a boy, any more than separation anxiety occurs particularly more in the female than in the male." In terms of metapsychology, are there any sexual differences that you do think you observe? Do you observe any significant characteristics distinguishing castration anxiety of males versus females?

LR: That's a thoughtful question that could lead to a new essay, because, frankly, my gut reaction is that it wouldn't be fair in the interest of equality to say it's all the same, even though many things are exaggerated in their differences. There are differences. For example, Erikson tried to show some differences innately in boys and girls with regard to phallic and oral predominance or characteristics. I think a lot of what he wrote is probably true and has an enduring quality. But he aroused the ire of the feminist movement, who thought he was belittling the little girl. Males opposed him, too, thinking he was giving them too much responsibility. That is inappropriate on both parts. He was trying to be a scientist.

But in following that example of trying to be a scientist, I would expect that there are characterological and intrapsychic differences. They are not differences of more castration anxiety in one than in the other; I don't think that counts. I think that experientially they both have it. Females have fainting reactions. A woman patient of mine, when she goes to the dentist, has to be tranquillized and even, she hopes, anesthetized because of severe castration anxiety. I know many males who don't share that reaction, but unconsciously they may have it in other ways. But I think there are differences. I'm not prepared to declare these off the top of my head, but that would be a good study for thoughtful consideration. I think I could come up with some interesting reflections on that, but right this second I can't in front of three women. You would all say, and rightly so, "Well, how do you know that?" or "What do you know about that?"

SRR: You said that "in the community of analyzed analysts, one cannot fail to be impressed by the seeming frequency of unresolved transference phenomena, which constitute a significant factor behind some of the existing problems in psychoanalytic organizational life." You have also noted Anna Freud's attribution of this to the technical deviation made necessary by the real differences between training and other analyses. We're interested in what you think about the difference between training analysis and regular or therapeutic analysis.

You wrote, "Many have also felt that mutual transference"—I think you've been talking about this—"and countertransference residuals, which continue to operate in a complementary relationship are responsible in part at least for problems not only of creativity but of productivity among analysts." And also, "One cannot overestimate the crucial importance of these problems in the future functioning of psychoanalysts."

We are interested in whatever else you are willing to add on this subject.

LR: First of all, there are, but there should not be, differences between the training analysis and therapeutic analysis. An analysis should be an analysis. To the extent that the training analyst, or the candidate-patient, or both permit the real relationship to interfere with the training analysis, the training analysis suffers and leaves the possibility of unresolved transference-countertransference residuals. Now, concepts are never applied puristically. That may be a desire, but it doesn't work in operation. Not with me, not with anyone else. I'm sure that every analyst unconsciously imposes his own impulses and wishes to justify his theory and his role in the institute, and his position among rival groups in the analytic community. He does the same in relation to his trainees, who also provoke that in their own way, although one shouldn't react to those provocations, but we all do.

Anna Freud's quote simply takes cognizance of the fact that in a practical sense these things occur, and I agree that they occur. I don't agree that in theory the two categories of analysis are different. In theory, they shouldn't be different, though in practice they are. To the degree that the practice wins out, and differences occur, the patient is left with some kind of acting out, which then persists. Recognizing the continuation of these complications in the postanalytic years, after my first presidency of the American Psychoanalytic Association, I instituted a postanalytic-postgraduate section, and established a Committee on Postgraduate Development in the American Psychoanalytic Association. I did not intend more postgraduate analysis, but a continuous study in depth of the problems of the postgraduate years.

The first few years of a young analyst's postgraduate life are very decisive, as it was in my own case, as to what one's future will be. Either one will be a writer and producer and a productive person, or a teacher or a nonteacher, or a good, practicing analyst or even a nonanalyst. People drift away from the field because in the first five to ten years, they pick the wrong patients; or they choose for the wrong reasons and soon become disillusioned; or they don't become teachers and then get angry at the institute; or they're not headed to be training analysts; or they're too much headed to be training analysts and not anything else; or they go to the meetings of the American Psychoanalytic Association or they don't. All of these have shaping influences on the development of a young analyst.

But the main thing that shapes his future development is the residual of his relationship to his training analyst and his teachers, especially his charismatic teachers. Some of these may do a lot more harm than good. A lot of charismatic teachers deflect the development of future followers because they become devotees and slaves instead of independent people. Although analysis aims toward autonomy, sometimes training and the training process inhibits autonomy. It's not any one person's fault; it's the subject as much as the people putting things into him. Anyone who allows that to happen to himself must take the responsibility for permitting it. And that leads to these conditions which lead to future splits. I once spoke, as President of the International Psychoanalytic Association, to the first meeting of a newly admitted Society. I sat before these twenty or thirty analysts in a small South American country—there's no reason not to name it; it was in Venezuela—and I looked at them and said, "I can see your future split. I know who's going to be on which side." And I've lived to see it come about.

LRAYMOND: It happened?

LR: Yes, years later. Why did I say that? Because I could see the incipient rivalries, hatreds, transferences—it was certainly not theoretical differences—right there. If you ever get a group of fifteen or twenty graduates who don't have that, that's very wonderful. But I don't think it's common.

LRAYMOND: You make this point in your castration essay: "Analyses on today's scene are empirically and theoretically more steeped in problems of attachment, separation, and relational issues than in bodily harm and loss. A hypertrophy of the interactional aspects of the psychoanalytic process at the expense of the reconstructive favors in principle conflicts between self and object over repressed sexual or aggressive intrapsychic conflicts." Do you think emphasis on the interactional versus the reconstructive approaches produces a different analytic result in patients who endured bodily harm with their primary objects?

LR: Absolutely, a more complete analysis. I don't reject the other, but I add this. Again, it's a question of one out of a duality being accepted and hypertrophied, and the other being atrophied or lost. And it's also an example of the fact that castration can be under separation anxiety. In other words, take a child from one to three who is dealing with a closeness to his mother about which he has problems. The problems, however, aren't that bad, and he grows into age four. Now he's a little bit shy and afraid to be alone. He has stranger anxiety in the nursery, or in the kindergarten, or in prekindergarten, where he is not a leader. He's not rambunctious, and that's his level. His anxiety level is wherever it is.

At four or five, he starts getting incestuous wishes and castration anxiety. He runs into much bigger trouble than he's had in the first three years. It's later, but it's deeper because it's closer to terror. In later analysis, he will much more quickly deal with the first three years of the separation than the fourth or fifth years of castration anxiety; they will come out last, not first. It isn't as if the analysis goes steadily backward, first to castration, and after you deal with castration, you say, you're afraid to be alone. He will say, "Well, that's nothing compared to what I just went through."

SRR: I'm thinking that the transference is also different, because when he goes to the very early years, in a way he's looking for a maternal, or benignly maternal response, or he experiences it, or might imagine it. Whereas, if he goes to the castration period, then it's much more frightening. For that reason, it's also easier to go back to the earlier time first.

LR: Right, that's a good way of realizing the developmental viewpoint, which is becoming so popular now. It doesn't necessarily mean from one to one hundred It might mean that five is worse than one. The numbers are different. Or even ten or twenty might be the worst. Suppose he was in an airplane crash at age forty. That supersedes the castration anxiety of age four or five, although it may unconsciously revive it.

LRAYMOND: Although this quote from Ferenczi is somewhat long, I want to know what your associations are to it from your own clinical experience. This passage is taken from Ferenczi's 1929 essay, "The Principle of Relaxation and Neocatharsis":

"But after we had succeeded in a somewhat deeper manner than before in creating an atmosphere of confidence between physician and patient and in securing a fuller freedom of affect, hysterical physical symptoms would suddenly make their appearance, often for the first time in an analysis extending over years. These symptoms included paresthesias and spasms, definitely localized, violent emotional movements, like miniature hysterical attacks, sudden alterations of the state of consciousness, slight vertigo, and a clouding of consciousness, often with subsequent amnesia for what had taken place. Some patients actually begged me to tell them how they had behaved when in these states. It was easy to utilize these symptoms as fresh aids to reconstruction, as physical memory symbols, so to speak, but there was this difference, this time. The reconstructed past had much more of a feeling of reality and concreteness about it than heretofore, approximated much more closely to an actual recollection, whereas till then the patients had spoken only of possibilities or at most of varying degrees of probability and had yearned in vain for memories. In certain cases, these hysterical attacks actually assumed the character of trances in which the fragments of the past were relived, and the physician was the only bridge left between the patients and reality. I was able to question them and receive important information about dissociated parts of the personality. Without any such intention on my part and without my making the least attempt to induce a condition of this sort, unusual states of consciousness manifested themselves which might also be termed autohypnotic."

I am interested in hearing your thoughts on this.

LR: Ferenczi is a wonderful author and yet he's considered the father of the deviationists; for example, of Alexander of the Alexandrian movement.

AR: You were in his house in Budapest. It's sort of an apartment, isn't it?

LR: We weren't inside, we were outside. We were in the courtyard.

AR: I wasn't able to go in, but you did. A family was living there. We were in Budapest with colleagues, and they drove us. I got sick there.

LR: It was an apartment house…

AR: …in a rather ordinary neighborhood.

LR: I bet it wasn't at the time he lived there. It wasn't inelegant. We walked into a courtyard, and they pointed to the windows, a little apartment where Ferenczi lived and worked. I don't recall that we got in. I don't think so.

I admire Ferenczi a lot. Alexander doesn't come up to him, even though he followed his example. You're going to have to picture the culture of the times, and their great conviction that there was a truthful reality that they were going to get to, and that he felt he was getting closer to it. Now, again, there's an example; he got to that truthful reality when the patient had a feeling of safety. Today, Stolorow, on intersubjectivity, would say the same thing. That first you have to soothe the patient, and then you'll get the real underlying material. The trouble is that the soothing is the whole analysis these days. They never get to anything like you just quoted. But also one does not know how convincing this kind of report is. This was in the early days of exhilarating anticipation of great certainty. How did he know? He sounds like now he can believe it more—what Wallerstein and Arnold Richards were talking about yesterday as correspondence truth rather than coherence truth. These supplant historical versus narrative truth. They felt in those days they were experiencing historical truth. I tend to go with Ferenczi on this. I'm not the cynical analyst who says all of this is screen memory or misleading. But what's interesting in terms of castration is the bodily interest, the paresthesias, and the tics. All the early patients were like that. Dora and Anna O. were like that.

AR: And dizziness. I think that could happen a lot.

LR: Yes, it did. It may be that Freud got to castration anxiety before he got to separation anxiety. Ferenczi, too. They got to the big thing, and then the field went off into Mahler and Melanie Klein and preoedipal and mother-child. In doing that, they got away from the castration, and the oedipal, too. They eliminated these further during the splits of 1951. They completely eradicated them, and went back to maternal transferences, and never came back to the other. They got excited again when the Kleinians and then Bion came to Los Angeles, and it was all charisma and transference, but nothing about castration anxiety. When I write an essay now, it's like bringing back an archaeological find.

LRAYMOND: Do you think it is hard for many analysts to tolerate sitting with that deep level of anxiety?

LR: I quoted, in one of my essays, that Ferenczi had adrenaline handy. That's an amazing thing. Ferenczi spoke as if he sometimes injected adrenaline. A patient could get anaphylactic shock.

AR: I wonder what Freud thought of these doings?

LR: Well, Freud eventually thought he was off the beam. But in the beginning they were all close pals. Freud listened to Fliess, a wilder person than Ferenczi, about the nose....

SRR: What were your experiences in your development as an analyst, your training, people who influenced you?

LR: Yes, it is a question first of influence. When you arrive in a city you notice its climate. We flew in from Los Angeles. As soon as we passed the Texas border and came into Louisiana, we could see it was absolutely wet. Even the sky was wet. The rest of the country was dry. We live in a dry climate, and here they live in a moist, humid air; you have to start shedding your clothes. Well, where you are now does depend on your large surrounding influence, and it focuses on your individual propensities and interests and what you do with your surround. It's just like the ego surrounded by the id and the superego. The ego decides what to do with all these influences. Living in New Orleans you decide what clothes to wear and what kind of an analyst to be. There are different analysts in different areas.

And so it is with generations. An analyst coming into psychoanalysis in 1940 in New York, and an analyst coming into psychoanalysis in 1990 in Los Angeles are two different breeds. So different that they are almost not in the same field. I am an analyst who started in 1940 in New York, and I'm my age, and I live with 500 analysts in Los Angeles, 400 or 450 of whom have come in at a time when all I can do is roll my eyes as to what they're exposed to. And none of them have done what you're doing; namely, look at the past. You're looking at the past from the ground up. It'll change you forever, I know it will. And so, that comes to your question, Who am I, this fictive personality? Who is the sum of my component parts?

What are my component parts? First of all, I came in roughly 1940, so it's over fifty years ago. Analysis is 100 years old. I've lived half the analytic century. Not only that I've lived it actively. I've been involved in it since I was a candidate because many of my essays started then. One of my first published essays—it was not my first—was with a then unknown author named Margaret Mahler. She and I wrote the first and only analytic essay on Gilles de la Tourette's disease. In 1940, I was a resident at P.I., the Psychiatric Institute at Columbia, and Margaret Mahler was a young staff member, a recent émigré from Europe. She was also at Mount Sinai in New York. I met her when she hospitalized a young patient from Mount Sinai at P.I., where he was assigned to me to treat. The essay was published in 1943, after I finished my residency, but the patient was treated in 1940. Mahler and I remained forever connected after that.

I left for the Army Air Force on New Year's Day, 1943. I had started my psychoanalytic training at the New York Institute in 1940, which gave me my first analytic seed. This remained forever important in my analytic identity. I'll skip ahead ten years to after the War, the Army, and my finishing my analytic training in Los Angeles.…Right after my graduation in 1950, I saw a little notice in the *International Journal* that there was a prize to be given for the best international clinical essay. Without thinking that I had a ghost of a chance, I submitted the analysis of a doll phobia patient I had treated as a candidate. I later received notice that I had won the International Clinical Essay Prize, and the essay was published as the lead essay in the next *International Journal*. You can imagine the spur this gave my career. If I could do this, if this was the best clinical paper in the world this year—which was not to be believed—that was a great spurt to my ego, self-esteem, perspective, and so forth. My fellow residents—we were all residents in neurology at Montefiore—who later became analysts at the New York Institute, were the most extraordinary group—Arlow, Beres, Victor Rosen; Brenner came later from Boston and joined the group after I had left for the Army—each had a different influence, and every one of us became Presidents of the American Psychoanalytic Association.…

LRAYMOND: You also trained in neurology.

LR: Yes, I took the Board in neurology, and that's part of the whole thing. That has to do with not only being an M.D., but being a board-certified neurologist. We were all neurologists, had all been residents in neurology. I think that influenced our way of thinking forever about the nervous system, its organic and its psychological derivatives. That's seen in my writings on psychosomatic disease. I wrote an essay on the heart, on cardiovascular disease, on pain, on various mind-body reflections—even in "The Intrapsychic Process," I discuss the mind-body subject. Then we became analysts, all of us going the route from neurology to psychiatry to psychoanalysis.

We all became leaders of psychoanalysis, and we remained close with each other over the last fifty years. Some are not here anymore, but a few of us are. We are the survivors of that group. I transplanted myself via the Army—I left New York; Arlow, Brenner, and others stayed in New York. I was their west coast counterpart, the one who came to the other coast.

Another formative person for me was Otto Fenichel. As a resident in psychiatry, I became aware of Fenichel's book. Now this was very important, I never had a transference to Fenichel, but to Fenichel's ideas, his book. That's a big difference.

I have a transference to what I call the charisma of ideas and not to the charisma of personalities. And therein lies a big problem with analysis: people have a transference to the theory of their idols or training analysts. I have a transference to Freud's works, Fenichel's book—I only met Fenichel for a day or two. He had died a few months before I got to Los Angeles. People think I'm attached to Fenichel. I don't know the man. I know his book. I met him once and shook hands with him. I got on his list to be analyzed by him, but he died before I ever got to his city.

SRR: Did he have something to do with your deciding to go there?

LR: Not exactly, but that's a good question. I was going there anyway, but that was the clincher. No, I had decided to go there, and then I was glad to meet Fenichel for that reason.

AR: When we met Fenichel, it was in Denver, Colorado, where Leo was in the Air Corps. We met at a colleague's house; Fenichel was there with his new wife, Hanna Fenichel. I don't know if you know her; she was a child analyst. They were on a honeymoon. We met them socially. Leo also met him at the hospital.

LR: He saw us give sodium pentothal interviews to prisoners of war. We were using analytic principles, and that's what he was very interested in experiencing firsthand. We met under those auspices.

AR: He was just in his forties. Of course, we thought he was quite old. He was very jolly, full of humor, and very lively. Leo thought so much of him, that he was quite inspired to meet him. Leo had known his work, of course, and his book.

LR: I started my training in New York. I was in analysis in New York and in the first year of courses when I went to the Army. Most of my other colleagues never went to the Army, so they were three or four years ahead of me, because I took that time out from analytic training. It was four years before I got back into it again. I was going to resume my training analysis. During the few days we were together in Denver, Fenichel and I met, and I got on his list to continue my training analysis with him in Los Angeles after the War. I only went the first year in New York, so I had a lot to go.

AR: But the time in the Army was not lost as far as analytic....

LR: It was very analytic.

AR: In the Air Corps, there was a man named Jock Murray,...

LR/SRR: Yes.

AR: ...from your part of the world.

LR: I never knew him personally, but many of the senior analysts in Boston talk of him.

AR: He was very dashing.

LR: He was very instrumental in bringing analysis to the Air Force, and I was one of those he used to execute it.

AR: And he was perfect for that.

LR: Did you know Dr. Valenstein?

LR: I met Valenstein a few years later. I'll come to that.

AR: But Murray was very influential.

LR: Valenstein is in my generation and about my age. We met when we were both young graduates coming to the American Psychoanalytic Association and starting to give essays on panels. We worked together and became very close because we have always seen eye to eye.

LR: He also talked about his military experience.

LR: He was not with me.

SRR: So you went to California.

AR: We met Jock Murray in Texas before we went to Denver. In Denver, Leo was part of a group that trained flight surgeons in psychiatry.

LR: First, in Texas, there was the consultation service. That was under David Leach. In Denver, it was in Fort Logan, Colorado, a school for aviation psychiatry. We taught analytic thinking to flight surgeons and to young medical officers, many of whom later went into psychiatric residency and became analysts. Many of them went from the Army and our course to the Menningers' in Topeka.

AR: We would have sessions at our house. They would do some reading, and you'd have these discussion groups.

LRAYMOND: That must have been a great opportunity.

LR: Anyway, Fenichel was a name, but not a personality, to me—a symbol of psychoanalysis. His book to me is still a bible. The other people who influenced me were also strangely people I was not personally connected with—Hartmann, Kris, Loewenstein. Again, you're going to hear an opposite thing tomorrow, which I'm going to correct on the platform. I never met Hartmann until after I graduated in Los Angeles and came back to the American Psychoanalytic Society on a panel in the 1960s at which I worked with Hartmann. However, by then I was known and looked to for different things, so that when Hartmann had his seventieth birthday in the 1960s, Masud Khan, the associate editor of the *International Journal*, decided to do a volume in honor of Heinz Hartmann, and he asked different people to participate. He called me or wrote me from London, and asked me if I would summarize the scientific life of Heinz Hartmann for his seventieth birthday.

I wrote an essay called "The Scope of Heinz Hartmann," which Hartmann's son, Lawrence Hartmann, who is now the incoming president of the American Psychoanalytic Association, told me—I don't know him much either, but I gave the Hartmann lecture in New York a few years ago and met him there—in a letter that his father had often said to him, "If you want to know about my scientific life work, read Rangell's summary." I got to know Hartmann from beginning to end in writing that essay. It's a very succinct summary of Heinz Hartmann, and so I came to have one analytic root in me of Fenichel, another was of Hartmann, and another was David Rapaport, again, someone I never knew or worked with personally. I met him at the Austen Riggs many years later. You must know Austen Riggs. Do you visit it from Boston much?

LRAYMOND: We're in Boston, but Austen Riggs is in Stockbridge.

LR: Well, Rapaport was a visitor in Los Angeles, who gave a few lectures, but I was inspired. His lectures followed and helped make a path for me; Freud, Hartmann, Fenichel, Rapaport, that's the line of my thinking that courses through all my writings. I'm very chagrined at how these people have been shunted aside. Freudian is a dirty word in Los Angeles—at best a very ambivalent word.

Hartmann is practically forgotten; even in New York, he's very much down. Rapaport was long ago the object of a revolt. When I came to Los Angeles I would say the spirit of Fenichel was in me through my whole training; then came the split, the Los Angeles split with Fenichel's thinking on one side and Alexander's on the other. I lined up with Fenichel's thinking even though my analyst was on the other side. My analyst was very disappointed in me because I didn't go where he went, I went to the other side. And I had written the doll phobia, which made me very classical because I followed the whole framework of analytic thinking of structural theory. That paper is built around the equidistant stand of the analyst toward the intrapsychic structures within the patient. If you believe in the analytic structural view in theory, I don't see how you can abandon it in technique.

The theory of technique follows one's theory of neurosogenesis. If you're a self psychologist regarding the development of neurosis, you should be a self psychologist in the treatment of neurosis. If you're not, you're inconsistent. I would prefer you to be consistent and wrong than inconsistent and confusedly right. So I'm consistently an analyst who believes in the metapsychology culminating in the structural point of view. After the split I became a very strong member of the Freudian group, the old group in Los Angeles, and, not unrelatedly, because I was a very consistent and prolific writer, I fortified my ideas.

There's nothing like gaining conviction as much as by writing essays. When you write essays, you put yourself down and commit yourself, you know what you think.

People who only listen to essays and agree with this one and that one and that one and that one, have no fulcrum of their own. They resent people who have a fulcrum because they think you're too opinionated if you believe in something. You're supposed to not have opinions or strong opinions. So I, by being a teacher, and especially a writer, and a panel participant, and a giver of essays, and a giver of plenary sessions, began to develop and expand and maintain and stand for my views in a very firm and strong direction, which enabled me to take a stand on all the controversies that came on later.

In addition, a lot of the controversies have to do with personal relationships that stem from my positions of leadership both at the national and international level. That led to my essay, "Transference to Theory," which I'm sure you know about, and which we'll come to. But it also led to other things. It also led to my essay on "Aggression in the Oedipus Complex," at the opening plenary session of the International Congress in Vienna. The reasons I wrote that essay were because I was giving a Presidential Address and the meeting was in Vienna. Vienna had suffered from malignant aggression, and the Freuds had been the victims of that social pathology. The Freudians and Anna Freud were returning to Vienna for the first time, and the Oedipus complex was central to Freudian theory. I got the idea to tie these thoughts together almost at the last second. My essays are always late. They're always last minute. Tomorrow's essay is not yet really written.

AR: Well, the whole theme of the Congress in Vienna was on aggression.

LR: Anita conceived of the theme. It was a very historic congress. That's not in the history books, either. We were sitting around with the program committee in our beach home in Carmel, after my election at the Rome Congress, preparing the fare for the Vienna Congress. What will it be on? Anita said, to our guests, "How about aggression?" Everyone picked it up. So, later I thought, What could be better than aggression and the Oedipus complex, putting them together, where they belong anyway. That essay shows how theoretically the aggressive drive, not just the libidinal drive, is contained within the Oedipus complex, and how the latter explains and fuels the aggressive as well as libidinal drives in its tragic unfolding.

AR: That was before self psychology was invented.

SRR: I have one more question. It's about your essay on friendship which was I found so stimulating. I'm thinking about this especially from the context of being analysts, considering the nature of the work and how straining it is. We hear a lot about how hard it is to have a peer group and the different strains there are in it. A supervisor of mine, when I had a very terrible, straining time with a patient, said, "It's good that you're having this while you're in supervision." He was talking about how taxing and lonely the work is, and one's having to keep it so private. I was thinking of that in the context of just how important friendships are. I'm interested in anything more you care to say on that subject. I'm interested in your friendships; obviously, this is your best friend right here.

AR: In fact, I think he gave me a little credit for that essay. There's a footnote because I remember looking up some things for you, and we talked about it a lot.

LR: I talked about the friendship essay this morning.

SRR: But I'm wondering about your own experience in terms of friendship.

LR: That essay was written in 1963. Do you know that it was then and is still today, in 1991, the only essay on friendship in the analytic literature?

SRR: It had quite an impact on me.

LR: It is the most frequent object relation. We hear so much about object relations, yet no one talks about friendships.

LRAYMOND: You're right.

LR: The subject came up in a discussion I led on an essay today. I talked about man-woman and woman-woman friendships because this essay had to do with the lack of referrals of men to women analysts. Elizabeth Mayer, the author of the essay, stated that even women referred men to male analysts rather than to other women analysts. Isn't that strange? Why wouldn't a woman refer a man to another woman rather than to a man. I said that some of the answer will be found in examining friendship patterns, male-male, female-female, and between men and women.

These were all in my essay, which is so old I don't remember what the whole thing was, but there were many vicissitudes of those relationships. The main thing about friendship patterns that is disturbing is their pathology. Some of the most painful experiences in life are friendship problems, and they're so unacknowledged. That is what you are asking us. We have experienced a lot of that, yes.

SRR: It also bears on—almost as a parallel with what we were talking about concerning some of your other essays—how the ability for action tends to be minimized. It seems to me that analysts tend to minimize the importance of friendships, if one hears about it in a clinical situation. When a patient comes in very upset about a friend, I think it's easy to start to think, where's the transference, rather than realize how...

LR: ...important is the extra-analytic present. That's a third field of observation and data—not just reconstruction of the past or the transference, but also the extra-analytic present—and here with friends as much as with spouses and others. With spouses you have to solve the problems, with friends you often avoid them. There is an example in my essay of the breakup of a friendship group that I would recommend you look up. It's amazing stuff we've been through, where a whole too-intense group splits.

Among many things, it has to do with heterosexual or homosexual acting out, or temptation and paranoid reactions. If they're not acted out, then you get paranoid about them. It's a very good example of the closeness between homosexuality and paranoia, this particular group that I reported. They lived around us, a whole little group, and within a few years everyone was everyone's enemy. Analysts were prominent among them; the outcomes had professional, even scientific group consequences.

SRR: Yes.

AR: Divorces and one testifying for or against another in court. It became so bad.

LR: And suicide. There was a moving picture that once affected me deeply called *King's Row,* about a small town where all this happened—suicide, murder, sexuality.

AR: Unfortunately, you don't have to go far for that.

LR: I think Ronald Reagan was in it.

AR: He was in it.

LR: It's a gripping picture. I've never forgotten it.

SRR: I know my friendships have changed since before I entered analytic training. Your identity and so much of your day-to-day experience changes. How has all that changed for you over the years?

AR: Well, you can just think of the friendships within the psychoanalytic groups here, and the psychoanalytic associations, the American Psychoanalytic Association, and the International Psychoanalytic Association, and imagine how much has evolved or changed. Perhaps you can imagine also at what costs.

LR: Over years, and incidents, and trials and tribulations, and tests of character which come up in innumerable crises—or even more in ordinary situations, at such high, busy levels of activities—the alienations, shifts of friendships, changed loyalties, and regroupings of people's relationships to each other are mind boggling—too much to be able to tell, and more than anyone would want to tell. One needs a certain strength, and a firm priority of values to endure it, or, even better, to overcome it.

AR: It was during his Presidency of the International Psychoanalytic Association that Leo started writing his book, *The Mind of Watergate*. Do you know that book? Well, I think you should send it to them. Besides its specific subject matter, that book grew very naturally out of the atmosphere and experiences we were immersed in.

LR: One way I think I dealt with the many personal pains and conflicts engendered by organizational problems I found myself surrounded by, was to try to understand them scientifically, and to write about them if I came up with anything I felt was worthwhile. It was no accident that my outgoing Presidential Address in Paris, after four years of the I.P.A. Presidency, was on "The Syndrome of the Compromise of Integrity."

The essay received a standing ovation, but I never felt it was referred to again commensurate with the validity and power of its message. In that essay, and in the Watergate book, which covered, respectively, our own professional lives and the wider political scene, both equally a slice of everyday life, I made the statement that compromise of integrity was as ubiquitous as neuroses in human affairs. I think it will take the next psychoanalytic century to catch up with the significance and standing of that subject.

SRR: We need that work. On a more personal note, how did you two meet? You have such a wonderful relationship.

LR: We met on a sort of crisscross date five years before we really met. It was on a double date when I was in college at Columbia. A high school friend, who was attending Ohio State, came home for vacation. We each had a date, and I borrowed my father's car. I had just learned how to drive, and I had my girl in the front, and my friend got out to pick up his date, and she came down. It was at night, and they came over to the other side of the car to get into the back seat. And he introduced me to her, and through the window, I saw her face. That's how we met. And here was this other girl, her best friend in a way, sitting next to me.

AR: Friendship.

LR: That was the only time we met. I finished college and went to medical school at the University of Chicago. I then returned to New York to intern. There was an intern's dance, a formal, and I wasn't going to go because I didn't have a date. As it came closer to the time of the dance, I met my friend again.

AR: I was about seventeen and you were nineteen at our original meeting.

LR: So, it was five years later, at twenty-four, when I was in touch with Neville. He had gone to medical school, too. He's now a dermatologist in Connecticut. I was talking to him, and he asked, "What are you doing?" I said, "There's a dance going on at the hospital." He asked, "Are you going?" "No," I said, "I'm not going." Then I said, "I don't know, I would like to go." He replied, "You remember that girl Anita I went out with?" "Yeah, sure I do." He said, "Why don't you call her? She's around, I just saw her." So I called her. I asked her if she remembered me. I then said, "There's a dance tonight. Are you free?" We went to that dance—that was April Fool's Day—and nine months later we were married.

AR: We got married just about the time he started his residency in neurology at Montefiore. At Montefiore, at that time, there were several people—Victor Rosen, Jack Arlow.

LR: We all met—it was quite a group—the day we started that residency. Since then, we've been together. This was 1939.

AR: In 1939, we got married; yes, 1939 is when you started.

LR: That's right, the internship was 1937 and 1938. It was January 1, 1939, when I started the residency; February 22 we were married. This interview is easily about both of us.

AR: Many people are threatened when their spouse goes into training, but it didn't work that way.

SRR: It's actually very important when you think of the people reading this book, to have that kind of knowledge about you.

LR: The introduction by Arlow mentioned that.

LRAYMOND: I was just going to say, it was so nice to hear.... When I say it's unique, it's also very much recognized by other people because everybody mentions you as a team.

AR: Well, it was an enrichment, an enhancement, and I'm just sorry I haven't done what you're both doing, but it didn't work out that way.

SRR: Could I ask just one more question? I just asked your husband, and I'd like to ask you, when does he write?

AR: Every single day, and just in between times, and at night....

SRR: Unbelievable; between patients.

AR: When I have dinner on the table, he's upstairs.

LRAYMOND: As I hear you two talk to each other, I'm curious how you have worked together over the last fifty years in exchanging and developing analytic ideas as a couple.

LR: Who are you addressing that question to?

LRAYMOND: Both of you.

LR: Do you want to start or do you....

AR: Oh, I think you should start.

LR: I think just as the unconscious directs the conscious, Anita directs me. It's true. She didn't get the prize; I got the clinical prize, but she deserved it.

AR: No, no. I really love analysis, and I enjoy it. It isn't just coming to New Orleans. I really come to hear the essays. I enjoy that very much and feel stimulated. He does express his thoughts and ideas; and I'm pretty tough about them and ask a lot of questions and worry about it, too. We go through all those phases. I like the people involved, and I find that very interesting. People from all over the world. We've had a lot of personal contact with people; in many ways it's like an extended family with all the likes and dislikes and problems.

LR: Anita knows them all, all over the world, has known them, and remembers things. She also has a fifty-times better memory than I have and remembers everything. She also has a big literary background and will frequently mention an example from music, literature, or art. She's into art, very strongly now. Anita is a docent at the Los Angeles County Art Museum. And she has an interest in the psychoanalysis of art—she does with art what I do in psychoanalysis. For example, she will try to attend the Munch workshop here; she's an expert on Munch, and will know as much about him as the presenter—I know that.

AR: I just wanted to make sure that he was including some of the points that I have enjoyed knowing about Munch. I don't know if you know about Munch.

LR: At my panel tomorrow, not panel but dialogue, I will bring in a discussion of new theories which oppose structure and even reality, which in fact have a parallel to deconstruction in art and architecture. That all comes from my exposure to Anita and her world of architecture and art. Also, we have a couple of architects in the family now. But the deconstruction movement—we just saw an example by Isozaki of a building that defies gravity; there are some buildings like that in our neighborhood in Los Angeles by an architect named Frank Gehry—I don't know if you know that name—...

LRAYMOND: No, I don't.

LR: ...where the top floor sticks out in such a way that you think it's going to fall down. And I think that some of the alternative theories do to analytic thinking, what some of these architects do to gravity. They act as if it doesn't exist. Or they're defying it. That's the main thing, they're defying it. Anita has widened my horizons on all of this immeasurably. You know many people write essays together, I mean, there are a number of pairs, or writing partners—Hartmann, Kris, and Loewenstein, Arlow and Brenner, Calef and Weinshel, and there used to be Sandler and Joffe—and it should be Anita and Leo, but it isn't. It's just Leo Rangell all the time, but she's behind them all. She's part of the alter ego, the ego, the executive functioning of these projects.

AR: So it's been great. I've enjoyed it, and I do have my own interests and my own world. I'm very happy to leave Leo at home where he practices and go to the museums I'm involved with. But I'm always glad to return to Leo and psychoanalysis. I don't ever really leave it because it's part of us, you know.

SRR: You state that "in the usual clinical course of events, the typical progression of unfolding insights requires what one could call a creative leap on the part of the analyst at the portals of the interpretation of castration anxiety. The final steps often depend on the firm, mutually respectful therapeutic alliance without idealization or depreciation or countertransference, but a common search for the sought-for goal. The creative interpretative therapeutic step depends on a triumph of secondary process over primary process thinking on the parts of both analyst and patient."

Could you say more about the process of work at this point and, more specifically, how you work and how you teach your candidates to do this kind of work?

LR: That's an amazing quote, too. By the way, the phrase "creative leap" was given to me by a patient. I think of somewhat contrasting two patients. The particular patient who gave me this phrase is rather flattering. He thinks I have the capacity to do that. Another patient doesn't use those words, but is always denouncing me for not having creative ability. He thinks he's with the wrong shrink because I'm not creative enough. He still hasn't achieved what he wants, and maybe the reason is that I do not come up with the necessary creative spark. Not necessarily a creative interpretation, but something original, which every analyst should be able to do. Maybe he's right. Though I sometimes say to him, which is no doubt defensive on my part, that I've given him a stream of ideas and interpretations, that he has all the insights, but he doesn't do anything with them. He replies, in effect, that that's a copout on my part. That's why in your quote I bring in both the roles of the patient and the analyst.

Analysis is a mutual effort and endeavor. The idea of the "creative leap," which came from a patient and is a concept I respect, applies not only to a distant interpretation, for example, of a creative leap to the primal scene. How do we ever know from a dream or free associations that the Wolfman—you know, people doubt that whole thing about the Wolfman's primal scene. They think it was Freud's imagination. It was never proven that he saw his maid bending over backwards and he wanted to mount her. These are "creative leaps." The question is, how creative and whose creations are they? Are they truth or the analyst's creations? "Creative" can be overdone, but a creative leap built on truth—this brings up the question of historical versus narrative truth.

I believe in truth and in history; that there are historical as well as distorted truths. Some say you can never get at the truth historically, you can only get at it in the here and now version. By the way, the creative leap is necessary in the here and now as well as in the past. Both in the production of clinical phenomena and in their understanding. Isn't transference such a creative leap, both ways? Like the example I gave you of a patient who had an argument with his wife and the analyst asked, "Why are you mad at me?" That's a very creative leap on the part of the analyst. In fact, it's so creative it might be completely untrue. Now, we want to be imaginative and creative with both the secondary and primary processes combined. Our understanding has to be inspired, intuitive, and correct, and cognitively accurate.

How do you impart this? There are two difficult things to impart in the training process. One is the analytic attitude. How do you tell someone what the proper attitude is? You don't sit in his chair; you don't know how he or she looks at a patient; what their faces express; what their hearts and affects are saying. The only thing you know is the feeling you get about what they are like. I could meet you two, and I could feel how you are behind the patient. The same with a supervisee. But your analytic attitude is different from anyone else's, so you have to be sort of a model. And one way that you demonstrate yourself as a model is how you present cases. That's another thing.

I too often hear cases presented where I have the feeling I'm listening to the analyst, not to the patient. It's the personalities one is seeing and hearing. One is too mild or too aggressive, too soothing or too harsh. The excitement of Freud's case reports was the seeming objectivity with which they were presented. You didn't think that he was wrong when he implied death wishes against a parent or incestuous wishes. If you did, analysis never would have gotten started. If people didn't believe Freud's case reports, or Freud and Breuer at the beginning, they would have dropped him as a madman, or crank, or neurotic, imposing his own problems on the patient. "He is a sexual pervert," they would have said. Instead, they came to feel that Freud was not only reporting accurately, but that the reports were of universal significance.

In today's world, there are analysts who present cases where you believe the clinical report, and others where I am far from believing them. This goes for supervision too. I mean, I believe what I'm hearing, but what I'm hearing is more the analyst than the patient, his distortions or defensiveness or even aggression. That's why the supervisee has to be analyzed in addition to being supervised. You can't analyze while you're supervising or vice versa. So how do you impart analytic functioning? It's a very delicate and subtle thing to do, and I think it's very rarely done effectively.

SRR: You have described a "distinction between analysands who articulate about the identificatory process versus those who don't."

Is the process of learning in the analysis different for these two groups? I'm assuming or postulating that candidates or analysts in analysis are more conscious of and/or verbal about this identificatory process.

LR: I think that what must be watched for is intellectualization as a defense. I don't think that someone who's intellectual is necessarily defensive. That's another important distinction. Intelligence is not intellectualization. Or, because an analyst tries not to be judgmental, does not mean he should discard the use of judgment. By the same token, a patient can be curious about the intellectual process of analysis without using this as a defense or distortion. The patient who criticizes me for not being creative enough is very interested in the analytic process and not in a way that is deflecting or aggressive. I think it's genuine. He's also very imaginative. He's a writer, and he has a writer's block. And just as he wants to put his intellect and intelligence into his writing, he uses them in the analysis. When he says he is with the wrong shrink, it's because he's thinking about what this shrink process is, how in the hell it works, and why it isn't working. I'm quite disturbed and baffled by it, because it's been many, many years, and he's still blocked. And I don't think he's without talent, or that he's in the wrong profession as a writer.

I give him not only the benefit of the doubt, but I inwardly really have faith that he's very sensitive, articulate, and has a lot to say. Yet he sits at his desk, or paces the floor for hours at a time, and can't write. All around him, people who seem much less talented are very successful—screenwriting, directing films—and things come out. They get notoriety, they make money. And he sits there, and I think he's better than they are, yet he can't do it. So he's also interested in the analytic process and I'm interested in his interest in the process. In contrast, a candidate in analysis you'd expect to be interested in the process, but he could be using it as a defense because he has to be analyzed to become an analyst, so you have to walk a tightrope between his interest in the process as a profession and his interest in his inner life. In each case, you have to be able to differentiate between intellect and intellectualization, using judgment and being judgmental.

LRAYMOND: In your essay on the "object," you note some of the potential difficulties in the training of analysts. You wrote, "I have described transferences to theory in analysts which play a part in determining theoretical preferences, as displacements from positive or negative attachments to objects. Such identifications with and transferences to theory come to be used in regulating self-esteem as well as determining group relationships among analysts." What has been your own experience of these phenomena?

LR: I've dealt with these problems by writing about them. But again, this doesn't have the effect that it should. I experienced these problems and issues personally by living in a city that was seriously splintered on the basis of transferences and shifting allegiances. For example, it was not an accident that for five years, the Institute was Kleinian. And then for three or four years, it was Bionian. And then for a few years, it was Fairbairnian. And then Kohutian, and partly Kernbergian. None of those phases were based on the sequence of clinical observations followed by theory formation. In each instance, it was a bandwagon effect behind a charismatic leader to whom there was a displaced transference. I say displaced because there was repeatedly a new leader. It wasn't someone they knew before. They imported a Kleinian from London, and Bion from London, and Kohut from wherever he came from.

They imported the new system, then went for it gung ho. Then they accumulated experiences, and then gave up the new current theory. In other words, the sequence was new theory, experiences, disillusionment. Why was the theory so exciting at first? Because it was wish-fulfillment. It was id-oriented, it was not ego-directed, not ego-planned, or judged properly. In those years, I knew many of the leaders of these splinters or cults intimately. I knew their histories, and I knew who their own transference leaders were, and who their cliques and bandwagons were—there you have group formations which were destructive of analytic unity and of analytic productivity. Instead, it became a group of competing social clubs, socioscientific organizations, all of whom referred only to each other, adding the economic factor, and who partied and socialized with each other, and more or less derogated, or even character-assassinated people from other groups.

LRAYMOND: It must have been difficult.

LR: That is an understatement.

AR: It's become worse, unfortunately.

LR: Are you familiar with what I'm talking about?

LRAYMOND: Well, in Boston, I know our institute, PINE, split from BPSI, but I don't know the specifics of how each analytic group related to the other in that split.

LR: Well, it was there, too, I'm sure. Not as bad as what I'm talking about, but it was somewhat there.

LRAYMOND: To follow up on your experience, how do you sustain yourself in that kind of atmosphere?

LR: It's very disturbing. I sustain myself by having a few good friends, my own practice, my own writing, and my own participation at levels at which I do have camaraderie and good exchanges. Through the years that was with the American Psychoanalytic Society. In later years, it became very exciting for me with the International Psychoanalytic Society, even though at the International level, I met a lot of people of different theoretical persuasions. But I met them on what I call common ground, which is not what you hear about as common ground from another perspective. Our common ground was an analytic quest for analytic understanding in common. We had a lot of marvelous experiences together on an international scientific level, and my writing, and now lately my putting together my writings into some books.

All of this gave me a sense of conviction, as well as a sense of sadness at how much of this is being splintered and eroded. As a positive example, two weeks ago, I had the experience of being a Visiting Professor for seven or eight days in Michigan. I accepted and was happy about it because Michigan happens to be a bed of analysis simpatico with my ideas. That's why they invited me. Some other professors who preceded me—there were five before me—were all, more or less, to my way of thinking, some more, some less. That week in Michigan was mutually gratifying. They were inspired and I was very thrilled because I had a back and forth exchange about my views and theoretical and clinical issues in about eighteen different appearances, lectures, and seminars from morning until night, several times every day, Monday through Saturday. I come home replenished, but where I don't have the receptive soil that I do there. So I again have my writings, and my friends, and my practice.

AR: He has a great practice, a very interesting practice, and he works at it very hard.

SRR/LR: Thank you very much.

SELECTED BIBLIOGRAPHY

Rangell, L. (1952). The analysis of a doll phobia. *International Journal of Psycho-Analysis,* Vol. 33, pp. 43–53.

Rangell, L. (1954). Similarities and differences between psychoanalysis and dynamic psychotherapy. *Journal of the American Psychoanalytic Association*, Vol. 2, pp. 734–744.

Rangell, L. (1954). The psychology of poise. *International Journal of Psycho-Analysis,* Vol. 35, pp. 313–332.

Rangell, L. (1955). The role of the parent in the Oedipus complex. *Bulletin of the Menninger Clinic*, Vol. 19, pp. 9–15.

Rangell, L. (1955). On the psychoanalytic theory of anxiety. *Journal of the American Psychoanalytic Association*, Vol. 3, pp. 389–414.

Rangell, L. (1959). The nature of conversion, *Journal of the American Psychoanalytic Association,* Vol. 7, pp. 632–662.

Rangell, L. (1963). On friendship. *Journal of the American Psychoanalytic Association,* Vol. 11, pp. 3–54.

Rangell, L. (1963). The scope of the intrapsychic conflict. *The Psychoanalytic Study of the Child*, Vol. 18, pp. 75–102. New York: International Universities Press.

Rangell, L. (1963). Structural problems in intrapsychic conflict. *The Psychoanalytic Study of the Child,* Vol. 18, pp. 103–138. New York: International Universities Press.

Rangell, L. (1965). The scope of Heinz Hartmann. *International Journal of Psycho-Analysis,* Vol. 46, pp. 5–30.

Rangell, L. (1967). Psychoanalysis, affects, and the "human core." *Psychoanalytic Quarterly,* Vol. 36, pp. 172–202.

Rangell, L. (1967). The metapsychology of psychic trauma. In: *Psychic Trauma,* ed. S. S. Furst. New York: Basic Books.

Rangell, L. (1968). A further attempt to resolve "the problem of anxiety." *Journal of the American Psychoanalytic Association*, Vol. 16, pp. 371–404.

Rangell, L. (1968). A point of view on acting out. *International Journal of Psycho-Analysis*, Vol. 49, pp. 195–201.

Rangell, L. (1969). The intrapsychic process and its analysis. *International Journal of Psycho-Analysis,* Vol. 50, pp. 65–77.

Rangell, L. (1969). Choice-conflict and the decision-making function of the ego. *International Journal of Psycho-Analysis*, Vol. 50, pp. 599–602.

Rangell, L. (1971). The decision-making process. *The Psychoanalytic Study of the Child,* Vol. 26, pp. 425–452. New Haven: Yale University Press.

Rangell, L. (1971). Obituary, Dr. Heinz Hartmann. *International Journal of Psycho-Analysis*, vol. 51, p. 567.

Rangell, L. (1972). Aggression, Oedipus, and historical perspective. *International Journal of Psycho-Analysis,* Vol. 53, pp. 3–11.

Rangell, L. (1973). On the cacophony of human relations. *Psychoanalytic Quarterly,* Vol. 42, pp. 325–348.

Rangell, L. (1974). A psychoanalytic perspective leading currently to the syndrome of the compromise of integrity. *International Journal of Psycho-Analysis,* Vol. 55, pp. 3–12.

Rangell, L. (1974). Affects and the signal process. Abstracted in *Journal of the American Psychoanalytic Association*, Vol. 22, pp. 612–625.

Rangell, L. (1975). Psychoanalysis and the process of change. *International Journal of Psycho-Analysis*, Vol. 56, pp. 87–98.

Rangell, L. (1976). Lessons from Watergate. *Psychoanalytic Quarterly,* Vol. 45, pp. 37–61.

Rangell, L. (1978). On understanding and treating anxiety and its derivatives. *International Journal of Psycho-Analysis*, Vol. 59, pp. 229–236.

Rangell, L. (1980). *The Mind of Watergate.* New York: Norton.

Rangell, L. (1980). A neglected classic. *Journal of the Philadelphia Association of Psychoanalysis*, Vol. 7, pp. 93–103.

Rangell, L. (1981). From insight to change. *Journal of the American Psychoanalytic Association*, Vol. 29, pp. 119–141.

Rangell, L. (1981). Psychoanalysis and dynamic psychotherapy. *Psychoanalytic Quarterly*, Vol. 50, pp. 665–693.

Rangell, L. (1982). Transference to theory. *Annals of Psychoanalysis*, Vol. 10, pp. 29–56.

Rangell, L. (1982). The self in psychoanalytic theory. *Journal of the American Psychoanalytic Association*, Vol. 30, pp. 863–891.

Rangell, L. (1982). Some thoughts on termination. *Psychoanalytic Inquiry*, Vol. 2, pp. 367–392.

Rangell, L. (1984). Structure, somatic and psychic. In: *Frontiers of Infant Psychiatry,* Vol. 2, ed. E. Galenson, J. D. Call, & R. L. Tyson. New York: Basic Books.

Rangell, L. (1984). The analyst at work. *International Journal of Psycho-Analysis*, Vol. 65, pp. 125–140.

Rangell, L. (1985). The object in psychoanalytic theory. *Journal of the American Psychoanalytic Association,* Vol. 33, pp. 101–334.

Rangell, L. (1986). The executive functions of the ego. *The Psychoanalytic Study of the Child*, Vol. 41, pp. 1–37. New Haven: Yale University Press.

Rangell, L. (1986). The psychoanalytic theory of affects. In: *Compendium of Psychoanalytic Terms and Concepts*, ed. B. D. Fine & B. E. Moore. New Haven: Yale University Press, 1989.

Rangell, L. (1987). A core process in psychoanalytic treatment. *Psychoanalytic Quarterly,* Vol. 56, pp. 222–249.

Rangell, L. (1987). Historical perspectives and current status. In: *The Significance of the Interpretation of Dreams in Clinical Work*, ed. A. Rothstein. New York: International Universities Press.

Rangell, L. (1987). Psychoanalysis—Where next? *American Psychoanalytic Association Newsletter*, Vol. 21(1), pp. 6–7; 21(2), pp. 6–7.

Rangell, L. (1990). *The Human Core*, Vol. I *Action within the Structural View;* Vol. II *From Anxiety to Integrity.* Madison, CT: International Universities Press.

Edward Weinshel

Edward Weinshel, M.D. was, until his recent retirement, a training and supervising analyst at the San Francisco Psychoanalytic Institute and a Clinical Professor of Psychiatry at the University of California School of Medicine, San Francisco. He was Chief of the Department of Psychiatry and Director of Training for the Department of Psychiatry at Mt. Zion Hospital and Medical Center. He is an Honorary Member of the British Psychoanalytical Society and a past Vice President and Secretary of the International Psychoanalytical Association. He was a visiting psychoanalyst for the Buenos Aires Psychoanalytical Association and has been plenary speaker for the American Psychoanalytic Association. He has also given the Rado Lecture of the Columbia University Clinic and the Freud Anniversary Lecture of the New York Psychoanalytic Institute.

Dr. Weinshel was on the editorial boards of the *Journal of the American Psychoanalytic Association, Psychoanalytic Quarterly,* Guilford Press, and the *Revised Edition of the Psychoanalytic Glossary.* He was also North American editor and consultant associate editor of the *International Journal of Psycho-Analysis* and the *International Review of Psychoanalysis.* Dr. Weinshel was interviewed May 9, 1991.

SRR: You have described the analyst's acceptance of the responsibility for self-observation as a contribution from the superego. You differentiate self-observation from self-analysis, which you consider a more deliberate, self-conscious effort. You propose "the achievement of an ego state which is neither solely affective nor an intellectual one. We would describe it rather as a state of readiness to hear and to experience and to do that which is necessary to maintain the analytic process in the patient."

You note that a willingness to live with ambiguity is inherent to this state. Can you discuss what it is like experientially for the analyst to live for long periods in this state, and can you describe it affectively? Also, do you have any thoughts about how living in this particular state over long periods of time impacts the analyst's psychic economy?

EW: That's marvelous, because I don't think I've thought of it consciously. On one hand, I think being an analyst is hard work; on the other hand, it isn't. I think it's very hard to describe exactly how it feels. Part of what makes it hard has to do with the superego. It also has to do with the whole question of neutrality. I've been very much influenced by Bob Gardner's *Self Inquiry*. Originally, when I wrote on these things I talked about self-observation, but I think that Bob's phrase is much closer to what happens. I think we're consciously asking ourselves all kinds of things about why this, why that, how this, how that. I think that's hard in itself, even after you get used to it, but I think even more, there is always an inner resistance to thinking so hard and questioning ourselves so hard.

To put it that there is a superego factor is probably a terrible oversimplification, but I don't know how to go beyond that. Vic Calef and I wrote about this in the 1970s. I would stress more now the idea of self-observation and self-inquiry as important in analytic work. It is consistent with what has been happening in the last decade with more emphasis on the analyst looking at his own work and his own feelings. Self-inquiry is so important.

Usually we talk about neutrality in terms of not making judgments or being sure that our judgments are neutral. This is just not true, because I think we are always making judgments. I'll stick my neck out further to say that we always have to make judgments. The point is that we have to check on our judgments and see how much we are fooling ourselves, or enjoying ourselves too much, or whatever it is.

I think that's where the hard work comes in because there is such a temptation not to analyze. The gross things are unpleasant, but it's that constant need to look at ourselves and check ourselves. There is such a difference between a training analysis and ordinary analysis. The training analysis has a tendency to pay more attention to those particular ego functions that are oversimplified. For an analyst, I think it's a matter of professional life and death, so to speak.

SRR: You have described evenly hovering attention as "an altered state of consciousness, a state favoring bursts of insight in many ways similar to the activities of creative artists and scientists." Can you discuss what that kind of experience is like for you personally, and can you say something about gratification in having that kind of experience?

EW: When I was a candidate, one of my supervisors said, "The only time you have a right to enjoy yourself in doing analytic work is when you and the patient think of the same thing at the same time. The idea of enjoying when things are going well is often a trap." Most of us are at least a wee bit suspicious of our thinking things are going really well, particularly when the patient seems inordinately pleased. On the other hand, I don't think that analysis needs to be grim. We often do get uptight about it, and there is a certain kind of relaxation and comfort in what we're doing that I think facilitates the work.

I don't think we're capable of doing it all the time. Just as a patient isn't always in analysis, I don't think we are always in analysis. We need some rest, even if it's for a second or two. I doubt whether any one analyst doesn't drift out of that feeling at least once a day or more. Sometimes it worries me, but one of the things I think is happening, as part and parcel of our looking at ourselves more, is that we are also becoming, little by little, a bit more charitable with ourselves. This is a consequence of a lot of things. Teaching is different, the role models are different, and the demands are not so rigorous that we do everything right. We don't talk so much about there being one kind of answer for everything. It's understood that people are different and that analysts are different. The analytic situation at any one moment is different, and there probably is no such thing as one correct answer or one correct interpretation.

I remember being genuinely relieved, when I was a candidate, reading Merton Gill's statement about "still recognizing one's friends after analysis," because in our own development we often feel we have to bring about these huge dramatic changes. I was as influenced by Gill as I was by some of my teachers. It's becoming more accepted that we're going to make mistakes.

I don't know if you've kept up with Dale Boesky's work. I think it is magnificent. He makes the point that mistakes may even be an absolute necessity for the analyst. I remember my friend Vic said, when I was a young analyst beginning to do supervision, "It's important that you prepare yourself for falling asleep with a patient." He wasn't recommending it, but he was saying that you are going to make mistakes. Unless you are prepared to accept that as part of the life of an analyst, you're going to have a hard time.

LR: That reminds me of a quote from your essay with Dr. Calef, "The Analyst as the Conscience of the Analysis." You wrote, "It would perhaps be more accurate to say that he (the analyst) places himself in the position of being ready to dream without actually dreaming (Fliess' [1942] concept of 'conditional daydreaming')…"

EW: See what Vic meant?

LR: Yes. The quote continues: "…or without permitting himself the luxury of uninhibited fantasy. The analyst tries to maintain a state of being able to dream while still awake and simultaneously controls, to a degree, both fantasy and dream—a control which precludes both inattention and sleep." Could you elaborate more on your own experience of this state of mind?

EW: I still believe it. I think we produce some of our best work in that state. It goes back to the previous quote and to the relationship to creativity. We should watch ourselves to see how close we are getting to being fully awake or falling asleep. Am I saying anything that may seem strange or different?

LR: No. You're describing a state of mind between dreaming and being fully awake which captures a type of empathic regression in the analyst, parallel to that occurring for the patient.

EW: By and large you are not aware. You don't think of how you are thinking and feeling unless you ask yourself for something that brings it about.

LR: Do you know what made you aware of this phenomenon?

EW: I wish I knew how it happened. Vic and I wrote together for a period of twelve years. We used to meet at least once a week, and usually for at least a half a day.

LR: It must have made a difference to have that much concentrated time to think together.

EW: I know. As we both said, it was very hard to know where the ideas came from. At the end of that essay, the thing I liked the most, frankly, is the metaphor of Sherlock Holmes. I'll be damned if I knew which of the two of us came up with it. I want to think it's me, and I bet Vic felt the same way.

LR: What was your experience like when collaborating with Dr. Calef? How did it evolve as a creative process and friendship? How has his death affected your own creativity and writing since then?

EW: Well, for reasons that aren't clear to me, I like to work with someone else. In a way, it has to do with a kind of loneliness; in another way, it's fun to talk. From a more objective viewpoint, talking about an idea and bouncing it back and forth are important. You can't do it with everybody, and not everybody can do it.

Vic and I were altogether different temperamentally. Yet we were able to write together. We never got into a fight about any of our essays; we got into fights over other things, but never about writing. It was a wonderful experience, and obviously we were very, very close. Our families were close, and we vacationed together. I still get depressed about his death. But I've also written essays with Owen Renik and Bob Wallerstein. I guess I just happen to like it, I'm not altogether sure why.

LR: How did your friendship develop with Dr. Calef?

EW: Well, we just knew each other. San Francisco is a relatively small city compared to others. I think it's more informal in terms of hierarchy. He was one of my teachers to begin with. We were both involved in Mt. Zion for a while, so we just became closer and closer.

The actual collaboration began as one of those freak things. We were talking to each other on the phone. In the course of the discussion I said, "You know, I had the funniest experience today with one of my patients." I described something about sexual feelings with the dead–what's the word?

LR: Necrophilia?

EW: And Vic gave a scream that could be heard four blocks away. He said, "That is the most amazing thing; so did I." And then we thought we ought to sit down and talk about this. That's how the more formal structure of our meeting together began. We also had been in some self-established study groups together for years and years.

SRR: It's wonderful that you had that.

EW: One of the nice things about that informality is that all the study groups I've been involved in have included candidates as well as senior training analysts.

SRR: That's so different than in Boston.

EW: Well, I think it's a social thing. I think San Francisco and Boston are very much alike in many ways, but there is much more formality in Boston. I remember I was on a site visit to Denver. I was chairman of the board at the time, and one of the site visitors from the east was going to turn them down because the candidates and instructors were using first names. It was straightened out, but there are differences.

I make big pitches at our institute for more than one teacher at case conferences. I think that helps everybody. Sam Hoch and I do a continuous case conference together. This past year was the first time it was done at our place, and it was a huge success. The fact that two training analysts can see things a different way and disagree without fighting made it easier for the candidates. There is something about our not being so very sure about most things that makes having two points of view helpful.

LR: In this quote from your "Conscience" essay with Dr. Calef, you describe the following "mobile translation" of secondary processing into primary and back into secondary again:

> "The analyst assumes the superordinate function of 'the keeper of the analytic process' in the face of the resistance against it (in himself and his patient.) To do so he suspends his personal conscience (biases), paradoxical though it may be. Avoiding the overestimations and overexpectations for the personal analysis, it is nevertheless expected that it will provide a relative resolution of conflict to permit certain ego functions sufficient freedom (secondary autonomy) for the development of the analyzing instrument which includes listening, observing, integrating and translating functions, and allowing a mobile translation of secondary into primary processes and then back again to secondary process thought and language. It is in the evenly hovering attention (an altered state of consciousness) which the analyst consciously permits himself that his resistances are temporarily suspended, old connections held in abeyance to potentiate the possibility for new ones to occur. It is a state of readiness to sleep and dream

though precluding inattention, sleeping, and dreaming while permitting limited fantasy formation."

Could you say more about this translation process and how you might teach supervisees to further develop this capacity?

EW: Where do you get these questions? It's very hard. I don't know if I have thought of them in those words, although I've sure tried. Particularly, I'm sure I do teach this to my supervisees by setting an example. You let people think freely. You tell a candidate that the goal is not to come up with one answer as much as to get as many possibilities as you can.

It may be a tangent, but I think there are many negative things about case conferences. I think it's perhaps one of the worst ways of teaching technique. The poor person presenting has fifteen supervisors; that's horrible.

SRR: It's very interesting.

EW: First of all, it's not how we do analysis. Think of how much we actually do remember of the previous hour. Then you get fifteen people together having taken pretty good notes on that hour. Suddenly you have an additional amount of data, and that certainly changes the whole structure.

SRR: Wouldn't that change when you move to a primary process mode versus a secondary?

EW: Sure. I think that's one of the ways in which it is taught. I don't care personally whether my students take notes or not. I know some of my colleagues are very tough about that. I think it has to do with how many different ways people think analytically. If you read about the lady analysts of the past, many of them did things like knitting. I'm sure it was not to be distracted, but it was their way of relaxing.

When I work, I use a prodigious number of pages of paper every day. Most of them are scribbling or doodling. Occasionally, I'll take some real notes when suddenly someone says things, but I keep this thing on my lap all the time. I rarely take significant notes, but that's the way I relax best. I think everybody develops their own way of relaxing, so that they can approximate that state of mind.

LR: When you are in that more relaxed state, do you notice if you prefer particularly sensory modes of association, for example, visual, auditory, or somesthetic?

EW: I'm not only very visual, but I close my eyes. When I see people face to face, they think I'm falling asleep, but this is not always true. I'm very visual.

LR: Could you give an example of how you might translate back from a visual image to an interpretation?

EW: I'll be taking my little doodles, and suddenly something hits me. I pay some extra attention. When I pay extra attention, I close my eyes or lean back, and then something happens.

LR: Something creative happens while listening....

EW: Of course, you can be distracted from time to time by noises, the patient's movements, or something else. No matter how conscientious you are as an analyst you are not always functioning on all cylinders. This creates some of the superego conflicts that we get into—what's best to do, for instance, if you are sick, feeling lousy, depressed, all these human foibles, should you cancel? When I have a cold, I know I'm not going to function as well as when I'm feeling tip-top. On the other hand, to cancel is a minitrauma, and I usually don't.

I admit we don't always feel really good, so we don't always function well in terms of how we think. We know the feeling of when we're on a roll and things are clicking with the patient, but we don't do it all the time. I don't know what percentage that is. I'm sure it varies with the analyst. We don't talk too much about that, how we don't always function evenly.

SRR: It's good for us to hear it discussed. In "The Psychoanalytic Process," you state: "Today we would probably say that appropriate psychoanalytic work with the patient manifesting a transference neurosis will result in a more effective resolution of crucial intrapsychic conflicts with less pathological, more adaptive compromise solutions than had been possible in childhood." And in "The Scope of Psychoanalysis," you state: "We rarely speak any more of psychoanalytic cures. We're much more likely to focus on changes, shifts or compromise formations." Could you tell us more about how you conceive of the adaptive compromise formations, particularly in terms of analysts themselves?

EW: You have no mercy. I think analysis has changed tremendously, but a little at a time. Part of it is my own bias. I'd rather see change because that's more glamorous or more revolutionary. But most of the changes that occur have been relatively gradual due to our changing ourselves from reading, listening, or working with our patients. Sometimes we aren't even aware of those changes, and sometimes they take a lot of time. For those of us who are older, changes in analysis over the last decade have not been easy to apply. It's difficult when you've been doing analysis another way over a long period, even when you are convinced of the validity of new theoretical aspects. There have been a series of changes which have to do with a more realistic, more modest approach. I think it was unfortunate that so much was expected and that we were so successful as analysts early on. Little by little it became apparent that we weren't going to be able to deliver the goods as consistently as people wanted them.

As a rule I don't think we talk anymore about cure because we know that we are not dealing with a tumor to be extricated. Please, God, we're always going to have conflicts of some sort or another. Joan Fleming was never my supervisor, but we worked together. One of her phrases that I love was about the re-solution rather than the resolution because it fits more closely to what happens. All we get is an opportunity to rework some of the problems under more advantageous situations.

The same thing holds in regard to what I said about the transference neurosis. I think there has been a lot of misunderstanding. Not everybody will agree about the transference neurosis. I think people tend to think of it much too literally as a precise kind of replication of what has happened. So often our colleagues think that the goal is to have a transference neurosis. My view is that it provides one with an opportunity to work though some of the older conflictual, oedipal problems, to analyze those particular problems. It's not a magical thing. It doesn't emerge in any mysterious way, and it doesn't provide a certainty that things are going to get better, unless those things are worked through.

The fact that somebody doesn't develop a transference neurosis doesn't mean the analysis is a failure. It's not whether the transference neurosis is obtained, but whether those things are analyzed. All it means is that you've analyzed some difficult things. That's why I put it in terms of compromise formations which become more realistic and more useful. I don't know how you go about getting compromise formations. They just happen, they are inevitable.

LR: You talk about the "unexpected" in your essay, "The Scope of Psychoanalysis." Here's the quote: "The structural theory's stress on conflict and compromise formation virtually guarantees an emphasis on multidetermination and a premium on searching for the unexpected." Could you say more about that?

EW: I think in my original version I had included a phrase that Ernst Kris had used about looking for roses. I forget exactly, but something like "an analyst works looking for roses in January." I think we do do that; we hope for something interesting. I think we are alerted to be ready for what is unexpected.

LR: Can you give an example of what you're describing?

EW: I can't give it from my own practice offhand. But two weeks ago, in one of the continuous case conferences, there was a patient who had been in analysis for four to five months. There was a feeling that something was being withheld, but there really weren't many clues. The patient started off obviously withholding, but then in the middle of that he blurted out that his wife had been in analysis with his analyst. That's what I mean by unexpected.

SRR: You've remained convinced that "persistent and effective work with the resistances in both analysand and analyst constitutes the core of the psychoanalytic work and process." You note that resistances are inevitable, and that productive work and resistances can take place simultaneously. Can you tell us more about the nature—here we go again—of the analysts' resistances? Are there certain common resistances that you find?

EW: Of the analyst?

SRR: Yes.

EW: First of all, it's idiosyncratic, and I avoid classifications. I know Freud's classifications of resistances are useful, but I think they also cause troubles. On the firing line, they are intellectual artifacts. On the firing line, I don't think we see the things as clearly as they are delineated in theory. That's also true of diagnoses. I think that there are two kinds of resistances: one that the patient has and one that the analyst has. It may be that they are actually the same. These are relatively new ideas.

As we learn more about enactment, it may be hard to detect where it starts and why it starts. I think it's a danger to fall back on the old idea that resistances are necessarily bad. It does have a negative connotation, and we will probably never get away from it. That's one of the reasons that people whom I respect highly don't like the term. I don't know if Arlow or Brenner have talked about it in print, but I know that they would prefer to put it all in terms of transference, and Roy Shafer has put it very vigorously that way. I think these are all a matter of taste.

Resistances and transference are part and parcel of the same phenomenon; these are abstractions in a way. But we see them together. We were discussing this at breakfast while preparing for a panel for next fall. I told a variation of an old story about a man who was having supper. His friend came in and said, "What are you eating?" He replied, "Well, I'm having cottage cheese and noodles." The other fellow said, "Why do you call it noodles?" And he replied, "Well, they look like noodles, they feel like noodles, they smell like noodles, and they taste like noodles. That's why I call them noodles." That's how I feel about resistances. I like them because they are observable.

At the panel in Miami, we discussed this while we worked on Freud's essay on technique. This was when Roy Schafer presented his essay. I suggested that resistances are external manifestations of internal conflict. It will be a very interesting ongoing debate for a long time. But it seems to be an observable phenomenon. No matter what subtitle we put to it, God knows that analysts are not always willing to do analytic work for all kinds of reasons, for all our various shortcomings and conflicts. It's hard work. One of the temptations of not doing analysis is that other things are easier.

LR: In your essay, "Further Observations on the Psychoanalytic Process," you quote Boesky's description of resistance in the analyst: "...I have in mind complex and lengthy sequences of interaction which only gradually become evident to the analyst as a resistance in the patient and to which the analyst has in some more or less subtle way contributed by his or her own behavior. The phenomenon to which I refer seems to me to include countertransference, but transcends that concept....It is useful to view certain behaviors of the analyst, which actually join in the creation of a 'useful' resistance, as a creative contribution which is necessary only for that analyst and would not be necessary for another analyst."

This seems to describe an aspect of resistance that is positive, but would also require careful self-analysis on the analyst's part to uncover.

EW: Vic and I touched on that whole thing, but we didn't go very far with it. We didn't have either the guts or the material Dale has done. I think it is one of the most exciting things in the business.

LR: How would you work with supervisees to increase their awareness of this type of resistance with their patients?

EW: Carefully and maybe too carefully. Part of it is that I don't want to butt in. The other is that it is part of the analysis. There are different ways of calling attention to it. We don't very often anymore tell a patient he or she is resisting. We try to point to the resistance without putting it as grossly as that. I think you can do the same with teaching. It depends on your relationship with the supervisee. Good supervisees, in particular, can tell by your expression. More often than not, they've picked up on their own resistance. But there are other times when you have to be more blunt about it. I don't know if there is any one way. Sometimes just by emphasizing certain things in the material.

SRR: We'd be interested in anything you want to share with us about your own development as an analyst, who influenced you, and any key experiences, mentors.

EW: In January, at Stanford, they had an exhibition of Freud's artwork. Have you seen it? It was a joint effort between Stanford and our institute. They had a dinner for all the people who had planned it, and they asked me to give an after-dinner speech. It was the first after-dinner speech I had ever given. Part of what I did was to talk about how I got into the business. There were a number of factors. One of the people who inspired me a great deal before I was really interested was Max Lerner, when I was still in high school. That was a long time ago. He may still be living. Eventually he wrote for the New York papers, but then he wrote a lot of relatively liberal articles about people. They were marvelous, and I was fascinated. Every once in a while he would write about Freud, whom he always spoke very well of. I started off wanting to be another Max Lerner, because I liked the idea of what he was doing. He was part economist, I think, and part writer for *The Nation* and *The Republic* and other fancy magazines. I went through a big disillusionment, however, and I decided to be a doctor.

A couple of years later, he wrote a book of essays. The first few chapters of the book dealt with ideas. His book was titled *Ideas Are Weapons.* He mentioned in those early chapters how powerful ideas are. Then he went through each century from the 16th on, noting that each century was connected with particular kinds of advancement in ideas. When he got to the 20th century, he felt that the most important ideas were those dealing with "the irrational." He said

Sigmund Freud was mainly responsible for those. Well, that perked up my interest.

When I got into the Army, I was sent to basic training. One day, there was a sign on the bulletin board. It said, "All those with a burning desire to learn more about psychiatry, sign here." I thought it sounded like bird watching. Then about two weeks later, almost a hundred of us took the traditional two steps forward. We didn't know what was going to happen. They told us that we were going to go to school for military neuropsychiatry in New York. I ended up at Bellevue, which was a marvelous experience.

The administrator for the three schools was Norm Reider, whom I got to know and like. Then I went back to Wisconsin, where I trained. I got a little tired of it, and I was looking for a residency elsewhere. I found out that Reider had been made head of the department at Mt. Zion. Those were the days when you didn't have to go through all kinds of monkey business. So I called him and asked him if I could have a residency for a year. He said, "Sure, come on down." It was marvelous. There were lectures given by Erikson, Bernfeld, and others who were really inspirational. So, eventually, I became an analyst. I think Reider was one of my first heroes.

My second hero, when I was grown up, was Max Gitelson. The first thing that drew me to him was seeing him at an early morning meeting of the planning committee for Reider's Festshrift. There he was, smoking a big black cigar. I figured any man that could do that at 7:00 in the morning was terribly impressive, so I began reading his material. I think he still is one of the best people in the business. He influenced a lot of people, but he didn't get much recognition.

LR: When did you first become interested in writing?

EW: I think it probably began when I was editor of my high school paper. It was obviously something I liked.

LR: In your experience, how do listening to your patients and writing about your observations work together? How does one process reinforce, or influence the other?

EW: I don't know. I think that so many unconscious factors come into play. I didn't do much writing until I had had a good deal of clinical experience. I felt more certain, then, more sure of what I was doing. I enjoy it.

SRR: You have described how the analyst does not immediately transmit information and assessments to his or her patient; rather, he retranslates the unconscious back into secondary process terms and then eventually into the language of the patient, to make his interpretive remarks. Can you say something about that ability? Can you tell us about the other abilities, besides intelligence, that the analyst uses in being able to do this? I'm thinking, in particular, about speaking the language of the patient. Do you see this ability as a particular talent or kind of creativity? Can it be taught? Do you try to teach it?

EW: I don't know. I think some people have an easier job of it than others. Is it simply an ability? I think it's complicated. I have more feeling about the other side. I feel sorry for the people in the business, particularly candidates, who don't write easily. I don't think there is a one-to-one relationship between the ability to write or to think or to analyze.

SRR: I'm not thinking about writing as much as being able, in the clinical work, to translate ideas into the language of the patient.

EW: I think it's very difficult. I think you learn by experience, but there are "naturals." I wish I were one of them. I'm sure you've seen people who seem to know how to do it from day one. I've always had the conviction that good students make teachers look good, and bad students make them infamous. Particularly in terms of listening and conversion of what one hears into secondary process. I don't know how some people can do it.

We have a marvelous group of candidates at the current time. They make me angry sometimes, how smart they are. It's a phrase I'm going to use tomorrow, what I call "unambivalent envy." It's that capacity. People who haven't read a lot can get right to the point quickly. It's one of those things that we don't know as much about as we should. Whether it can be taught, I don't know. I worry more about those who can do good analytic work, but can't always explain what they are doing. They often have a harder time in training than those who are verbal and even more glib.

SRR: Back again to "The Conscience of the Analyst" essay. You state: "It is theoretically conceivable that specific circumscribed areas of psychopathology could, in a given candidate, facilitate his doing psychoanalytic work, a topic sorely in need of further elaboration and clinical documentation." Can you say more about this?

EW: Not very much. But it still intrigues me. The most gross psychopathology is not as applicable to analytic work as other types of clinical work, for example, with schizoid and psychotic patients. There is something about the access to one's unconscious that does help. We were talking about that before in other ways in terms of the countertransference, the transference that the analyst has to the patient. That is closer to the way we tried to talk about it twenty years ago. There is something about the way people are able to use their illness to connect to a patient in one way or another, but I don't know more about it.

LR: When you are with other senior analysts, is this ever a topic of discussion or is it avoided?

EW: Talk is to analysts like an onion is to a martini. It just is. I don't know if you know about CAPS and even more, Aspen—endless talking. Analysts like to talk, particularly when they are away from home because then they can talk about their cases. In fact, at lunch today we were talking about confidentiality and what do we do with it? Are we overemphasizing it? How do you protect it? It's a time bomb. So, writing a paper these days is like crossing a minefield. How do you do it without ending up in court or offending someone? But most analysts love to talk about their work in one way or another.

LR: You bring up the concept of candidates' accepting assessment in their training analyses in your essay with Dr. Calef, "Reporting, Nonreporting, and Assessment in the Training Analysis." You say, "We suggest that the future analyst must understand and accept this 'reality' in order to participate in the working alliance of the training analysis, just as all patients must accept the 'reality' of time, money, vacations, and assessments. At the same time, the training analyst must be willing to accept his responsibility for those assessments which bear on the candidate's capacity to be analyzed and to do analysis."

You also point out: "The understanding of the development and operation of those (ego and superego) functions together with their assessment by the analyst with his candidate must become a core part of the training analysis, a process that should be investigated with the candidate's knowledge and participation and reported first and foremost to the candidate." Are these views you still hold?

EW: I still believe in that theoretically, particularly how important assessment is. Assessment is part of what we talked about at the very beginning today. How do we work? How do we know we are doing the right thing or trying at least to know? I think the idea of the analyst reporting is an ideal, and I'm not sure it can be achieved. There are all kinds of reasons for it. Now there is so much bad feeling about it that candidates look upon you as Borgia if you are a reporter. I know only one or two in our own institute who still do. This is contradictory in a way, but there has to be absolute security that nothing gets out. If you report, you worry about your report being disseminated in some way. I don't mean openly, but in some way or another. And then you really have done wrong to your patient.

I think there is also a misunderstanding about what constitutes reporting. Many of my colleagues and many candidates have the idea that reporting is telling all kinds of sordid stories about the analysand's past or present. That's not at all what Vic and I had in mind, or what we practiced, which was really just to get an assessment of what was going on. It doesn't seem as comfortable as it used to be, so I don't do it anymore.

SRR: Do you think it has something to do with a change in culture or generation?

EW: I think that's an important point. I think the analysands speak up a lot more. They have access to the records and want to see them. It doesn't happen too often, and it has always been a controversial thing.

SRR: You said, I think it's in the same discussion, that "it's by no means infrequent, if it isn't altogether universal, that candidates come to analysis with a history of certain delinquencies committed early in life, certain latent perversions that are covered by reaction formation or other quasisublimation, and that these defensive sublimations seem to be relatively effective forms of mastery or cure, but these patients are nevertheless plagued with the feeling of being impostors, dishonest perverts. We are not referring here to actual perversion, but to neurotic fears and fantasies which negate their pregenital nature and which have to be dealt with in every analysis."

I think you've already discussed some of this in terms of the change in culture. You state that dealing with such psychological structures may become more problematic when the analyst has promised not to report. It also made me think about the whole question of training versus nontraining analysis, and differences you observe on how these issues are dealt with and resolved.

EW: It's another big topic. It's something we all experience in one way or another. I think most analysts have a sort of split personality. That is, they are tempted to treat their patients with much more understanding and much more support in indirect ways and are much more tolerant of this list of things than they do themselves. I think one of the reasons that the analysand-candidate is usually against the idea of reporting is that they feel that there is a terrible exaggeration of what happens. The crimes are usually very negligible, and maybe negligence is one, but this is part of the difficulty.

I'm sure there must be some exceptions, but most of the candidates I've run across and I worry much more about what has happened in the past than in the present. With their patient they are altogether different. Isn't that true? The analysis of those things, of course, is terribly important. These are some of the significant resistances when doing training analyses. Let's face it, more and more of the student control cases are really training analyses. I don't know what the statistics are in Boston, but about two-thirds of the candidates I have in supervision are dealing with other kinds of potential analysands or therapists, a lot of our potential analysts. So the idea of training analysis is no longer limited to a relatively small number.

I tried to deal with the whole business of the differences between training analysis and other analyses in an article I wrote for the I.P.A. a few years ago. I tried to approach it in terms of resistances and the nature of resistances. There's currently in the American Psychoanalytic Association a workshop for training analysts. This is a good idea because it's always been such a terrible secret. Not everybody agrees, certainly. I'd say it's about 50/50—the people who feel that training analysis is only a very good analysis, and others including me, who feel that there are differences. I think just the reality of the situation makes a difference. Not just the reality of what Vic and I called the "fishbowl" analysis, which is important, but it's just harder work for the analyst.

In the analysis itself, a patient may say to you, in one way or another, "I want to kill you." If a candidate says that, it's not just the fantasy, because a training analyst does have some power even in nonreporting institutes. If the analysis doesn't work out, the chances are the candidate will not be able to carry on in the profession. When the candidate in a sense does replace the training analyst, those are more than quantitative issues. The conflicts may be the same, but in a training analysis I think it's different.

LR: You also wrote about the possible "negatives" of the "institutionalization of psychoanalysis and psychoanalytic training" in your essay, "The Functions of the Training Analysis and the Selection of the Training Analyst." You wrote: "Some of these problems may contribute to the creation of an institutional ambience which can interfere with the training procedure; some may contribute to splits in the transference which may complicate the personal analysis; some may facilitate a regressive infantilism in the candidate which stultifies analytic individuation, independence, and creativity." From your own experience where do you see these problems manifesting themselves in the training process? How might they be prevented?

EW: One I've already alluded to is supervision. It is a natural setup for a split transference, and it happens very often. Without being very conspicuous, what often happens is that supervision starts out as a friendly relationship and ends up in a split, in which the supervisor is the good guy, and the analyst is the bad guy. That's not uncommon and is fairly easy to deal with, as analytic tasks go.

Another thing that happens is that certain training analysts develop cliques; some are more important than others in a sense. There are arguments about this, what I have called the attempt to establish a therapeutic community within an institute. I think that an analysis is not necessarily a pleasant thing. There is no question that along the way there has been bad treatment of candidates, a kind of abuse at times. That's one extreme. The other is treating the candidate as a child very specially; I think there is an in-between that is more appropriate. That's what I had in mind.

SRR: That's helpful. Just one more question about that same essay. This is following what you've been saying. You talk about the fact that the analyst is a real object as well as a transference figure for the candidates, and that this puts particular pressure on the analyst, the analysand, and the analysis. How does this shape the termination phase, given the ongoing nature of the relationships.

EW: Again, I think it varies tremendously. On one hand, in a small place like San Francisco, it's probably different than in a place like

New York. We are brought together more and more frequently and closer in a sense than in a great big place. I think it's something that has to be worked out first, as best one can, in the termination phase. But I don't think it can be done entirely. You are supposed to deal with all the resistances and transferences, but you don't want to tangle too much with those transferences having to do with the analyst's analyst. That's one of the things that is tricky in the termination phase.

SRR: I'm not exactly sure what you mean.

EW: There are certain things about the analysand identifying with the analytic attitude. We don't rush into disturbing that particular identification. As the analysis proceeds, some of that gets worked out. The patient will recognize that there is an identification there. Then you can work a little more with why that particular identification has developed at that time. Again, the timing of that is important, and we don't want to destroy it altogether. There is no question that it happens badly at times because some negative feelings interfere with certain parts of the overall analysis.

Then there's the whole stage of what happens afterwards. Usually I have fairly decent relationships with my candidates. I have to confess that I've seen three of my own analysands here. I was really pleased to see them and chat for a little bit. I don't have close relationships with any of them. I've been on committees at the Institute with some, but it's an interesting thing. There is an inevitable amount of social contact due to various functions. Actually, for the first time I'll be going to our graduation dinner dance because I'm fed up fighting with my friends. I'm not altogether comfortable, and I enjoy functions like that more without having candidates, especially current candidates.

LR: You discuss Dr. Calef's concept of identification with the analytic process versus with the analyst in your essay, "Some Observations on the Psychoanalytic Process." You quote him as saying, "The outcome of analysis may be dependent (not so much on the identification with the analyst per se but) on the nature and extent of the identification with its process and on the nature of the transferences that persist postanalytically." You indicate that he "broached the provocative question that the absence of such phenomena may indeed indicate areas of analytic incompleteness or failure." Could you say more about this from your own experience?

EW: Well, I think that's one of those subjects that has been debated for a long time. I think Arnie Pfeffer's essay in the 60s was really important for lots of reasons, not only because of what he found, but for the questions that he posed. I think when Freud insisted that the crucial thing in the analysis was a resolution of all of the transferences, it made a lot of difference what the real relationship was. There was originally a much more stringent attitude about how an analyst should behave, but this has changed gradually because there is more recognition that you can't ever have a complete resolution of the transference. Arnie Pfeffer pointed that out, and Vic's point of view was essentially along the same lines.

What they both said in different ways is that some of those transferences are very important and will persist. If I remember correctly, Vic even said what we all know. We hear it from our patients along the way and afterwards. At times, when they want to solve problems, they'll say in so many words, "How would Dr. So-and-so do that?" Is this perfect? No, it's imperfect. But if you look at it from the vantage point that maybe a certain amount of imperfection might be important, this is hardly a new idea in the history of ideas. There has been a relaxation in stringency for some of us.

SRR: You stated that "irrespective of the therapeutic success of the personal analysis, the candidate can never be entirely free of conflict created either by internal or external stresses or pains originating from physiological and/or psychological sources." You were talking about this much earlier. "The analyst learns to understand the inevitable reality of such pains and conflicts while maintaining a particular attitude towards his work." Are there ways that we could learn early in our analytic experience or training to be prepared for that eventuality and are there ways that you teach or supervise with this in mind?

EW: I talk about this frequently with my supervisees, especially at the beginning. I think supervisees tend to be very, very hard on themselves. I'm not against being critical, but I think there are times that it gets out of hand. Their expectations are often too great. This is something we talk about quite openly. Incidentally, I don't know if I mentioned Betty Joseph. She was one of the big influences. She comes from a quite different school of thought. Talking to her and getting to know her really well helped me feel a little more tolerant toward other analysts and other schools of thought, that we didn't know everything. American analysts tend to be relatively provincial. European analysts, for instance, know more about what goes on in American analysis than we do, let alone Latin America. She was a very special lady and was certainly important.

LR: Did you meet her in San Francisco?

EW: No, I met her at an I.P.A. training analyst conference, but she did come to San Francisco.

SRR: I don't know if you'll have anything to add to this because we've talked about it some already, but you also mentioned in this essay the shortcomings of the training analyst and how little is focused on or discussed about that. I wonder if there is anything more you might add?

EW: You mean about how little it is talked about?

SRR: Yes.

EW: I don't know the answer. I don't even know how to approach it. You usually don't begin being a training analyst until you start to flirt with senility. Then, in our institute, we are limited to three candidates at a time. I would guess that the average training analyst probably doesn't have more than twelve to fifteen analysands in their professional life. There are institutes where they don't have any limitation, which is marvelous. There is no better way, however, to start a clique than having one analyst have fourteen to fifteen analysands. We don't have access to the data to see how other analysts deal with it.

We had a revolt of the younger training analysts a year or two ago. They were furious that the older ones wouldn't talk about their cases. It wasn't an easy issue to resolve. They felt that we knew from experience what goes on. Some institutes have special courses and training in training analysis. This is a good idea, but not the same as the data and having the opportunity to share experiences.

In South America, they do this much more often than we do. They go with colleagues to each other's countries and talk with each other about training analysis issues. I think it's beginning to happen here with the establishment of this workshop. If I remember correctly, it has quadrupled in size since it started, so it reflects a need for training analysts to have more. But they still don't talk freely.

LR: You suggest the need for more systematic study of these problems in your essay, "The Analyst as the Conscience of the Analysis." You wrote: "It is imperative to find effective methods of gathering specific psychoanalytic data which would permit a more accurate dynamic formulation of the ways in which the 'realities' of the institute (in respect both to the problems of institutes in general and to the operational milieus of individual institutes) foster specific resistances which might either interfere with or actually defeat the analytic work." What has been your experience with study groups on this topic with other training analysts?

EW: Well, a large part of what goes on in the Board of Professional Standards is related to those issues. There are many study groups on all varieties of problems in different aspects of analytic training. Site visits, for instance, permit an institute to get a better idea of what its problems and issues are that might interfere with training. Usually the focus is on those things.

I had a marvelous experience just recently. We permitted the president of our society to come to the training analysts' meetings. He was completely taken aback by what happened because he had an altogether different idea of what went on at those meetings. He pictured something quite different. In turn, his feedback was very helpful. Training analysts on the whole take their own work very seriously. I've always been impressed with that.

LR: You discussed termination in your essay, "Further Observations on the Psychoanalytic Process." You say, "The agreement to terminate the analytic meeting, then, is best understood not as a decision to terminate the analytic process but as a judgment that the analyst's input is no longer required to adequately maintain the analytic process." Could you say more about this?

EW: It's so hard to decide when to terminate an analysis. There must be at least 400–500 different reasons suggested. It's not so much that you have done everything that you can do because you know damn well that you haven't. It's more related to whether you can continue the self-observation and self-inquiry beyond analysis. When you feel that the analysand can do that, that he or she is perfectly able to carry on, then you consider termination. It's not a more arbitrary matter of what particular things you'd change.

SRR: Do you think of self-analysis formally? I know you talk in terms of self-observation, do you think of it as a separate kind of work?

EW: I know I'm probably a minority, but I just can't conceive of self-analysis. I'm sure you've heard the joke about the difficulties of the countertransference. It's true. Analysis really needs two people, not just two internal objects.

SRR: I'm interested in your thoughts about the match of patient and analyst.

EW: I think again it's one of those ideals. God, wouldn't it be wonderful, but I think it's so hard. We know by experience that we don't do too terribly well in predicting, whether it's predicting what will happen if you make a certain interpretation or what's going to happen in terms of getting somebody started in analytic training.

I suppose all analyses are in a sense begun as trial analyses, whether we call it that or not. I think most analysts have been fooled awfully. You can feel that this is a virtually hopeless case that you'll pick up and work with because somebody wants you to, and it turns out to be a joy. Other times, my predictions have been a complete flop. Those are more painful, the ones we think are going to work out and don't. I don't know about the match.

LR: I liked your description of the "not-so-good hour" in the essay, "The Scope of Psychoanalysis." You wrote, "...What I have in mind by 'The Elevation of the Not-so-Good Hour' is an increased recognition of an attention to the less glamorous and exciting exchanges that take place daily at the interface of the analyst-analysand interaction, the more prosaic and 'quiet' elements of that interaction, and how the analyst and his interventions assist the patient's analytic efforts—instead of so much attention to those 'frames' in the analytic work which feature the analyst in a starring role. I believe that such a position is not only technically wise, but is a very practical application of the counsel of modesty." I am interested in any further thoughts you have about this.

EW: It's work in the trenches. After I gave that paper, I got a letter from a colleague who said, "You're right, of course. Unfortunately, so many of our colleagues would rather be involved in more glamorous things." I think that's one of the pitfalls. We do enjoy exciting hours, but whether they are the ones that are really the most helpful, I have my doubts. It's the daily work. This is why I think that some of our best analysts are those who aren't necessarily well-known or who write a lot. Each institute has one or two people like that who are not known outside their own society. The ones that analysts go to when they have troubles either with themselves or with their patients.

SRR: Do you tend to think that they are less known for some reason that they are people who are less inclined to being public?

EW: No, they are not known outside of their own society.

SRR: I may not be making a relevant connection, but are you suggesting that these are people who are less apt to be writing, that are more private people?

EW: I'm just saying that it's not necessarily those who are best known around the country who are the best analysts. I know in our own society, and I'm sure in yours, there are people who are relatively quiet, who carry on in life without all kinds of things, whom others go to when they are in trouble.

LR: You wrote about reanalysis in your essay, "Some Observations on the Psychoanalytic Process." You made a comparison between your experience with patients who return for more analysis with you and that with patients who had been previously analyzed by someone else. You mention that it is a subject that warrants more careful investigation. Have you done any further work on this topic?

EW: I haven't done it yet.

SRR: Though it also brings up the whole question about reanalysis.

EW: I think that reanalyses are really interesting because when you find out what's happened in the other, you start to think about how you would handle something like that and might handle this particular patient. It's a complex thing because there are those whom Bob Wallerstein calls the "lifers," who are going to be in treatment of one kind or another forever. Another variant are those who come for analysis but refuse any other kind of treatment because their relationship is with analysis, not with any particular analyst.

Sometimes the issue is why they didn't go back to their original analyst. They often undergo relatively brief psychotherapy, and then they go back to the analyst where there was some immediate resistance. Sometimes there is resentment about what happened before and having to deal with the realities—a kind of continuation of the termination process that hasn't been cared for. Some turn into psychotherapy because analysis isn't necessary. Where a new problem is visible, sometimes what's needed is just to guide somebody who has had a good analytic experience a little bit, so they can sort out the pieces. The question of reanalysis is a whole category, not just one thing.

SRR: When you do psychotherapy with someone whom you've analyzed, is the work now more secondary process-focused rather than primary process?

EW: It's more the secondary. It's a different kind of thing. It used to be that there was nothing but psychoanalysis. It's a whole fascinating topic, learning the differences—to accept the fact that there is no such thing as pure self-analysis. People are starting to think and talk more about what the psychotherapeutic things are that go on in any analysis. I think this questioning is healthy, rather than demanding protectiveness of the process.

SRR: Since we've got you for a few more minutes, any thoughts about the future of psychoanalysis for people such as us, just beginning in terms of practicing?

EW: Can I tell a story?

SRR: Yes.

EW: When my son was about twelve or thirteen years old, I was head of training at Mt. Zion, and my wife dropped me off after lunch at the hospital. I said, "Goodbye." My son said, "Dad, I know you'll do what you have to do, but don't tell them how hard it was when you were a resident." You see, it's just the other way around. I feel guilty when I think of how easy it was for us compared to the people of your generation. That was a period where a lot of people went into analysis because it was stylish.

What has happened in the last five to six years is that the quality of candidates is awesome. We're getting the real cream of the crop. I don't know what's going to happen. My hunch is that the focus in health will be more on social issues, not just in terms of money, but how the money is spent. I don't think we have a lot of influence. I don't know. I wish I did. There is no question that the candidates who are coming in now are dedicated and better prepared. God bless us.

SRR/LR: Thank you so much.

SELECTED BIBLIOGRAPHY

Weinshel, E. M. (1952). The psychotherapeutic aspects of schizophrenia. *Journal of Nervous and Mental Disease,* Vol. 115, pp. 471–488.

Weinshel, E. M. (1966). Severe regressive states during analysis. *Journal of the American Psychoanalytic Association,* Vol. 14, pp. 538–568.

Weinshel, E. M. (1970). Some psychoanalytic considerations on moods. *International Journal of Psycho-Analysis,* Vol. 51, pp. 313–320.

Weinshel, E. M. (1970). The changing identity of the psychiatrist in private practise: A symposium with L. C. Patterson, I. Philips, L. Schwartz, & D. Schwartz. *American Journal of Psychiatry,* Vol. 126, p. 11.

Weinshel, E. M. (1970). The ego in health and normality. *Journal of the American Psychoanalytic Association,* Vol. 18, pp. 682–735.

Weinshel, E. M. (1971). The transference neurosis: A survey of the literature. *Journal of the American Psychoanalytic Association*, Vol. 19, pp. 67–88.

Calef, V. & Weinshel, E. (1972). On certain neurotic equivalents in necrophilia. *International Journal of Psycho-Analysis*, Vol. 53, pp. 67–75.

Calef, V. & Weinshel, E. (1973). Reporting, non-reporting, and assessment in the training analysis. *Journal of the American Psychoanalytic Association*, Vol. 21, pp. 714–726.

Calef, V. & Weinshel, E. (1975). A paradigm and a credo. *Contemporary Psychology,* Vol. 20, pp. 33–34.

Calef, V. & Weinshel, E. (1975). A neglected classic II. Siegfried Bernfeld's "The facts of observation in psychoanalysis." *Journal of the Philadelphia Association for Psychoanalysis*, Vol. 2, pp. 38–40.

Calef, V. & Weinshel, E. (1976). Transference Neurosis. In: *The Encyclopedia of Neurology, Psychiatry, Psychoanalysis, and Psychology,* ed. L. Wolberg. New York: Aesculapius.

Weinshel, E. (1977). Plenary discussion of the report of Commission IV (Child Analysis) to the 1975 Conference on Psychoanalytic Education and Research. In: *Psychoanalytic Education and Research,* ed. S. Goodman. New York: International Universities Press.

Weinshel, E. (1977). "I didn't mean it": Negation as a character trait. *The Psychoanalytic Study of the Child*, Vol. 32, pp. 387–419. New Haven: Yale University Press.

Weinshel, E. (1979). Some observations on not telling the truth. *Journal of the American Psychoanalytic Association,* Vol. 27, pp. 503–533.

Calef, V. & Weinshel, E. (1979). The new psychoanalysis and psychoanalytic revisionism. *Psychoanalytic Quarterly*, Vol. 48, pp. 470–491.

Calef, V. & Weinshel, E. (1980). The analyst as the conscience of the analysis. *International Review of Psychoanalysis*, Vol. 7, pp. 279–290.

Calef, V. Weinshel, E. M., Renik, O., & Mayer, E. M. (1980). Enuresis: A functional equivalent of a fetish. *International Journal of Psycho-Analysis*, Vol. 61, pp. 295–305.

Weinshel, E. (1981). Book review: *The Mind of Watergate* by Leo Rangell. *International Review of Psychoanalysis*, Vol. 8, pp. 121–124.

Weinshel, E. (1982). The functions of the training analysis and the appointment of the training analyst. *International Review of Psychoanalysis,* Vol. 9, pp. 434–444.

Calef, V. & Weinshel, E. (1983). A note on consumation and termination. *Journal of the American Psychoanalytic Association,* Vol. 31, pp. 643–650.

Calef, V. & Weinshel, E. (1984). Anxiety and the restitutional function of homosexual cruising. *International Journal of Psycho-Analysis*, Vol. 65, pp. 45–62.

Weinshel, E. (1984). Some observations on the psychoanalytic process. *Psychoanalytic Quarterly*, Vol. 53, pp. 63–92.

Weinshel, E. (1986). Perceptual distortions during analysis: Some observations on the role of the superego in reality testing. In: *The Science of the Mental Conflict: Essays in Honor of Charles Brenner*, ed. A. Richards & M. Willick. Hillsdale, NJ: The Analytic Press.

Weinshel, E. (1987). A discussion of the various contributions. In: *The Interpretation of Dreams in Clinical Work,* ed. A. Rothstein. Madison, CT: International Universities Press.

Weinshel, E. (1988). Structural changes in psychoanalysis. *Journal of the American Psychoanalytic Association,* Vol. 36 (Suppl.), pp. 263–280.

Weinshel, E. (1988). Play and playing in adult psychoanalysis. *Bulletin of the Anna Freud Centre,* Vol. 11, pp. 108–127.

Weinshel, E. (1988). The many borders of borderline: On the virtues of modesty in psychoanalytic diagnosis. *Psychoanalytic Inquiry*, Vol. 8, pp. 333–352.

Weinshel, E. (1989). On consolability. In: *The Psychoanalytic Core*, ed. H. Blum, E. Weinshel, & R. Rodman. Madison, CT: International Universities Press.

Wallerstein, R. & Weinshel, E. (1989). The future of psychoanalysis. *Psychoanalytic Quarterly*, Vol. 58, pp. 341–373.

Blum, H., Weinshel, E., & Rodman, R., eds. (1989). *The Psychoanalytic Core: Essays in Honor of Leo Rangell, M.D.* Madison, CT: International Universities Press.

Weinshel, E. (1990). How wide is the widening scope of psychoanalysis and how solid is its structural model? Some concerns and observations. *Journal of the American Psychoanalytic Association*, Vol. 38, p. 275–296.

Weinshel, E. (1990). Further observations on the psychoanalytic process. *Psychoanalytic Quarterly*, Vol. 59, pp. 629–649.

Weinshel, E. & Renik, O. (1991). The past ten years: Psychoanalysis in the United States, 1980–1990. *Psychoanalytic Inquiry*, Vol. 11, pp. 13–29.

Weinshel, E. (1992). Therapeutic technique in psychoanalysis and psychoanalytic psychotherapy. *Journal of the American Psychoanalytic Association*, Vol. 40, pp. 327–347.

Horowitz, M., Kernberg, O., & Weinshel, E., eds. (1993) *Psychic Structure and Psychic Change.* Madison, CT: International Universities Press.

MERTON M. GILL

Merton M. Gill, M.D. was, until his death in 1993, a training analyst at the Western New England Psychoanalytic Institute and the San Francisco Psychoanalytic Institute. He was Professor of Psychiatry at the Abraham Lincoln School of Medicine, University of Illinois, Chicago and received a National Institute of Mental Health Lifetime Research Career Award. Dr. Gill taught at Yale University and the Downstate Medical Center and served on the staffs of the Menninger Clinic and the Austen Riggs Center. He was the posthumous recipient of the Mary S. Sigourney Award of the American Psychoanalytic Association. Dr. Gill was interviewed May 10, 1991.

SRR: We are very interested in your personal experience in the process of renouncing psychoanalytic metapsychology and in breaking with David Rapaport, who was such an important person to you, how the experience of taking such a strong individual stand changed your own development, and how you were affected by other people's responses to you. I imagine that publishing your critiques of Freud's case histories was quite a bold act at that point in time. I'm also curious whether you ever had a transference to or idealization of Freud?

MMG: I am reminded of an episode that took place some years ago. I was in a kind of a workshop, which was led by a very prominent analyst I will not name, and he suggested that Gill and a few other people, like George Klein and Robert Holt, in order to declare their independence of David Rapaport to whom they had been so submissive beforehand, were demonstrating their independence and newfound freedom by rejecting Rapaport's ideas. And I'm delighted to be able to tell you that I said, "Would you keep your interpretations to your office, please?" That's a beginning answer I think.

It was not difficult for me in a certain sense despite the problems that are involved in departing from the ideas of somebody who was a beloved mentor; but I was able to do it by way of identification with him because he would have been the first to say, "That's very interesting, Merton, now let's see, what are you saying?"

SRR: That's nice.

MMG: At least that's how I knew him. There are others who disagree with that view of him. But as far as I'm concerned they didn't understand him. They were too occupied with demonstrating independence to be able to see that what they experienced as invasiveness was also genuinely collaborative and respectful.

SRR: I remember you read Freud as a college student.

MMG: Oh, Freud, yes. Did I idealize Freud? Yes, to begin with. I still do. I also have a bone to pick with him. Although it's not fair. He was a child of his times—who is not? Did you hear the lecture?

SRR: This morning, you mean? No.

MMG: Well, I won't dilate on that. But, Freud in some ways, was, in my opinion, too opinionated. I don't know that a true genius, which Freud was, could make such a bold, unheard of, unprecedented step in the history of human thought without being opinionated, but I still don't like it. And in a certain way, he must be excused for making the body so central in his theory, because the body is indeed so central in the human psyche. To have expected him to make the leap from the soma to what I think of as a hermeneutic view of the soma is asking too much even of a genius. My identification with Freud, I'm going to be personal, remains strong. I take pleasure in being regarded as a heretic, and the identification takes that form.

SRR: Having worked in very different ways, conducting both classical or more traditional analyses, as well as more "here and now" transference-centered analyses, can you discuss with us the different experiences of these analyses from the analyst's perspective? For example, do you now find yourself less focused on or attuned to your own unconscious fantasy in your clinical work? Is the concept of "even hovering attention" still relevant to your work? More directly, is your feeling of engagement different, not less or more necessarily, but somehow different?

MMG: I will answer that, but first I will take exception to the way you put the question. I don't want to be stereotyped as somebody who thinks only the "here and now" is of consequence, but you said it in a way that that could be understood that way.

SRR: I don't want to be saying that.

MMG: All right. Yes, it's very different. It's not a different form of engagement. It's a greater engagement. I carry things to extremes. When I was a classical analyst, I thought, "Look, you're not supposed to have a relationship with the patient. Okay, I won't say hello and I won't say goodbye." And I didn't. Now I think that's nuts, but I tried it.

SRR: Can I ask how long you practiced classical analysis? Was it for a brief period, say several years, or was it longer?

MMG: Well, you see, I've never done much analysis, and I always hesitate to say that because I think some simpleminded people will say, "So, what gives you the right to talk about it?" But I've done a fair amount of it. I was a training analyst in San Francisco for many years. I was first a training analyst in New Haven at the Western New England Institute—Winnepesaukee, we called it. So, I've done a fair amount, but not what some of my critics do, eight to ten hours a day year after year. And I don't pretend that I have. But I don't think that that diminishes my right to speak. If you read my chapter in this new book by Oremland, you will see that I concede that Oremland has had much more experience in what he is describing than I have, and I still think he's wrong on an important point. You see, I'm by many people considered to be a very arrogant person. They're right, but they don't see my modesty, which in my judgment is at least as powerful. You don't want to hear about that.

SRR: Your classical analytic period was relatively brief?

MMG: How long did it last? Well, you see, I graduated from an analytic institute in 1945—very young, by the by, as analysts go. One reason for that was because I wasn't in the war because of a physical problem. So, I was able to continue at a time when many young people were being interrupted because of their military service. And I practiced that way, never really full-time. I've always done other things. There are those who say if you don't practice full-time analysis, you don't understand analysis. With this, of course, I disagree. I think there are a lot of people practicing full-time analysis who don't do analysis. One of the things that made a difference fairly early was that I wanted more analysis after my training analysis, and I found the styles of my various analysts, and I've had more than just those two, so different, and so different in their significance to me. That idea of the relationship in psychoanalysis began to loom very important.

Quite early in my career, I can't tell you when—I could check back in terms of research applications I made to NIMH—I got the idea of studying the interpersonal effect of an interpretation. It seemed to me that the interpersonal effect of an interpretation could often be much more important than the cognitive nature of the interpretation. So I was already on my way towards abandoning classical analysis. How many classical analysts there really are, God knows. I think many people who call themselves such really don't practice it, because it, in a certain sense, is so nonsensical if you really take it seriously—like you don't say hello or goodbye and so on.

SRR: You seem to be suggesting that your experience of engagement with the patient has become more intense in your more recent and current analytic practice?

MMG: I feel that if I don't feel related to a patient, something is very wrong.

SRR: Did you experience more sense of engagement in your second analysis? Did that experience catalyze the shift in your own work?

MMG: No, my first analysis was also in medical school, and that was dreadful. Then I had a training analysis, and then I got into trouble, and I went back to my training analyst, and it was very unsatisfactory. What did you ask me?

SRR: I am so interested in what you're saying that I'll have to think for a minute.

MMG: I have no objection to that!

SRR: You were saying that you realized....

MMG: It wasn't until I had a period of analysis quite late in life, actually it was in 1971—I was born in 1914—at age 57, which was the age at which both my parents died, that I had an analysis with a man where there was a relationship, although his description of his analytic posture was "detached," and he was anything but detached. And there's another illustration of the fascinating paradox of a man who described himself as detached because that is supposed to be how you're supposed to be, but who, nevertheless, was very involved. He dealt with that paradox and inconsistency in his own thinking by saying that there are two relationships that an analyst has with an analysand—the analytic one and a personal one.

SRR: As Freud would say.

MMG: Did Freud say that?

LR: We took a course this last semester on the relationship between Freud and Ferenczi.

MMG: With whom?

LR/SRR: With Axel Hoffer.

MMG: Oh, with Axel; you're lucky.

LR: It was wonderful. We read some of the letters between the two of them, and he would make the distinction between their analytic relationship and their friendship, saying to Ferenczi in essence, "You're my personal friend."

SRR: I'm curious. Concerning the truly meaningful analysis which took place when you were 57, was your analyst about your age or was he much older?

MMG: He was a couple of years younger. He's dead now. That wasn't the last period of work I had. That was the last analysis I had. Since then, I've had other, what some people call psychotherapy. You know how I feel about that. Actually this last period of psychotherapy has been personally the most rewarding of any therapy I've ever had. Whether that's because it built upon what had happened before, or because the relationship was different, or because I was now able to do things I couldn't do before, I don't know. I only know that it's wonderful.

SRR: What you're saying makes me think of the notion of the life cycle. I think about how certain persons, like yourself, retain the desire to pursue self-knowledge in their later years. I am reminded of—was it Fairbairn who was in analysis with Winnicott?—...

LR: Guntrip.

SRR: ...Guntrip, and you know the kind of....

MMG: With Winnicott and with Fairbairn, and he wrote about the differences between the two, and astonishingly, it was the reverse of what he had expected it to be.

SRR: But it was following Winnicott's death, I believe, that Guntrip discovered a key childhood memory never accessible before. This was quite late in his life. Guntrip's description of this event and its significance to him was quite moving. I have a similar experience of you, as an individual, continuing to grow.

MMG: I don't really know what the reason is, but I know. I'm fairly ill physically. I have et cetera. I don't want to get more into it, but I could have a stroke, et cetera, and besides I am getting along. It's like fuck 'em, I mean. Say what I think.

SRR: We appreciate your openness so much. As you must be aware, we hear so little, really, about the personal experience of the analyst. Our curiosity about this, in fact, is responsible for this project. I wonder how you would describe your concept of the "analyzing instrument"? Perhaps you wouldn't make use of that concept at all?

MMG: I had lunch with Evy Schwaber yesterday, and we agreed that in an analysis which is truly worthwhile the analyst changes significantly and is not the same person—we assume a better person. So, I agree with her that the analyst is an instrument, but as an instrument, nevertheless the analyst undergoes significant changes because if he is, or she—those pronouns please excuse me—…

SRR: Oh, please don't worry about it.

MMG: …is what I think an analyst should be, the analyst will accept being analyzed by the patient. It's still the patient who is the analysand, you understand, but the analyst ought to learn more about him- or herself in an analysis that has been truly worthwhile.

SRR: What you said leads naturally to our next question. I imagine that your sense of yourself must be greatly enriched by your patients' perceptions of you. I wonder about the effect on the analyst of being so informed about him- or herself?

MMG: I'm grateful. It spreads out into the other aspects of my life. I behave differently with my wife now. She's not always tremendously pleased about that, but I am.

SRR: Does the patient's awareness of having an impact on the analyst become a central aspect of the clinical work?

MMG: I don't have any more patients really. I have two patients now once a week. I don't do any analysis anymore. But your question is, are they aware of their impact on me?

SRR: Or on the analyst?

MMG: I am suddenly reminded of an episode with a current patient. He said, "You seem very worried about this. It's all right, I decided myself. You didn't make me do it."

SRR: Are you supervising now?

MMG: Yes, not in our institute, that is to say, the establishment institute. But I do have two candidates from our division 39 branch, which has a training arm. And I do a great deal of supervision of so-called psychotherapy. I can't even say the word anymore, because for me, you can practice once a week sitting up and do analysis, and you can practice five times a week lying down and do half-assed psychotherapy.

SRR: You must observe your supervisees develop in response to the feedback from their patients. I would think that it would be a most significant experience for the patient to recognize that he or she has an impact on the analyst, that this would foster a sense of mutuality.

MMG: Absolutely.

SRR: I'm wondering whether this dynamic becomes consciously articulated, whether it is discussed in the analysis?

MMG: Do you mean conscious to the candidate?

SRR: To the patient.

MMG: To the patient? I don't know. You know with patients, it's a very common complaint—"This is so unfair. I mean, I've got to tell you all about myself, and I know nothing about you." There's a case report by Frederickson in a recent *Contemporary Psychoanalysis* where he took abuse from the patient month after month, maybe year after year, and finally he couldn't stand it anymore, and, he said, they were standing nose to nose, and he bawled the shit out of the patient. And the patient said, "Thank God, you're a human being." That is to say he had influenced the analyst. The analyst had to admit that he had been influenced by this attack. I think that's terribly important. That's part of its being a relationship. And if there's a relationship, two people influence each other. Remembering that there's an analysand and an analyst, but it's not a symmetrical relationship, I tried that. I don't know if I should tell you that, but.... Speaking of Ferenczi, I tried mutual analysis twice.

LR: Did you?

MMG: Disaster.

SRR: Well, it's very useful for us to hear that. That's a learning experience we would never get to know about.

MMG: There were certain complexities that would make me hesitant about generalizing to the idea that it is absolutely impossible. Actually I have a supervisee now who is conducting a mutual analysis with a friend, mostly by telephone, and it seems to be working, although she seems to be getting a lot more out of it than he, so I don't know. But the two times I tried it, it was a disaster.

SRR: What made you decide to try it?

MMG: That's the kind of guy I am. I always do things to extremes, and as I became more and more impressed with the centrality of the relationship, I would naturally say, "So, let's really have a relationship." An analysis has to remain asymmetrical, I believe. Though I remind you I said there were circumstances that would make me loath to generalize. Maybe some people could carry it off. It would depend on the couple, of course, and what their prior relationship was and so on. Maybe peers could do it, maybe a couple of analysts of a particular kind of temperament could do it with each other, I don't know.

LR: You had touched on this in your interview in the *American Psychoanalyst*.

MMG: It's not an interview, it was an essay. You see, that's characteristic of me, too. I won't let even such a small slip go by. I know you know it was an essay.

LR: Actually, I didn't remember it as an essay, but I don't mind your correcting me.

This is the quote I wanted to ask you about: "One is the controversy over the range of applicability of the psychoanalytic technique in terms of frequency of sessions, chair, couch, type of patient, and experience of therapist. I believe it can be demonstrated that with the changed view of transference which follows from the person point of view and the concomitant recognition of the centrality of the analysis of the transference as the decisively defining feature of psychoanalysis, the range of applicability of the psychoanalytic technique can be much extended." As you have tried different arrangements, that is, different portions of the patient relative to the analyst or different numbers of sessions per week, what impact do you think those differences in arrangement have had on the relative intrapsychic and interpersonal experiences between you and the patient?

MMG: I don't think generalizations are possible. Let me emphasize that I wrote of analytic technique, not the carrying through of a "full" analysis. Perhaps I should better speak, as Roy Schafer does, of the "analytic attitude." To begin with, as an indication of how strongly I believe that, I teach that to psychiatric residents. You can imagine how some of the other supervisors feel about that. They say I'm trying to make little psychoanalysts out of them. There are those who say, "You would teach a resident to analyze transference? That's very dangerous, and so on." I don't think so, and I get good results, and the patients get far more, in my opinion, than they ordinarily get from the usual kind of psychotherapy that's taught to a resident. But, then, of course, the frequency and the posture, and so on, are important influences. I would be stupid to deny that. But how much analytic work can be done is a matter of the couple. Like I said a while ago, there are people on the couch five times a week in whom no analysis goes on, and it's not always the analyst's fault, although, just between us, I think it is. That's something of an exaggeration. There are persons who simply can't bear it. So you do what you can with them. Supportive psychotherapy has a place in this world, and so does Elavil and all the rest of that stuff. It's just not my bag. I wouldn't belittle the enormous relief many suffering human beings have gotten, but symptomatic and supportive therapy are not what I'm interested in. Have I answered your question?

LR: Just more of your thoughts, with particular patients....

MMG: Now, for instance, I have something to say about that. Ernst Kris once said to me, "If I can't see a patient five times a week, I feel I lose touch with the unconscious." I think that's rubbish. I can see somebody once a week and with the right kind of person, where things are moving, from one week to the next, it's a continuous process. There's no hiatus, there's no Monday crust, there's no weekend crust. But it depends. There are people, of course, with whom frequent contact is necessary. In fact, that's what I said in my 1954 essay, which some people think is classical and the high point of my achievements, after which, as I said once from a public platform, "Everything else has been downhill." In 1954, I said, "The frequency of sessions is necessary to keep open the wound into the unconscious." I believed it; then, I was a classical analyst. In the first place, I'm not so sure you have to wound the unconscious. In fact, if we take seriously our beliefs about the nature of the human psyche, we could very easily translate that into a sadomasochistic interaction that we make wounds into the unconscious. I lost my train of thought.

LR: ...About the frequency of sessions and the 1954 essay.

MMG: In 1954, and how I radically altered my views in an essay in 1984. That's the one where everyone thought, "Merton has lost his marbles." I was on a panel on converting psychotherapy into psychoanalysis, where I had the good fortune to make that quip that, according to my fellow analysts, I've been going downhill since 1954. Of course, my position on the panel was, "Why do you talk about converting psychotherapy to psychoanalysis? If you do it right, you're always doing psychoanalysis. You don't have to convert anything." But that's not accepted dogma. There's going to be an exchange of letters between myself and Robert Wallerstein in the new issue of the *International Journal* on this subject, because Wallerstein wrote a long piece on the history of this problem of the relationship between psychoanalysis and psychotherapy in which he implied that he, too, saw me as going downhill. The way he expressed that sentiment was by saying that whereas I used to see the difference between psychoanalysis and psychotherapy, I now blur them, and I have regressed to the position of Franz Alexander. I didn't like that for some reason! And so, I wrote a letter to the *International Journal*, and they agreed to publish it with his reply.

SRR: You no longer consider the achievement of any regressive state necessary or necessarily desirable in an analysis. Is that correct?

MMG: That's a hard question. I'm still thinking about it. I don't know.

LR: Could you say something about your process of thinking about it?

MMG: I have referred several times to what Arlow, a "classical" analyst, said, "It's not a matter of regression. It's just a matter of regressive tendencies that were always there becoming more available and open." And in that sense you could say, it's progressive. Actually, Schaefer has written in an illuminating way of the dialectic between regression and progression. That—just simply think—I have a bit about it in my chapter in the Oremland book—there is, in classical analysis, an unnecessary additional iatrogenic regression, I feel pretty sure, and for that we are indebted to Leo Stone and his quite remarkable monograph entitled, "The Psychoanalytic Situation." Whether the concept of regression to the infantile neurosis makes sense, I don't know. In the first place, the whole idea of the reinstatement of an earlier phase of life is under heavy attack. In addition, my tendency is to feel that the regression is there, and palpable, and ready to be worked with, and there is no need to increase it. But I'm hesitant.

LR: In your experience do you think the quality of the regression or the need for regression is different for individuals who have undergone specific significant traumas?

MMG: My experience does not entitle me to reply.

LR: One of the thoughts I had as I was reading your essay in the *American Psychoanalyst*...

MMG: She learns!

LR: ...is that when you're working with this current transference....

MMG: Transference is never solely current.

LR: Right. Do you think that you might discover the interpersonal effect of the trauma sooner in some ways if you're paying consistently close attention to what's getting enacted with you in the room in the here and now?

MMG: I will make a very arrogant remark, along with a few other arrogant remarks. Freud said, "There's only one way to make analysis shorter." Remember? "Do it better," he said. In my opinion, this is doing it better, and it will be shorter. I would say that's likely, but I don't have the experience that would enable me to say, "Yes, I have cases with a specific trauma at such and such an age, and so on." It's like I told you, I haven't done as much analysis.

SRR: When one regards the transference as closely involved with continual plausible speculations on the patient's part about the analyst's inner state, one must then conceive of psychoanalysis as an intensely dyadic relationship. So many analysands demonstrate longings in analysis for a greater intimacy with the early mother, to be attuned to the mother's inner state. From this perspective, psychoanalysis could be conceived of as offering a new opportunity for an experience with a certain similarity to the original desire. If we think of analysis in this way, doesn't the real person of the analyst assume a vital importance, as well as the particular match between analyst and patient?

MMG: I'm inclined to say yes, but once again, I feel hesitant. I think.... What's her name is doing research on it—Judy Kantrowitz —on the match. Yes, I think we are all of us so inevitably children of our own culture, that if we are working with someone from the same culture, there will be manifold commonalities that will pass unnoticed because they are held in common. You know the old saw about if a fish were a scientist what's the last thing a fish would discover? Water. It's the same idea. And in that sense, to work with persons of other cultures and colors must be—I haven't had the pleasure—a fascinating and broadening experience, because some of these taken-for-granted assumptions that we haven't made explicit might rise to awareness. I have a little bit of that now. I have a friend, an analyst, an Indian. We meet once a week. He has the idea that some of the things I think should be recorded for whatever, and we talk. And some of his Indian background, not much, unfortunately, because he's quite Americanized even though he grew up in India, some of those things, for example. He doesn't understand what's all the fuss about one theory, and that is related to the polytheistic Indian culture as against our monotheistic of which we are so proud.

He can't see what all the fuss is about: "We have lots of gods. It's nicer, I mean, if you don't like this one, you like that one." It's interesting. He thinks I'm caught up in my insistence that we're going to have to decide between self psychology and ego psychology and adopt what, following my friend, Irwin Hoffman, I call the social constructivist paradigm. My Indian friend thinks of himself as much more tolerant than I. He says that his position is so much more consistent with the notion of relativity of truth than mine. It's as if I think we're going to have to find out what is really the way to do analysis, and that's related to his comfort with polytheism. That's all. But that's the only illustration I can give you.

SRR: Have you found over the years that you were a better match for certain patients?

MMG: Better match with than with others?

SRR: Yes.

MMG: I had an interesting illustration the other day with one of my patients, who came in waving a copy of *Newsweek* with an article on the man beaten up in Los Angeles and said, "You know, …." He was obviously on the side of the police. And I lost my cool. I regained it, fortunately, and we were able to work on it. But for a bit, I lost my cool and I couldn't stand what he was saying. But I don't think that's bad, if you can catch it before you've wrecked something. But altogether the analysis of the transference is primarily a retrospective activity. If you accept the dyadic nature of the analytic situation, you will be able to function—this is something that I owe to a significant degree to my friend Irwin Hoffman—to be more spontaneous, even though you still maintain analytic discipline, so to speak, whatever that is. With that greater spontaneity, you will inevitably engage in, well, you're always interacting. But many think if you're silent, you're not interacting, which is of course nonsense. But, there are many different kinds of interacting. And if you allow yourself greater spontaneity, you will get drawn into more of what Sandler calls "role responsiveness," and you'll have to deal with that by looking back on it. You can't do it in the moment. In addition to which, the complexities of interaction are such that even if you tried to do it while it was happening, you'd only be able to see this or that facet, and it's only over time that you might become alerted to another facet of it. I don't know what started me on that. What was the question?

SRR: About the match.

MMG: Yeah, okay.

LR: I want to ask you about Dr. Hoffman because you've mentioned him twice. How has your knowing him and working with him influenced your own development as an analyst?

MMG: He was never really my student. He is my collaborator, and he is often my teacher. I predict that he will be one of the most prominent analysts of his generation, prominent in the sense of making important contributions. When we were both…when he was still at the University of Illinois in Chicago, which is where I am now, he was already finished with his internship, or whatever you call it. We began to meet more and more regularly, and then we began a kind of research that eventuated in a coding system that we developed in common, and it just became more and more obvious to me that he is my superior. I take some pride in the ability to recognize that.

SRR: It's a strong word.

MMG: Well, he's smarter than I am. He's more careful than I am. His mind is more dialectical and complex than mine, and he teaches me. I'm delighted. I mean, I don't think many people are lucky enough to have somebody like that when they get to be fairly old. There are interesting complexities, you understand, in such a matter. After all, there still is the Oedipus complex, but we're managing. We talk about it. That's what makes it possible.

LR: What is your creative process like together? In to what do your ideas evolve when you're together?

MMG: I come up with an idea, and he says, "Yes, Merton, but…." That's what usually happens. And his contribution clarifies, extends, elaborates, and makes more dialectic what I had thought I understood. I just wrote an essay that I'm going to give in Italy, and I asked him to look it over. There's a hurry, and so far I've only gotten back from him the first sixteen pages. In those sixteen pages, there's one place where he says, "That's a good idea, Merton." I can show you at least a dozen other points in the essay where he says, "You didn't understand this," "This isn't quite right." Now whether that is the correct ratio, in general, I will not bother myself with.

LR: This is a quote that I selected from his review of your work, from the chapter by him: "The point is that they repeat patterns of interaction; patients have reason to believe that the analyst's inner experience and outward behavior are colored by the pressure they exert to make the relationship repeat those patterns." In your experience, do you think patients are aware of the pressure they exert on the analytic relationship?

MMG: Usually not, because they feel they're not supposed to. It's your job to make them aware of it. That's part of a very important aspect of analysis that I think is not as widely understood as it should be. You have to show the patient that you want to know all he is experiencing about you, and the only way you can show him that is by interpreting the implicit references that he makes to how he's experiencing you. After a while then, when the patient understands that you really want to know, he'll tell you.

LR: That was the second part of my question. How do you help a patient discover his or her internal experience of you?

MMG: You have to show them that you want to know and that you can take it, even if it's critical.

SRR: That brings to mind Dr. Schwaber's work.

MMG: Yes. Dr. Schwaber and I have been struggling for quite a while to come to some integration of our respective views. We respect one another. We feel that there's a disagreement, and we're trying very hard to figure out what it is. I think we made a little progress at lunch yesterday. In fact, I thought I had an idea about it this morning, but that probably should be discussed with Dr. Schwaber.

LR: I want to ask about your coding scheme in your essay, "A Method for Studying the Analysis of Aspects of the Patient's Experience of the Relationship." How much did that scheme develop over time? Did you find it useful?

MMG: I'm embarrassed to say that we dropped it.

LR: It seemed elaborate, as if great effort had been put into developing it.

MMG: I would disagree with that to some degree. One of its assets is that it is as simple as it is in contrast to the usual kind of scheme of that sort. It's comparatively quite simple. We dropped it. We don't know its reliability, we don't know its validity, we don't know its usefulness. There was a study conducted at Menninger's by Horowitz, who used the scheme with some elaboration. It was simple enough that he needed to elaborate it, and found it of some use. There has been, in a certain sense, further work on it in terms of related concepts, the two principal ones being Luborsky's "the core conflict relational theme," CCRT, and Hartvig Dahl's "frame analysis," which you may not know about.

LR: I don't.

MMG: For that, you would have to read Dahl. So, in that sense, it has been carried further by certain persons who are using closely allied concepts. Why didn't we carry it further? Because neither Irwin nor myself is an empirical scientist. As I said in the essay, "It's not my temperament. It's not my skill." I'm sorry. I think it's a good beginning for what could be important research, and I hope someday somebody will pick it up. But Irwin and I are much more interested in "conceptual" research.

LR: I have a second question from that same study. It is in describing some of the theoretical background for that study, and this is a quote that I found interesting. You are talking about the patient: "But he will just as often disavow his perceptions, because they are so intimately, even if indirectly, linked with repressed infantile wishes and conflicts. The patient's absolutizing of his own experience, his sense of its necessity often depends on a disavowal of situational factors to which he has been selectively responsive. Conversely, his sense of the relativity of his experience and of his own perspective, and therefore of alternative possibilities, is enhanced to the extent that he becomes aware he has selectively attended to particular facets of reality."

MMG: That's a mouthful.

LR: What I find unique in the concept is the idea of selective attention.

MMG: That's ours only, as it applies to analysis.

LR: That was the question I had. I wondered if you had developed that concept after working with Rapaport?

MMG: No, it's Irwin's. This is Irwin's substitute for "distortion."

LR: I find the concept interesting in that it seems to incorporate both cognitive and affective elements.

MMG: Absolutely.

LR: Could you elaborate some more?

MMG: It's Irwin's invention. I don't know what there is to elaborate. It just says.... The idea that the patient is distorting what's going on is not correct. It is true of the many possible ways of understanding what's going on, that the patient chooses a particular one, and he chooses that particular one as a result of both his neurosis, or infantile experience, if you wish, and what's going on now in the relationship. It becomes the.... There's an interesting way of putting it in an article by Protter. He says, "The analyst's function is to make the patient a psychoepistemologist." If a patient is really analyzed, the patient becomes a relativist. The possibility of righteous indignation is almost, only almost, gone, because righteous indignation should still be acceptable, as well as certainty. That's Irwin's. People think...or many people seem to feel that it follows that if you adopt a hermeneutic, constructivist position, you can never be sure of anything. It might be this, it might be that—that you will be left in an obsessional quagmire. That's not true. Pragmatically, you have a right to be certain, but you should always also know you could be mistaken.

LR: One question I have is what follows from the analyst communicating this idea to the patient? Does the patient become more aware of this pattern, and...?

MMG: Yes, and in time becomes a psychoepistemologist.

LR: In your experience, do patients feel any liberation of affect at the time that they become aware of the choices they have been making? Is there a connection between the cognitive capacity to see choices and the affective capacity to experience them?

MMG: That is a consummation devoutly to be hoped for.

SRR: How do you conceptualize psychic change?

MMG: Like I just said, or to express it more specifically, the range of empathy that a person develops with other human beings broadens. They can catch themselves more quickly when they are about to enact an old neurotic pattern, and sometimes even stop doing it. I mean, all this talk about structural change, it seems to me, is so abstract and mechanical that I prefer to speak in the kinds of terms that I am now using. To some extent, now the data, by the by, the experiences in follow-up studies by—who's the New York man? Pfeffer—the repetition of the transference neurosis in brief and rapidly with the interviewer in a follow-up study. I mean, the notion that the neurosis is dissolved is nonsense. You're just in a better position to catch it before you do these things that are going to hurt you and other people.

SRR: Do you think in terms of mourning?

MMG: I don't think of it in those terms. When you ask me the question, it makes perfectly good sense. I presume that a significant change in a human being must be accompanied by the severance of some old loyalties. And I can't imagine a person doing that without feeling sad. I mean, neurosis is also like an old shoe, and the new shoes squeak for quite a while. Sure. There's another point that Irwin insists upon—I believe correctly—the notion of new experiences against old experiences in the psychoanalytic situation is an oversimplified way of putting it. There's always the old in the new and always the new in the old. Well, there's always the old in the new, whether there's always the new in the old, it depends on whether you're getting anywhere.

SRR: You have already discussed this to some extent; the question concerned what it is that is internalized through the process of psychoanalysis. You spoke about internalization earlier, so I wonder...?

MMG: I have strong feelings about that. There's an amusing passage in Stone's book to which I referred a bit ago. It said, "The classical analyst holds that if you pass your former analyst on the street, you should have no more feeling than if you had passed a brass monkey." Now, that's an interesting remark to think about. In the first place, if you pass a brass monkey walking down the street and have no feelings, what the hell is the matter with you? In the second place, the implicit remark that maybe your analyst was like a brass monkey should also not be ignored. I mean it's very funny. Of course, Stone says that's utter nonsense. No, you carry your analyst around with you for the rest of your life. That's not a bad thing if you had a good analyst. And they're not all good. I'm a bit of a ham. I imagine it's obvious by now, maybe more than a bit. And that was released by analysis. I was quite inhibited. I couldn't tell a joke. It works sometimes.

SRR: We're interested in your thoughts about the role of the superego.

MMG: Robert Knight, my training analyst, in his presidential address, I think it was—he was president in 1952, I'm terrible on dates, I know the date, because I looked it up recently in another connection—said, "The time has come to rise above principle and do the right thing." You understand the reference to the superego. Proper superego....In the first place, the superego should not disappear, but it should become more flexible. You should be able to tolerate things that you used to find unbearable. You shouldn't live solely on the basis of foreordained, cast-in-marble principles. They say that that's what makes women better than men, better human beings than men. It depends on how you look at it. There are those who say it makes them better human beings, and those who say that shows how corruptible they are, that women have holes in their superego.

SRR: Holes or more flexible superegos?

MMG: I say, it depends on which viewpoint you take.

SRR: Which is yours?

MMG: My view? I think generalizations about the sexes stink to begin with. I'm very fond of women; I'm also very fond of men. I'm more fond of women than I am of men. How that happened has something to do with my personal history, but be that as it may, I hate these generalizations. Some women are impossible, some men are wonderful. Even with regard to the superego issues. When I read essays, women are this way, and men are this way, generalized ideas about mother transference and father transference, I get a little sick to my stomach.

SRR: We're interested in your thoughts about training analysis. What do you consider most important in terms of the analyst's development? Do you believe that a training analysis can serve as a full therapeutic analysis, given the particular problems inherent to training analyses?

MMG: The sins of the fathers shall be visited on the sons unto the seventh generation. That's one of the difficulties with psychoanalysis, that it's an apprenticeship. And the influence of your own analysis on your subsequent analytic work is so profound that if your own analysis is cast in a rigid mold, you're going to have to fight like hell to overcome it. That's why so many people have a second analysis. Whether the first analysis can be a good analysis, which you asked me, is an interesting question. I think it's possible if you have a good analyst, but I'm not—this is arrogant, you can include it if you like, I don't give a damn, I mean I do care—but I don't think there are so many good analysts running around.

SRR: I don't know that that's arrogant.

MMG: Well, it sounds like, "I know, and there are very few like me," and stuff, but I don't think there are. And it shows in the next generation. My hope is, and I think there is some evidence to back it up, that analysis is slowly, establishment analysis is slowly beginning to recognize that it is a dyad, and that that's at the heart of understanding it, which is not to deny the centrality of a one-person psychoanalysis as well. That's a mistake I made for quite awhile. As I began to see what was wrong with a one-person analysis, in my usual impetuous, exaggerated way, I threw away the one-person analysis in favor of a two-person analysis. Irwin would never make that mistake. That's how he's my teacher. There's a one-person analysis, too, and a one-person psychology, which, by the by, is significantly related to the fact that man is a biological organism as well as a person. I hope the implications of that are clear, but anyhow, that's an important part of it.

LR: I think it would be helpful to hear you spell that out a bit.

MMG: I'd like to tell you an aphorism I invented that I'm proud of. I have to make sure I say it right. The human body does not come about....The human body is not created by social intercourse, but by sexual intercourse. You're supposed to find that funny, but it may take a little while to sink in. The prominence that is progressively being given to the social aspects, as it were, of the human psyche, unfortunately, is leading some former analysts to abandon the centrality of the body, which I tried to say in that essay. It's as though man is created through a social interaction, but the body is there, too, and the body came from sexual intercourse, not social intercourse. That's the meaning of the aphorism. It occurred to me while I was listening to a self psychology presentation at the last meeting of Division 39. You are a psychologist, and you are a physician. Evy told me that. I didn't look up your biographies. The reason I agreed to do this is that I so liked the interviews I read.

SRR: Thank you.

MMG: I was listening to a presentation of an essay. It was a panel, a self psychology panel, and they were telling about a patient, who was liberated to the point where he could buy himself a Corvette. And he said it was wonderful. He could play with it like he couldn't play with things before. I mean the phallic, masturbatory implications were just so obvious, and they completely ignored them. That's when it occurred to me. Incidentally, I got up and said so. I didn't use the aphorism, and so on. But that was when it occurred to me. I'm sorry, but that related to the whole business, you said you wanted to ask me, one of you did. What did I mean by that remark about the self and the body? I forget....Did you ask me that in a letter or...?

SRR: Yes.

MMG: It's a question of the relative superordinacy of the relationship between persons and biological organism, and that's where, in my judgment, if I understand him correctly, Freud went wrong. A friend of mine wrote a book recently which was initially entitled, "Where Freud Went Wrong." The publisher talked him out of it. I'm not sure Freud went wrong altogether even on this matter. You see Freud is such a complex genius that you can quote him on almost any side of a question that you care to. Why did Freud insist that he was talking about psychosexuality and not sexuality?

Because he knew there was something wrong with a concept of sexuality in which the soma, the body, was the regnant factor. I think he knew that somewhere. But the denial of the significance of the body was so paramount that I think in reacting against that, he had to take the position he did. If you read the—I know this, I usually don't remember things this way, even when I was younger—but the fourth preface to the "Three Contributions of the Theory of Sex" says, "It's lovely that people have accepted my ideas about repression, but I remain convinced that the other bio..."—no, he didn't say other biological factors, but simply that biological factors are equally "valid." And the instinctual drive is a borderline concept, and so on.

And, by the way, something that occurred to me not long ago, which is an insight of some consequence, is that Freud's change from the first anxiety theory to the second one in "Inhibitions, Symptoms, and Anxiety," was a hermeneutic shift in my opinion. Because, whereas the first theory said repression of libido leads to anxiety, the second theory says anxiety leads to repression. How much more sense, intuitive sense, the second theory makes. If you're nervous, if you're frightened, you try to forget it. Now, if you don't discharge some energy, the energy is converted to anxiety. As he said in his metaphor, like wine turning to vinegar. The change is a hermeneutic turn.

LR: To be sure I understand, can you explain what you mean when you're calling it a hermeneutic shift?

MMG: I mean that the body is very important in terms of what it means, not qua the body. When you start talking about the fact that it's important in terms of what it means then you're talking hermeneutically. If you talk about orality, anality, as if you're talking about the mouth and the anus, instead of emphasizing, you mean what the mouth and the anus have come to mean to this person. If you talk about it as such, that's not hermeneutics. That's old-line classical analysis.

SRR: When did you make that shift?

MMG: Which?

SRR: In terms of meaning, what you just described in terms of the meaning of the body. It's such a profound....

MMG: I don't know; I don't know. An early step was that I said the body is being—the issue is like with the one-person and two-person issue, and they are related. I said, you know, they're making a fuss about the body. It's just not that important. And for a time, I abandoned a central tenet of classical analysis. God be praised, I was able to come back to it. Like in a workshop yesterday, a case was being presented of a woman who blushed uncontrollably whenever she performed. And I said to the group, "I'm going to take a chance and say something. Do you think it's possible that this blushing...?" You see, the very fact that I'm giving you this illustration means that it ain't all hermeneutics; I'm still puzzled. I said, "Do you think it's possible that the blushing was a displacement to a different part of the body of the engorgement of other parts of the body in preparation for the sexual act?" And they all said, "Of course!" And I was astonished because I, in my experience, maybe because I live in Chicago, think many people don't believe that anymore. They all said sure. They wondered what was the matter with me that I was raising it as something that they might disagree with.

But you see, even just thinking about it now, makes me think I haven't really...I haven't made it yet, because to say that it's an engorgement of another part of the body is quite somatic, so it's not just...the meaning of the body, it's the body too. I appreciate this invitation, this invitation not only because I love to talk about myself and I love to talk about my ideas, but because I'm going to have to think about that. I didn't think about it before. That's one of the things I'm proud of. If I talk, I run up against...I suddenly realize that I don't understand that or that I've been in my impetuous way too, if you'll forgive the expression, cocksure about what I think. I'll think about it some more.

SRR: What is stimulating for us is hearing how you continue to ponder, to question. You don't hesitate to turn the idea upside down, to say, "I see it differently now."

MMG: I don't know where I got it from, but....I don't believe in higher powers, but if they exist I thank them for it.

LR: I have a question about training analysis. In the Hoffman chapter, he describes one of your positions. He says, "Instead of being concerned about managing his own behavior so as to promote a nonspecific regression on the one hand and a spontaneous, specific transference on the other, Gill's attention as a clinician is devoted to identifying the various disguised expressions of transference, such as displacement and identification."

My question is, how does one deal with the defense of identification in a training analysis? What are your thoughts about identification as a defensive process in the treatment?

MMG: Nothing is simple. Identification can be defensive and at the same time liberating. I said your analyst lives in you, is in you as long as you live. The question is, can you cope with it? Can you disagree with him if necessary? Which means that a very heavy burden lies on the training analyst because the whole setup is designed to make the candidate submissive. A training analyst who is a good training analyst has to conduct the analysis in such a way that the candidate is free to disagree with him. We don't see that much. We see that when cliques are formed in our institutes, they cluster around a charismatic or at least an analyst with clout and his analysands. That's not nice. It's the kind of thing I call obscene. I don't think the ordinary obscenities are the worst obscenities, these are the worst obscenities.

I mean, if a candidate is a clone of his training analyst, it's been a lousy analysis. So, you say, how do you deal with the identification? Every time you see it rearing its ugly head as an idealization you should nip it in the bud. Well, better let it go for a while, though not like Kohut says. You know, I don't know if he ever got....He says you let it flower and then later you deal with it. And I'm not sure in some instances it's ever dealt with in Kohutian analysis. But I should say a word about self psychology before I'm through, lest I be misunderstood. But anyhow, about the training analysis, yeah. In just the same way, in the analysis of an ordinary person, you have to help the person see that the person has a right to comment on your behavior and your experience, and criticize your behavior and your experience, and you have to listen to that in a genuine way, genuine to the point, as Schwaber emphasizes, that it will even change you. That obviously should take place in spades in a training analysis where it's more difficult, but should be done.

It reminds me of something I'm accustomed to saying about a training analysis, with regard to the termination. An ordinary citizen has gone through four, five, six years of the most intimate kind of relationship, and one day they decide they will never meet again. How can a candidate possibly empathize with that when he knows that he's going to remain in contact with his training analyst for the rest of his life. Well, I rub it in because I would try to help him see that he is having an experience that is so different from what his patients will be having that he should be especially tender and gentle with them on the point. I'm not saying that means you should always have a tapering off period, as Stone suggested might sometimes be desirable.

Again, my experience is inadequate to permit me to speak with any sense of authority on the subject. I don't know how an analysis should end. I only know that even in the best of circumstances, it must be experienced as such an incredible abandonment that maybe analyses are supposed to end in some other….I had an experience of that sort once that I paid for in blood. I'll tell you it's a personal experience, but I don't have to name names and I don't have to reveal myself particularly to do it. In one of my later analyses, I was with a man who obviously was attracted to me—I don't mean, well, of course homosexually, too, but that's not important—sufficiently so, that as we were going to end, he said, after much thought, I've decided to do something I've never done before. I agree that I will have a relationship with you after the analysis is over. I paid for it because it was a manifestation of a very important aspect of the analysis that was not dealt with—I'm willing to say—my mother. He enacted with me that, which meant that I was fortified yet further in failing to deal with some of my feelings about my mother, and I had to deal with them subsequently. Happily, I was able to with another person.

So, you see, I'm saying, it's not all black and white. There is something about the termination that should be a termination too. As Modell says, what is this strange kind of business where you enter an intimate relationship with the understanding that it has to come to an end. Where else do you do that in life? Analysis is a little nuts. I mean, it's a remarkable invention. Freud's genius lies as much in that invention, as much as in what he discovered about the human psyche, this strange thing, method. That you start with another human being, you want that human being to express himself or herself as intimately as possible. You become involved, but it's still asymmetrical, it's not mutual, and it's understood that it will come to an end. That's a remarkable invention. We don't exclaim about it often enough.

SRR: But with training analysis, termination is different.

MMG: One of my two patients asked me the other day, "What's the difference between psychoanalysis and psychotherapy?" He seemed to notice the couch for the first time. He sits once a week. And I said, "That's an important subject. We'll talk about it next time, all right?" He began the next hour by saying, "You know, you kicked me out last hour." I said, "You mean when I said we'll talk about it next time." He said it jokingly, but he meant it, and he didn't mean it, you know. And he asked me about the difference, and I told him about the frequency. And he said, "But, I come much more often than once a week," meaning by that, I think about it in between. Doesn't that mean I'm coming more often? But that's when things are going well. The patient works in between, which has something to do with my feelings about this rigidity about frequency. I was answering a question thereby. Now what was the question?

SRR: You were talking about termination.

MMG: About termination. And the analyst and identification. Okay, that's an aspect of identification.

SRR: And about what transpires after termination, due to the existence of the institute.

MMG: That the candidate never experiences the poignancy of a separation. Although the ordinary patient does have the analyst in his heart, the candidate doesn't really understand what a violent rupture complete physical separation is to a human being, especially since issues of separation are so central.

SRR: You've described interpretation as being in part an expression of the analyst's psychic reality. Apart from listening to the patient, how can the analyst best gain as full access to his or her own psychic reality? Would you think of self-analysis? Do you practice it?

MMG: I don't do it in any kind of a systematic way. Partly because of my pleasure in introspection. I'm thinking about myself, and I enjoy myself very much. I keep thinking about what it means when I talk to somebody in all my life situations. I'm not thinking a lot about you two young women, but I'm thinking about it some. I imagine you're enjoying me, not just because of what I say, but because I make jokes, and I'm funny. I'm kind of attractive for an old man, and so on. I'm assuming that, and I'm displaying myself to some degree for you. And I think that's all right. That sort of thing. I think about it all the time. In all my life relationships. I don't understand how a good analyst could help himself. I mean, that's the kind of thing you're interested in, no? Do you think you can shut it off for a while? I can't.

SRR: Do you think that most of us are like that, or do you think…?

MMG: Not enough of us are like that.

SRR: I think you are unusually….

MMG: Perhaps. Perhaps, maybe that's because I find myself such interesting company. I'm always reminded in that connection of something Bernard Shaw said. He spent a lot of his time reading instead of meeting with people, and he said, why should I talk with ordinary people when I can converse with the mighty dead? I know how arrogant that sounds. What did you want to ask me?

LR: I was very interested in the work you did with Margaret Brenman-Gibson on hypnosis. I want to read to you a passage from Ferenczi's 1929 essay, "The Principle of Relaxation and Neocatharsis." Similar to you, he seemed to be trying to determine the similarities and differences between the patient under hypnosis and under the influence of the transference. This is what he said:

> "But after we had succeeded in a somewhat deeper manner than before in creating an atmosphere of confidence between physician and patient and in securing a fuller freedom of affect, hysterical physical symptoms would suddenly make their appearance, often for the first time in an analysis extending over years. These symptoms included paresthesias and spasms, definitely localized, violent emotional movements like miniature hysterical attacks, sudden alterations of the state of consciousness, slight vertigo, and a clouding of consciousness often with subsequent amnesia for what had taken place. Some patients actually begged me to tell them how they had behaved when in these states. It was easy to utilize these symptoms as fresh aids to reconstruction, as physical memory symbols, so to speak, but there was this difference, this time. The reconstructed past had much more of a feeling of reality and concreteness about it than heretofore, approximated much more closely to an actual recollection, whereas 'til then the patients had spoken only of possibilities or at most of varying degrees of probability and had yearned in vain for memories. In certain cases these hysterical

> attacks actually assumed the character of trances in which fragments of the past were relived, and the physician was the only bridge left between the patients and reality."

That particular piece brought your work to mind. "I was able to question them and received important information about dissociated parts of the personality. Without any such intention on my part and without my making the least attempt to induce a condition of this sort, unusual states of consciousness manifested themselves, which might also be termed 'autohypnotic.'"

I wonder, as you hear him talking, whether you have any associations or reactions to his observations?

MMG: Where is that from?

LR: It's from his 1929 essay, "The Principle of Relaxation and Neocatharsis."

MMG: He was a great man. What would I have to say about that? Well, there is an important essay in the literature—I was trying to think of the name of the author; I can't; it's a woman—in which she—Macalpine, Ida Macalpine—said that psychoanalysis is the slow induction of a hypnotic state, which it can be. But if it is, the analyst is behaving like a hypnotist, and is not recognizing that that's going on. It's cloning, cloning the patient. I haven't seen that kind of manifestation of hysterical attacks, but to some extent that's because of whatever are the cultural reasons responsible for the fact that hysteria is something we read about in books mainly. Although I have a resident now who has a woman with blindness who is recovering from it through the analysis of the transference, so blind that her workplace has made all kind of arrangements to make it possible for her to work, and so on. So it still happens. I don't know that I would have much more to say about it, other than that there are some interesting essays in the literature about altered states of consciousness in analysis. In fact, there's a book recently by Bollas, called *The Shadow of the Ego,* or something like that....

SRR: *The Shadow of the Object.*

MMG: ...*The Shadow of the Object*, a quote from Freud's essay, "Mourning and Melancholia." "The shadow of the object has fallen on the ego," where he describes states of reverie. Come to think of it, I'm glad you asked me that question because it didn't occur to me when I read it that these might be hypnotic states. I don't think Bollas sees them in that context, and maybe that's so. But Dickes has written about that. I knew him at Downstate many years ago. Altered states of consciousness. And I wrote an essay once on spontaneous regression on the induction of hypnosis, which is in a way related to it, and we had trouble bringing the man back. The only bridge to the present. He remembered a perfectly dreadful scene. I won't describe the details of it. That's an important statement. It's less common knowledge because something has happened to hysteria. But that's another indication of the brilliance of the man. Except that, I don't think he says there, I would have to read the article carefully now, that he was inducing a hypnotic state.

LR: No.

MMG: So there you are. So the duality he wasn't seeing yet. That would be a nice thing for you or somebody to write an essay about.

LR: How did you get interested in hypnosis?

MMG: It was because of Margaret Brenman that that happened. We met at Menninger's. She was a lowly psychology something or other. I was a doctor, a medical doctor. When they call psychologists lay analysts, I get very angry. Why is a Ph.D. more of a lay person than an M.D.? I said that in a speech, a few remarks. Division 39 gave me an award at the last meeting, which I was very pleased to get. But I was thrown off by my involvement in my person. What was I talking about? Oh, I was telling you about Margaret Brenman. So I met her at the Menninger Clinic. She had done her Ph.D. thesis using hypnosis and the Zeigarnick effect, which you might know what it is.

LR: I don't know what that is.

MMG: Remembering better unfulfilled tasks than fulfilled tasks is the Zeigarnick effect. So we got to know each other, and I was very interested in hypnosis. And we began to do some hypnoanalysis. That's how it began.

LR: I've wondered if there's a particular state of mind in both the analyst and the patient, when the work is going well, which lies between primary and secondary process, between remembering and experiencing, and between dreaming and waking; that is, a state of mind which is fluid and which might allow for greater receptivity to both conscious and unconscious thoughts between the two.

MMG: They go into a mutual hypnosis sometimes? That's interesting. It's related to Bert Lewin's ideas about the analytic situation, although, as I remember, he deals with it only in relation to the effect on the analysand of different kinds of interpretation. [Gill added this point about Lewin after reviewing the transcript.] My preference is that I want the analyst to stay awake.

LR/SRR: Thank you very much.

SELECTED BIBLIOGRAPHY

Gill, M. M. (1951). Ego psychology and psychotherapy. *Psychoanalytic Quarterly*, Vol. 20, pp. 62–71.

Gill, M. M., Knight, R. & Brenman, G. (1952). Spontaneous fluctuations in hypnotic depth; ego function. *International Journal of Psycho-Analysis*, Vol. 33, pp. 22–33.

Gill, M. M. (1954). Psychoanalysis and exploratory psychotherapy. *Journal of the American Psychiatric Association*, Vol. 2, pp. 771–797.

Gill, M. M. & Rapaport, D. (1959). The points of view and assumptions of metapsychology. *International Journal of Psycho-Analysis*, Vol. 40, pp. 153–162.

Gill, M. M. & Brenman, M. (1959) *Hypnosis and Related States: Psychoanalytic Studies in Regression.* New York: International Universities Press.

Gill, M. M. (1963). *Topography and Systems in Psychoanalytic Theory* (*Psychological Issues*, Monogr. 10). New York: International Universities Press.

Gill, M. M. & Klein, G. S. (1964). The structuring of drive and reality: David Rapaport's contributions to psychoanalysis and psychology. *International Journal of Psycho-Analysis*, Vol. 45, pp. 483–498.

Gill, M. M., Simon, J., Fink, G., Endicott, N. A. & Paul, I. H. (1968). Studies in audio-recorded psychoanalysis, I. General considerations. *Journal of the American Psychoanalytic Association*, Vol. 16, pp. 230–244.

Gill, M. M. (1973). Introduction to George Klein's "Two theories or one?" *Bulletin of the Menninger Clinic*, Vol. 37, pp. 99–101.

Gill, M. M. (1976). Early interpretation of transference. *Journal of the American Psychoanalytic Association,* Vol. 24, pp. 779–794.

Gill, M. M. (1976). Metapsychology is not psychology. In: *Psychology versus Metapsychology. Psychoanalytic Essays in Memory of George S. Klein* (*Psychological Issues*, Monogr. 36). New York: International Universities Press.

Gill, M. M. (1977). Psychic energy reconsidered: Discussion. *Journal of the American Psychoanalytic Association,* Vol. 25, pp. 581–598.

Gill, M. M. (1977). Early interpretation of transference. *Journal of the American Psychoanalytic Association*, Vol. 24, pp. 779–794.

Gill, M. M. (1978). The two models of the mental health discipline. *Bulletin of the Menninger Clinic,* Vol. 41, pp. 79–84.

Gill, M. M. & Muslin, H. (1978). Transference in the Dora case. *Journal of the American Psychoanalytic Association*, Vol. 26, pp. 311–328.

Gill, M. M. (1978). Freud's concepts of unconsciousness and the unconscious. In: *The Unconscious* (Vol. 1), ed. A. S. Prangishvilli, A. E. Sherozia, & F. V. Bassin. Tbilisi, U.S.S.R.: Metsniereba.

Gill, M. M. (1979). The analysis of the transference. *Journal of the American Psychoanalytic Association,* Vol. 27(Suppl.), pp. 263–288.

Gill, M. M. (1979). Psychoanalysis and psychotherapy: 1954–1979; Atlanta, October, 20, Psychoanalysis and psychotherapy: A revision. *International Review of Psychoanalysis,* Vol. 11, pp. 161–180.

Gill, M. M. & Hoffman, I. Z. (1980). Psychotherapy process. Some views on effective principles of psychotherapy. *Cognitive Therapy Research,* Vol. 4 (Special Issue), pp. 271–306.

Gill, M. M. (1981). The boundaries of psychoanalytic data and technique: A critique of Gedo's *Beyond Interpretation. Psychoanalytic Inquiry,* Vol. 1, pp. 205–232

Gill, M. M. & Hoffman, I. Z. (1982). A method for studying the analysis of aspects of the patient's experience of the relationship in psychoanalysis and psychotherapy. *Journal of the American Psychoanalytic Association,* Vol. 30, pp. 137–168.

Gill, M. M. (1982). *Analysis of Transference, Vol. 1: Theory and Technique* (*Psychological Issues,* Monogr. 53). New York: International Universities Press.

Gill, M. M. & Hoffman, I. Z. (1982). *Analysis of Transference, Vol. 2: Studies of Nine Audio-Recorded Psychoanalytic Sessions. (Psychological Issues,* Monogr. 54). New York: International Universities Press.

Gill, M. M. (1983). The distinction between the interpersonal paradigm and the degree of the therapist's involvement. *Contemporary Psychoanalysis,* Vol. 19, pp. 200–237.

Gill, M. M. (1983). The point of view of psychoanalysis: Energy discharge or person. *Psychoanalysis and Contemporary Thought,* Vol. 6, pp. 523–551.

Gill, M. M. (1984). Psychoanalysis and psychotherapy: A revision. *International Review of Psychoanalysis*, Vol. 11, pp. 161–179.

Gill, M. M. (1984). Robert Langs on technique: A critique. In: *Listening and Interpreting: The Challenge of the Work of Robert Langs,* ed. J. Raney. New York: Aronson.

Gill, M. M. (1984). Transference: A change in conception or only in emphasis? *Psychoanalytic Inquiry*, Vol. 4, pp. 489–523.

Hoffman, I. Z. & Gill, M. M. (1988). Critical reflections on a coding scheme. *International Journal of Psycho-Analysis.* Vol. 69, pp. 55–64.

Gill, M. M. (1991). Merton Gill speaks his mind. *The American Psychoanalyst (Newsletter of the American Psychoanalytic Association)*, Vol. 25, No. 1, pp. 17–21.

Gill, M. M. (1994). *Psychoanalysis in Transition: A Personal View.* Hillsdale, NJ: The Analytic Press.

Albert Solnit

Albert J. Solnit, M.D. is Commissioner of the Connecticut Department of Mental Health and Sterling Professor Emeritus (Pediatrics and Psychiatry) and Senior Research Scientist at the Yale University Child Study Center. Dr. Solnit is Honorary President, as well as past president and secretary-general, of the International Association of Child and Adolescent Psychiatry and Allied Professions. He is a past president of the American Psychoanalytic Association, the American Academy of Child and Adolescent Psychiatry, and the Association for Child Psychoanalysis. He is the recipient of the American College of Physicians' William C. Menninger Award, the First Irving Phillips Award of the American Academy of Child and Adolescent Psychiatry, and the Cornerstone Humanitarian Award. Dr. Solnit had a Chair endowed in his name at the Yale Child Study Center and a nursery school named in his honor at the Anna Freud Centre in London. He is principal editor of *The Psychoanalytic Study of the Child.* Dr. Solnit was interviewed May 11 and December 1, 1991.

SRR: I'd like to start with a number of questions about play, beginning with a quote:

"The play involves physical and mental activity and in a sense is always between thought as trial action and an action designed to solve problems and always with an underlying fantasy or state of pretense. It may be a preparation as well as a part of mastery, defense, and adaptation. The maturational and developmental characteristics change as the child and adult capacities advance in regard to the complexity of understanding skills probably pertaining to a continuity with earlier forms of such play activity or playful attitudes. This latter could be viewed as a unique style or analogous to a central organizing fantasy that is uniquely characteristic for each individual beginning in childhood and in various modifications continuing throughout the life cycle as a component of progressive development."

I was very interested in this and in knowing your thoughts about the individual's unique lifelong style. It made me think about Lichtenstein's formation of an identity theme. And it sounded like you have a similar perspective, a way of looking at the shaping influence of the early object relations.

AS: By the way, we are just getting together a book on play. Dr. Ritvo is writing a chapter called, "The Play Signature."

SRR: That's great.

AS: Dr. Ritvo's title captures the concept. The way in which the primary love objects have introduced play, and the use of pretend, and the use of toys is most dramatically seen by how they invest transitional objects and help promote transitional objects. One could say that children, out of their own kind of rhythm, impulse, expression, and ego regulation, have a preferred way that they practice playing, because it is so pleasurable. It has so many satisfactions for them. There is a tendency to go along with that which you are familiar with—to practice it, deepen it, and broaden it.

In that sense, it's a way philosophically to explain why each person is unique, because we use what we have in preferred ways. The history of our emotions, thoughts, and endocrine system is always individually unique. Even in identical twins, a unique integration and synthesis finds expression. Play is a wonderful way of being able to express uniqueness. Think of yourself personally—how there are a number of complicated or simple functions that you always start the same way because it's familiar, pleasurable. Suppose you were raised in California, and salad was served first. If you moved to Boston, you would probably still prefer the salad to be served first. Now, that's a bit of conditioning. But it's more than that. After a while it becomes a preference.

Certainly masturbatory activity and the central organizing masturbatory fantasy are unique to each person. You can look at it from the point of view of play, of sport activities, even the point of view of aesthetic preferences—that at some level there is a synthesis of all those factors. So, I think, in play in particular, you have access to the fantasies of a child that tend to be primary or recurrent ones, as well as the variations and the explorations of new fantasies. In the psychic economy of the normal child, the ability to work at and practice toward making thought a trial action is very badly handicapped if you can't use play as a major avenue towards achieving that.

SRR: You have described play as "trial action of a different source of thinking/imagining, etc., because in childhood play is behavior that characterizes what the child is feeling without expecting it to be perceived as behavior that is consequential, responsible, or unchangeable. Play can always be redone. We could say the same about playfulness in adults." Could you say more about the function of play in the adult and the range of play in normal adults.

AS: I just gave my Brill lecture on playfulness in the adult, and it's going to be published in *The Psychoanalytic Study of the Child.* There I took a look at two patients, the same two patients that are in that other essay, but looked at from the viewpoint of playfulness. It's really amazing how it's not only playfulness, but playing at certain activities in the one adult that I described. The man became drawn to play. He couldn't resist it. He has become a very good golfer, and he just cannot feel that things are going right unless he has a chance to play golf regularly.

Playfulness is a mind activity, allowing yourself not to use the body, which for children is important. Probably the more we study it in children, the more we could say that it isn't really play unless there is action involved. So the playfulness has roots, both genetic and related to the temperament factors listed in the essay. In addition, it reflects any significant new experience because it may be an add-on or a modification based on very severe deprivational or traumatic experiences in adult life such as a change of primary love objects, not a change of the original one, but the replacement through falling in love, marriage, divorce, remarriage, and so on.

I have a hunch that in the satisfactory remarriages, you'll see at least some evidence of the new relationship beginning to have an impact on how playful the person is. You can just think immediately of people you know in your everyday life, who tease some people they know and not others.

LR: That's very true.

AS: I have a sort of game I play. I was on the plane and one of the attendants was very charming. She teased me a bit. I said to her, "I can tell you've had a brother who must have teased you." She said, "How did you know?" I said, "Because you tease the way a person does who has a brother who teases." So that was playful on my part. She laughed and thought that was very funny.

SRR: What about play in the analytic relationship?

AS: I think that it's not called playful because it's often very serious. You can't free associate unless you can pretend that what you're going to say has no consequences.

SRR: That's perfect. Yes.

AS: If your analyst says something stupid, you don't have to use it. So play and free association are really first cousins.

SRR: So, maybe, following that, if a patient in analysis had not been able to play as a child....

AS: They are very resistant. We have people who are so tied up that until you can begin to help them be aware of their anxieties, their tolerances, and their resistances, they are frozen. They are very difficult. Sometimes the analyst sits them up for a while. The change visually will give them more permission to pretend. Pretending is the basic ingredient of play.

LR: What do you think is happening for the patients when they can actually see the therapist?

AS: Often it's not analysis. Often it is the use of suggestion. It's the use of sport, the use of reassurance because you are there, and you're not doing anything. I have had patients the other way. When they lie down, they can really talk to me. When they sit up, they can't.

LR: How would you explain the difference in these patients?

AS: Well, it's an individual matter. Ones who can talk freely when they are lying down but can't talk to me when they are sitting up are so socially anxious that they keep misperceiving my neutrality as evidence of approval or disapproval. They keep reading into it.

When they can't see my face, they gradually hear that I am quiet, listen, and am attentive. They are released from whatever the visual experience is evoking.

You have to go back and find out why vision was the pathway through which that particular kind of anxiety was evoked. Then there are the patients who can talk only when they are sitting up. That I think is the matter of reassurance that they are strong and that magical beliefs and drives are not going to get out of control.

SRR: I also wonder about teaching candidates. It seems to me a very difficult thing to learn how to make a patient safe for free association or play.

AS: Is that supervision or seminar teaching?

SRR: Supervision.

AS: I have a very clear style of supervision. It was first enunciated and published when I was the chair to the 1969 pre-Congress conference in Italy on training, the one on supervision. I let my supervisees know that I'm not there, they are. I am not there to criticize, but I am here to learn. If I can help them learn, then they should feel free to (1) disagree with me and (2) to realize that if what I say is useful, the timing and the mode of using it is not something I can tell them about. I play very much the role of collaborating. My supervision is offered, not imposed. I do not run the case because I don't think I ought to.

SRR: So, you are working in terms of relaxing the supervisees, which then helps them.

AS: It also makes them anxious because they are in charge. It's not just to relax them. It's also to make them aware that it's their patient, not mine.

SRR, LR: Yes.

SRR: You talk about the meaning of play for children of different developmental capacities and tolerances, observing "it is clear that all agencies of the mind are represented, though the mix is usually characteristic of a particular period of development." Would you say the same for an adult? That when an adult plays, the play is stimulated from all the different parts of the self?

AS: I don't know for sure if you mean playful or play?

SRR: Play.

AS: You mean, for example, when an adult plays a game of golf, or....

SRR: No. Something more creative.

AS: When they play charades?

SRR: Yes, maybe charades would be good.

AS: They are influenced much more by the context as well as by their innards. They often are embarrassed by their innards. Context produces competition. So for them it has social consequences or is perceived as such.

SRR: With the artist, somebody who works creatively, is it still play or is it a mixture of play and work?

AS: Well, there is a very interesting article by a Finnish analyst about the way in which a performer experiences his activity while playing the violin. I read it and thought he was talking about play. I referred to him in the essay. He's a very sound analyst and musician.

I think that the artist and the performer, both in singing and playing musical instruments, are engaged in an adult extension of play. It's no longer play—it's serious—but it's an extension of the same capacities for pretend and for using the body and mind in this pretend way. They are playing music in the sense that their mind and body are working together and that they are using their imagination for interpretation.

I think it's useful to consider that a kind of play. It may not hold up. There are some essays by people who have looked at this, not analysts. Dance, which is even more interesting—how does the dancer interpret the choreographer's direction?

SRR: A few questions on play. I was thinking about the parent. Let's say a parent is playing with a four-year-old, playing a game of dolls. Playing, but not being fully in the experience like the child, but still somehow both playing. Let's say my own sense of play, and also empathizing with where the child is in the play. I'm wondering how you conceptualize what that psychic...?

AS: Well, that leads to a very interesting question, why some people can't be child therapists. They cannot permit or tolerate the regression necessary to enter into a pretend game. A child therapist/child analyst is constantly allowing regression in the service of the ego to enable them to pretend, to talk in the child's language and to do what we started with—to try to understand how it feels to be a child, that child—to put himself in the skin of the child while remaining adult.

SRR: I had an experience. Reading your papers made me think of this. Reading a story from my childhood to one of my children and suddenly feeling a certain affect state, an affect state from my childhood take over. And I have heard other people talk about that. I just wonder whether you would think of that.

AS: How old was your child when you were reading to him?

SRR: But it was more of a book for myself. I had actually both of my children.

AS: You were reading to them?

SRR: Yes. Once I was reading *Alice In Wonderland,* and once it was *Little Women.*

AS: Were you reading to them or reading with them?

SRR: To them. And it was almost a flooding, with one it was the affect of the story, but with the other, it was some kind of identification, awareness, hard almost to put words to it of myself at that age.

AS: And you were able to remember or recall what it was like for you at the age they were, and maybe a little more closely how they felt.

SRR: Well, the thing that was so interesting was that I didn't feel I knew what they felt. I felt suddenly in touch with....

AS: You were transported.

SRR: Yes. And it was surprising. It just came out of the blue. But it made me think about it, even though it wasn't exactly about play.

AS: Was one sitting on your lap?

SRR: No.

AS: They were sitting beside you?

SRR: Yes.

AS: But skin to skin, body to body contact.

SRR: Yes. And there was a great satisfaction of introducing those books to them. The experience with the *Alice in Wonderland* was more complicated it seemed, even than affect. I don't know how to describe it, but just "this was me."

AS: Well, the subject matter might have helped too, but there is a literature, not very large, very small, about the psychology of reading to children by parents. It's not in the analytic literature; it's mostly in the children's literature. I gave a couple of seminars on that once at the University of Connecticut—a seminar on children and reading.

First of all, what is clear to me from the observations I made is that when mothers or fathers sit with their children, have them on their laps when they are very young, and it is calming, not overstimulating, and a sharing of an experience, those children have less trouble learning to read than the children who don't. There is some kind of identification that takes place, not only through the intellectual and verbal, but also through the body experience. The "Oooh, this is such a pleasant easy time!"

LR: It seems parallel to your concept of proactively using memory to prepare for trauma.

AS: The sense of the mother really being with her children, that she's really mothering. And not only mothers, but fathers do it. They are with their children having a good time together. It's an experience that links their past to the child's present and to the mother's present. I think it's dynamically very powerful. It achieves a kind of communion in which empathy isn't a sufficient term to describe it. It is an ability for the adult to regress sufficiently while being the reading adult (parent) that they are on the child's level of emotional and intellectual experience. For the child that's very reassuring.

For my own children, I was never good at reading because I was always too tired and would fall asleep. They would wake me up eventually. But my wife, Martha, is a terrific reader. They all used to just look forward to the end of the day when she would sit down and read to them. They would cluster around and listen to stories that were just right for each age.

I am quite convinced that it's a very good sublimation of breast feeding, of intimacy at a well-regulated level. It produces a sense for the child, which we were talking about earlier on, that, "Now I feel important, now I feel worthwhile, I feel well-fed." That is the kind of great experience that when you get into trouble later on, you realize that you are a pretty good person because you had that specialness with a special person. And there will be another time you can do that. I am trying to remember the quote that we talked about, how you reassure yourself that you are all right.

LR: The one about coherency?

AS: Yes. See, it is one of the ingredients. If you have sufficient experience that you're all right, that your mother's all right, and you are a good and worthwhile person, it becomes a resource available to you in such times when chaos, trauma, and deprivation require you to wait, to have faith. You can work out a better deal for yourself. They are connected.

SRR: Another question on play. You talk about a play state. Wouldn't there be, just briefly different kinds of play states? I was thinking about the link between play states and affect states.

AS: Do you remember the context in which I mentioned play states?

SRR: I don't remember right this minute.

AS: I think that was my groping for the same thing. There are boundaries to this. If you are playing, and the play suddenly goes out of control to a state of aggression, hostility, masturbation, or whatever, it's no longer play because it's not pretend. A play state is one in which there is sufficient comfort and security to be able to pretend. Now, it's true that children under terrible conditions can pretend and need to pretend in order to be able to tolerate what's happening. Denial is a kind of pretense, "It doesn't exist." But the play state is one that is much more positive. You have the time and the lack of hunger or pain to be able to pretend and try out new things.

SRR: So it has its own kind of affect with it, perhaps?

AS: It's usually when there isn't a storm, when the affect is not disrupting thinking.

LR: Thinking about the play state, I was interested in your describing the quality of consciousness that goes with it. In your essay, "The Psychoanalytic View of Play," you wrote: "Play is a unique capacity for combining thinking and acting (behaving). The mental component is between primary and secondary process thinking, tapping into the primary process while relaxing the censoring, orderliness-demanding, and inhibiting influence of secondary process thinking and reality testing. Play allows thinking and acting (or behaving) to flow into each other with a looser connection, developmentally and experientially, than nonplay thinking and acting usually permit; but it is a much tighter or more cohesive and coherent connection than, e.g., in sleepwalking."

You seem to be describing a similar state between primary and secondary process that some analysts, such as Weinshel, have noted while listening to patients, without the component of acting (behaving). You continue in the essay: "As we speak and think of the dream state, a waking state, and the sleeping state, I suggest we explore how the concept of a play state would facilitate our study of the many meanings of play as well as its uniqueness as a mental and physical activity." Could you say more about this?

AS: It's built on two things. One is the suspension of reality, which is necessary in order to pretend. That already means that you have to drop some of the requirements of secondary process thinking, the logical and consequential. This is the invitation for certain primary process thoughts to come in like strong affects, like irrational condensations and telescoping of ideas, and can even lead to certain kinds of humor. It leads to incongruities which ordinary secondary process thinking tends not to tolerate. So, that first sentence or two talks about primary and secondary process, but the suspension of reality is really a condensed way of putting it all. Now what was next after that?

LR: If you can elaborate further on your description of the mental state of play as somewhere between dreaming and waking.

AS: Between sleep and awake. If a child is playing with his fingers, or is not yet verbal, maybe six months of age, biting his toes, or masturbating, he may be doing it in a very playful way. While a child is still at the breast, he may play with the breast, for example. That's a kind of a play state. I don't think that's play yet because we can't confirm it. So, developmentally, I think it's useful to consider calling that a play state. In that sense, it's between dreaming and being awake.

LR: I'm interested in how play and its accompanying state of consciousness can be distorted by trauma. You address this in the same essay: "Play that reflects or is coping with a previous trauma may be constrained by being influenced disproportionately by past experiences and its effects on both the thinking and the behavior of the individual. For example, past trauma may evoke more of the remembering than the exploring functions of play."

AS: Trauma often leaves an unsettled state as a residue. There is an effort to overcome that restless, uncomfortable, fearful feeling by trying to find, usually in a disguised way, experiences that will reproduce the equivalent of the trauma so that it will come out differently than in the previous trauma. It's like that old joke where the man goes to the same movie all the time because he wants to see what really happens during some torrid sex scene. The movie doesn't show it, so he keeps going, hoping they will show it.

We don't really understand in detail why they do that. We understand the economic reason for it, to try to feel better, to try to have it come out differently. But why should a traumatized person go back to the equivalent of the trauma? Why don't they try to find an indirect way of overcoming that? Instead we do go back. It has something to do with repetition-compulsion that goes back to familiarity—going back to what you know.

I think that play that does that tends to be constrictive. It goes back to the same old thing, and it doesn't explore as widely or as elaborately as it might if there weren't this trauma that needed to be mastered. So the body and mind go back to master it. It excludes other ways of being able to use the imagination and the body. In that sense, it can be constricting. On the other hand, I don't want to be dogmatic. It is entirely possible that a trauma could lead to a person returning, but then becoming quite inventive and creative—never overcoming the trauma, but always out of that trauma doing interesting, creative things at great burden to them, with great pain and anguish. So you have to be careful not to say there is any linear or recipe quality to it.

LR: Ferenczi wrote about the connection between remembering and an "autohypnotic" state of consciousness in certain adults he treated. I want to read this excerpt to you from his essay, "The Principle of Relaxation and Neocatharsis." I am interested in any associations you may have to his observations, particularly in terms of your own clinical experience with children. He wrote:

> "But, after we had succeeded in a somewhat deeper manner than before in creating an atmosphere of confidence between physician and patient and in securing a fuller freedom of affect, hysterical physical symptoms would suddenly make their appearance, often for the first time in an analysis extending over years. These symptoms included paraesthesias and spasms, definitely localized, violent emotional movements, like miniature hysterical attacks, sudden alterations of the state of consciousness, slight vertigo, and a clouding of consciousness, often with subsequent amnesia for what had taken place. Some patients actually begged me to tell them

how they had behaved when in these states. It was easy to utilize these symptoms as fresh aids to reconstruction—as physical memory symbols, so to speak. But there was this difference—this time, the reconstructed past had much more of a feeling of reality and concreteness about it than heretofore, approximated much more closely to an actual recollection, whereas till then the patients had spoken only of possibilities, or, at most, of varying degrees of probability, and had yearned in vain for memories. In certain cases, these hysterical attacks actually assumed the character of trances, in which fragments of the past were relived, and the physician was the only bridge left between the patients and reality. I was able to question them and received important information about dissociated parts of the personality. Without any such intention on my part and without making the least attempt to induce a condition of this sort, unusual states of consciousness manifested themselves, which might also be termed autohypnotic."

AS: Autohypnosis is a hypnagogic phenomena. Rather important for certain patients, but in children I don't see that very often. I would think it would be unusual. I will tell you a funny story, which is not an analytic case. It was a child therapy. The boy was about, I think, eleven or twelve years old. He had problems with schoolwork and some nightmares, phobic reactions associated with going to sleep. The question came up as to whether he had an epileptic condition, temporal lobe epilepsy. He came to see me over a period of time.

I couldn't find any evidence, nor could the neurologist, that he had psychomotor epilepsy, although he might have had it. But what became clear was that he had a lot of castration anxiety. He could gradually play it out and even talk about his fear of being hurt and of losing control. One day he came to see me when I was in an office that had very high ceilings. It was long and narrow, not very big. He said to me that he wasn't sure if he could trust me to help him.

This day he came with a little bag. In the bag there was one of these cages that they sell parakeets in. He had bought one with his father's help. He opened it up, and he let the parakeet fly all around the ceiling. Then he said, "Now, what are you going to do?" To me, symbolically he was saying that the bird's in danger because of you: "You have to kill him," or "This is no place for him. He can't eat, and he can't sleep. What are you going to do?" And that dramatization was his way of trying to come to grips with his castration anxiety, to see if somebody really could help him. Also to test whether what we had been telling him was essentially true, "There is nobody under your bed"; "If you go to school, your father and mother (who were having terrible marital difficulty) aren't any more likely to hurt each other than if you were there." And he was sort of testing this all out.

Now, the end of the story is that I not only had this funny office, but the funny office had a funny couch and a funny pillow with it. I got on top of my desk and caught the parakeet in the pillow slip. We put the bird back into the place where he could get air. And he said, "You know I am glad to see you do that because I think maybe I can trust you." I only saw him a few more times, and the symptoms cleared. I don't know if they recurred. The reason I tell this story is that this was not an epileptic attack. It was a dramatization. Now, was that play? It really wasn't play. It was serious. It wasn't pretend. But it was a serious dramatization.

LR: That sound like an important distinction. Can you say more about "dramatization" as opposed to play?

AS: Well, I think when a child plays with you a long time, especially if they are young children, they finally begin to create dramas in which you are actually invited in. In those dramas, they let themselves and you know what is on their mind and where some of the areas of trouble are. In that sense, this older child, eleven or twelve, was still using an infantile, much more regressive model of trying to solve problems.

Why couldn't he talk to me about it? He wasn't quite old enough, and he wasn't raised in a family where a child was invited to use thought as a trial action, so he acted it out. Now if an adult did that with you, you'd tell him to catch his own bird.

SRR: You have described the search for a social conscience as one of the major processes that enables each adolescent to relinquish childhood ties with primary love objects, to rebel and somewhat independently to experiment and explore socially, sexually, and aggressively, "forging individual values and self-esteem as the individual moves toward the integration of his or her adult personality." I wonder what you think about when an adolescent demonstrates a lack of social conscience.

AS: I think that since it isn't the only major reason or method for achieving the integration of the personality, it isn't a necessary condition for it. I don't necessarily think of it as something I need to bring into the treatment, diagnosis, or consultation. It's only that when it is something that the adolescent has shown an interest in and has had experience with, I understand it as one of the avenues toward adulthood that is worthy of understanding in a positive way. In other words, I was trying to make the point that while there is always some defensive element in it, it isn't only or mainly a defensive mode of being able to cope.

SRR: I am thinking about instances in which an adolescent has a strong social conscience and is involved in that way, but his or her values are very similar to the parents, so that it doesn't function as much as a rebellion. I assume that still promotes growth but doesn't promote....

AS: Usually for the adolescents I've gotten to know, who both indirectly and directly acquired the same values as their parents and the same identifications with certain social issues, they've rebelled in other ways. They've rebelled in terms of work choice, love choice, or lifestyles. Within a given social movement that has meaning for social conscience development, adolescents can still be quite different and not have the same cookie cutter for the other parts of their personality.

SRR: Do you think it's necessary to rebel in some ways?

AS: I don't think it's necessary to physically rebel. I think that's where analysts have had trouble being understood. I think adolescents often can rebel in quiet, internalized ways in terms of the way they fantasize, the way in which they have different tastes or hierarchies of values. It may be a similar set of values, but with different priorities given to the values. I think there has been a misunderstanding that unless you dramatically and physically rebel, there is no evidence of rebellion. It's the old argument I have with Daniel Offer, a well-known psychiatrist in Chicago. He has tried to be critical of psychoanalytic theory in adolescence by saying he has studied thousands of adolescents and has discovered that those who are doing very well often are not rebellious.

AS: I've said to Dan, both privately and publicly, "You don't have to be overtly rebellious to ward off regression and to find and explore for oneself one's own psychological terrain. Sure, I know a lot of healthy adolescents who have never been known to be rebellious but in whom, if you had a chance to analyze them or to see them in a particular life situation which forces into view some of the derivatives of fantasies and the hierarchy of their values and longings, you can see the real disagreement with their parents. It may not last, but it's there, transiently at least, and sometimes permanently.

SRR: In terms of social conscience, what are your thoughts about the social conscience of the analyst?

AS: I have a very strong feeling about that, which has been elaborated and consolidated since I last saw you. I did a review of a book that will appear in the *International Journal of Psycho-Analysis* on a symposium that was held in Boston. It had to do with psychoanalysts against nuclear warfare and the use of nuclear weapons. They make very clear to me what I have always felt, which is, first, that the analyst need not be from one cut of social conscience or social values. The analysts ranged all the way from the most reactionary to the most liberal and radical, but the question is, do they analyze and do they understand analytic theory within the limits of our knowledge?

Secondly, I would never have thought that somebody who is a psychoanalyst would look for the absence of social conscience because of their social conscience and then put it into the treatment. I tactfully criticized one or two of the essays in that symposium, which said that if it's absent, conspicuous by its absence, you better bring it in as something that the patient is unaware of. I think that's really not warranted unless it is conspicuous by its absence, meaning there are other reasons to believe that it's there, but it's been defended against or there has been a reaction formation against it. There are a lot of people who in their normal growing up do not relate personally to some of the most terrible problems of our world. You may remember that we discussed this argument between Bob Coles and John Mack.

LR: Could we review it, because I don't remember it?

AS: Well, they had an argument that appeared in print in the *New York Times.* John Mack's group at The Center for Psychological Studies had done a study that showed that children were aware of the threat of nuclear warfare, that it preoccupied them and turned up in their nightmares, and so on. Bob Coles said that he never found that when he talked to kids, that it only came up with certain families, but not the majority. He felt that the Mack group was creating artifacts.

You are free to look at that argument and make your own choice. I think there are a lot of children who have other things that preoccupy them more than the threat of world destruction from nuclear threats. I think it depends on whether it's proximal or distal. Children must have had some sense of cataclysmic events that human beings bring about in Nagasaki. On a smaller scale, in urban settings, it may have more to do with their experience of proximal violence.

SRR: I don't remember the studies very well, but I thought it had something to do with the children of parents who were very involved.

AS: Yes it did, but they generalized from it and said that when parents weren't as involved, then the concerns still existed for children, and that it was a burden for them. Bob Coles took exception with which I agree. You ought to talk to Bob and John about it; John's an analyst, and Bob isn't.

SRR: I have noticed that some analysts have a very keen awareness of the adolescent transference in adult patients. We had an interesting discussion in a seminar in which a number of analysts said they don't see it and other analysts....

AS: Don't see the transference of what?

SRR: An adolescent, the transference of adolescence in their adult work.

AS: You mean they don't find it coming up for construction or that what is transferred is not from the adolescent period.

SRR: Exactly. And I was interested in your experience. We were hypothesizing.

AS: Well, I think that that has been commented on in the literature. I think Anna Freud at one time noted how many adult analyses did not bring into view reconstructions of the adolescent period, whether in transference or repression. She wondered why that was, and she speculated that it was so close to adulthood that the threat of regressing to the most recent period, from which a young adult has come through, might make it more highly charged.

I have done adult analyses where I haven't heard much about adolescence or adolescent transference, and I've had some analyses where it's very clear that the transference is a residue of an old struggle in adolescence. I think that there are two or three speculations. One is that analysts aren't sensitive enough to it and tend to not hear it when it comes up. Anna Freud thought that was possible and likely.

SRR: Would there be any reason why that would be, why analysts would have more trouble with that particular period?

AS: I think some analysts might have trouble because they might not like patients who are too rebellious in the nonchildlike way. We don't quite have the right handle on it yet. We need research to explore whether the kinds of defenses and transformations at the juncture from adolescence to young adulthood have particular features that are difficult or uncomfortable to get at, or else are still so accessible that there is no conflict about it. One can see and hear youngsters who explore and feel that they've had it with their parents and their childhood, but who feel in particular conflict about it. I think there is a wide spectrum of possibilities.

LR: My question follows on that one. I was wondering how you technically decide to respond to a patient's experimenting or individuating in a way that recalls adolescent development. Do you treat it with historical reference or do you consider it newly emerging adolescent development?

AS: Well, I just went over some old notes of an analysis I did many years ago. I technically remember being quite respectful of the reappearance of adolescent issues that were being resolved somewhat differently than they had been. I remember thinking that to overemphasize the analytic interpretive perspective would be a risk, because it would give the wrong impression transferentially that I had brought it about. The man was in analysis from age 35 to 45, a father and a spouse. While recovering some memories of early puberty and adolescence, he went into a frenzy of activity deciding to build a workshop. He often seemed so preoccupied that I felt there was resistance.

But as we watched that drama unfold and could analyze parts of it, he was redoing something that he had not been able to do as an adolescent because of both rather severe trauma and unresolved oedipal problems that had been a heavy burden during his adolescence. I remember his last comment. The place was finished, and everyone was really terribly pleased. He was quite proud, and he said something like, "I suppose you would like to say the analysis helped me." And then he said, "Well, in analysis you can play around with ideas like that." I didn't say anything.

LR: Yes.

AS: And I think that is what a child analyst does. They tend to be very respectful of the reappearance of or of the resurgence of developmental momentum. They avoid making the analysand self-conscious about the analyst's involvement.

SRR: I was thinking about the comment also as perhaps representing the adolescent transference as well, his worry that you would somehow want to take it away from him.

AS: Well, transferentially it showed up in a different way later. It didn't seem to me that transference was a resistance there. He was telling me, "You know, it's no bother to come here when I'm having such fun building. I don't know why I have to come here 4–5 times a week, but, OK, if you want me to, I will." So there was resistance, but I didn't interpret it because he kept coming and working on things. I didn't see the transference as a resistance.

SRR: That's interesting. I was wondering about paralleling the adolescent's need to individuate with the task of the analysand individuating from the analyst and wondered about the special issues, about individuation and training analysis.

AS: That brings us right back to the personal analysis whether it's a training analysis or one not related to becoming a psychoanalyst.

SRR: Exactly.

AS: Well, the training analysis is both a clinical and an analytic experience, but it also carries with it the mentorship, teaching by example, at least of the analyst for the analysand. I was just talking about that the other day to a colleague on our education committee. An analyst had said, when asked, "Well, the training analysis is quite different than the therapeutic analysis. I've had both." He first had a therapeutic analysis without the training, then the training analysis. They happened to both be by training analysts, the first one was when he was a good deal younger and had some symptoms that he wanted to deal with. He gave less credit to the training or didactic analysis as a therapeutic experience. He said it was too complicated by the fact that this was also a person whose work he was trying to learn how to do.

The training analyst has to constantly be aware of his ambitions for or disappointments in the analysand. Analysts may want the analysands to be extensions of themselves in some way, and they have to analyze that in themselves to make sure it's as little a burden to their analysands as possible. For analysands, the way you set up your office as analysts, the way you say hello/goodbye, arrange for payments, all of those become expressions of personality and of taste and of lifestyle that are observed and experienced by the analyst and analysand; they are either welcomed or rejected.

I can't tell you how many trainees have said to me when I'm supervising them, "Well, I always do it this way because that's the way my analyst does it. It seemed like the right way, so I do it, and I'm comfortable," whether it's handling the bill or how they arrange their office or whatever it is. That's where Loewald's idea that the analyst is a real person is certainly apt, keeping in mind that it should not be allowed to play a major role and that it can be analyzed. But for the analyst to pretend it doesn't exist can be a burden to the analysand.

SRR: You mentioned how this person felt that the therapeutic analysis and the training analysis were quite different. What do you think about that in general?

AS: Well, I've only had one, so I would not judge it. For me, personally, the training analysis was much more comfortable because I felt I was doing it for the training, until I got into it and realized what it was really doing. The entry was easier for me because it was an institutionalized form of learning a profession or method. Others who had had a therapeutic analysis worried that they might be criticized, given a low grade, or expelled in a training analysis.

At the Western New England Institute for Psychoanalysis, we don't have our training analysts report on their analysands to the education committee. It's a nonreporting institute, so that candidates don't worry about being discussed by a Committee.

SRR: In *The Psychoanalytic Study of the Child*, you noted that certain analysands with a definite sense of their analysts as real persons also gave the clearest evidence of a full-blown transference relationship and the most intensely felt mourning. You noted that when a transference/real person balance did not exist, however, mourning evidently could not occur. This seems to support the importance of a real relationship. I'm interested in your thoughts about....

AS: That was a three-authored paper in the *International Journal of Psycho-Analysis.* My own experience has been limited in terms of the number of people I've analyzed. It was a consensus by the three authors, Ruth Lord, Sam Ritvo, and myself from the literature and from our collective experience, two of us being analysts.

Theoretically it holds up because I don't believe it's possible for an effective analytic process to go on in which the analyst as a real person doesn't appear. By definition, there would be something peculiar about that analysis. Therefore, if the analyst died and was only an imaginative figure, you might see some evidence of longing or disappointment. I think in that situation the real identification with the analyst would not be a significant factor. You were saying something about it if weren't a real person?

SRR: I wasn't even thinking about the experience in terms of the death. I am interested in your thoughts about the ideal balance, that the analyst has to be quite a bit real but not too real.

AS: You know, I think that's one of the places where art replaces science. It's a matter of style, and I think an analyst, who goes out of his way to keep everything so neutral and who thinks he is not coming through, deceives himself.

LR: You must see in your supervisees a range of people figuring out how to be analysts and still be themselves with their analysands.

AS: Absolutely.

LR: Would you say that you encourage your supervisees over time to be more real, less neutral?

AS: In my supervision, in recent years, I find that I am doing two things rather repeatedly. One is trying to help the analyst do the analysis inside his or her head before they decide what to say. I have found that approach enables them to be freer without necessarily getting excessively active. So I say to them, "This is what I thought about when you were telling me these materials. This is what I tried out in my own thinking, saying this, thinking that. By the way, don't do anything I'm doing, but I want your own mind to be giving you that kind of feedback. And then you can decide what and when to interpret.

I have one analyst supervisee now, who for a long time almost said nothing. I supported that, and now she's becoming much more active. Occasionally, I say, "You shouldn't have said that, you should have thought it." I think one of the most intriguing things about different analyses is that the degree of verbal activity on the part of the analyst is so variable. I'm on the whole relatively quiet, and my teachers ranged all the way from very active to very, very conservative. My own analyst was relatively conservative.

SRR: We'd like to ask about training. We are very interested in your formative experience in terms of your own.

AS: My own training?

SRR: Yes. What was most important to you, and who....

AS: Well, I had an early interest in children from the time I entered medical school because of my family and early experiences. My family was very devoted to children—to their own and to other children, as well. And I wanted to be a pediatrician. I didn't want to be a psychiatrist or an analyst. When I was in the military service, I decided I should learn some psychiatry because I realized from my internship and assistant residency in pediatrics we didn't know enough about development or about the psychological side. So I went to Schick General Hospital in Clinton, Iowa. They said, "What would you like to do?" I said, "I'd like to learn some psychiatry." Later I learned that the commanding officer said that anyone who wanted to go into psychiatry was nuts.

As it turned out, I had a lot of experience with infectious disease at the time. They had a serious infectious disease ward, and they were low in personnel. But he didn't think of pediatrics in terms of infectious disease. So I began to learn psychiatry more formally after medical school in the military. They sent me to a school of military neuropsychiatry.

During my last six months, I was sent overseas to Germany. I had three ratings because of my background. I was a neuropsychiatrist for three air fields; I had already been an instructor in the flight surgeon school and in the school of Aviation Medicine; and I had a pediatric background. They found the perfect place for me. They found a community in which the first dependents were being brought overseas after World War II to join their husbands. So, there were children and mothers. I took care of the children and the mothers because there was a dispensary for them where I was quartered.

There I began to realize there was a useful mix in combining psychiatry, pediatrics, and general medicine. That intrigued me. So, I went back and finished my training in pediatrics at San Francisco General Hospital. Then I got the idea, a seed which was planted just before I started medical school. A close friend of mine had given me my first analytic book, the A. A. Brill translation of Freud's

Psychopathology of Everyday Life and Dream Book, all in one. When I came back, I intuitively said to one of my friends, "You know, I think I ought to get analyzed because I think I could be a much better pediatrician if I were analyzed." I didn't particularly have any florid symptoms sending me into treatment. I had the usual neurotic difficulties, I suppose, the usual worries. I actually tried to see if one of the analysts there had some time. He didn't. By that time, I had decided to go back east for a year to learn psychiatry more formally, with the understanding that I would be working in pediatrics and psychiatry.

When I finished my adult training, I was the first child psychiatry trainee at the Yale Child Study Center. I had to make a decision between going there or going to Boston to the Roxbury Putnam Children's Center. I decided to say in New Haven. I thought it would be worthwhile to be associated with a new center. At this point, the first person who more systematically advised me, was Samuel Ritvo. He was my first teacher in child psychiatry, and he encouraged me. Each teacher I had influenced me in a different way. So my identity has always been a sort of mixed one. I have always done more than one thing at a time. For the first ten years at Yale, academically I spent six hours a day in the pediatric clinic. I had a deep conviction, along with Milton J. E. Senn, that we must teach pediatricians in the outpatient setting. I was there every day. I knew every medical student that went through Yale for ten years, because they had two stints with us, junior and senior clerkships, before we started sending them to other clinical clerkships.

I learned an enormous amount about children, about pediatricians, and about medical students. At one point, I was chairman of the Curriculum Committee of Yale's School of Medicine and chairman of the Medical School's Ad Hoc Committee on Governance that developed a model of governance that included medical studies. I was known to be restless as a child, and to some extent I still am. It's one of those traits that you have to learn to harness. That's probably why I took the commissionership.

SRR: I think that's wonderful.

LR: That is so great for someone with your experience and overview of psychiatry to be heading the Department of Mental Health in Connecticut.

AS: I have always been interested in it. You know, when the Governor finally convinced me that I should take this job, I had turned it down at first, in January 1991. He called me back a week later and said, "Listen, I let you off the hook, but you are just the right person."

SRR: Good for him.

LR: Could you talk just a bit about your analysis if you feel free to do so?

AS: What do you have in mind?

LR: Maybe just from the more general perspective of your analytic training, how it shaped your interests, and what you eventually pursued in your career? I know that your practice involves a lot of consultation outside of analysis, working with pediatricians, educators, and the public. You've written about your work with Drs. Lustman and Ritvo.

AS: And now, more recently, Dr. Neubauer.

LR: We are interested in any of your thoughts about how these various people have shaped your analytic identity over time.

SRR: Going back, I remember from the other interview, that you mentioned you were assigned to Dr. Hartmann?

AS: That's right. I didn't know who he was. I knew he was a person who was well-known, but I didn't really know who he was because I was relatively new to the field. I knew who Freud was, but I didn't know who Hartmann, Kris, and Loewenstein were, other than that they were important in *The Psychoanalytic Study of the Child.*

SRR: Could we ask what he was like?

AS: Well, he was a very handsome man, who was obviously very intelligent. Socially, he was very courteous, thoughtful, and very conservative. He expected me to use his presence to hear myself and to be in touch with myself, and he facilitated that. I think he practiced what he said, which is that in analysis the analysand and analyst gradually learn to understand each other better, and they make an arrangement to work together.

They are able to work together much more effectively as the analysis goes on. He never used jargon. He was very parsimonious. He didn't give long explanations. The point was to get you to hear yourself clearly and to facilitate your going on. He would tend to confirm or question the understanding that he thought you had arrived at by the way in which he listened.

SRR: He was such a major theoretical thinker. Did you get to know his thinking from your analytic experience with him?

AS: Not in any explicit way. I learned about him by reading later on and in conversations I had with him after I finished the analysis. It was the extraordinary way in which he listened and helped you listen to yourself.

SRR: That makes me think of your own style as an analyst as it developed over time....

AS: Well, my major teachers in supervision who had a real influence on me were people like Ernst and Marianne Kris, in particular; Phyllis Greenacre; and, in a very interesting way, Bert Lewin. Edward Kronold was my first supervisor. But the major influences on my clinical work were the two Kris's. They became close friends, and I felt like part of the family.

SRR: At what point in your analytic progression did that happen?

AS: Well, Ernst, in particular, was the cooriginator and the director of the Yale Child Study Center Longitudinal Study. Marianne started with it, and even before I had gone very far in my own analytic training, I was a member of that team. They used to meet once a week for at least a day, sometimes more than a day.

SRR/LR: A whole day every week?

AS: A whole day in New Haven to follow up your observations of these children and these families, the parents. And we had long conferences and discussions. Marianne was always modest, but incisive. Ernst was always expansive and articulate in an extraordinary way—most inspiring. He's the person who impressed me as the most gifted psychoanalytic teacher. He had a tremendously open mind and was able to articulate his thinking. Hartmann and he were well-matched.

Hartmann was also very open minded, especially with much more sophisticated awareness of the biological input. His writings are classics. He was a man who was so bright that in a theoretical discussion if you didn't understand it right away, he wondered why you couldn't; Ernst Kris, on the other hand, was a very energetic teacher with a full discussion of questions.

Marianne was the master clinician of them all. If you had a clinical problem and went to her with it, you came away realizing how complicated people were and how much respect you should have for their complexity. My other supervisors were very good and helpful, but they didn't influence me as much as the Kris's did.

LR: Are there particular qualities of their characters which influenced you?

AS: Marianne never would come to the point with you until she heard as much as was available. Then she always could think of possibilities of human behavior and development that other people might not have thought of. She had an enormous tolerance for human capacities, for the vicissitudes of human experience.

Ernst put clinical observation and direct observation of children together with theory. He worked it over in an exciting fashion. In a very scientific way, he introduced us to what science is about—that you make speculations, you make predictions, and then you check out your predictions. Marianne was much more practical; that is, "This is what you need to understand in order to be helpful." His approach was, "This is what you need to understand in order to make theory much more understandable or in need of modification, refinement, or elaboration."

In the later years, the work with Anna Freud was also shaping. We spent hours, literally hours, both in England and Ireland, in London and Walsberswick, where we would not be bothered by time, talking about issues having to do with children's needs, children's rights, children's interests.

LR: What a wonderful experience!

AS: Joseph Goldstein, who was really the leader of the study, was never intimidated or awed by her. He was like a junior colleague that was very highly respected by her. I was, as she said, the mediator. Joseph Goldstein was fully trained analytically, but he had never practiced beyond his own control cases, so she would often turn to her own experience or mine for confirmation about the clinical experiences in our discussions and writings.

I often would disappoint her by saying, "Well, I didn't quite understand that," or sometimes I didn't quite agree. She was a constant clinician. Her ability to intensely study human issues around given observations was really so sharp, focused, and highly organized that she influenced me in regard to keeping clear where you are and knowing the limits of your knowledge. My two other supervisors were Samuel Ritvo and Lillian Malcove. I'd like to say I was supervised by Berta Bornstein, but you couldn't call it that. I told you that story, didn't I?

LR: No, I didn't hear it.

AS: I felt in my period of becoming a child analyst that if you didn't have supervision from her, you hadn't had all that you should have. I went to her. By that time I was a graduate, and I now had the time to try to do that. She said she would love to meet with me regularly, but she wouldn't call it supervision unless I would supervise her in her work, and she would supervise me in mine. So we used to swap stories. I learned a great deal from her.

SRR: Could you characterize what she was like in particular? You had so many great teachers.

AS: Oh, she was very dramatic and really had a wonderfully imaginative way of describing how she understood her child patients. She was so enthusiastic and full of interesting questions. I don't know what she learned from me, but I learned a great deal from her.

SRR: They were both women, do you think that made a difference?

AS: Well, my sample is too small because I didn't have enough men teaching me child analysis. Maybe.

LR: I'm curious how you began writing? What role did it play in your elaborating your own thoughts? Did you write in order to figure out things with certain patients or was it more to reflect on what you'd experienced with them?

AS: My earlier background had been to earn a Master's degree studying the endocrine system of rats and the use of radioactive phosphorus. I was at Berkeley, and we were looking at the interaction between progesterone and estrogen as it affected bone metabolism. I had been steeped in the physical experimental method. In order to produce enough progesterone, because progesterone itself was too expensive, I had to use a purified extract of the anterior pituitary, prolactin, a hormone which would turn on the progesterone phase of the female rat's ovary to produce huge amounts of progesterone on a sustained basis.

I had learned technical things about chemistry and the endocrine system, about controlled experiments, and I thought I was pretty good at it, but I didn't enjoy it very much. It wasn't my forte. I took a year out of my medical education to finish my Master's thesis, but I found that I really didn't like laboratory medicine. I liked clinical medicine instead. I liked people who told me stories. So, my writing includes a Master's thesis, which is biochemical, and then I wrote two senior theses for graduation from medical school.

LR: I don't remember that, no.

AS: Well, it's sort of a window into my own way of functioning. The original problem that I tried to deal with came out of a bacteriology course. I had the idea that when people scrubbed for surgery for five minutes, they didn't know whether they were scrubbing evenly and thoroughly because even if they looked they couldn't tell. So I devised a technique in which we used lampblack and blindfolded them. We knew that if you watched you could remove the lampblack in five minutes of scrubbing, meeting the standards of a surgical scrub. We also knew that surgical personnel scrubbed for five minutes while not looking or keeping track of where they scrubbed. We were about to develop an invisible fluorescent material that would glow under ultraviolet light, revealing where you had not scrubbed.

I was a junior when I was doing that. One of the sophomore students came and said he wanted to learn research, and the Department Chair of Bacteriology said he should join me in this study. He turned out to be Henry Kempe of battered child fame. He helped me do it, and actually he made the drawings of the hands with the blind spot because he was a better artist than I was. It would surprise you that the hypothenar eminence was one of the most commonly overlooked areas. We mapped it out by frequency with a class of sixteen. Everybody cooperated, and it was playful and fun. I didn't feel satisfied with that.

Henry Kempe became a much more well-known person than I did because of his research on vaccinia; he was really a superb virologist and pediatrician. More importantly, he later described and did research on the battered child syndrome. I used to say that Henry and I had worked together. I found blind spots interesting and became an analyst, and he found blind spots interesting and looked for viruses, microscopic creatures.

The professor of neurosurgery, who was the chairman of surgery and of bacteriology, accepted my research thesis for graduation, but I wasn't quite satisfied and decided to do another one. I think I partly wasn't satisfied because I felt I had to do something alone. Henry had been so bright and helpful that he allowed me to coast a bit.

So, I did another problem. This is the way my mind works. I had been a clerk in anesthesia. A five-year-old child had died of a brain cyst. It was an *Echinococcus* cyst. So I studied the treatment of that disease, Hydatid Cyst Disease, caused by the parasite *Echinococcus* and transmitted by infected sheep. In the liver, it takes twenty years to show up, and in the brain it takes a few years. I did a study of the incidence of the disease in California by going to all of the hospitals that might have been capable of making the diagnosis. I turned up forty cases. Until then it was thought to be a rare disease. They had a lot of sheep in California. That was my senior thesis, showing that sheep were the reservoir, demonstrating incidence, ages, sex, and what appeared to be the contacts. Dogs were also transmitters. They didn't suffer from it, but they would often eat the sheep livers.

SRR: Did your interest in research begin very early?

AS: Yes, I always had an interest in research, but I found the more formal physical laboratory research somewhat tedious. I enjoyed what you might call natural science research. Psychoanalysis seemed to me a wonderful natural science.

SRR: Were you surprised to find that you were a theory maker as well? Was that something you just discovered when you became a psychoanalyst in training, that you also were very much inclined toward theory making?

AS: Well, I think a number of things I wrote about required theoretical thinking and theory building, as I would call it. I don't think I was a natural born theorist—I'm an empiricist. I see something; it intrigues or arouses my curiosity, and I want to find out more about it. The theory then follows. For example, one of the projects, which I initiated but didn't spearhead because I didn't have the time, was accidental ingestion of poison by young children who turned up in our emergency room. It was the beginning of my interest in abused children. I knew these children weren't being abused, but they were neglected in a sense.

The pediatricians were following a necessary idea, which was to get bottles that the children couldn't undo. It was an engineering approach. Make the product safe. Then even if they wanted to, they couldn't have it.

I got a small group to start following successive children brought into our emergency room for accidental ingestion of poison. I gradually developed a theory, which I still think is quite good. When a mother is sad, depressed, and overwhelmed, the protectiveness of her psychological presence tends to be less effective. I hypothesized that on the basis of psychoanalytic theory.

It was Ernst Kris who taught me this, that as children get into the second and third year of life, they don't need the mother or father to be concretely there to keep them safe, but they have to have the parents' psychological presence available to them. The younger the children are, the shorter the distance they need between physical and psychological presence. The older they are, then it's a matter of object constancy which I've written about. As children mature, they can have a radius of protective presence that is longer if that protective presence is still available, even if the mother is in the next room rather than in the same room. My hypothesis was that in accidental ingestion of poison and other accidents of childhood, something had interfered with the protective presence of the mother and father. In that case, the child did not have available the ego resources to sufficiently avoid what the parent had told them was dangerous, or to understand the consequences of such behavior.

I'm still convinced that is the major reason for the high incidence of accidents in childhood. Well, I stated the problem, developed the theory, and wrote an essay. It's related not to cruel neglect, but to subtle neglect with a depressed or overwhelmed parent.

SRR: It sounds like it also requires an understanding of internalization.

AS: That's right. I couldn't have done that without my analytic training. That came after I finished my analytic training, the ability to understand what is the nature of the relationship. I was curious about the story of lives.

LR: What analytic ideas in particular have you found useful in your consultation with pediatricians, educators, movement therapists, and others?

AS: I think the derivative theories around object relationships are the most powerful for being applied in child rearing, child education, and child care. That doesn't mean that the theory of instinctual drives or other facets of ego defense or of ego adaptation aren't important, but you can get their attention with object relationships because it immediately moves into an area of their competence.

The bedrock of this teaching includes the psychoanalytic theory of identification as an outcome and characteristic of certain relationships. Along that line, I view myself as having been most deeply interested in the application of psychoanalytic theory to the experience of being a child and being a parent, in a wide variety of settings—education, family, law, that kind of thing.

LR: How do you find yourself translating psychoanalytic concepts for nonanalysts? Is the translation sometimes difficult?

AS: Well, like my most important teachers, I don't use jargon. You are hearing me use terms like protective influence and psychological presence, instead of identifications or object constants. My technical essays have the more technical terms.

I noticed in my own psychic economy that if I'm not seeing analytic patients, I feel there is something missing from my ability to confront other issues and problems. The clinical analytic thinking I do enables me to think about chronic schizophrenics in back wards of state hospitals. I'm doing a few things that are quite unconventional in my commissionership, which I don't think I would have done had I not been a psychoanalyst with a certain confidence that the understanding of the individual is what you build everything on.

LR: Can you give an example of something you are attempting?

AS: Yes. Within a couple of days after starting as the commissioner, I had a call from the Connecticut Civil Liberties Union and from the Yale Clinical Legal Group saying, "You may not be aware of it yet, but there's a class action suit against your department." I said, "Well, can I find out about it before I ask you what is being done?" They said, "Sure, but we're not going to wait long." One of the class actions was against putting people who were mentally retarded and psychotic into our institutions because the Department of Mental Retardation didn't have an adequate place for them.

According to the class action suit, they were being deprived of their constitutional rights for appropriate treatment because they were being treated for their psychoses, but not adequately for their handicap—mental retardation. They were being kept in too long. The presumption was that if they were restored to proper health, they would have been able to go back into the community, to their family, or to a neighborhood-like setting. I thought about it, worried about it, read about it, and I called them. I said, "Listen, I don't quite know how to answer this, but I think the way I would like to approach it, if you will allow me, is to have a weekly conference in which the commissioner of mental retardation and the commissioner of mental health both meet with the staff of this hospital, which has a large number of such cases. We can listen to case-by-case presentations, so we better understand it, and we would like the lawyers representing the plaintiffs and the lawyers from the attorney general's office to be present also."

The attorney general's office was very uncomfortable with that because they might be listening to things that would strengthen their class action suit. I said, "Listen, we're into this in such a bad way now, it's been so neglected that we need to look and see what we are doing. Otherwise, they are going to move towards a motion for finding us in contempt and will put us under a panel of monitors that would be very difficult." So finally, over a few sessions, the attorney general's office became comfortable. Now the Yale law group and the attorney general's office are part of our team of keeping track of and improving the care of individual patients until we have finished the thirty cases of the class action.

We'll then go to another hospital and do the same thing. I don't think I could do that if I didn't believe that understanding the individual is not only enormously exciting and important, but from it you can learn for others.

LR: It's a wonderful model.

AS: There are over thirty states that have class actions of this kind, but mostly they have well-organized institutional forms of responding and attacking, responding and attacking. We have an alliance with our opponents who have written, "We're not going back to court as long as this is going on this way; this is what we want. We want better care for our patients."

LR: That's great.

AS: Now, that's a success story. There are some other stories that aren't quite as successful. But I approach it as a clinician. That's what the governor said, "I need a clinician. We haven't had a clinician in there for a while."

LR: It makes a lot of sense. I want to ask you about two other areas you have considered in your writing, which are often neglected in the analytic literature—the role of the father and of siblings in an individual's development, and the possible connection between aggression and failure of the mother-infant bond.

AS: I can't give you a good conceptual frame of reference, partly because I'm not sure I understand it. But I can give you some particulars. First of all, we're in a period of enormous clarification about the fact that the theory of bisexuality has never been carefully understood, so that women can be paternal, and men can be maternal. I have believed in that for a long time. I think I learned it from Freud, from Kris and Hartmann, and all my teachers, and I think the feminists have made us wake up. Not always have they led us correctly, but they helped us wake up.

My wife has helped to educate me better, and we have three sons and one daughter. Our three boys have learned to understand, under a much better and different way than I did, the role of men and women and the way in which they live together, work together, and take care of children together. I think there has been an influence from cultural change. Powerful cultural expectations can have a lot to do with what's going on. My own family had a humanizing influence on me.

I have thought more and more about Freud's two attitudes, one is that every person is bisexual—the predominance of most people being either toward a male or toward a female. With the extraordinary revolution we have in this country about the tolerance for and understanding of homosexuals, I also think of Freud's extraordinarily wonderful statement, which I'm not sure I can remember, but in which he said that homosexuality shouldn't be treated as a sickness. He implied, I think, that it could be understood as a developmental issue, but not as an illness. Of course, a hundred years later the American Psychiatric Association agreed with him. Now, I don't think the last word's in on that; I think there are biological studies that are going to help us understand why individuals are different and how they happen to shape up.

I had the good fortune to be able to encourage Kyle Pruett to pursue his study of fathers who decide to stay home and take care of their children. His latest article will appear in *The Psychoanalytic Study of the Child.* It describes his follow-up of these children, what their latencies are like, and, for most of them, the fathers have continued to be the person most available to them physically. The mothers have continued to work, and those families have been relatively stable in terms of constancy. The latency of those children doesn't look that much different, although there are some differences.

Kyle raises questions about the role of aggression, that men's aggression comes out differently than women's. Perhaps it's more biological style than the strength of aggressive drives or of the options available for their expression, but men's musculature, endocrine system, and maturing capacities are on a different track than women's. The difference can't be ignored and shouldn't be, but it also shouldn't be used to create stereotypes.

LR: What are some of your thoughts about siblings?

AS: You know, we studied siblings under the direction of Marianne Kris. We published in *The Psychoanalytic Study of the Child.* They kept kidding me because I kept looking for what was normal about sibling experience instead of what was pathological. For example, I emphasized the community of interest, the way in which they were more like each other than they were like their parents, the sense of being able to vicariously know how the world was through the eyes of your friendly sibling, as well as through that of a rival. In our opinion, rivalry is anchored in terms of siblings' competition for the attention and priority of the parents. It is true; I'm more turned on by what quietly works rather than what doesn't work.

LR: I wonder if siblings play an even bigger role now in households where both parents work?

AS: Single children can grow up wonderfully and have the imagery and fantasies of siblings and use the knowledge of how siblings are through other people's eyes.

I think, though, that the sibling experience can be a very positive, as well as a challenging, experience. In general, when it works well, it's enormously useful. You see, I think at bedrock I'm probably defensively an optimist, more identified with my father than my mother. My father was an inveterate optimist, who would deny some of the most threatening things. Usually he was able to prove he was right, so I'm still trying to follow his example. That's the most personal thing I'll tell you.

LR: Your comment about your father reminds me of your noting in your essay, "Early Psychic Development as Reflected in the Psychoanalytic Process," the constancy of the influence of the primary love object throughout life. You wrote: "Examining the origins and development of love object choice in the constructions and reconstructions of the psychoanalytic process provides a useful view of early psychic functioning. Further, the view indicates how the choice of love object, a vital aspect of libidinal development, unfolds from earliest childhood into adulthood; while the influence of the primary love object changes and elaborates in complexity, the choice-process has powerfully influential ways of remaining constant. The uses and limits of psychoanalytic treatment to modify the influence of early psychic development in the adult personality emerged from this research as a related issue and as a feature of how the method of investigation has an impact on what is being studied."

In your clinical experience what helps promote psychic growth both in and outside of analysis? What relative roles would you assign to life events, intrapsychic factors?

AS: There is a rather large range of sources. The most natural, logical, efficient ones are based on a good relationship with a loving protective, guiding parent or parents. That doesn't always work since there may be unexpected losses. Achieving replacements is difficult. In our child analysis study group, we are trying to understand what promotes development. What do you understand and what do you say that promotes resolution of neurotic difficulties or other difficulties such as borderline conditions?

LR: That sounds interesting.

AS: Some children, depending on the constitutional capacity of their ego, can extract what they need from small amounts of nurture and stimulation. But if they are not well-equipped constitutionally, that may not be enough from which to extract. And we need to keep in mind that the nature and nurture thing is never solved. It's only refined and elaborated. Analysts have a better basis for understanding that, especially child analysts, than any other discipline I know. Maybe geneticists have that capacity. That's why it's not surprising that one of the most interesting books on genetics is written by a father and son, Peter Neubauer and his son, Alexander, *Thumbprints,* a study of identical twins.

SRR: I hope you don't mind if I make this comment, but I was thinking about "Notes on the Superego," by Hartmann, Kris, and Loewenstein.

AS: That was a powerful article.

SRR: I remember it was very powerful for me reading it. They talked about change occurring outside of the treatment catalyzing development, ongoing development, so I'm thinking that when you talk about normal development, how your earlier teachers must have inspired you in this direction as well.

AS: You see, Hartmann and Kris were dedicated to the understanding of the body and the mind. Hartmann was a very sophisticated biologist and neurologist, and Kris had always longed to be a physician. When any young person came to him and wanted to be an analyst, he said, "Go to medical school first, even though some parts of it won't be what you want." Are you both physicians?

SRR: No, I'm a psychologist.

LR: I'm a physician. What was Kris' training?

AS: He was an art historian and psychoanalyst.

SRR: I remember that. Right.

AS: He is still recognized as the world expert on cameo painting.

SRR/LR: Thank you so much.

SELECTED BIBLIOGRAPHY

Ritvo, S. & Solnit, A. J. (1958). Influences of early mother-child interaction on identification processes. *The Psychoanalytic Study of the Child,* Vol. 13, pp. 64–86. New York: International Universities Press.

Ritvo, S. & Solnit, A. J. (1960). The relationship of early ego identifications to superego formation. *International Journal of Psycho-Analysis,* Vol. 41, pp. 295–300.

Omwake, E. B. & Solnit, A. J. (1961). "It isn't fair," the treatment of a blind child. *The Psychoanalytic Study of the Child,* Vol. 16, pp. 352–404. New York: International Universities Press.

Solnit, A. J. & Stark, M. H. (1961). Mourning and the birth of a defective child. *The Psychoanalytic Study of the Child*, Vol. 16, pp. 523–537. New York: International Universities Press.

Solnit, A. J. (1964). A tribute to Heinz Hartmann. *Psychoanalytic Quarterly,* Vol. 33, pp. 475.

Solnit, A. J. (1966). Some adaptive functions of aggressive behavior. In: *Psychoanalysis—A General Psychology,* ed. R. M. Loewenstein, L. M. Newman, M. Schur, & A. J. Solnit. New York: International Universities Press.

Solnit, A. J. & Kris, M. (1967). Trauma and infantile experiences. In: *Psychic Trauma,* ed. S. S. Furst. New York: Basic Books.

Solnit, A. J. (1968). Eight paediatricians and a child psychiatrist. In: *The Teaching of Dynamic Psychiatry*, ed. G. L. Bibring. New York: International Universities Press.

Solnit, A. J. (1968). Child analysis and paediatrics: Collaborative interests. *International Journal of Psycho-Analysis,* Vol. 49, pp. 280–285.

Solnit, A. J. (1970). Learning from psychoanalytic supervision. *International Journal of Psycho-Analysis,* Vol. 51, pp. 359–362.

Solnit, A. J. (1970). A study of object loss in infancy. *The Psychoanalytic Study of the Child,* Vol. 25, pp. 257–272. New Haven: Yale University Press.

Solnit, A. J. (1972). Seymour L. Lustman. *The Psychoanalytic Study of the Child,* Vol. 27, pp. 3–7. New Haven: Yale University Press.

Solnit, A. J. (1972). Aggression: A view of theory building in psychoanalysis. *Journal of the American Psychoanalytic Association,* Vol. 20, pp. 435–250.

Solnit, A. J. (1972). Youth and the campus, the search for social conscience. *The Psychoanalytic Study of the Child*, Vol. 27, pp. 98–105. New Haven: Yale University Press.

Solnit, A. J. (1973). Commentary on movement therapy as a psychotherapeutic tool. *Journal of the American Psychoanalytic Association,* Vol. 21, pp. 344–346.

Solnit, A. J. & Priel, B. (1975). Psychological reactions to facial and hand burns in young men: Can I see myself through your eyes? *The Psychoanalytic Study of the Child,* Vol. 30, pp. 549–566. New Haven: Yale University Press.

Lord, R., Ritvo, S. & Solnit, A. J. (1978). Patients' reactions to the death of the psychoanalyst. *International Journal of Psycho-Analysis*, Vol. 59, pp. 189–197.

Solnit, A. J. (1982). Early psychic development as reflected in the psychoanalytic process. *International Journal of Psycho-Analysis,* Vol. 63, pp. 23–37.

Solnit, A. J. (1983). The sibling experience. *The Psychoanalytic Study of the Child,* Vol. 38, pp. 281–284. New Haven: Yale University Press.

Solnit, A. J. & Provence, S. (1983). The sibling experience promoting development: Vicarious mastery. *The Psychoanalytic Study of the Child,* Vol. 38, pp. 337–352. New Haven: Yale University Press.

Solnit, A. J. (1983). Anna Freud's contributions to child and applied analysis. *International Journal of Psycho-Analysis*, Vol. 64, pp. 379–390.

Solnit, A. J. (1984). Preparing. *The Psychoanalytic Study of the Child,* Vol. 39, pp. 613–632. New Haven: Yale University Press.

Solnit, A. J. (1984). *Memory as Preparation: Perspectives.* London: University College.

Solnit, A. J. (1987). A psychoanalytic view of play. *The Psychoanalytic Study of the Child,* Vol. 42, pp. 205–219. New Haven: Yale University Press.

W. CLIFFORD M. SCOTT

W. Clifford M. Scott, M.D. has been on the staff of the Maudsley and Cassell hospitals in London, where he maintains a private practice. Dr. Scott taught at the London Psychoanalytical Institute and the University of London Institute of Psychiatry. He resigned the Presidency of the British Psychoanalytical Society to return to Canada in order to introduce psychoanalytic training at McGill University. From that time, his primary work has involved the development of the Canadian Psychoanalytic Society and Institute and their branches. An ongoing focus in Dr. Scott's work has been the study of instincts and their vicissitudes in children and adults. Dr. Scott was interviewed June 20, 1991.

LR/SRR: We'd like to first ask, looking back now and considering your own development as an analyst, how you were introduced to analysis and what have been the highlights for you?

CS: Well,...I heard of analysis when I was a high school student in Toronto reading Bernard Hart's little book called *The Psychology of Insanity,* which I saw in the public library. In high school, I was more interested in physics and chemistry.

My father was a minister, and I grew up in a small town and across the road from the one doctor in town; Dr. Z had no children, and I was over there all the time. I didn't go to public school until I was seven and a half years old because both my parents had been school teachers. I was taught at home, being the first boy, the first child, too. But, eventually, I went into a new six-year course in medicine, which gave me a chance to study liberal arts subjects on a voluntary basis. I started in psychology, mathematics, and philosophy.

During these first three years, before we did clinical work I began to wonder if I wanted to become a doctor. I took a two-year fellowship in gross and microscopic anatomy, and I also became more interested in analysis, psychiatry, and hypnosis. I remember being at a tea party one Sunday afternoon. When I was told to show the group hypnosis, I had the courage to try to hypnotize a young girl. She certainly went under, so much so that we had difficulty waking her up! So, then I said I won't do more hypnosis until I learn more about it.

After two years of anatomy I went back into medicine for the last three years. A new professor in psychiatry came and gave brilliant lectures and knew about analysis. I learned a lot about psychiatry in the next year and a half as a student intern in a small psychiatric hospital of sixty beds. I wanted to train in psychiatry right away, so I didn't take an internship in medicine.

I was offered a post at Hopkins; I couldn't afford to take it—they weren't paying anything. So I went for 14 months to Manhattan State Hospital on Ward's Island, New York City. It was an 8,000-bed hospital, and I saw a great many intake patients. I also spent one month when the female doctor went on holiday in a 400-bed unit for chronic, catatonic schizophrenics, all of whom had to be "seen" twice a day. I saw much clinical phenomena that I hadn't seen before. Many of the staff of this 8,000-bed hospital lived on the island, so I did some general work, helping the full-time intern in charge, the visiting surgeons and other specialists, giving anesthetics or doing whatever was needed. I then went to Hopkins in September 1928.

Adolph Meyer, who was one of the first analysts in America, joined the first group there and helped form the American Psychoanalytic Association. He had been in Vienna during the 1928 summer, and he had brought Paul Schilder back to Hopkins. As a junior in charge of a ten-bed female ward of restless, retarded, and excited suicidal patients, I admired Schilder for daily discussing my patients and using them for teaching. Schilder wrote two books that year—one on the relationship of psychiatric symptoms to brain function and the other on the understanding of the relationship of psychoanalysis to physical troubles.

Meyer gave a very intensive course for each of the four years of medical students and for all first-year interns. You had to learn and say clearly what is the problem and what is the complaint. Within twenty-four hours of admission you began an intensive examination. At the end of a week, you had to know enough to write a formulation for Meyer with all the data you could present. You also had to write a formulation for the referring physician, for the patient's family, for all the medical auxiliaries, for the psychologist, for the social workers, for occupational therapists, for the nurses, for the significant relatives, spouse, children, and for the patient in language each could understand. When you do that forty times in one year with new patients, you certainly learn something. You also had to write what he called a "personality study" because he believed in the genetic development of individuals.

Meyer talked to me about my career, and he advised that I apply to the Boston Psychopathic Hospital where his previous chief assistant, MacFie Campbell, was then professor. I came to Boston in September 1929 and worked very hard as a senior intern. I was interested then in the biological aspects of depression, and I wrote a little essay about one of my patients who was so depressed that she had very little appetite. I found that this patient had no hydrochloric acid in her stomach. After testing her with a drug supposed to enable secretion of hydrochloric acid, we didn't know if she just had too severe inhibition or if the drug simply didn't work.

When I came to Boston, I wanted to treat somebody intensively and see what analysis was like. Campbell said, "Fine, go ahead, if you have the time and the energy." So, I picked a 35-year-old woman who was a civil service secretary. She had been brought in having run away with her cat and some food, because she thought she was going to be kidnapped by "white slavers." Behind that she felt that her boss was arousing her sexually, and her mother was telling her that she should get married and have a baby. I saw her for the next two years for about 500 hours. She got somewhat better, but not well enough to leave the hospital; she was still very scared, shy, and sad. A social worker, if available, might have helped her with a lot of these problems.

When I came back to Boston in 1954, I went to see her in the hospital. I hadn't seen her in 30 years. She was in a ward for chronic women and looked the same, except 30 years older. She felt I did, too. I had a very uncanny feeling, it was like the next interview. And she said to me, "You know, we tried to do too much too fast." That was a very interesting projection. She had tried to do too much too fast, and she was there in the hospital because she couldn't learn enough fast enough to find her way outside. All her relatives had died, her persecutors had died. Now she had no one to look after her dental care and her glasses, and she couldn't make friends in the hospital. It was a pitiful sight. I saw her two or three times. She didn't fight me as she had, but she had not become hopeful. She was sad and didn't know how she could adapt to any situation in Boston; she had no contacts. Eventually, when I went to see her later, she had been discharged; I couldn't find out to where. She was one of the ones that was lost. I learned a great deal about schizophrenic development and chronic secret masturbation from her.

I had planned to stay in Boston only one year, but I was offered a three-year teaching fellowship in psychiatry at Harvard. In the second year, I could go overseas to have some analysis because there was no one else in Boston except Martin Peck and no organized analytic teaching course. And so I moved into Vanderbilt Hall, a new residence for medical students and visiting faculty. I continued my analysis of this patient and discussed her repeatedly with a group of people.

I became interested in writing about the unconscious. Of course, I read a lot of Hartmann's volumes, which were much better on the unconscious than others. Campbell attended some of my discussions but also taught concepts of the unconscious, having studied philosophy and anthropology before medicine.

I corresponded with Ernest Jones about my possibilities for training in England. He said, "Oh yes, come to England, don't get mixed up with any American groups." Eventually, I went to London and saw Jones and Glover. Jones asked me who I wanted as an analyst. I didn't know, so they sent me to Melanie Klein. I saw her, and my analysis began.

SRR: How did they decide on her for you?

CS: I don't know. I think she wanted a student. I was her first student. She had many analysts in analysis, but I was the first person she analyzed who had not had previous analysis. You find out about analysis when you try to accept being an analysand in the hands of an analyst, wondering, What's he or she doing for me? Will I be able to do it myself, learn something about self-analysis? Freud did. I was also going to the National Hospital for neurology and clerked for Holmes, Riddoch, and Symonds.

SRR: Could we ask about your experience with her?

CS: Well,...her room was her drawing room. She had a couch with a head at the top which was on a hinge. She sat behind me, and I lay down. I can't tell you exactly what she said at first. She introduced herself to me and we arranged times and money and so forth, and she said, "Lie down." I can't remember whether she told me to tell her everything that was on my mind or not, because that was assumed. I began to talk, and I talked about her, the room, about her not being a doctor and that she was a Jewess, and I mentioned her being a woman. And she said, "I'm a Jewess, I'm not a doctor, and I am a woman. Anyway," she said, "you can choose; are you going to go on with analysis with me or not?" I waited not very long. I said, "Yes, I will."

So it was not the first interpretation or first confrontation, but it was an interpretation of the fact that I could stop or continue. It was a very important thing that you are not demanding but offering something.

And then I began to get dizzy. I'm flying this way and that way. I began to feel like I was going like this and with the dizziness like that, and she gave this a sexual interpretation immediately. "You've made a mistake, you're head over heels." I was heels over head. "As if you want to be all over me. This is a normal childish reaction in connection with excitement." I don't know whether she laughed or not, but I laughed. She certainly could laugh. She had a great laugh. And I chuckled at this situation. And then we went on. Soon I began to talk about my Boston patient in analysis, as I had tried it. And for six months I talked a great deal about my patient, using my 500 hours trying to understand so many things that I couldn't understand. And she referred always back to my history. I don't remember what the first thing was she did, but I didn't take notes.

There was so much to think of after each interview, six interviews a week, that I didn't sit down and write notes until I had patients in supervision. It was more than six months before I began to talk a great deal about myself in terms of continuity; each of the anxieties of my patient had led to something in my own life. That year I was allowed to attend lectures and seminars, and about half-way through the first year, I started to take a patient under Jones' supervision. Technically, I needed two to become a member. I started one, and then I had a second under Rickman.

But as the time went on, I became more interested in the analytic situation there. Her book *The Psychoanalysis of Children* came out that year in German and soon after in English. She gave me a copy in German before I could get a copy in English, but I couldn't read it very well. I wanted to get child training. And it so happened that that year, in my first summer, 1932, was the 100th anniversary celebration of the British Medical Association.

Campbell from Boston and Meyer from Hopkins were two of the chief speakers. They were asked to come over and give addresses on psychiatry to the psychiatric section of the British Medical Association. I was able to arrange for both of them to interview Melanie Klein. Both of them told me the same thing—that she's an amazing woman, but that they didn't know whether she was projecting all these ideas into these children or not. Time would tell. Either this is all craziness, or people will wonder why they didn't ever report this work with children before. Time has told us that she was right about it.

It was all a little bit different than what happened when Freud presented his material to a medical audience. They said this is a matter for the police. This isn't a matter for a medical meeting. I felt then that time would move a little bit faster than it did. Campbell was there, and he was the one who determined whether I was going to go back to Boston or not in September. I pleaded with him to allow me to stay to take child analysis, and he begrudgingly did. He said, "We don't want people to get too interested in all this."

That was 1932. And then 1933 came along and that was a very bad time, the Depression. The next year, in the spring of 1933, I was trying to get a job to come back to, but I couldn't get one in Boston or in New York. I was going to be broke without my scholarship, and I didn't have a license to practice. I needed a medical license, so I took and passed my exams and got a job at the Maudsley hospital.

Jones said, "If you're going to practice, you'll get patients. I'll send you patients, and people will also come knocking at your door late at night saying, 'Somebody's in trouble, do you know anybody who could help them?' but it often turns out it is they who want to be helped. They don't want anybody to know that they are in trouble or seeing an analyst." And this turned out to be true; later, of course. I was qualified in twenty-six months as an associate member of the British Psychoanalytic Society. A couple of years later I gave an essay and became a full member of the Society. I began to supervise before the War, but during the War I was out of analysis. When I came back, I became a supervisor and training analyst.

SRR: Where was this now?

CS: Back in London in 1946. In late 1952, MacLeod, a recent London graduate analyst who had moved to Montreal, visited London looking for recruits for psychiatry and analysis in Montreal. In the summer of 1953, Professor Ewen Cameron visited London and wanted me to come to Montreal. I went there for a week in the fall of 1953, then came in 1954 to try to introduce training in analysis in the Department of Psychiatry at McGill in Montreal along with Hans and Friedl Aufrieter, who were Viennese-trained members of the British Society.

We believed that we could have an ongoing training program if we had two more training analysts. We soon ran into trouble, though, when Cameron wouldn't agree to the appointment of the fourth member of our group. In the meantime, analysts who'd been trained in the States, England, and France, began to return to Montreal, and the society, sponsored by the British, began to develop. It was eventually recognized by the International Psychoanalytic Society.

After our group was recognized as a society, we decided to form an institute. Though at first it was an English institute, later we had two branches training in Montreal—one in French and one in English. Both have continued until the present. It was 1958, the year before I resigned from McGill, that the institute began. At that time, you could not work at the University if you worked at the Institute. Professor Cameron had hoped to continue the work I had started, but when this didn't happen, he gave in, and the English Branch Institute began to cooperate with the University to some degree.

SRR: And the philosophy of the school or institute in terms of theory…?

CS: It was an eclectic group: English and Viennese training, some with middle-group English training; others trained in the Klein group, others with Anna Freud, some from Paris and the U.S. At first, there was psychoanalytic training under the auspices of McGill, which ended in 1959 when I resigned. The training then began under the Canadian Psychoanalytic Institute. There were no branches at first, just the Montreal group with some of the members of the Canadian Society in Toronto coming up to teach. Later, other branches developed in Montreal, Toronto, and Ottawa.

SRR: Could you tell us about some of the other analysts who were important to you?

CS: One of my teachers was Ella Sharpe who came into analysis by way of teaching; she was head of a girl's school. She's the one analyst whose voice I can hear when I read her. She was a beautiful teacher, a beautiful head mistress, and a beautiful teacher of English. And she was—well, I just think of the pleasure and poise of an English girl's school.

LR: While we're thinking of people you've known, I noticed that you mention Balint in several of your essays.

CS: I knew Balint early, when he first came to England. During the War he went to Manchester and he did some extremely important experimental work with babies. Earlier I had read Middlemore's book on the nursing mother. I don't know whether you know that. She was an analyst, writing about the varieties of mothers and varieties of babies and their adjustments in the first months; it's a beautiful little book. She died young. And Balint? He came to one very interesting conclusion about the differences between babies, which he called positive pressure feeding babies and negative pressure feeding babies. Do you remember that?

LR: No, I just remember your mentioning in your essay on blathering, that it might be more of a positive pressure expression. It struck me as I had never thought of it in those terms.

CS: Some mothers pump milk into the baby's mouth and the baby has to latch onto the breast to keep it from leaking out. Others have to be sucked and hold tight on the teat to keep air from being sucked in. I don't know how quickly babies adjust to which it's going to be. Some have a nursing mother who has to get at her baby or the milk would go six feet across the room. And Balint was the one person that was most interested in discussing it with me.

I have also been interested in mood. If a person is angry, he can get angry at being angry, and then become even more angry. Each reflection brings a new complexity of interrelationship from one part of the self to another part.

People can forget whether they want to remember. If they forget that they've forgotten, then it's not there. It's like repression, sometimes what we call "the deeply repressed memory," which hasn't been there for a long time and then it suddenly is there and may appear from the forgotten quickly. Other people want to remember and then realize that they wanted not only to forget, but to forget that they've forgotten.

LR: It reminds me of your writing about memories connected to "mourning for what might have been."

CS: You asked the question earlier about Balint. Well, he was very interested in the body in neurological terms, as well as psychological terms, but he didn't elaborate the concept of the body image as much as I had hoped.

With regard to this instinctive activity, sleep has a beginning and an end. We all remember when we woke up today, we have some anticipation that we are going to sleep tonight, and so we think of it as repetitive. At the beginning, we have to separate the difference between going to sleep and what we later called death. Often children are told they are going to die, to sleep forever and dream forever. But they ask "What's beyond the dreams?"

In his book on the skin, Anzieu views skin as one aspect to the body. The body has its solidity, its holes and cavities, this idea of the container. We hear that psychosomatic patients don't have fantasy, but they are full of fantasy; the way they describe their body is fantastic. They never separate what we call the body reality from their fantastic ideas.

LR: Your essay on the body schema was interesting to me, as you indicate that patients' body representations in fantasy have deep psychological roots. In your experience, do patients tend to focus their representations on particular levels of the body schema? For example, one person experiencing fantasies related to skin, another more focused on the digestive tract?

CS: There is so much more to it, and that brings me back to one of Meyer's phrases: "Beware of the falsity of pseudosimplicity" or of coming to a closure too soon. There is a difference between senses and a remembered image, or an anticipated image. We do separate senses, and some people become extremely sensory. But that varies very much. Along with it is fantasy, and where does that come from? Isn't it a question of what we call "dream"? What is the difference from the "waking up" and "sensing"?

Dreams always contain what we call day residues from the world, with light and dark furniture, other people's flowers, and the sun and moon, so that is something I have thought about a lot—the conflict between sleeping and waking. We know we do the same things we do with other instincts which we try to modify, and so forth. Sleep has its vicissitudes, but at the same time we say it is a compliment if we see someone who is "sleeping like a baby"; we're continually thinking of secondary process and the primary process, and what are the earliest forms of sleep and dreams.

Winnicott quotes me in one of his essays on body schema, and he quotes Jones on the mind. In his last essay, Jones talked about the mind not being an entity, but a myth that we should give up. He liked the enigma of existence, the soul versus the mind.

SRR: That brings up a question. What are your thoughts about working with people at different points of the life cycle, whether the process of mourning is different when people are older versus younger?

CS: Yes, well, it's like Piaget or Isaacs. At every stage, a child begins to have some continuity. They may go back and fumble the way they did at their best at other times. They are comparing themselves to someone else who was developed to another stage, and they are very impatient about practicing, taking their time with each one. For instance, my mother was always saying the cure of adolescence is time. It takes ten years to go ten years. You can try to do it faster, but you can't do it faster. So the ideals of mourning at any time are continually changing. When you come to geriatric analysis you can analyze people in their eighties, and self-analysis at eighty-eight is different from what it was at twenty-eight or forty-eight.

SRR: Does the nature of transference change when you're working with patients who are older?

CS: If you are analyzing transference in terms of people in the past, you have to think of the age of the person who appears. For one woman the transference appeared to be a man. When the man appeared first in analysis, he was forty, but her knowledge of him was from twenty to forty, and so he was a different man at forty than at twenty. As soon as she began to deal with the relationship with him at twenty, before she actualized the relationship at forty, she became confused about her memories of what she had anticipated and what actually happened. This woman is now almost sixty. Her husband almost died in her arms some months ago. That was a unique experience to her because that was apparently the way she wanted to nurse her father to his death but didn't, because she wasn't there. There are certain scenes that differ, like the primal scene, which is different from childhood to later life. So it is with the child's idea of what it is to watch a birth or to be born. The child is different at different ages. If you've seen somebody killed or die when you are at different ages, it is quite a different experience.

LR: You gave an interesting example in one of your essays of a man who, having lost his grandfather at age 4, seemed to experience himself "dying" as an "internalized death experience" when he reached the age at which his grandfather died.

CS: He was depressed, saying "I'm going to die," and then he would disidentify saying, "I don't want to die. I can live longer than he did."

LR: Given such an observation, how do you think the unconscious timetable keeps track? At times, it seems uncanny.

CS: Time is one of the most difficult problems to keep in touch with in analysis or in general about the body scheme, because there is such a thing as real time. The sun and the moon, from the time we are born, haven't changed very much, and day and night have been there. We even know there is rhythm. We think of objects as a mass rather than as a continuation of a change in mass, and that's where we get so mixed up in connection with function.

In fact, there is a lot of this in my essay on time. I was describing the fantastic or the realistic of time. Recently, a patient discovered in his fifties that he had believed he was going to live to 120 and that he wouldn't retire until he was 90. There is an old Jewish expression he had heard as a child, *"Leben sie ein hundert und zwanzig."* This became part of his belief, "I'm going to live to be 120, and I'll retire at 90." His partners wanted to change the rules of retirement. He was quite like a psychotic, but it was his own way of keeping in touch with what he knew about people. He came to know that this was more a metaphor instead of a good judgment of fact.

SRR: How do you conceptualize what analysis does that allows people to grow or change?

CS: The process of analysis is searching for the new truth, searching for everything and finding something. We know we've forgotten a lot, and we've forgotten that we've forgotten a lot—the repressed. If we remember our life, then we may find that we can have a second chance. I'm reminded of a very intelligent patient who wondered what would have happened if she hadn't stopped school at twelve. She said, "I can't make up for all I've missed." You see, it's a tremendous amount of mourning. She still writes like a twelve-year-old. She has never developed a script, and she writes slowly. In her analysis, she's developed a much greater vocabulary and she's quite a talker. She argues with her son who is going to college, and she's getting a great education from what he's learning in college.

LR: You have talked about body schema being represented psychically as a continuum in time and space. How does early childhood trauma, emotional or physical, affect the psychic representation of body schema and is the continuity disrupted in significant, detectable ways?

CS: You see, we are talking about ideals in terms of continuum. Sometimes there are big gaps in a person's life related to repressions. This whole problem comes up in connection with multiple personalities. They ask "How many lives have I lived?" I read yesterday that the Dalai Lama was at Harvard quite recently, talking about consciousness in terms of the continuity of a different life and interests before, beyond the bodily consciousness. The body scheme of the Dalai Lama includes that you're going to die sometime, but you're going to come back again.

I think you caught how my thinking has changed a little bit in terms of the way people talk about God. God has come to mean a three-letter word for everything. Just as patients switch from remembering earlier events to anticipating later events, they also switch from talking about everything to talking about the whole versus a part and a nothing. Their switching is searching from their remembering of earlier events and anticipations of later events; it's switching also from some way of talking about everything to talking about something that's a whole versus a part and a nothing.

SRR: I was struck in your essays by your freedom and respect for patients' being able to express the nonverbal parts of themselves through noise, through movement, and focusing on it. How, in your own experience and training, did you develop that kind of ability, both to observe and to enable that kind of freedom.

CS: Partially, it goes back to my first interview with Klein when I had brought the memory of dizziness—it had all sort of history in my lifetime. One of the tricks my father used to do was to flip me with my hands between my legs. I also remember when I romped in my parents' bed. It's a wonderful thing, to stand on two feet, balance, and then fall down. It's great to learn that if you're going to take one step, you have to balance on one leg while the other leg takes a step. Only then are you able to learn to run and skip and jump, and so on.

I always advise students to try at least to analyze one child, particularly one two to five years old, who is learning so much during that time. Eventually I don't think people will be qualified until they show their capacity for child analysis—it would be like not knowing medicine until they know pediatrics.

In fact, pediatricians started an institute in Montreal to teach pediatrics because it wasn't taught in the University. When the University saw that they were really going to have it outside, they brought it into the medical faculty. I wonder if that will ever happen with analysis. I'm a nurse, fundamentally; I'm a philosopher. I'm a psychologist rather than a professional psychoanalyst.

SRR: That brings us to another question. What are your thoughts about the future of psychoanalysis, where do you see it heading, what would you like to see occur, and what do you worry about?

CS: Actually, one of the contemporary worries is whether analysis is a profession. For instance, in the British society at the moment they make only the medical doctors Doctors. All the psychologists want to have their Doctor titles. In Canada, our roster has no prefixes. We're all analysts. But the problem is, What is analysis? How different is it? There's also the problem of watering down to short analysis, to something less than the best we could make in every working day. What is the essence of analysis? Confidentiality, the truth, discovering new mechanisms, and not knowing what's going to happen. When you analyze a child, you have to have somebody in the environment to support that. With a schizophrenic, you have to have a better environment than a custodial mental hospital to help a patient get better. In other words, we want to be an ally to provide a holding environment, just as we want the patient to be able to hold himself. Often we say, "Oh, if you have never felt this way before, this is not a memory. It may be in the beginnings of this as a child you learned to control or postpone its continuity. Nothing has happened and now you want something new to happen." At the end of the interview I'll say, "You want something oral, but we don't know what yet."

The best example of that was a man who began to laugh in the middle of the interview and couldn't stop. It was such a laugh—I would say, he had never laughed like that before. All I could say at the interview was what I just said to you: he has controlled such capacity before and he can again, and wants to contain it (luckily) till tomorrow. He left. He came the next day, and the door was barely closed when he began to laugh again. He closed the door, and he wanted to lie down. He laughed the whole interview. After ten minutes into the third interview I could see he was trying to speak. After another fifteen minutes he did speak, saying with tremendous relief, "I am not my mother." It was like the man who said "I am not my grandfather." Well, his mother was a chronic schizophrenic who had been deserted by her husband when he was an eight-year-old with older siblings. She had collected the family urine and stools and had boiled it for breakfast for them all. She was called crazy and sent to the hospital. She came back and did the same thing again. Then she went back into the hospital and has never been out.

He got better. I had a letter from him many years after he finished his analysis and he said only one thing: "I think you may have realized, I have come to realize, I was more manic than you realized when I laughed so much." He had been dealing after the laughing with mourning and the previous denial of his hopelessness about his mother.

LR: You write about working successfully with manic-depressive patients in analysis in a hospital setting. Could you tell us more about those experiences?

CS: Yes, it was at the Cassell Hospital, a sixty-bed hospital with six of us, each with ten patients. I was able to begin analysis there after being an intern at the Maudsley and before I went into private practice. Some manic-depressives have a psychotic core, and some people are intensely manic-depressive. These may have some obsessional symptoms, or they may regress to almost a paranoid state, or a megalomaniac state, in contrast to self-reproachful and manic states. I have had patients like that for many years. There are many unsolved problems about regression and progression and oscillation between alternative states.

LR: What was your sense of how long these patients were able to maintain their gains?

CS: Well, I've had failures. Once earlier in my career I gave an essay on how many I treated had improved and how many didn't. The problem is that people vary so much, just as schizophrenics do. You don't know who you are able to help until you try. There is so much to be learned. The problem is how any patient can be helped in any way. There is a history of spontaneous recoveries. But what is spontaneous? It only means that something happens quickly. When Janet gave a paper in New York, he called these quick changes "psycholeptic." We know many of these psychotic states change tremendously, sometimes very quickly.

LR: What are your thoughts about the contemporary emphasis on biological treatment of manic-depressive illness? Is it the same in Canada, as in the U.S.?

CS: That's one of the problems of the future. It's going to change. I remember Meyer saying hormones have a great future. They can do so much good and harm. Thyroid extract was the first, and it was addictive. Now it is still legal, but I haven't seen it used for decades. We've got a tremendous drug problem in our country, not just drugs for psychotic patients. General practitioners give so many people so many drugs that are legally prescribed, but there are so many recreational drugs. People want the fast track. Children are growing up with so many drugs at home, on T.V., and in shops, and are being taught that. At the same time there are many sorts of different temptations; alcohol and tobacco are always there, but you know there are new drugs always coming.

LR: Is analysis well-received in Canada? Are analysts able to practice more full-time analysis?

CS: There is not the difficulty in Canada there is here. Here there are many sorts of psychotherapy. But what is psychotherapy? In England, they have a government commission to define what psychotherapy is. They have taken about eleven groups, of which analysts are one, to determine how psychotherapy can be defined and regulated. I don't know what's going to become of analytic parameters. It's hard enough for us to say what our own standards are and what the difference is between any other kind of treatment and analysis. When I was called up for war, I could only see patients for a week at a time. Seeing them every day for a week or twice a day for a week than if I had seen them less frequently, I could make analytic interpretations more often.

SRR: What do you think is the most important part of training for people like us beginning our analytic careers? What do you recommend as the best learning experiences?

CS: Well, first clarify why you chose analysis. Then consider what's analysis. It's a changing thing. What is its "work" on "sublimation"? What do you want it to become? Now come back to the question of the training. First of all, you are selected. Then you get some introduction. The more history you read, the more autobiographies you read, the more you learn surprising aspects of people. I'm just reading *The Silent Lectures* by Professor Salmon Campbell. It was given to me the other day by the wife of a neurologist in Boston. Do you know who Salmon was? Salmon was the chief psychiatrist in the American services during World War I. He was quite an enthusiastic person, and he died shortly afterwards. His friends made a collection of enough money to give three lectures a year by some prominent psychiatrist and have a book published. Well, I'm just reading Campbell's lectures about the history of psychiatry. He addresses the very topic we're discussing—the need for a more interesting, humane, and pluralistic attitude toward the psychoses.

Freud, himself, said maybe drugs will become bigger business. Who knows what drugs are going to do? They have a terrible and tremendous effect. Freud gave himself and his wife cocaine. Meyer used experimental drugs. There are going to be discoveries. I grew up in Toronto. I was taking my anatomy when insulin was discovered—it was amazing. There are going to be discoveries and tremendous mistakes. Perhaps lithium is a tremendous mistake to use without knowing more. But it's cheap. What are the cheapest, and what are the most expensive? We rarely know. ECT is still used. Often it was advised as a preventative. But it was too dangerous to become a bathroom "use as needed" accessory to keep spirits from becoming too low! And talk about fits [seizures]—that's one thing that very few analysts report: analysis of people with fits. I know of a very successful recent analysis of a person with fits. They turned out to be substitutes for one aspect of her sexual activity. At a certain stage in her sexual development, intense orality had been inhibited and she had a fit instead. Eventually, a new partner in sexuality was more tolerant and finally they came together, and she's a very successful person now.

LR: Do you think candidates now are missing important experiences which you had in your own development as an analyst?

CS: I don't think they have the courage to risk getting the best understanding of themselves. Nor do they feel that they are going to make a good living because they aren't sure they will get patients. They can get patients if they look for them and analyze them well. If they learn to analyze them better and better, their successes will present them with new patients. It's what Jones told me: have the courage to go into private practice. They will be supported. But there are so many more analysts and other experts now. There is so much money going into child research, which will find again what child analysts have found out before. That is one place research should go. The facts of analysis of children can be made public more easily than with adults.

Somebody's already given money to award a prize of more than $100,000 a year for the best contributions to adult analysis in the last ten years. I don't know who, or what kind of group of people are going to get together to give anyone such a prize for work with children. The American Psychoanalytic Association lost a court battle recently in connection with the training of analysts without a medical background. When I returned to Canada in 1954, I was not allowed to become a member of the American Psychoanalytic because I was proposing the training of nonmedical analysts, of professionals from other fields trying to help people with problems and complaints in a new way.

SRR: I'm a psychologist, so I really appreciate hearing this.

CS: Are you a psychologist?

LR: I'm a psychiatrist.

CS: When I went into psychiatry, only selected doctors said that it was right to train nonmedical doctors. Some from the beginning thought that if analysis was going to go to the university, the selection had to be broader than for doctors because analysis was something so different and new. These views led to my being interested in why analysis wasn't discovered centuries ago. It's so simple. What do you think? Somebody is writing a book about the history of analysis. Aristophanes' comedy, *The Clouds*, depicts Sophocles almost inventing analysis. Many priests devoted time listening to confessions and learned much and helped many, but their work never had the professionalism, or acclaim, of medicine or surgery. The Benedictines, in the time of Queen Elizabeth I, giving prolonged confessions to scrupulous penitents, really discovered analysis, but the switches in the manic-depressives posed complex problems.

Psychoanalysis as a developing science has made a beginning. I cannot imagine it disappearing, only becoming better. Those who became interested in trying to help scrupulous penitents unable to accept absolution were, to me, really dealing with agitated depressions. Priests gave them long confessions, but they stopped for some reason. Most of the literature in Latin has not been translated, but there is one, Masterman, who has translated quite a bit. One can read between the lines. I think they got scared when some of their penitents suddenly changed and became manic and felt they were in touch with God, more in touch with God than the confessor was, and that led them to the sin of false pride and got them into new trouble. Analysis is observation. Galton, in 1879, wrote an article in *Brain*. Oddly enough, *Brain* is still being published as a journal of neurology, while *Mind* is still being published as a journal of philosophy. Both journals started about the same time. Galton was a medical school dropout who eventually became professor of genetics at the University of London. He began to experiment on himself with free association. He was trying to categorize statistically what happens when one thinks freely. He only wrote one article saying this isn't possible scientifically, and there is no future to it because the details would be too intimate for anybody to make public.

Talking or writing to anyone, including oneself, may become so secret and intimate that an analyst might be willing to go to jail rather than divulge what the analysand has said. Of course, later the analyst or analysand might change his attitude. I remember it being said that Meyer was against analysis, but in my opinion he felt that it was such an important procedure, it should be reserved for those patients who could not be helped otherwise. Then it should be really confidential with no hospital notes other than those stating the fact of there being an ongoing psychoanalysis in progress. Another psychiatrist would care for any other in- or outpatient treatment needed. The nearest treatment to analysis was what he called "distributive analysis." With this method, associations were kept to the complaints and problems rather than being "free."

A student, Finesinger, who became Professor of Psychiatry at University of Baltimore, became an analyst. He had an obsessional patient telling his story who talked, and talked, and talked. Finesinger could never give an interpretation because the patient always gave it to himself first, and he could never catch up. Eventually, after several years, the patient said: "I think I'm finished. I can do this myself now." He said, "Goodbye and thank you very much, Doctor," and he had never been given one interpretation. That to me was an example of good distributive analysis. His free association wasn't interfered with.

On the other hand, Meyer did advise analysis. I remember one patient, a late adolescent girl who had fits. After much examination and treatment the staff didn't know whether they were epileptic or not. Anyhow, Meyer said, "We'd better try analysis." He gave her a female doctor and said that the patient will eventually become confident, and there will be no records of this endeavor. The patient got better. Years later she gave her analyst permission to tell the staff, who had known her when she was ill, about her history. She had been her father's favorite. Her mother died and her father remarried a woman who was very jealous of his children. She turned out to be homosexual and seduced his daughter into homosexual activity. Out of this developed her fits and her secrecy. That kind of problem may often be in the background. You find people willing to take a challenge and risk much. Some get the help they can use, and you may learn a great deal from the ones that accept the help you can offer.

LR: As you talk, it is clear how much you have maintained your enjoyment of analysis and people.

CS: Well, I don't know whether I've written about it or not, how loving your work is one of your loves. One of your love's works is analysis.

LR: How do you think about the personality of an analyst? Are there particular qualities which you think are most helpful or important for an analyst?

CS: I've just written a review of a new book that's coming out on psychoanalysis and culture. I've wondered about the difference in personality and culture. We're born into a civilization, we're born into a family, a nation, a culture, religion, politics, and so forth. All those shape personality. Who from Yale wrote the book called *The Person*?

LR: Lidz.

CS: Lidz, yes. That's an excellent book. There's a new edition that's better. His idea is that behind a person is the self, the "I," the "me," and the "what are you going to call it?" One long-term patient of mine became angry, saying, "You know, you've never given me a name." And I was put on the spot by her. What did I think? Had I given her a name? So I broke my habit and said "Yes, to me you are '__________.' That's going to be your name." And she said, "Well every doctor should be a little more like you are."

So analysts must be interested in people, in children, in life histories, and they mustn't be too hung up or ill. Everybody has their quirks, but they must do something to try to get rid of as many as they can, and focus on how they can further develop.

Somebody may complain about you, as professors have complained about me, because I was too interested in words. I just read an autobiography of Piaget who said he didn't want to get too interested in patients because he might become too autistic. He had to stick to experiments! As Freud put it, "You don't want to become identified with your patient." The more ill they are, the less you want to become them, but the more you want to understand them. It's as if you've made some links between something you've reached in your own self—you have some common bond. That's talked about in this country as "empathy." Well that was an interesting introduction from the German. It's a German invention.

Freud wrote Fleiss, "A man, Lipps, the psychologist, knows too much about dreams. I don't want to read what he writes." And oddly enough, the word sympathy (sympatisch) dropped from the German language for quite some time, a German professor told me. Lipps invented his own word for putting yourself in the place of the artist: What is the artist trying to do? Are they trying to get help, or are they trying to learn to do something themselves? Everybody wants to make a new discovery about himself, sometimes with help from somebody else, so he can carry on with life. Ross said training and analysis is like getting your Ph.D. You have to make a new discovery, and in analysis you have to make a new change in your personality which you are going to grow with for the rest of your life.

LR: You are talking about how analysts observe themselves. It reminds me of your paper on sleeping and waking, how they are often parallel processes. Could you elaborate more on how you make sense of an analyst's sleepiness in relation to the patient?

CS: Yes, it's a problem, just as it's a problem to discover the patient's fight against his sleepiness. Winnicott told me a patient felt that he was so sleepy one time that she left, saying: "You lie down here and take the rest of our interview for self-analysis. I'll give you a present." I never had a patient do that. One of my candidates, who is now an analyst, has written a book about his life. He and his wife were both in concentration camps before the War and were released. They married afterwards. When the War began, they were sent to Czechoslovakia. Sometimes he felt I was asleep, so he began to speak in Czech. When I asked him to translate, he looked around, apparently surprised that I was just looking up. Once I had a patient turn around and take a picture of me.

LR: Yes, you mentioned that.

CS: If you are sleeping, should you excuse the patient and say, "I'll see you tomorrow?" I often wondered who ever did that because a patient bored him or he felt he could make better use of his time: shades of Lacan. The problem is greater than that, though, because when all instincts come into analysis in one way or another, memories of sleep and anticipation of what's my next sleep, and so on, keep coming.

One interesting thing is that as I age and have more time for self-analysis, I become more interested in analysis of the aged. What helped was waking-up around 4:00 A.M. and trying to understand more about the way as a baby I had coped with early morning hunger. What do they do? They begin to daydream or return to sleep, or wake and daydream of what they want, or of what others want, and discover they want to sleep. I realize I don't always want to sleep, but parents do so often want children to sleep. It's a problem. So that comes up in analysis. It's very difficult for patients, who often say: "I don't want to sleep here; I'll never sleep here." But then you find they almost fall asleep. They are on guard against it, as if there is something wrong with it. But in case they fall asleep, it is better to know how would they like to be wakened, because some may sleep through to the end of the session!

LR: In your monograph, "Remembering Sleep and Dreams," you made a distinction between countertransference and an analyst's appreciation of his or her own shifting repetition of unconscious and preconscious attitudes in response to different patients. Could you say more about this distinction?

CS: Yes. Well, countertransference has a long history. We know something about self-analysis, and we know something about the attempts to analyze a developing transference and the analyst's defenses against doing so. When we are with a patient, some of that self-analysis goes on. At the same time, it is mixed up with the fact that we are thinking, Are we or are we not going to give an interpretation? Does this interfere with our listening or not? What we think about this analysis and analysand all become related and perhaps confused. Is that part of our self-analysis? By saying something to myself, did I miss what the patient may have said? Did I say something like it that I didn't hear precisely?

To use such self-analytic material with patients without having analyzed it sufficiently first is trying something new. Under what conditions do you ever use it? Do you ever tell a patient a bit of your self-analysis which is very important? For instance, when you've made a mistake and you've said something to a patient with whom you've confused another patient or somebody else you know. It is one thing to say to a patient, "I made a mistake; I was doing something, and you don't need to go into what I was doing." But it's another thing to tell the patient what was going on and to ask him to associate to what you said. It gives you the opportunity to analyze what he thinks of your making a mistake. The problem is, can you maintain the analysis and admit you've made a mistake? Can you risk what might be a different kind of mistake, involving your patient in wanting to analyze you? I don't know of any instances in which the analyst has said, "I can't go on with this analysis. I want you to analyze me if you want to." I've heard that it happened once—after an analysand became an analyst, he then analyzed the analyst. Have you ever heard of that?

LR: No, never.

CS: In fact, when I heard that from the informant, I didn't want to know with whom this ever happened. I didn't want to complicate my life; you see what I mean? It's like Freud, when he said to Jung, "I'm not going to talk to you so much anymore. You know too much about me already." I didn't want to know whether anyone in England had been analyzed by a previous analysand because I hoped that I would never ask a student of mine to do it. You can't cease to be a real person or not have your feelings. Some might say what is important is the amount of emotion that you show and whether your patient sees. Once I got a cable that my sister had died overseas. I didn't stop my practice that day, but I'm sure I looked sad; my patients observed it and talked about it.

LR: You've mentioned self-analysis several times. How have you used it over the years and in what ways has it evolved for you?

CS: I went back for two periods of analysis. Both of them helped in the sense that I did more concentrated self-analysis in those hours than I ever did by myself. It's a very hard thing to talk to yourself and keep at it. That's a discipline.

LR: Thinking of self-reflection, what do you think makes it difficult for us to talk to ourselves alone? What are the inner obstacles?

CS: When this comes up in analysis, I have an experiment that I do. I tell the patient, "I'll go out for five minutes, and you can tell me what happened when I come back because I think you've been practicing self-analysis with me, and you'll get a chance to really show yourself how good you are at it when I leave." And then I go out. What do you think is the most common thing patients say when I come back?

LR: That they couldn't do it.

CS: Why?

LR: They couldn't really talk to you, so maybe they couldn't talk to themselves either.

CS: Why? The walls have ears. They believe that I'm listening. They regress to being like a child, crying and believing that everybody hears them. You learn to believe that there are secrets and that you can only be heard by others if they are a certain distance from you. Pull the covers over your head and then whisper away to yourself, as a child will whisper or talk to itself. You are told as a child not to do it, and it brings up all sorts of other inhibitions.

LR: I am interested in your focus on the role of action in speech. You wrote about encouraging patients to practice in the analytic situation what they would say to someone. You link together with the patient his slips, errors in speech, and so on. You also talked about your interest in what body movements communicate. Can you elaborate on this more?

CS: Yes, action can be put into words. If your hand could speak, what would your hands say? Or, if your foot could speak, what would it say? You can speak for it.

LR: Or, as you described encouraging a patient, "If you can't find words, make any noise."

CS: Yes, "Guess some word and that will lead to an association, and if you can't guess a word, guess a noise." They will eventually be surprised about the importance of noise. Or, I might say, "Get going. This is part of the missed child analysis. You see, what we are doing now is something that couldn't have been done years ago. What would it have been like earlier? This is a memory of the trouble you were in, and you didn't make a noise." The youngest child I analyzed came because he didn't speak. He made noises with objects, but not with his voice, until finally he took a stance in the middle of the playroom and listened. He looked around, took a big break, and gave one scream. When he finished, he didn't move. There was no echo! And he burst into a beautiful smile.

LR: It sounds as if you can reach deeper levels of communication with people in a unique way.

CS: Well, we all know only a bit of our uniqueness. I remember Joan Riviere who was an analysand of Freud. In her first interview with Freud, she didn't know what to say. He said, "At least you had a mother and a father. At least you can always interpret that you've made lots of noises as a child." Every child makes noises except the one I saw who had stopped when she was three days old. But I found out later that when children are born they make noise. Learning to breathe is really noisy, but not always. It's amazing how people can learn to be silent or can be deluded about the difference between their gut and their lungs. I discovered a patient had the delusion that she didn't need to breathe to speak. Another patient—a peptic ulcer patient—said that he vomited a little after he woke up before he could eat. Eventually, he did so in my room into a wastebasket which I stuffed with a newspaper. It was only a little spittle, but the noise led him to feel he was vomiting. It was from his lungs; he was just yelling. It took him ten days before he could accept that it was from his lungs, and the yell was that of a hungry and angry baby.

LR: How do you encourage the candidates you supervise to work with patients at that level, who are having difficulty speaking?

CS: I help them learn what I've learned. I do that with any difficulty that the patient has that I have had any experience with. Sometimes they bring something that I've had no experience with. You must keep on with analysis until you discover something new.

SRR: Did you ever come back to Boston for a period of time?

CS: No, I never have. When I first came back here, I gave one of my body schema essays, at the Massachusetts Psychiatric Society, I think it was. I wasn't acceptable because I was a Kleinian graduate, but had ceased to be a "Kleinian" for some reason. The most critical remark Klein made to me was that I ceased to go to her seminars as much I had. I was too busy; at least that was my excuse. She said, "You're not as closely in touch with my work as you once were." But we always got on well together. We agreed to differ about certain things, like the existence of primary narcissism, the primary destructive instinct, and primary object relations. We agreed on there being much to learn. The things that we differed about we could laugh about. Winnicott always called her a "Eureka Shrieker." She always made the most of any new idea. She was very responsive. She also said, "I can't know everything," because I knew a lot that she didn't know. She was a frustrated doctor. We agreed she had much experience which I lacked.

LR: You have written about different states of consciousness between sleeping and being awake. How do you understand your own fluctuating states of consciousness with particular patients?

CS: I don't know how to give names to them except being awake or asleep. There are various stages people describe: "I want to go to sleep, but I can't;" then they wake up the next morning remembering that they had been asleep. They may talk about their conflict about staying awake versus going to sleep; then they switch and talk about what it is like to wake up. "Am I waking or am I dreaming? Or daydreaming? Do I want to get up or do I want to go back to sleep?" You have to take the story of that transition in its complex forms and conflicts.

How slowly or how fast can you wake up? Some people learn to do it very quickly. Janet called these sudden changes psycholeptic. People say, "I just touched the little one on the sleeve." There is much observation on sleep, but they can't tell from the EEG when the person is asleep, as researchers once believed. You can't wake a person up by saying, "Tell me how you are waking," because you will evoke in that person all the conflicts related to the disturbance of sleep—of wanting to cooperate with experiments, wanting to discover more, wanting to bring new harmony to sleep and waking, and wanting to avoid the paradox of being in both states at once. The EEG status in waking is also complex, but we can't correlate that complexity with our work.

Podvoll was trained in Washington. He went to Riggs and then he was depressed and accidentally went to a Buddhist retreat in Vermont, and later became Director of Psychology at Naropa University, Boulder, Colorado. He started in that department training psychotherapists. His coteachers are analysts of different types. He is going on with his analysis and his analytic practice at the same time. This year, with his wife, he is on a sabbatical in Tibet. There is a long history in Buddhist philosophy or psychology of seeking answers to what you are asking about sleep, meditation, and stages of waking. At Naropa much previously untranslated

Buddhist psychology is being studied. And it's interesting that in their last translation of the Tibetan *Book of the Dead*, which is read to the dying and to the deceased, the publishers, in the introduction, discuss how this book could equally be a story of the beginning of life, as if all Buddhist fantasies and beliefs are related. They attempt to put into words what it must be like to be dead and be reborn.

SRR: Another question. You have such an ability to allow or enable patients to regress. I've always been curious about how some people seem to enjoy regressing, even have an affinity for it or a capacity for it and some people seem less interested or drawn to it.

CS: One aspect of regression is going to sleep, but this does not say regressing to where—the "I'm going to sleep" is not specific. How many ways are there of going to sleep? There are many sorts of other regressions, of doing things in more primitive ways, though they may want to repeat it instead of remembering doing it. Now I am more awake to the good memory of having been asleep versus repressing it, projecting it, or introjecting it. We usually don't remember where dreams went when we woke. A good example of the confusion between remembering and projecting dreams was in a patient who, as he woke up, experienced his dreams disappearing into a closet at the end of his bed. He was not supposed to open the door of this closet. Earlier dreams had disappeared into the wall. As he talked about this he did not want to remember and became confused about his memories of his particular fantasies of what went on in the room beyond the wall.

SRR: Do you find that people have very different capacities to regress, some people are…

CS: …able to remember so differently. Yes. People have very different capacities to remember. I remember very vividly sometimes. People also have different capacities to imagine; they learn in analysis how their mind works, whether they will think in terms of an image, fantasy, fact, memory, or anticipation.

LR: You made an interesting statement in your monograph, "Remembering Sleep and Dreams." You noted that patients often need less sleep during analysis without their knowing why, but that there were no patients who seemed to need more. How do you understand that observation?

CS: Some have thought that they sleep too much because they were often told to sleep on a problem. They probably went to sleep and tried to dream on it rather than daydream to find a solution. Usually they were disappointed. During the War, when too many had too much to deal with, you could always instruct people to go to a safe place, take some sedative, go to sleep and dream of a better way of coping with what is too much. Then, if they had a bad dream, at least they would wake up in a safe place.

LR: What did you hear about Sandor Ferenczi during your training in England?

CS: A lot of it has only recently been translated since I saw him at the Weisboden conference. He was there with his pupils around him. He was a sick man then, and he died shortly thereafter. We heard about him from Balint and his associates. I never talked to Klein at great length about what she thought about his technique or ideas.

SRR: Outside of Freud, who would you recommend reading for a beginning analyst or a student entering the field?

CS: Instead of reading Freud I'd tell them to read Jones' three-volume biography. It is the best textbook because there is so much of Freud quoted in it. It gives a picture of the past. That's a big book—it would take them quite a time. Jumping from Freud to somebody like Klein or Ferenczi is more difficult. On the other hand, if they are interested in children, I'd ask them to read the good biography by Susan Isaac. I'd then ask them to read Klein's papers. I wouldn't read the biographies about Klein, but her first essay in which she introduces the problem of seeing a child. She's clinical from the beginning.

SRR: Is there anybody in particular writing now that you especially like?

CS: It's interesting to read Segal on Klein. So much of the literature is in terms of arguments. The British Society has a monthly bulletin, and in the last, somebody was talking about analyzing a manic-depressive woman who was depressed. As soon as analysis started, she began to have manic attacks, and she had seven or eight manic attacks in three months. I've tried to write a long letter to the author because I've written many things that are apropos. He doesn't talk about the manic attacks in an interpretive way. It's amazing why she isn't schizophrenic from the material, but she has a manic-depressive history. So many people can be saved from being schizophrenic very early in life. So much of the content of her analysis is connected with the last three months of prenatal life, when babies become so active, drink so much, and urinate so much.

LR: You had mentioned these prenatal bodily movements in some of your essays, that they may actually reappear in regressing psychotic patients.

CS: That's something to think about in the future.

SRR/LR: Thank you very much for your time. The breadth of this interview is remarkable.

CS: It reminds me of 1938 when everybody in London was digging trenches in the parks, and war seemed imminent. Melanie Klein came down to Kent to stay with us, and she was so upset. She thought she might die when there were so many British students to teach. All that she discovered could be lost and never be discovered again. The opposite question that raises is why wasn't this discovered earlier? Why hadn't analysts had more courage to listen? I think it goes back to their personal histories, as well as ongoing intimacies. Much of an analysis is so intimate, but you want to tell the world what you've discovered. Often, there is nobody to tell because most people will think you're crazy.

LR/SRR: Thank you very much.

SELECTED BIBLIOGRAPHY

Scott, W. C. M. (1924). A pathological anomalous thyroid in the Barn-Door Skate. *Contributions to Canadian Biology being Studies from the Biological Stations of Canada, Nova Scotia*, Vol. 2, pp. 131–134.

Scott, W. C. M. (1926). The relation of the iodine content and the histological structure to the growth curve of the thyroid gland of the Barn-Door Skate. *Transactions of the Royal Society of Canada*, Vol. 20, pp. 229–237.

Scott, W. C. M. & Katzenelbogen, S. (1931). Functional achlorhydria and the Histamine Test. *American Journal of Psychiatry*, Vol. 10, pp. 829–837.

Scott, W. C. M. (1941). The soldier's defence and the public attitude. *The Lancet*, Vol. 2, pp. 271–274.

Scott, W. C. M. (1946). A note on the psychopathology of convulsive phenomena in manic-depressive states. *International Journal of Psycho-Analysis*, Vol. 27, pp. 152–155.

Scott, W. C. M. (1947). On the intense affects encountered in treating a severe manic-depressive disorder. *International Journal of Psycho-Analysis,* Vol. 28, pp. 139–145.

Scott, W. C. M. (1948). A problem of ego structure. *Psychoanalytic Quarterly*, Vol. 17, pp. 71–83.

Scott, W. C. M. (1948). A psychoanalytic concept of the origin of depression. *British Medical Journal*, Vol. 1, pp. 538–540.

Scott, W. C. M. (1948). Some psycho-dynamic aspects of disturbed perception of time. *British Journal of Medical Psychology,* Vol. 21, pp. 111–120.

Scott, W. C. M. (1948). Psychiatric problems amongst evacuated children. *British Journal of Medical Psychology,* Vol. 21, pp. 171–174.

Scott, W. C. M. (1948). Some embryological, neurological, psychiatric, and psychoanalytic implications of the "Body Scheme." *International Journal of Psycho-Analysis,* Vol. 29, pp. 141–155.

Scott, W. C. M. (1948). Application of psychoanalytic principles to the treatment of in-patients in mental hospitals. *Journal of Mental Science*, Vol. 94, pp. 767–772.

Scott, W. C. M. (1948). Psychopathology of anorexia nervosa. *British Journal of Medical Psychology*, Vol. 21, pp. 241–247.

Scott, W. C. M. (1949). The "Body Scheme" in psychotherapy. *British Journal of Medical Psychology,* Vol. 22, pp. 139–150.

Scott, W. C. M. (1951). Indications for and limitations of psychoanalytic treatment. *British Medical Journal*, Vol. 2, pp. 597–600.

Scott, W. C. M. (1952). Patients who sleep or look at the analyst during psychoanalytic treatment—technical considerations, *International Journal of Psycho-Analysis*, Vol. 33, pp. 465–469.

Scott, W. C. M. (1952). Psychopathology of depersonalization (Proceedings Premier Congress Mondia de Psychiatrie, Paris, September, 1950, Psychopathologie Generale), Abstract, Vol. 1, pp. 260–262. Paris: Herrman & Cie.

Scott, W. C. M. (1954). A new hypothesis concerning the relationship of libidinal and aggressive instincts. *International Journal of Psycho-Analysis*, Vol. 35, pp. 234–237.

Scott, W. C. M. (1955). A note on blathering. *International Journal of Psycho-Analysis*, Vol. 36, pp. 348–349.

Scott, W. C. M. (1956). Sleep in psychoanalysis. *Bulletin of the Philadelphia Association for Psychoanalysis*, Vol. 6, pp. 72–83.

Scott, W. C. M. (1957). Discussion: Leo Kanner's, "Early infantile autisms, 1943–1955." *Psychiatric Research Reports,* No. 7.

Scott, W. C. M. (1958). Therapeutic results in psychoanalytic treatment without fee. *International Journal of Psycho-Analysis,* Vol. 39, pp. 64–68.

Scott, W. C. M. (1958). Noise, speech and technique. *International Journal of Psycho-Analysis*, Vol. 39, pp. 108–111.

Scott, W. C. M. (1959). The impact of Meyerian psychobiology and psychoanalytic theory and practice in the development of child psychiatry in Great Britain. *Canadian Psychiatric Association Journal*, Vol. 3, pp. 120–131.

Scott, W. C. M. (1960). Symposium on depressive illness: "Depression, confusion, and multivalence." *International Journal of Psycho-Analysis*, Vol. 41, pp. 497–503.

Scott, W. C. M. (1961). Differences between the playroom used in child psychiatric treatment and in child analysis. *Canadian Psychiatric Association Journal,* Vol. 6, pp. 281–285.

Scott, W. C. M. (1963). The psychoanalytic treatment of mania. *Psychiatric Research Report*, No. 17, pp. 84–90.

Scott, W. C. M. (1963). A finger-licking, finger-flicking habit. *Journal of the American Psychoanalytic Association,* Vol. 11, pp. 832–834.

Scott, W. C. M. (1964). Mania and mourning. *International Journal of Psycho-Analysis,* Vol. 45, pp. 373–377.

Scott, W. C. M. (1966). The mutually defensive roles of depression and mania. *Canadian Psychiatric Association Journal* (Spec. Suppl.), Vol. 2, pp. S267–S274.

Scott, W. C. M. (1975). Remembering sleep and dreams. *International Review of Psychoanalysis,* Vol. 2, pp. 252–354.

Scott, W. C. M. (1981). On positive affects. *Psychiatric Journal of the University of Ottawa,* Vol. 2, pp. 79–81.

Scott, W. C. M. (1982). Melanie Klein 1882–1960. *Psychiatric Journal of the University of Ottawa,* Vol. 7, pp. 149–157.

Scott, W. C. M. (1984). Primary mental states in clinical psychoanalysis. *Contemporary Psychoanalysis*, Vol. 20, pp. 458–464.

Scott, W. C. M. (1984). Psychoanalysis of a boy of 26 months with a 20 year follow-up. *Journal of the Melanie Klein Society,* Vol. 2, pp. 3–8.

Scott, W. C. M. (1985). Narcissism, the body, phantasy, fantasy, internal and external objects and the "Body Scheme." *Journal of the Melanie Klein Society,* Vol. 3, pp. 23–49.

Scott, W. C. M. (1986). Mourning, the analyst, and the analysand. *Free Associations*, Vol. 7, pp. 7–10.

Scott, W. C. M. (1988). Repairing broken links between the unconscious, sleep and instinct; and the conscious, waking and instinct. *Free Associations*, Vol. 12, pp. 84–91.

Scott, W. C. M. (1989). A note about adopted children. *Melanie Klein and Object Relations*, Vol. 7, pp. 22–23.

Scott, W. C. M. (1991). Le sommeil et le reve de l'enfant. *P.R.I.S.M.E.* (Psychiatrie recherche et l'intervention en sante mentale de l'enfant), Vol. 1, part 3, pp. 81–85.

Scott, W. C. M. (1992). Making the best of a sad job. *Melanie Klein and Object Relations,* Vol. 10, p. 1.

JAMES McLAUGHLIN

James McLaughlin, M.D. is Director of the Staunton Clinic of the University of Pittsburgh School of Medicine and Clinical Associate Professor Emeritus of Psychiatry at the University of Pittsburgh School of Medicine. He is a training and supervising analyst at the Pittsburgh Psychoanalytic Institute and Society. Dr. McLaughlin is a past president of the Pittsburgh Psychoanalytic Society and of the Pennsylvania Psychiatric Society. A particular emphasis in his work has been the transference–countertransference interplay. Dr. McLaughlin was interviewed December 20, 1991.

LR: In your recent essay, "A Clinician's View of Empirical Research in Psychoanalysis," you describe how your particular analytic stance gives you a sense of authenticity in your work: "The more I have tried to analyze from a steady base in the reality view (the psychic reality) of the patient (McLaughlin, 1981), the more I witness the patient's spontaneous drift to and assimilation of the transferential past by which he shapes his own reconstructive thrust in the analytic endeavor. When this happens, there is an authenticity to the work that I have not experienced when I have attempted to construct the analytic knowing from my theory and expectations."

I wonder if you could say more about the ways you work to create analytic conditions for authenticity. How do you monitor authenticity in an analysis? How can you tell if it becomes derailed?

JM: I'm still trying to explore how far I can go in that. It's something that I got caught up in back in the 70s in trying to understand where I was not making good contact with patients; where I was contributing to things happening that were unnecessarily estranging or dislocating. I could see where my often fumbling efforts to articulate an idea derailed us. This could occur so often when I started from the basis that I was supposed to provide the ultimate statement to a patient that would somehow bring something into focus. This was to evoke an ah-ha!, happy! reaction in the patient and in myself; then we would both feel affirmed and delighted with each other, ready to go off to the next hour. Instead: clunk! And it was that sort of clunk of awareness that I'm not really where the patient is.

I wondered if other analysts kept running into these clunks. So, I worked to share these things with other people trying to get feedback on how they, too, saw it. I became more pleased with the idea of trying to make sure that I had tapped into how the patient was looking at his own concerns, in his own perspective. I tried not to read another level of meaning that I presumed was there and that I should apprise the patient of. So, instead of trying to cut below the surface to deal with underlying drives and conflicts and instincts, I tried to remain at the surface to learn where the patient was. What could happen, then, was a shared sense of "yes, we see something pretty much in the same way." Then the patient's best "yes" was not just a "yes" but a "Yes, but." For then would follow a twist to it that suddenly gave a much less generic quality to what we were looking at—a glimpse of the patient's own special signature and coloring. It's then, at that moment that we both can sit and feel, "Yeah!" And especially if I had found ways to acknowledge that there is something there I hadn't seen before, and here we're finding it. "Your voice gets a little lilt in it. Do you hear that little lilt?" The patient gets engaged in that, and then the associations you get are more honestly and cleanly taking off from that moment, and then it's beautiful the way a patient will think about some aspect of the outside world or the past.

I remember Bert Lewin's old Venn diagrams about this that were so enchanting. You go where the patient goes, and the patient takes you to something about his past I hadn't heard before and hadn't the slightest clue was there; often, an event in adolescence that I might have otherwise leaped over entirely had I been pursuing the ineffable. And then when you get that, I don't know how we can find better authentication, working within our analytic frame, than that kind of drift. Because with it comes an affirmation of what was being worked on here, often the focus has been between the two of us looking at each other, but often it's what has been going on in a chunk of this mother's relationship with her child or her husband and off you go. The transference gets lighted up and off it goes.

LR: That's a wonderful description.

SRR: That leads right into my question about the nature of the transference. I don't know whether you still think in terms of a transference neurosis? Also, I'm curious whether working the way that you do, you get less of a certain kind of negative transference or a certain loading of the transference, whether the entire analysis therefore evolves in a different way?

JM: Yes, it does. I think that I evoke less iatrogenic turbulence by trying to find ways to put ideas to patients that do not pin them with the idea, or "lay it on them," but put it up there where it can float between us. By doing that, I think I minimize a lot of that inevitable anxiety anybody feels about having somebody, however well-intended, come into their frame of reference, their psychic space, or whatever metaphor one wants to use. You hope to come in with an offering, with your hand opened, palm up. Yet, you find that the patient feels you're coming in with a pointing finger on the end of it. People, none of us, like that point. We want the hand that offers, not the hand that points. So that makes a big difference. But good intentions do not make for Panglossian glow. You're really always into a potential for hurting—no matter how well-disposed, there are times when the patient will or must find something. But when they do, it's a little bit easier to see where that something has been occasioned in a twitch or a tone that reveals I've put a spin on it. And then we can deal with that. And because the quantity is less, there is a chance of making a focus on what I have put between the two of us. In Isakower's terms, there is a moment when the minds of two people work as an instrument sensitized by optimal shared intensity, and hope, and expectancy. I'm adding my own stuff to that.

Then, a lot that is painfully, painfully, shamefully there can more easily be addressed, in a fashion I don't truly comprehend. But it is delightful to wonder about, this lighting up of the transferential aspect, which I would be reluctant to call transference, at the initial time of working. What we call transference becomes so much more evident, the past now alive in the present, when the analyst can provide a field that's just a little bit cleaner, its affective tone a little more positive. And I think we need more that is implicitly supportive in our basing of our work.

SRR: As you're speaking, I'm wondering, wouldn't it be very possible that if an analyst wasn't sensitive to what we might call the "pointed pain," then he or she might attribute the patient's negativity or anxiety exclusively to the patient or to the transference and interpret accordingly. In other words, the analyst would understand the patient's distress to be a function of his or her neurosis, rather than something induced in the analytic relationship.

JM: Exactly! I think we do that much of the time out of our own need to be in charge, to feel we are mastering the situation. We're protecting ourselves when we use our theory for defensive reasons, frightened reasons. It is then that we do override the patient's view so much of the time. And to me that's what we have tended to do in so far as some of us were taught more catechistically than others, schooled to obey the major precepts of those essays of Freud's on technique. There are two very different qualities of Freud in them: the assured analyst working with a superior knowing, versus the not-knowing analyst seeking to be informed. He plays back and forth between them with wonderful Viennese footwork, then comes down on the side of law and order, constraint and abstinence.

SRR: You have described the analyst's "growthful" participation in the analytic work. I'm curious about whether and what you have observed of the patient's awareness or responsiveness to this growthful participation of the analyst. You describe the analyst being enriched and enlivened in the process of the work. That reminded me of Lichtenstein's ideas about the child being the instrument of the mother, and that infant having the sense of that mother's pleasure and mother's needing in a certain way that enlivening experience, that being part of the infant's growth, whether your patients are aware or intuit in some way your growthful experience.

JM: I think early on I was not free to consider your question. Let me back up a little bit. One of my supervisors was Robert Waelder, in Philadelphia, one of the most magnificent, flexible thinkers in analysis that I had ever run into, and he used to say, "Jamie, you have a lot of emotion." I'd say, "Yes." And he would laugh, and he never said it was wrong. But mainly I learned to be very muted about that. Then I began to hear my voice delivering interpretations or interventions, coming across as flat as a cake of ice. I thought, "What is this?" I was playing out the character of a very decent, controlled, detached analyst and I couldn't stand it. And I began to shift—I had to, for my own sake—and I think the patients began to notice it. I know they did. I had some people come back for a second analysis, mostly graduate analysts coming back for more work. And after about a month or so, they'd say, "We're not having the same kind of analysis." I'd say, "Gosh, I guess we're not." Because they're being able to say "We," their being able to say "We're not having..." said so much.

LR: That must have been gratifying.

JM: It was a little bothering while it was gratifying. You see I am the product of two highly sacrosanct organizations where I came from, an institute trying to survive a split while sponsoring a new training program, establishing itself in the skeptical climate of academic medicine. And it took a long time to come free of that. In coming free, I was helped by mixing it up with people around the country, some of whom were every bit as uptight in their training as I was. Others, like some whom had worked with Val [Dr. Valenstein], were much more relaxed, "Let's try it and see"—more of the Viennese panache. And that was an eye-opener for me. I also began to see that some of those who spoke the most profoundly and in the most beautifully shaped phrases were not listening to the data. They were spinning some kind of a nicely articulated prayer wheel of generalizations that could be turned when some familiar clinical picture came up. What little I could see in that picture was often so superficial in contrast. Gradually, I began to feel better about that surface, that manifest content. So, with that came an ease of doing things differently; but always with a little sense, "Am I seeing it right?"

And then I realized that, as a training analyst, I imposed some of that uncertainty by my silence and staying back and not talking as much. So, outside my office I became a great talker about what I do. I still am. I want the candidates to know how I work; I want my fellows to know how I work. I want us all to show what we do, training analysts especially, so that we can all see we're in the same spot together. It has helped in our institute to break down some of the hierarchical constraints about showing and telling. I know I'm going all over the lot on this, but this stance has to hold—from where you work with a patient to how you work with your colleagues, how you work within your family context—how much do you show?

LR: It sounds as if you felt more authentic when you could express more of yourself.

JM: That was what was going on in me, and I couldn't keep it from being there. And when I kept it quiet, what came out sounded so phony, like decaffeinated coffee in the container. There's a lot there that you're not smelling yet. You need to get it warmed up. I have had a lot of trouble with those very quiet, restrained people, who say, "This is the way it helps you work best." I believe they can work that way. I can't, and that's as far as I want to take it. Because I believe a lot of beautiful work gets done by the silent ones, by a patient and analyst who sense a fit. The selection process goes on for both sides in the early interviews. Those early impressions determine who stays or flees, who is chosen, who is eased off. We get the patients we deserve.

LR: In that same essay on empirical research in psychoanalysis, you brought up an important question about our potential "blind spots" as researcher-clinicians: "How can we do our analytic work in a way that minimizes the analyst's presumption of knowing, that maximizes his open search to see what he did not know to look for, to learn what he did not even sense he did not know?"

What are your thoughts about how we can discover "blind spots" in ourselves? How do you teach this kind of awareness in supervision? How do you try to maintain it yourself in your own work?

JM: I profoundly believe in what you just said as questions. And the answers, I think, are not easy. To me it's a constant effort to keep, not an inhibiting eye on how you're doing, but a kind of an eye that is interested and absorbed, doesn't interfere with the doing. And it's somewhat like, when you're into your best tennis or skiing, simultaneously into what you're doing with at the same time that wonderful, exhilarated sense of watching something happen that you are not cognitively trying in any way to control. You're riding with it, you're going with it. It's that way with patients. And it's tricky because you can get into too much enthusiasm with what you think you're seeing. And then I learned—and Evelyne Schwaber's been wonderfully helpful to me in this regard—I've learned to drop back and find out from my patient, "How are we doing?" And there are hundreds of ways to try to get at that, but "How are we doing?" or "What is happening between us?"

We made contact with each other about 1980 or so, when I brought out that essay about transference and psychic reality. I found a clansman who had been working on these matters from her viewpoint, and in ways technically beyond my scope. So, I get telephone consultation with her once a week on my analytic cases. I'm constantly shocked: When I'm thinking I'm doing so well in not getting in the way, I find I put a spin on something in trying to get patients to "see" something that I think would be so good if they knew it, they'd just feel so much better. And then I can see where the subsequent behavior of patients, either in the session, or, more alarmingly, outside the session, will show that the turbulence that I've created has spilled over and moved them in some way that is unnecessary and disruptive.

She and I have a difference about this that goes like this: She feels that by sustaining the work in the one-person psychology of the patient she maintains the cleanest possible stance of the analyst—you have the best possible working conditions. I say, "You're a wonderful mother. You've got all those wonderful and so different sons. So you know what it's like in ways I don't. I've got to come at it differently." To me, analysis ought to be done as you're doing; and I'm trying my damnedest to learn how to do that because I believe in it so. I also feel there are times when patients, for their own sake, will find it good to have me banging up against them in a different way and from my viewpoint. And then they beat on me in their different way. Then we're into recognizing each other's very individual differences of viewpoint. I think when we've got that then I will have the best of both worlds.

SRR: She's a wonderful teacher. She also told us that we must read your essay on the Hippocratic oath.

JM: Oh, that was fun. I still like that essay.

SRR: Our next questions come from that essay. In it, you describe the developmental motives of the physician who becomes an analyst and, in particular, "a sublimative or reactive alteration of destructive and erotic strivings into a serving, preserving and the healing of others, which constitutes a reparative identification with the nurturing mother, an effort to please her and placate the father."

You discuss the reemergence of aggressive competitiveness manifesting in "efforts to usurp the paternal prerogatives of knowledge and benevolent conquest disguised as service to others." That raises a number of questions. First, you're describing male physicians.

JM: That's all I had in the sample during those times.

SRR: I assumed that. I wondered if more recently you've been able to analyze enough female physicians to have a sense of the differences between the female and the male dynamics.

JM: Oh, yes. Although I don't think I have quite the sense of the illusion of clarity of knowing that I enjoyed when working with male physicians, many of whom were raised in the same general context as mine. When I think of my own work, I do think the sex of the analyst makes a difference both in terms of what the patient is able to get from the analysis overall and how its unfolding and shaping take place, but also how much the analyst, as man or as woman, is able to encompass and relate to experientially and take care of in the patient. And I think much of our growth in that regard as analysts comes only with a lot of experience and effort to be open to our own bisexuality and multiple identifications. I was helped by having a second analysis with a very fine woman analyst who let me engage her sexuality and gender differences with generous openness. And that was a wonderful eye-opener for me.

So, yes, there are differences that I see in woman analysts whom I have seen in analysis. First, they show a different kind of competitiveness toward me. It can be with the father, but it's apt to be more heavily loaded in relation to the mother. And some possess and use more sensitively than I, those qualities of holding and containing that some patients so very much need. They will seem to me sometimes to be excessive in offering these, just as I will sometimes when I'm feeling very womanly. They have a surer sense of these matters than I when I'm doing it. Like being much more confidently appraising of a woman's tears than I am able to be. I, much less certain, have to watch the patient more closely.

So, I think, if I'm answering in any way your question, it would be that yes, over time when I got a different cohort and open cadre of analysts-to-be, I was able to see that a lot of the assumptions I had made about the dynamics of the healer that seemed to be generally valid enough for men did not have to be that way for women. Some women didn't have to get into the fierce oedipal level competitiveness with men. And if she had also come out of the early relationship with her mother with a comfortable feeling, "Yeah, it's very nice to be a woman," she had a base of comfort from which to approach her patients, less reparative necessities; different from my struggles to cope with men at all the levels at which we must try to engage each other. I know that I'd never write this essay this way again. In the first place, I was hiding behind too many abstract words. You had better damn well do that back in the 1950s and act as though you're sure of what you're saying. I'm still delighted in the parallels between all that mythological material about medical healers and what I was finding in myself.

SRR: Being a psychologist by training, I was particularly interested if you had a sample which allowed you to develop particular formulations about the non-M.D. analysts, from the same kind of perspective as in the Hippocratic oath.

JM: A sample, meaning?

SRR: Of non-M.D. analysts, who might have had similar motives but chose different routes than medicine to satisfy them.

JM: Oh, indeed. First though, I think I would like to stick with a generalization that I would put like this: The people I work with, irrespective of their basic professional identity, who are in my mind the most patient-centered of therapists, are what they are for very personal reasons from their early development. I do think that dealing with a depressed mother or a distracted mother, who basically had a lot to offer but often had to be somewhere else, evokes in the little one a yearning for that engagement that he knows is there but isn't always going to be there when he needs it. So, he learns how to go after it. And I think the best therapists are the ones who hang in there and go after it. Now, do I think they are best because they are like me? Hell, yes! But I get a feeling of a resonance in such people about this seeking that I think is authentic; for me it's authentic. And I know it's based on a lot of shared primary feelings of all kinds. Like, Why do I have to work so hard at it? Is it going to be there when the patient and I get there? I sense this striving in those who turn out to be therapeutically committed. That kind of person is going to make a good therapist whose zeal is going to have to be acknowledged and measured, like, "Jamie, you have a lot of emotion."

I have learned to enjoy the discipline and the willingness to try to adapt that come from my medical training. I went to a school that did not have a lot of superheroes, who knew it all. Most of my teachers at the University of Pittsburgh School of Medicine were clinicians. We had a few we saw as heroes, like Davenport Hooker, a Ph.D. known for his studies of embryonic movements, miscarried human embryos. But most of our clinical teachers were private practitioners. I learned some of the best and the worst about how to be a doctor. I didn't come out congealed or fixed as to what is a good doctor because these people were obviously fumbling, trying. The ones I took to would acknowledge they were fumbling and would try again. And that's my picture of a doctor. Therefore, it makes sense to me to keep trying. Don't be satisfied, be able to be satisfied but don't stay satisfied.

It's been a natural tendency to see different sides. When I think about it, I didn't have a father to bang up against and depreciate and aggrandize. He was aggrandized by dying. But I had two wonderful, very human, very different uncles. And they taught me their ways about "how" and "what" that I still love to resonate to. When I have all that going on, and besides I'm ambidextrous, where do I come up with, "This is *the* way it is?" I cannot do it. I can't do it. I've got this hand, and I've got this hand.

LR: That's terrific. It comes down to your basic biology.

JM: It really is. I can write mirror image with this left hand. It's useless, but it's fun. I put that in an essay on the metathetic and antithetic because I hear and see so much antithesis. Everything you are is of use to you. This is probably why you're hearing me talk so much; because I don't have any single, definitive thing to say.

SRR: It sounds like what you're saying in terms of my question about the M.D./ non-M.D. is that there are many different ways of getting to a similar place, many different paths, and that so much of the motive is in very early experience.

JM: You're saying what I would wish I had said. I got stuck in the opening dimensions of it, about what I see as pretty common to the good therapists that I have the pleasure of dealing with, irrespective of their professional background. But the differences in professional background among analysts are profound and exciting. For a long time we've enjoyed having nonmedical trainees in our small institute, those coming primarily from psychology, but also from art therapy, child development, the academic disciplines. They come at the whole picture of the human condition differently from us physicians with our cadaver in our bones. Bertram Lewin's old reminder, "Hey, our first patient was a dead one," is profoundly true. I spent a whole year going down one side of a cadaver, resting my lunch on his chest. That does something to your picture.

SRR: You have described the "near ubiquitous" patterning of identifications and needs that draws us to become analysts. To me, this is a real limitation of training, the fact that the analyst has his or her own motives is neither recognized nor examined. I wonder if your work has facilitated these issues being discussed more freely at your institute?

JM: I think I spun out on your second curve. Are you talking about how we can help each other address the motivations for a person being an analyst, or at what time, or at what point can one think of oneself as an analyst?

SRR: No, about the motives for being an analyst.

JM: Mind you, those things were difficult to talk about, thirty years ago, particularly in my local institute. I found it easier when I teamed up, first with Lucia Tower, then George Klumpner, to do ongoing workshops at the national level on countertransference and other behaviors of the analyst. Stan Olenick, of Washington, wrote a beautiful essay in the 50s about the psychology of the analyst and the ubiquity of a history of having had a depressive mother. But he tucked it away in the *British Journal of Medical Psychology* because he wanted to have it flagged by him, but not to be too noticed. That's what he said when I asked him about it, and I think he was being very forthright, he being who he is.

I think that it is still a bit risky to try to write and to teach in a self-revealing way about these matters. Ted Jacobs and I will often get whacked for being exhibitionistic, narcissistic. But if it's done for good reasons, then I'm going to do it. But it's not a safe, popular, salutary thing to do. I don't care at this stage in my life. I have nothing to lose. And if anybody's willing to listen and feels they're getting something from it, there's a good reason.

And then I feel less isolated. Those words of the Peruvian shaman, which I used as the take-off for my *Psychoanalytic Inquiry* article: "You can learn from me. But you cannot follow me. If there was suddenly a great light, you would only see one man going through the brush. There is no path to be followed." I didn't realize the fit until I heard it. That's been—that's really me basically—a solitary person. I spent so much time as a little kid on my own in the autumn, winter skiing by myself, doing things on my own, yet with contentment. I came to see that I did these with the sense of an ambient other within me—those uncles who had meant so much.

That's why I'm utterly hooked on the concept of the importance for self-analytic work that transference sanctuaries provide. These places and doings bring us into enhancing resonance with the most positive aspects of early relating to those once central to our best identifications. We call upon these to renew our therapeutic identity each time we work with a patient. When we have stretched it to its limits, we need some way to get back inside ourselves and check out what's in the stretching. And that's when some new chunk of old problems and materials comes alive again. And when you settle it, there's rarely a great profundity of insight; but there's a fine easement in going back into the work with a little more sense of freedom to range across those fields and use your peripheral vision to pick up patterns that you won't ever see if you're looking beady-eyed at the problem of the patient. You know this from skiing, I know it from hunting. I know it from tennis—to be relaxed and open-eyed behind the couch is so much more fun and so much more taken in.

Now, what have I said there? That to discriminate across a wide range of possibilities in patient and analyst alike, a range coming out of rather narrow, simple motivational urgencies in each of us, is the way people ideally would want to be, so that they don't get caught in a little pea patch. You've got to be free to keep moving and always seeking for something not yet seen. I don't know what I'm seeking. I know that I'm not going to settle for the usual basic things I already know.

I think that for me, to see what is unique in the patient and between us—that's a wonderfully reviving thing. I so much want my patients to discover this, that I have to watch myself, because I don't want to go winging off into the night with them on something of my own, when they'd just as soon stay home and put their feet up against the fireplace. So that's the "furor sanandi," or my particular version of it, to guard against.

LR: You're describing analytic listening in an interesting way, as having parallels to different visual approaches—having blind spots, using very focused, "beady-eyed" vision, or using less focused peripheral vision. There's almost a "feel" to the way you try to find the right analytic stance for maximally "seeing" and "hearing" the patient.

JM: An uncle of mine taught me something about that when I was about nine or ten. Both of them did; both were great hunters. Uncle Frank said, "You'll never see anything you're hunting for if you look for it. You just let yourself get open, and you'll see that mallard coming in. You'll never see a track on a hillside if you're looking for it. You'll see it if you don't look for it. Just let it come in." That's been such a useful metaphor. It works. It really works out in the field. Don't ever look at the tip of your skis, just look out ahead.

LR: Given your interest in the antithetic and metathetic use of words, I was struck in your essay, "The Analyst's Insights," by two examples of double-meanings you gave to words. In the first example, you were talking about how you use woodworking as a "sanctuary" to further reflect on your work with patients outside the analytic setting. You chose a hand-sanding chore while thinking of a patient about whom you had imagery of a clam and a beach. I wonder if the "sand" parallel had been conscious for you?

JM: That wasn't deliberate. Jack Arlow wrote me a little note saying, "Did you notice that?" That delighted me; his personal, close and cognitive touch.

LR: There was a second example in that essay in which you gave double-meaning to the word "match": "However differently in degree the struggle stirs and sounds both participants, it is the richness and vitality of what goes on in this struggle that must be joined, this match that must be made, that strikes the faint sparks of insight to be fanned in the tinder of relating."

JM: Isn't that fancy?

LR: Were you aware of doing that? How would you understand that capacity for wordplay?

JM: That's the Irish in me. I'll see it later when I'm editing, and see that I was trying to make it something, make it a little more vivid. I can't stand reading dull stuff, and I hope I don't produce dull stuff. And this is one way. I just love to let the ideas go and then go to the literature. I refuse to go first to the literature, so that's another point. No, those are accidents. I like to think that they capture something I didn't try to make. It's there, I'll enjoy that it's there, but in Roy Shafer's terms I ought to take full credit for it or responsibility for it. But you know the feeling—I don't know where it's coming from and I don't care, just so it's there.

LR: It seems similar to your being ambidextrous. As a reader, I felt several different layers of my mind being appealed to simultaneously, like having one's unconscious tickled. It was a funny mental sensation.

JM: You read closely. I think we all do what we…I do not have a good, easy access and grounding to a lot of the poetry of people who really are poets. I had a rather short undergraduate education, and I've rounded it out with a lot of personal reading and exploration during World War II and ever since. The imagery that naturally comes to me comes out of my own personal doings. And obviously, there's a lot of activity in these. I don't have good visual imagery that allows me to come up with beautiful visual metaphor, so it's a different kind of metaphor, I think. It's more grounded in motion, kinesthesia, smells of things, and tastes, that just naturally affect the way in which ideas take their idiosyncratic shape. It delights me to hear that somehow you find these evocative, the way strawberry jam can be evocative, or the smell of peanut butter.

LR: You mentioned in that same essay that you do not "ordinarily have much visual imaging capacity in the fully awakened state," but that in relation to that one patient, you did experience a stark visual picture of the gleaming protrusion of a clam in sand. Can you say what was happening intersubjectively between you and the patient that might have led to visual imagery in particular at that time?

JM: I drifted into a reverie state. I didn't want to get too explicit about details, but this man was dealing with a lot of painful material around his father's death, a very significant loss for him, although it happened to him in his 20s. But his pain and yearning tapped into some old stuff of mine. This had not so much to do with my father because that was too ghastly, but pain and anger around an uncle who left when I was 12 or 13. I didn't see Uncle John again until 20 years later and he barely remembered me. He was very important to me in my earliest years. I think I was having trouble for a while letting myself be open to my patient's pain and get inside that pain; too much like my pain. So I tended to stand off, trying to evoke it from the patient rather than getting in there and adding ideas and the responses in *my* mind that could resonate, help him feel that I was there with him. I was hung up and hanging back and waiting for him to do more. He was hung up and hanging back and waiting for me to do more. And we kind of puddled or piddled into this deadened state.

Something had to happen, and I don't know how these things take place except they come from some mutual….He had to hang there with me while I was trying to hang there with him, and somehow there came that moment when we came up with these parallel images, such a railroadlike way, railroad tracks, and I don't like it. But it does capture something that's going on. When that image happened, to me, I tapped into something about us both. I still don't know what a clam siphon really looks like in a real sense. I only used what came to me as a kind of a—it had obviously a kind of phallic imagery, a mouth imagery, the hint of something underneath that was ineffable, and do I want to see more of it or not? I don't think so. I only wanted to see it enough to dry it up. I think it was pretty obvious that something was down there. So we just, I just tapped into it while he was tapping in.

The imagery that went back to Clavell's *Shogun* really opened up all this sadomasochism, awful things in both of us that, I don't know if they're there to that intensity, but surely not absent. You know, they're in every one of us. I didn't want to go any further than that. So, he and I had some kind of a thing that allowed us—me—to get moving. These events happened at a time when I was still trying to figure out things that I hope I have a little better handle on now. Like how to overcome this abstinent, quiet waiting that we think is so benign. And once you get over such an illusion and don't have to live by it, the world opens up wonderfully.

LR: In your experience does the appearance of visual imagery while listening to patients alert you to particular emotional processes in you, the patient, or between you and the patient?

JM: Oh, yeah. I think I've gotten much more open to things that had been dampened in me from adolescence. The more I've worked with patients, the freer I am to feel, to stay with what's going on. My visual imagery has sharpened, opened up, so I don't need to be in quite a reverie state. Visual imagery still comes in flashes and usually from off to the sides. Usually I'll see or hear off to one side or the other. And yes, I do assume that these are signals of something that I think is me. They often have relevance for what the patient is talking about, sometimes not—I just can't make it. I don't try to impose on it. At other times, it's as though, "Geez, an art gallery just popped up in that flash."

SRR: Here's more. I found the descriptions of your experiences gardening or working in your workshop very evocative. You wrote: "We tap into transitional phenomena similar to those shaped by the analytic situation, whereby those latent traces of the nurturing and releasing aspects of our experience with one or both parental figures are raised once again to living intensity in each of us." Do you think of analysts as people who are particularly drawn towards the reexperiencing of transitional phenomena, like artists or certain writers? Or do you think of the strain of the analytic work as intensifying our need for refinding that kind of soothing experience?

JM: Probably both. My own ways of using my sanctuaries are for natural replenishment, more often when I am having a strain in my personal family relationships or with patients. And I'll end up down in the shop working on something that doesn't desperately need to be done. The bigger the writing project or personal conflict, the more I'm apt to get into something fairly major in a crafting fashion. It will often be, "Save the house," something that takes on its own urgency. I think I'm answering your question in this way. The basic function for me is that it puts me in a context where I'm very much in touch with some of the best of what was between my mother and myself, between my mother and my sisters, but they are not in the shop scene as much. Mainly gardening was very much my place with her in the background, in the joy with whatever I could grow.

The carpentry and plumbing were with Uncle John, and we did all kinds of things together, like cleaning out septic tanks. On one occasion, our kitten fell down the outhouse. I was so little and skinny, and somebody had to retrieve that kitten. My uncle held me by my ankles. And I got lowered down and got this cat, and he hauled me up. Cat and I both were in need of some cleaning up. I get into a state in woodworking, in digging where the smells, the feel, the rhythms, are me. Make anything you want out of this, and you're going to be right, because he was a rich, very earthy guy, who taught me a lot. There I feel so good, not consciously. I can bring this up, and enjoy being, I think, honest about it, for all that is where there is so much of me.

So, once I'm there I find it easier to approach the strain that I'm dealing with, and I liken that to what I'm trying to do, with what I think works in analysis. Don't put me out on the edge of a cliff and ask me to reflect upon something that's straining me. Give me a place of comfort, then I'll do my work. Now, maybe I can be wrong in putting my own preference on the patient. But I'd far rather work from that assumption than send me or the patient out on a desert ordeal. Did I say desert because it's sand? You know, I don't know. Don't do that. Put me where I can feel good, familiar. Does that make sense?

SRR: Yes.

LR: That's similar to your imagery of the open hand versus the hand with the pointing finger.

JM: That's right.

SRR: That brings to mind Winnicott's description of the child playing in the presence of the mother. You have both experiences—the "doing with" with your uncle but also the gardening and playing in the presence of your mother.

JM: Yes, I had very much the sense of her approval as well as her disapproval. The worst thing she would ever do was not sending me out to get a switch that I was to cut that was just the right size to whip my legs for something I had done. I'd come back with a little bitty thing. She'd say, "No, you'd better go get a better one." No, the worse thing she did was…refusing to talk to me, her silence. I have trouble asserting silence with a patient and some trouble receiving silence because there is that old resonance. So now you can see why I might not be so silent, comfortably silent as an analyst. To me silence was proscriptive. It was oblivion, and that's the opposite of transitional object.

LR: It would be interesting to know how therapists/analysts rework their own issues of silence as they gauge what is tolerable for their patients.

JM: I wish I had answers to that. It would be good to have the kind of fraternal context in which these things could be freely talked about. I don't know that it happens very often, what with our group reticence. I have found good talking with a very few, very close colleagues around this country, particularly in that context that I don't much talk about called CAPS.

SRR: Sheldon Roth has told us about that.

JM: CAPS has been a very precious thing. Except it has the connotation of elitism. Whoever goes there is asked to come and join. And some of my best growing as an analyst happened there. I was sorry I couldn't acknowledge that. I kept mention of CAPS out of my *Psychoanalytic Inquiry* essay on how our work shapes us. I was told I would come across as being too damn much of a snob and an establishment man if I wrote like that. Politics does get into things. But there, meeting people twice a year fostered an intimacy over distance that has been immensely important. I could say things to

Carl Adatto, Paul Ecker, or Morty Reiser—I can name a whole bunch of wonderful people, some of them now dead, with whom I could talk like this and they to me. I didn't have it in my home town because we were so uptight, trying to do it right, and all the competition.

LR: You gave a very moving description in your essay, "The Play of Transference: Some Reflections on Enactment in the Psychoanalytic Situation," of the many nonverbal behaviors you observed in your patients during analytic sessions: "Hand in hand, hand to heart, to mouth: these small doings lead us to the limitless knowing and telling that lie in holding and being held, in the unity of beholder and beheld."

You also described some interesting differences in right-sided versus left-sided motions. Could you say more about the observations you made?

JM: There's a long piece of shaky methodology and research behind that, which went on for several years. With as many patients as I could, I tried to make little squibs and little signs above the written process material. I wanted to show the play of their physical behaviors on the couch as they spoke. This was possible only with patients who were quiet enough in their nonverbal activity and not talking my leg off. One yield came in being able to validate some of the old findings about right and left that Felix Deutsch described in his posturology papers. His observations were so good, but ill-respected or ignored. What I came up with by trying to capture the simultaneity of the verbal and these small kinesics, legs and arms and hands in relation to the body, was, I think, a nice contribution. It's very hard to prove any of it, of course. I'll ask people, "Do you mind trying it for yourself?" and have had people say, "Oh, I tried it for a day or so. I couldn't see a thing." That's right.

It takes a lot of looking over time to see a patterning of verbal and kinesic. And peripheral vision is best for recognizing patterns. You don't make them. They're going on. The words are coming out. Patterns are getting played out. Pretty soon you see something that's been going on and on in the words and action. And then, when you note it, it turns out so often to be appropriate for the patient's dynamics, and also in line with the tendency we humans have, cultural or inherited I don't really know, this tendency to lateralize, to assign meaning and value to what is sinister, what is dextrous, what's right, what's left.

LR: Did a patient's particular gesturings sometimes appear to be a reenactment of some early dyadic relationship with his or her mother?

JM: I think I saw this in the small, background kinesics in retrospect more clearly than when it was happening. At the time I see that one hand is holding the other thumb or scratching that hand. Then I find that this hand that is scratching or twisting is the dominant hand that the patient uses when talking about his father.

Repeated over time, such things take on some relevance. I don't make the connections if I can help it. I try to record these things right along with the verbal carrier. And then later on, I'll go back to look, trying to think about it and see, "What has been wrought here?" The trouble with doing this work is that it could be such a deflection of my involvement with the patient that I thought it wasn't being helpful. What I saw and heard could be helpful in shaping the metaphor for what I would say to the patient. This is always tricky because I'm looking at it from outside the patient's observational field.

And the way to get back into his is through the verbal content, enhanced by this metaphor, rather than to make reference to the non-verbal behaviors directly. The big gestures are more easily approached because the patient will become, or already is, somewhat aware of them, and is ready to become curious about them. Once they get over the initial sense of having been narcissistically attacked or touched too closely by my speaking of the actions, so literally touchy, once you get beyond that and the patient can engage, then we can get rolling with it.

LR: In your observations were there individuals whose gesturing didn't match the affective content of their words? If so, does such a disjunction possibly represent "trauma" of some kind, where nonverbal processing of the experience may have become dissociated from its verbal or affective aspects, or where different developmental needs or issues may have become unintegrated?

JM: Gee, that's a really good question. I do have the feeling that the very small gestures do often relate to the very earliest matters of holding and being held, being attacked and hurt, wanting to attack and hurt. They're very hard to talk about usefully. You can sense a lot, but the data are complicated. The verbal carrier may be complementary or contradictory. You still have to approach it the same way you would any other, through the verbal medium and perhaps speaking more of conflict when you discern contradictions between the two.

Most of the kinesic data that I've watched over analytic time change, not because I addressed them directly, but because I've addressed and worked with the issues that the person has been able to put into words. By working in those usual dimensions, a very tight immobile patient will show a wonderfully freeing-up—expect to see it. I think they show a nice opening up of their kinesic expressiveness....

LR: Over time?

JM: Yes.

LR: That must be exciting.

JM: It is fun to watch. That chapter of mine in the Mahler-Achtar book—that man was a finger-banger, nothing was going on kinesically except for his hands. In a year, he was gesticulating; he was still on the couch, but no longer still. It has been exciting to watch him loosening psychologically, as he loosens his gesturing. Another man, a tight obsessional, was motionless excepting for getting into this position (heel of right foot on top of toe of left foot, both vertically in line.) What would you think of that?

LR: That he can't go off a line?

JM: Right. What else? The attitude, the body context, like he's talking in a light, in a balloon fashion, and you can't pick up any affect.

SRR: Perhaps some agitation about being there or....

JM: I'm sitting there. All I'm getting is this gesture with his feet—one foot on top of the other, heel to toe. And I'm bored.

LR: He wants to kick?

JM: In many ways, all hidden. It's not easy to be around a patient who flattens all affect. It's surprising on a couch how uncomfortable holding that foot position can be. Try it sometime. There's a lot of latent homosexual tension in it. I'm not reading that into it. It's there, it shows up in the other data. And, on the other hand, it's riding along on top of mamma. So, there are all kinds of meaning I don't try to read; they're just going on. And you don't need to pay direct attention to it, but I think it enriches. For somebody without affect who doesn't have a lot of visual play, these small things add a lot.

LR: Could that position be some place of comfort for the patient, where he can rock himself, even if we can't picture it?

JM: This man was a runner. His moments of tranquillity came from running. I don't know how often you've encountered that in your work, now that running is so commonly abused. People for whom it becomes a haven will let you know. I don't run like that, but I hear about this running, that carries them into an ego state of a special quality of peaceful nowhereness. They say it's different if they're running with someone else, and they're talking, all kinds of loose.... There's a kind of free associative process that goes back and forth, and they wonder, "How did I say that to her or to him?" My patient had a little of this.

He also tried to have it both ways. There were times when he would run from his home of wife and two children, run a solitary three miles to his mistress, trying to make that running a time-space of very different sanctuary between wonderful problems on both ends. No, I think he didn't have very many places of quiet sanctuary, not even the couch. His had to be running from, running to, and transitional, not necessarily in the Winnicottian sense, but in a contextual sense: needing to be always between.

LR: The way he holds himself, supports himself is awkward. It makes me wonder if it reflects any earlier experiences with his own mother's holding if she were awkward or on edge herself.

JM: I like that. He was an immensely self-conscious and physically klutzy fellow. It later came out—again, this was somebody in a long analysis. It looks like he was inadvertently molested by her in the way some mothers will accidentally play with the little boys' genitals and get all whipped up about them, and then one time or another proscribe the boy's doing it. That kind of molestation. That's why the teeter! You picked up on the teetery quality there! It's not a stable position, although he could hold it for an hour, fifty minutes.

SRR: I would think it would take a certain kind of vigilance to hold it, in some way it would also be a way of distancing oneself.

JM: Very much so, the tension in this very rigid man, who could allow so little looseness and flex in his life.

LR: You wrote about play in your essay, "Some Observations on the Application of Frame Theory to the Psychoanalytic Situation and Process": "It is postulated that these complex capabilities are related to the child's learning to play with both words and actions, and specifically with those acquisitions of play capability that need to be acquired in the postoedipal and latency phases when adaptation to the cultural surround is being accomplished."

JM: Gee, that sounds stuffy.

LR: How do you nurture and encourage the capacity to play in your analysands and in your supervisees?

JM: I think it's easier in supervision because it's vis-à-vis, and I have a greater sense of freedom anyway. I like my supervisees to get the impact of how I feel about the work and how I see it, and the pleasure, the deep pleasure and the deep pain that you get into. I want them to know that, but I don't want them to feel they have to emulate that. I often don't know how to make sure of what's going to happen because I don't know what they're going to do with what I'm putting out. I don't want them coming out as a clone, but I do want them to feel that playful quality—to turn things around, to turn yourself around so you can be where you didn't expect to be. That's really good play, and I think you can teach that. It's a little harder with patients.

You'd have to be so careful that they don't feel that your playfulness is somehow at their expense. So, I've learned to be somewhat cautious. I guess that's fair enough; I want to be sure. I have a rich history in my family of wonderfully tendentious wit. The Irish family uses words to play with each other. We have to watch that because we could kill each other with this kind of sharp, incisive swordplay. So, modulate that, and turn it on yourself. Make yourself the center of the little fun that's going on. Or I laugh at my patients, at and with what they're saying that is funny. I was taught you know, not to respond to the patient's humor. If they say something funny, they can hear me laughing. And I'll say, "Geez, that was great!"

Now is that analysis? Yes, I think it is because it's spontaneous. It's genuine. I'm talking about all sides of their affective life. I think we have killed ourselves and our patients to the extent that we decided we were to go after the negative. I think you go after the positive too, and you've made a play area because you acknowledge contrasts. And play is working with contrasts and boundaries. So you stretch those boundaries with what you choose to laugh at, cry with. Do you cry with patients? I do. And one of them saw the tears in my eyes the other day as she was going out the door. I said,

"Yeah, we've been somewhere, something special." Now I think that I still twinge a bit because my very strict upbringing about "don't show too much, don't declaim" with training that says the same thing: constraint, discipline. How do you escape then? For a while I didn't want to escape. I was kind of happy, hunkered down, coming out of combat in World War II. It was nice to be hunkered down. Does that say anything about play?

LR: Yes. I particularly like your idea of play in relation to "contrasts."

JM: And the words that come out, the patients' words, the words I find—they become the essential toys and playground. Because people learn your pleasure in words and your susceptibility to words, and that offers the playground for those who have the incipient, at least, freedom to play.

SRR: My mind seems to go to developmental terminology. I'm thinking of play as creating building blocks of experience as a base for all the hard work.

LR: With humor you have more of a mattress to fall down on.

JM: That's nice. We cushion our pain with humor. You're so right. And the mattress suggests having two people.

SRR: Your discussion about the impacts of your two analyses stimulated a number of questions for me. I am interested in your thoughts about training analysis versus therapeutic analysis, the impact of one long analysis versus two analyses, the experience with a male versus a female....

JM: My first analyst was a dignified man of very advanced age, trained in Germany, who had one of those short analyses doctors in this country got over there. His idea of a lengthy exposition was clearing his throat. I clear my throat a lot, but I've got more reasons than identification—I've got Pittsburgh postnasal drip. I learned how much work I could do in his quiet mode.

I felt him to be a very benign gentleman. He was. At least I never had any reason to think otherwise because he never did anything unkind or thoughtless except to retire too soon. He was a good, useful man for me. You can see how what he was would key into distant fathers. He left town, retired before my analysis was completed and went off to Atlantic City. He joined the other organization than the one I had stayed with when the split in Philadelphia occurred. And we became good friends, as far as one could for someone of his remoteness and austerity.

SRR: Does that mean he left the analysis?

JM: Yes. I was left with an incomplete analysis. And at the same time, I had a kind of arrogance about me that came out of having survived a lot of tough stuff in the War, and I didn't have any concern about this being a training analysis, an evaluation. I went over for my qualifying interview in Philadelphia en route to skiing in Vermont. I'll just drop by, get interviewed, then go off to what I'm really eager to do. It didn't occur to me that they wouldn't want me. In retrospect, I think they had reason to think they might not have. But I didn't sweat about this as an evaluation of me. In the first place, we were sitting in Pittsburgh, he was connected with Philadelphia, and I was getting some kind of training credit over there, so far away, and I was getting a very interesting analysis that helped me a lot in dimensions that were useful at the oedipal level. All of which made it very nice because I was freely doing it.

Then I sought more analysis because I could feel the need. This time I went to work with Charlotte Babcock, who was the co-director of our provisional institute. Chicago trained, she came from a different tradition. Hers was a more active analytic stance. She asked questions, she reacted, and she was also short in stature like my mother. And, honest to God, I played out over about three years there, played out a lot of the preoedipal things, got into much better contact with my own feminine identification, which you can imagine was very strong.

That's part of the basic ambience for me out of which I come. And she, Charlotte, did a great job of helping me get loosened up and much more comfortable having your nipples tingle when you're feeling a very feminine, wonderfully receptive, giving mood. I know what that's like. It bothered me at first, now it's just the way we are. And that was a great help. And it also taught me that you can actively do good solid analytic work while still being quite a restrained, careful person. Compared to what I had gotten with George Smeltz, this was kind of "hog heaven" as far as what I was getting in feeding and so forth. Later on, she became incapacitated, and it fell largely to me to be guardian to her and to her husband in their terminal years. I could pay back.

It was good to be able to take care of her, of them, in our home for a long time and then during the nursing home years. So, that rounded off well, and I was able to mourn her in a very special way. These things all become part of your living resonance. You live with ghosts, but they're good ghosts. Are we through?

SRR: No. I'm just moved by what you're telling us and taking a minute to let it in. You're describing such powerful experiences with this person who was so important to you.

JM: There's a lot of love that goes into our work. I think we do everybody a disservice to the extent to which we deny that and minimize it. When I say love, I'm talking about self-love as well. I need my patients every bit as much in my way as they need me. And that's why, at age 73, I'm not reluctant to go on. I'm very reluctant to stop because I get fed by it. And I believe that if we can't acknowledge that, we're just destroying the large part of what we try to do.

Now, you asked early on, when do you think you're an analyst? So help me God, I was prepared to think of myself as an analyst while I was on George's couch, because I was busy doing and trying. Now what's an analyst to me? Somebody who's trying. I don't have any sense of having arrived at the place where I'm going to say, "I am now an analyst." I'm an analyst who—I don't know what else to do—who tries to go on seeing what more you can see. And I have no illusions about how great I am.

I think I'm pretty good at times, a pretty good analyst at times, but a pretty awful analyst at times because in my own enthusiasm I lose track of where the patient is at certain moments. Then I go back, and try to repair, to get back together and go on.

SRR: I'm deeply affected by what you said about the love and about your relationship with your analyst and what you had said about your mother. I was thinking that you were so fully mothered that, in a certain sense, you could know that you were an analyst because you knew that you had so much to give. I think that many analysts have to go through some kind of inner struggle to discover or develop that sense of conviction.

JM: I wouldn't have put it like that, but I think you're right. I've had a feeling of being very lucky in having been well-mothered. No doubt about that. I was the only son; three older sisters. They all pecked at me and loved me and did all the things that older sisters do. I learned so much from all of them. One died with schizophrenic problems that began when she was about ten. My oldest sister, a gem of a woman, convent-raised like the second one, damaged by our father's death, both having to go off and be in the winter months at a Catholic boarding school from the time they were just little girls. She brought back such a richness of words and books and things, that gave me a basic investment in reading that I've never gotten over or ever wanted to. She's in a nursing home now, and we take care of her.

Things, I guess, are circular. You're giving and getting all the time. I think that's the way it is with patients, too. Now, I may be sounding a bit maudlin. See, that's where my background was such that you don't talk a great deal about this. You keep it inside. You may have been raised the same way, I don't know. But I think it's fun to put that aside in moments like these.

SRR: It's more than fun. I think it's profound.

JM: Freely associating: one son. You can imagine the troubles I would have in what should be spontaneous. My wife was such a help. "Hey, hug him more." I was glad to hug him because I wanted to in the first place, but I didn't know how fundamental it was for him. I'm not quite phrasing it. And it's great to have that kind of help because she knew. She had a different, lively father who fathered her. She knew what it was like. I was glad to learn from her. So, that's gone very well. But it's that kind of easy learning from women that I learned to be very comfortable with. I enjoyed my sisters, although this middle one gave me a lot of trouble. But the others were so facilitating most of the time.

And that's been a nice thing. It made it easier to enjoy and appreciate women. My older sister was an intellectual model and, in a way, my mentor. She wanted to see that I used words fairly and clearly, and she taught me to try to complete my sentences when I speak. I think the problem for me has been how to discipline the wanting to give, the wanting to reach, the wanting to heal; those are the liabilities, if you were to ask me where do I fall short. It would be in those areas of overdoing. I really think I'm accurate in saying I don't see myself as having a hell of a lot of hostility in me. I can't stay angry at anybody for any length of time, and I'm saying, I think, that people need their aggression. I don't have that much problem being aggressive and assertive when I need to. But truly, I think I don't want to hurt anybody.

LR: I want to get back to your reaction to one of your quotes. You said, "Oh, that sounds so formal or stuffy."

JM: That's when I see that I'm protecting myself with large words.

LR: You describe how much you've changed as an analyst over time in being more relaxed and accepting of yourself. I think it's reflected in the language you use in your current papers compared to that in your earlier work. You sound more present and direct when you write now.

JM: You're right. You can see it better than I, so that I'm very pleased at what you're saying to me. I do think that's so, and there is a funny gimmicky thing about this. At Christmas two years ago, I got myself a Mac. Pouring ideas into a word processor and having the freedom to throw the words all around, it's a delight. It makes me more verbose. Everybody I know who has one writes longer letters. But it's been fun.

LR: You've been playing.

JM: Yes, You're playing. The damn thing talks to you. "Come on. Come on, try it again. Give it another whirl. Do you really want to do it this way?" And there's such a freedom. Do you have that same experience?

SRR: Oh, yes. I think people have very private relationships with their writing, like yours with your garden.

JM: That's right. I can see where the Mac and the garden provide that different digging.

SRR: But you can play with the paragraphs, you can play with words.

JM: And with a wonderful sense that there is no settled form.

LR: What do you think has allowed you to grow as much as you have, to search inside yourself and to keep trying.

JM: You know, I don't know how to answer a question like that without giving an essay. That feels right to me when you say it, and I think it's because we—I—learned how well you can hide behind words. That was the model of the 60s in much of the American. Don't say what you do, say it in language that masks what you do. Now, there were wonderful exceptions to these, but the model of the training was such as to encourage the cramping tradition of the American. When I first cut my teeth and got my butt beaten working in this organization, the model was very constraining. And I think it's been a matter of throwing off those halters while loosening up old constraints of my own. What's pressed me especially to free up is living with a lively wife, a lively son, and patients above all.

Because we allow patients to come at us in our openness, while at the same time trying to discipline our reactivity to them, there's not the freedom of give and take that we claim with a wife and family. The therapeutic stance shapes big differences in the introspectional impact, the necessity to stretch. I think that without the commitment to be a healer, it wouldn't work because why bother? Why bother? You step back, and you think to yourself, You've one lifetime that you're spending on these few people who become so important. At some levels that we know and have to think about, they are interchangeable. If it had been somebody else who had come into my office, that person would become just as powerfully invested. One might say the same thing about best friends, wife and family, so it's not a very easing position to take. It places our motives for loving, relating, and helping others somewhere within our own core. And I don't know why I'm saying what I'm saying except that it's a way of saying, "Hey, we are only what we at best are able to." And you can say, "Gee, that's not very much," or "Isn't it wonderful?"

And what are we going to do with that? Going back to your discipline. I deal with existential psychologists coming out of Duquesne University's world of Merleau-Ponty and Sartre and Heidegger. Oh, they beat me over the head with wonderful, clarifying questions and challenges that make me rethink each of my favorite theories and presumptions. At heart, I see how we keep doubling back to this existentialist dilemma, "What's it all about?" And the only answer I keep coming to is: don't use the question for holding back. If we don't invest, we don't ever get. It's as simple as that.

SRR: What you're also saying is that the extent to which we invest depends so much on who we are and what we have experienced in our lives. To underrecognize that is to lose part of the whole experience.

JM: I almost forgot this because I get caught up in how stimulating you are in your responding. That wish, that awful need to try to communicate and teach somebody, say something. I hope that people of your age and with your potential will be freer to speak of what is in you. I know I imposed my own inhibitions. I know others were imposed by my training. I tried to say this as gently as I could and as clearly in some of my recent articles because in my cramped ways I did a disservice to patients and certainly to my own pleasure in the work. For a long time, I didn't write. In my off hours, I planted and crafted. I did my uncle's side of living because I couldn't truly see and savor what I was doing. And if you don't feel it in your own doing, there's no bloody use in talking. Then when you do feel you're doing something, it is good to say it, but don't proclaim it to be a given truth. Let it just be told as the way it feels right to you.

I'm so glad we have the freedom in our field now to talk about what the analyst is doing, and bringing and not bringing to the work. It is exciting now to be able, across our analytic world, to do close sampling and following of analytic data so as to capture more of the analyst's doings. In telling our ways to each other, lies our best hope of teasing out the essentials in all the diversity of our efforts.

I hope you will come upon many useful glimpses and clues through this project of yours, this skillful drawing out from the differing lot that we are, so much more than we knew to say.

LR/SRR: Thank you so much.

SELECTED BIBLIOGRAPHY

McLaughlin, J. T. (1961). The analyst and the Hippocratic oath. *Journal of the American Psychoanalytic Association*, Vol. 9, pp. 106–123.

McLaughlin, J. T. (1973). The nonreporting training analyst, the analysis, and the institute. *Journal of the American Psychoanalytic Association,* Vol. 21, pp. 697–712.

McLaughlin, J. T. (1975). The sleepy analyst: Some observations on states of consciousness in the analyst at work. *Journal of the American Psychoanalytic Association,* Vol. 23, pp. 362–382.

McLaughlin, J. T. (1978). Primary and secondary process in the context of cerebral hemispheric specialization. *Psychoanalytic Quarterly*, Vol. 47, pp. 237–266.

McLaughlin, J. T. (1981). Transference, psychic reality and countertransference. *Psychoanalytic Quarterly*, Vol. 50, pp. 639–664.

McLaughlin, J. T. (1982). Issues stimulated by the 32nd Congress of the International Psychoanalytic Association. *International Journal of Psycho-Analysis*, Vol. 63, pp. 229–240.

McLaughlin, J. T. (1983). Some observations on the application of frame theory to the psychoanalytic situation and process. *Psychoanalytic Quarterly,* Vol. 52, pp. 167–180.

McLaughlin, J. T. (1987). The play of transference: Some reflections on enactment in the psychoanalytic situation. *Journal of the American Psychoanalytic Association,* Vol. 35, pp. 557–582.

McLaughlin, J. T. (1988). The analyst's insights. *Psychoanalytic Quarterly*, Vol. 57, pp. 379–389.

McLaughlin, J. T. (1989). The relevance of infant observational research for the analytic understanding of adult patients' nonverbal behaviors. In: *Significance of Infant Observational Research for Clinical Work with Children, Adolescents, and Adults,* ed. S. Dowling & A. Rothstein. New York: International Universities Press.

McLaughlin, J. T. (1991). Clinical and theoretical aspects of enactment. *Journal of the American Psychoanalytic Association,* Vol. 39, pp. 595–614.

McLaughlin, J. T. (1991). A clinician's view of empirical research in psychoanalysis. Presented at First Research Conference on Research in Psycho-Analysis, International Psychoanalytical Association, April, 1991.

McLaughlin, J. T. (1992). The search for non-verbal cues. In: *When the Body Speaks,* ed. S. Kramer & S. Akhtar. Northvale, NJ: Aronson

McLaughlin, J. T. (1993). Work with patients: the impetus for self-analysis. *Psychoanalytic Inquiry,* Vol. 13, pp. 365–389.

McLaughlin, J. T. (1993). Work with patients and the experience of self-analysis. In: *Self-Analysis*, ed. J. Barron. Hillsdale, NJ: The Analytic Press.

McLaughlin, J. T. (1995). Touching limits in the analytic dyad. *Psychoanalytic Quarterly,* Vol. 64, pp. 433–465.

Rebecca Solomon

Rebecca Zinsher Solomon, M.D. is a Clinical Professor of Psychiatry at the University of Connecticut School of Medicine and a supervising psychiatrist at the Institute of Living. She is a training and supervising analyst at the Western New England Psychoanalytic Institute. Dr. Solomon is a past president of the American Psychoanalytic Association. Dr. Solomon was interviewed December 20, 1991.

LR: We could start by asking how you became an analyst.

RS: What got me started in medicine was curiosity. I chose medicine in an attempt to answer certain questions which I had raised in a broad, naive kind of way, such as, What makes the human body work? This had always intrigued and puzzled me, so I thought medicine would be a way to learn. I didn't think that medical school was the only way I could go about it. There were other sciences, biology, but because of the Depression I had an opportunity to go to medical school. There wasn't very much money. I married when I was very young, and my husband, who is now deceased, was very supportive. He was older than I and thought it wasn't fair for me to be married so young. We lived near Yale. So he said, "Would you like to go to medical school?" I said, "I'd love it!" It was as simple as that. He helped me and that's how I got into medicine. If Yale hadn't been in New Haven, I wouldn't have been able to go, because we could not have afforded board.

LR: Were there many women in your class?

RS: No, there were just four. One dropped out, so there were three of us who graduated. It was a small class, only fifty. In those days the classes were small. And, again, it was almost a gimmick that I was accepted. Very few women were. Years after I was admitted, the dean told my husband, who was also a Yale Medical School graduate, that he decided to admit me because he thought I'd be a good doctor, but that it was most irregular. I agreed, because I hadn't even finished college. I only completed three and a half years. So I have to say it was fate.

LR: How did you become interested in psychiatry?

RS: Well, I went through an internship and a residency and practiced medicine for a while. That's a funny story, too. My husband was a psychiatrist, and we both agreed that he ought to go to the War. We were both very committed to the Second World War; it was very different than people feel about war now. In order for him to go, he had to have a substitute for his job. There weren't many people around, so I said, "I'll substitute for you." I had no training in psychiatry when I began working with delinquent boys. When he returned, I decided it was time to get some training. So I entered formal psychiatric training. As you see, it was a very maverick way of going about things. Of course, practicing medicine had also made me feel the need for psychiatric training. I was impressed with the number of psychological problems that patients who came for medical help presented. I went into analytic training towards the end of my psychiatric residency.

SRR: Did that seem a continuation of the psychiatry training or was that a separate decision?

RS: For me it was a continuation. As I studied psychiatry I kept wanting to learn more, and the way to do it was to go into analysis. In those days, analysis was the ultimate. It still is, except not so many people share the enthusiasm for it. However, it seemed to me the best way to learn more about the human psyche, so I was glad when I was accepted for analytic training. It was a real continuation.

LR: Could you tell us about your experience of analytic training and if there were particular people who influenced you?

RS: I trained at Western New England, which meant commuting to New Haven from Hartford. That wasn't much of a commute; I've done that forever. However, it was a time when Western New England was both in New Haven and Stockbridge, so that meant a second commute. Robert Knight, Brenman, and Rapaport were all at Stockbridge. Rapaport was on the staff at Austin Riggs and very important. It was an opportunity to study with all of those people, so we used to travel from New Haven on what was known as the Sigmund Freud Highway. I was the only one coming from Hartford. As you know, we've had an easy winter, but we had some terrible winters then, which meant cutting Saturday morning classes.

SRR: How long a trip was it?

RS: It took about two hours from Hartford and an hour and a half or two from New Haven, except when there was snow. We'd get up at 5:00 in the morning for a 9:00 class, because you never knew how the weather would be. We didn't want to arrive early, so we'd go slowly. Of course, Erikson was there, too; it was quite a group. We had a class on dream analysis with Erikson. Here we were, half asleep because we'd gotten up so early, carrying reams of books because Rapaport would expect you to come with all kinds of documentation. We'd come in with eight or ten books, and Erikson looked at us; I guess we were all kind of droopy. He looked around and said, "Now I know why all you people are in analysis." It really was crazy, but it was fun.

When you ask me who I remember from that stellar cast, I have to say they were all excellent, and each quite different. Rapaport was a stickler for detail; Erikson was imaginative and far-ranging. Rapaport would tell us about his and Erikson's arguments. He would try to pin Erikson down, and Erikson would say, "Can't do it, it's just there." And they would argue about whether it was something that one could document, or whether it was imagination and intuition. It was fun. And Knight was sort of in between the two. You don't know him, I'm sure. He was in between in the sense that he was both theoretically minded and very practical. We were very lucky because the program has since disintegrated. Although there are very good teachers at Western New England, the affiliation with Stockbridge stopped about the time of Knight's death. It's been in New Haven mostly since then. I've been on the faculty and a training analyst, which I've enjoyed.

LR: Did you ever go back to your work with delinquent boys?

RS: No, I didn't because we moved from New Haven and from Meriden, where the school was located. We moved to Hartford, and I had no contact with delinquency as such, though I've seen many personality disorders since then in a variety of settings.

LR: Did you begin your analytic work at the Institute of Living?

RS: No. Let's see, I was in analytic training in 1960, and I had just finished training when I went to work at the Institute. That came about because I was living in Hartford and an analytic colleague of mine, named John Higgins, had been working at the Institute full-time. He was a friend of Dr. Braceland, who was the Director-in-Chief. John moved to St. Louis, and there was no other analyst available at that time, so he suggested me to Dr. Braceland. I worked there part-time while I finished training, and it was an opportunity to use what analytic knowledge I had. I always continued in the general practice of psychiatry, which I enjoyed too. Also, while supervising there I learned a lot about psychotic patients, which I felt was helpful in using and learning about analysis. Knowing analysis helped me with the patients, too, so it was a good mutual relationship for me. I've been there since approximately 1961, I think. It's just 30 years, which is a long, long time. Since then I've been supervising and teaching, using my analytic knowledge.

LR: I'd be interested to hear what you found helpful from your analytic experience in working with psychotic patients.

RS: The thing that I found most interesting was being able to understand what seemed impossible to understand. That is, using analytic knowledge, knowledge of conflict to become able to learn what patients were talking about. That's the thing that I found most useful. You have to make big jumps, and you can't always be sure. But as I listen to residents present their work with psychotic patients, I think I've been able to help them to see that it isn't all that meaningless. They can say that it's just crazy talk, but as we look at it and think about it, we find that it isn't, that patients are really telling us something. And, so, in that way, it's been very useful to me. I have to be careful, because, as you both know, it's so easy to read into the production of psychotics what makes sense to you, which may not be true. But analytic training has made me feel more at ease and able to work with people. I found it very useful.

LR: Did your experience with psychotic patients help you, in turn, with your analysands?

RS: Yes, because it's really using primary process; isn't that what it's really about? When we listen to nonpsychotic patients whose egos are intact, we are still influenced by primary process, so it does help that way, too. It's the complement, I think; it's sort of a play with primary process. This is an aside. One of the things I like about Bob Gardner is that he does that so effectively. He plays with it, listening. Yes, I think it helps both ways.

LR: I'm curious about what kinds of differences you have noticed in your supervisees' capabilities to think in primary process? How do you help facilitate that kind of listening?

RS: I think there are great differences, whether in front of persons or behind the couch, tremendous differences in people's capacity to be comfortable with it. I don't know that I'm very good at facilitating it. I try to clarify it or interpret it, but if the person doesn't follow it, I find it difficult to make the point. So I don't think there is any "open sesame" to it. I keep doing it and hoping that it will take, and it does with some people. They can see a different way of looking at what they are saying. But sometimes it's just a "dud"; it just doesn't work, so we go off on something else. I wish there were an open sesame.

SRR: You talked in your essay, "Man's Reach," about the limitations of psychoanalysis. I'll give you a quote: "The inevitable limitations, frustrations and disappointments in our work have led some among us to overemphasize and elaborate some aspects of psychoanalytic thinking and disregard others in the belief that their formulations are the answer to our problem. There is often merit in both the old findings and views, but the narcissistic investment of both the initiators and followers of a restricted point of view have sometimes led to unnecessary theoretical schisms and organizational splits as groups have pitted themselves against each other as the repositories of truth."

RS: It sounds like such a big sentence.

SRR: You made a point about the strains of the work leading to this need for the truth.

RS: Right.

SRR: I'd like to hear more of your thinking about that. It seems like you could have written that right now, with all the different kinds of schisms going on.

RS: Well, I think they were all going on right then, too, obviously. Your question is, what did I have in mind?

SRR: Yes, and what your thoughts are about that now.

RS: I think what I'm referring to specifically as the schisms would be self psychology and object relations, which I don't think should be seen as schisms. I think people look for an answer, so, they say,

"Well, the answer is in the broad psychoanalytic principles. But if we take one out from the others, we'll get the answer. If you take the self out of the rest of the purview of psychoanalysis as a whole, what we'd have to talk about is the whole tripartite view, that's the answer." But to my way of thinking, you can't do that. It doesn't work. You can do it, but it's invalid, and that's what I had in mind. I think it grows out of our eternal desire to find an answer, whether it's in psychoanalysis or anything else. Certainly, in politics it happens all the time. To say, "If we concentrate on this, then we're going to find the answer. If one gives up drive theory and accepts self psychology, that's going to be the answer." I don't think you can accept self psychology and exclude drive; however, you might want to modify your conception of it.

SRR: Do you find with candidates that there is more of a desire to have an answer, or to have one way you go about things when one doesn't have that much experience? Or, do you think at that point that people are more open to taking in different viewpoints?

RS: No, I think the openness grows with experience. I think the early tendency is to want an answer because you feel so lost, we all do. We all remember the days when we didn't know at all. Now at times we don't need them. I teach first year residents, and one of their complaints is that they can't take all of this in, they've got to know where we're going. Although I appreciate that, I think if you stick to that too much, you narrow your viewpoint and overlook. I think it's a real problem in teaching. Not so much, perhaps, in analytic training because people have had a lot of experiences and are more open. But, certainly, in teaching psychiatric residents I want to give them as broad a perspective as possible because I think they are getting so misled by the limited view that they are being taught now. I think there is hope, if we can make them curious, if they can think about the problem as more than biological or narrowly dynamic, and if they can see the work as a process which we work at together and which constantly changes. I do think it is the younger person, who in his bewilderment says, "I have to know where I'm going, give me a road map." It is with experience that one is willing to go off the usual path.

LR: Do you also teach medical students?

RS: No, not at this point, just residents.

LR: If you were to advise first year psychiatric residents how to listen to a patient, what might you specifically tell them?

RS: I think the way of teaching is by demonstration, by example. In other words, the way I do it is listen with them in an interview and then communicate my trend of thought, where my thoughts go. I don't know ahead of time what I can say because I don't where my thoughts are going to go while I'm listening. So, the only way I do that is by demonstration. We're both listening to the same thing, and then we can question each other about it. That's where skepticism comes up, which is fine, but it's really by demonstration. That's the way I learned.

LR: I understand that you were once a president of the American Psychoanalytic Association.

RS: Yes.

LR: I was wondering what you might have discovered in that political position about trying to get analysts to listen to one another?

RS: Again, I can't really answer more specifically than to say that I would listen to what they were saying. I listened for content, but also tried to hear what people were struggling with, what the competitive or narcissistic issues were that I seemed to be hearing. This may sound self-aggrandizing, but just the other day I met somebody at a meeting whom I had never met before. It was at a dinner meeting, and he said, "I can't forget how it was when I listened to you conduct a meeting. You seemed to be able to know what so many people were talking about." It's been over ten years since I've been president, actually 1980. I don't know if his observations were accurate or not, but he said, "You seemed to be on top of what people were saying and could reflect it." So that's my attempt to answer you.

LR: Have there been other women presidents?

RS: Yes, one just got elected today, Judy Schachter of Pittsburgh. Let's see. Grete Bibring was president once. I think I was the third or fourth.

LR: Do you think your being a woman affected your style of conducting the meeting?

RS: I think it had to do with my getting elected, I really do. It was at the height of the women's lib movement, and everybody was eager to show that they were going to give a woman a chance. I think that was part of it. I didn't find it particularly hard. I don't know if you know the term they use, "queen bee"—have you heard that? I've been accused of being a queen bee.

LR: That's hard to believe.

RS: I can't believe it. I can't accept that, anyway. I've also been accused of being "unfaithful to the women's movement" because I don't feel as strongly about some issues as many women. I don't mean to deny that we're discriminated against, but, personally, I haven't felt that much discrimination. I'm sure that there are funny ways that I've been discriminated against. For example, Dr. Braceland, who was the head of the Institute, had a lot of trouble accepting women as analysts; so when he'd see me, despite our professional association for many years, he would always say to me, "Where is the most beautiful woman analyst?" I didn't know how to deal with that; it was so obviously a put-down, but I didn't want to be antagonistic. So I'd say, "I don't know, who are you talking about?" I kidded about it, and he quit.

One time we were at a meeting with some residents, and one of them said to him, "You know, she can teach, too." I haven't really felt at a disadvantage, but that might be because I haven't been sensitive to it. I feel that I've had a reasonable chance. What I haven't been able to do, things I would have wished to have done, has been due to my own limitations, which I talk about it my essay. I think there are plenty of men who feel they haven't done what they wish they could. I think I've also had advantages because I'm a woman. I think I've had more drinks paid for than most men, for instance. So it works both ways.

SRR: How do you deal with women who present problems concerning being women? When you see these kinds of explanations serving defensive purposes, how do you deal with it technically?

RS: I deal with it analytically. I deal with it as if they came in and told me they had problems at work or marital problems. Men or women, I try to understand the issues that the people are describing. Women who have women's problems are as varied as men who have men's problems.

SRR: I wonder if women try to enlist you more in a certain way in terms....

RS: Yes, I think they do. I think some chose me because they thought I'd be more sympathetic. I don't know if they are disappointed, but it's going to be different from what they expected it would be; I think that is just as well. Personally, I don't think, man or woman, you can approach psychological problems with a gender bias. So, I just try to understand why they feel as they do. There are so many reasons, you know, genetic reasons, psychogenic reasons, all kinds. I can't go along with this business that you need a woman therapist or that you need a Catholic therapist or a Jewish therapist; it's just as invalid in that sphere.

LR: How do you think it works out for women who may choose you to be a role model?

RS: I think they are going to be disappointed if they do come because I don't feel that I am a role model. As I said, I don't feel the gender bias is valid. I'm only a role model for what I think a psychoanalyst, a humane person, can be. I have nothing to offer that would say that this is the way as a woman you can achieve whatever you want to achieve because it's so idiosyncratic.

LR: What about the issue of women identifying with you, if their own mothers were much less developed emotionally or professionally?

RS: I think that may be implicit. It's nothing I deal with directly. When someone says what you just said about her mother, that would be an analytic issue, the disappointment. I would deal with the disappointment and the longing, which could be shared with a male analyst, too.

SRR: Yes. In your paper, you point out that, "the narcissistic wounds and issues of self-esteem regulation are associated with all levels of psychosexual development." You say that, "the manifestation of the disorder of self-esteem varies with the development level and will reflect the struggle with the crucial issues of various stages at which it occurred."

RS: That was from Edward Bibring's paper.

SRR: Do you see the self-esteem issues in patients you treat, or the cases you supervise, as very similar to those of some decades ago? You know that people write about these problems differently now.

RS: Yes, I know.

SRR: I wondered if you see differences in the population, or do you think it's more in the way people theorize about it?

RS: I don't think it's different. I think the setting is different. But the problems, as I indicated, are problems of narcissism. It's not a dirty word; I think too often it's used as a dirty word. But I think the problems are not really any different. We are still struggling to attain what we think is some kind of ideal of how we'd like to be, struggling with our wounds, and trying to understand why we don't attain these ideals. And then we project, and we deny. We do all kinds of things, but I really don't think they are any different. The case I quoted lived a long time ago, and he was struggling with a lady who was cuckolding him; so that's certainly not a new situation.

SRR: Do you see it more as a consequence of changing conceptions?

RS: The change is in the sociology of it. The fundamental issue, I think, is the same. A man's omnipotent needs, megalomaniac wishes, a woman's, too, have endured forever. And I don't think they are the same for men and women, although the principle is the same. They take different forms because of the biological and psychological differences—which I don't think we really are all that clear about even yet—what the innate psychologies of women and men are and what is culturally determined. I think both are there. I think as analysts we can't tease it out, and I don't think we need to, because we are just trying to understand from the person's point of view.

If we were sociologists, we would be in a different position. I think the basic needs and desires of men and women are really not that different. For example, Andrea Del Sarta and Robert Browning are a century apart. However, since the very beginning of recorded history myths have described people's desire to be in control. I don't think there's an underlying difference in terms of how we're put together. That doesn't mean that we can't exclude the impact of the culture of the time because that appears in analysis all of the time. One is not trying to be a sociologist, but in listening to patients it's important to understand their struggles in the context of their cultures. For example, I don't think one can listen to women these days without having knowledge of the women's movement, an understanding of what it is and how it evolved. One couldn't respond to the patient without this understanding. We can't just go back to conceptualizing dynamics according to Freud, whose papers were based in another culture. We have to know

Freud, but we also need to know what has happened since—how technology has changed, and how because of that the whole position of women has changed. Without that knowledge, we couldn't work with or help women.

I think, in a similar way, one has to have an appreciation that there are other areas that require a fuller understanding to be able to be helpful, even if one doesn't really have an expertise; for example, in appreciating someone's religion. It's in these areas, where one doesn't know as much, that the abilities to listen with the third ear, to hear what's primary process, what's individually versus culturally determined becomes so important. This is what makes our business so fascinating. One receives the opportunity to look at all the different levels. We talk to people from different places and different points of view and hear their complaints, or gratifications, or frustrations in light of what they bring, but the reverberations are the same. So, I think that this is where we are lucky. We can have patients of all kinds of persuasions, and what we learn can't be reduced; we can share it in the learning.

LR: I particularly liked, in your essay, "Man's Reach," your description of the "good enough mother." You said, "The 'good enough' mother conveys confidence in the child's potential for growth. She knows that growth does not occur without a struggle, and it cannot be hurried. She is available for help but does not intrude. Her help and understanding create an affective bond without which growth is not possible (Friedman, 1978)." You then say, "Similarly, a bond between patient and analyst is based on the analyst's implicit belief in the patient's potential to master his problems and by the analyst's offering, by way of his interventions, a framework in which this can be accomplished."

You identify the issue of the "space" that the analyst needs to leave for the patient to grow and struggle while still being helped. I wonder if you have had further thoughts about this? I am also curious how you might teach that concept of "space" to your supervisees?

RS: Yes, I think the issue is unlearning the tendency to impose one's point of view—for example, one's view of what a good mother is, or how and what one should accomplish and achieve. One has to be willing to disbelieve, to give up one's own frame of reference and to recognize that people grow at their own pace. A simple example of this would be deciding that one has to feed a child every three or four hours. It just doesn't work. Or the child must eat vegetables or whatever the current fantasy is. That's the kind of thing that I had in mind. One sees this when supervising, when the candidate or therapist wants to impose a certain way of looking at something on the patient. I would then ask, "What makes you feel that that's the way it should be?"

LR: What is it like to try teaching issues of timing and nonintrusion?

RS: Well, I think, again, it is taught by example. If one makes a premature clarification or interpretation, the patient just doesn't accept it, so that becomes an illustration of the necessity to wait for a time when somebody is ready to hear it. By addressing the material, we can see if there are some clues, which the candidate or the student might hear, that would lead him or her to recognize that it was not appropriate to do that. That would be the way. Mostly, I teach by example.

LR: In that essay, you also discuss the issue of therapeutic impasses related to a patient's disapproval of himself. You say, "The patient may not be fully aware of his disapproval of himself. The analyst's task is to assist in making these attitudes explicit and not to participate in their denial. Failure to recognize the patient's negative judgments about himself can lead to a therapeutic impasse, as the patient may interpret the analyst's silence as a lapse in understanding or as concurrence with his negative judgment, which the analyst wishes to conceal, and the patient may be reluctant to further reveal himself for fear of the analyst's disapproval." Could you say more about the way you see these kinds of impasses?

RS: I think that we see the most striking examples working in psychiatric settings. A patient complains that someone is criticizing him or her for not doing something; for example, not getting some work done, to take a very mundane situation. The patient might come in and present this story to the supervisor, or colleague, or parent, about how mean so and so is because he or she didn't like what I was doing and was hard on me, and so on. It can be an error to go along with the patient and say, "My, you poor thing, isn't that too bad; people don't appreciate you, they don't like you, they are critical of you." It's an error to go along with these patients and not recognize that behind the complaining is the patient's own disapproval of himself. That's what I had in mind. And it happens all the time, producing a false view of what we call empathy.

What we are not acknowledging is the patient's denial of his or her awareness of the truth of the criticisms. We can easily get caught in this kind of thing. The patient may make compelling pleas to enlist our help in order to reinforce his defenses. But that's what I meant, that's where the impasse occurs. One is trying so hard to be nice. If one accepts his or her viewpoint, the patient gets more and more frustrated and has to prove how terrible he or she is because he feels that you don't understand. And it may not all be conscious. I'm making it appear much more conscious than it is.

SRR: I'm reminded of an essay I heard several years ago on Freud's surgical metaphor, describing how at times the analyst has to say something to the patient knowing it's going to cause pain. Here you are describing the wish not to hurt.

RS: Yes, it's the wish not to hurt and to be kind. It brings to mind a kind of extremely troubled psychiatric patient we see, who comes in and blasts us, saying: "How can you do this to me? You don't understand." We understandably succumb, not realizing how angry and dissatisfied the patient is with himself or herself. I'm sure this happens more frequently with troubled psychiatric patients than with analytic patients. The analytic patients can cover it more; therefore, it becomes even more important to recognize it.

SRR: Again, in this essay, you discussed how Freud's earlier definition of transference, as the interplay between the preconscious and the unconscious, helps to explicate preoedipal transferences. You state: "Since the events and fantasies on which the attitudes and beliefs are based antedate the acquisition of language, they may not be retrievable in verbal form. They may be inferred from screen memories, and particularly from the analysis of repetitive behaviors which may appear pointless, but which are actually attempts to master (what Frank had described as) the unrememberable and the unforgettable experience."

Do you consider these phenomena to be an important part of most analyses or do you think there is greater attention currently being given to these issues, again because of the change in the analyst's way of observing?

RS: That's a tricky one. I really don't know how to answer that directly because what I'm really referring to are the enactments. This goes back to Arthur Valenstein's paper, in which he discusses those very early experiences. We do have some people who don't think these experiences could have such influence, like Brenner or Sandor Abend. His thinking is really very good, but he sticks very much to the notion that we are dealing primarily with oedipal transferences. It's really a difficult question. I think, though, that there are some behaviors that are best explained by Freud's concept of primary repression. According to Freud, there are certain impressions, engrams, or however you want to describe them, that are laid down and must influence behavior. These impressions can't be retrieved, because they originate at a time before speech has been learned. One can only accept the idea as a matter of faith. So, if it's true, and I do think it is true, it helps us to understand the behaviors of those with really severe character disorders, who get involved in behavior, the origin of which they cannot tell us. The behaviors can't be associated with anything that we know about but are so destructive.

SRR: What about in the analyses of healthier patients? Do you find yourself here, too, working with a good deal of preoedipal material and observing what you describe as preoedipal acts?

RS: As you know, it gets so mixed up in the course of an analysis. It's so difficult because if our theory is right, you can't disentangle it. Again, I think I'm basing it on the assumption that there are probably some kind of unrememberable memories that do influence people so that early, early experience does have a bearing. Yet, again, we're in trouble if we try to pin it down too much because we see people who had horrible early experiences and yet do well; they can work and love and get along quite satisfactorily. It's so hard to know. I think it's important at certain times to be able to recognize that the patient may be talking about something that he or she cannot put in words. This is not a time to be keeping in mind our theoretical perspectives. I don't think that it's intuition exactly because I think that we can tease it out. But we have to be prepared to hear things from patients that we can't put into words, yet we know are affecting them. To that extent, I think it is a helpful point of view, but I can't say it explains everything that we don't yet understand about a patient's behavior.

SRR: Do you think that certain patients' intense affect states require more attention or preoccupation from the analyst or draw on different parts of yourself?

RS: Let me put it this way. I think one has to be aware that they may exist and be aware of the fact that there may be certain experiences the patient has which are laden with terrible affect, although they can't tell you about them. And so I think this is where true empathy comes in. That one then takes a jump, on the basis of one's appreciation of what the patient is struggling with, to offer it as a possible way of understanding what's going on. So that, for example, if a patient has had early experiences with a loss of a mother and then has affective experiences that he or she can't understand, it can be useful to suggest that perhaps this does have something to do with what went on when your mother left. Or it may be a later experience, in adolescence or latency. It can be helpful to keep in mind that that may be the basis, or that the current affect of later experiences may be related to that earlier time. I think that can be useful.

Again, I would call upon that Frank essay which you referred to and to Val's work. I think that's what he's talking about. It's only because he is aware that something of that sort happened that he can help his patient become aware of it, although he can't really delineate it. As I remember it, he's not specific. He just states that this kind of thing went on, and I think that's certainly very valid. It does explain the intense affective states for which patients don't have memory. And that's what I think of as the preoedipal emphasis, although again one can't really interpret it.

SRR: Do you think that some analysts are more attuned to those things?

RS: I really do, and I don't think it has anything to do with their validity as analysts, because I think that it's so complicated. You can have somebody, who has a very keen mind but who may not be as aware of these kinds of preverbal things, yet can be extremely effective as an analyst. I think that we can all be attuned to patients in our own ways, but not for every patient. We don't all succeed with the same patients. I think that we are each attuned to our patients in our own particular ways, and not to the same extent with every patient. For example, one analyzes two patients; let's say that one starts with both at the same time. My technique doesn't vary that much, and yet the patients will progress at a very different rate. It doesn't have to do with what I do. It has to do with their putting what I offer together in their own ways and with how they resonate to what I say or provide, whether it's interpretation or clarification. It's another puzzling thing because it varies so much.

LR: You're describing differences in how patients make use of you and grow. In light of your clinical and supervisory experience, what do you think are the essential elements for psychic growth?

RS: I think that it's a fortuitous circumstance the way these things come together—that by virtue of the contact with you, the patient has a different kind of experience, that involves a different way of viewing things. I'm practically quoting Loewald because I like his view of it, how he puts it into words. It reminds me of a statement that I think Freud made a long time ago, about observing that a patient doesn't learn anything new in analysis. As patients will say to you, "I knew this all the time." They don't learn anything new, but they do learn. As we think about our own analytic experience, it's a new way of putting it together. I don't think it's the recovery of memories, for example, as Freud once thought, but it's reworking memories, seeing them in a different light. I think that's what the essence of the therapeutic impact is.

LR: Taking the other side of the question, what do you think prevents people from growing?

RS: They're stuck. They can't give up their own way. As I hear from them, they can't relinquish their fantasies, their hopes, and their wishes, which are based on fantasy. What happens is that you may make all kinds of interpretations. Patients may go along with you, but when it comes to modifying behavior, they are scared. They don't dare rework a way of looking at a relationship because it's dangerous, and it means giving up. I think that's a point Val makes, too, in the "attachment to painful affect" essay because what that means is losing not the affect, but also the attachment to the person. I think of a patient of mine who is absolutely stuck in the issue of failure. When he succeeds, he can't succeed because to be a success means he has to give up his mother. He has long since stopped living with her, but he fondly, and I say that advisably, remembers how she told him he could never be a success and that he'd always have to come home to her. It's just too dangerous to think that he can relinquish that. So that would be my answer to you.

SRR: I'm thinking about what you've said regarding Loewald's formulations of growth in analysis. It brings to mind Loewald's conception of the analyst as a new primary object.

RS: Loewald and I had a lot of discussions about that. I think that his statement can be misinterpreted. It's not that the analyst is a new primary object, because that could take us back to Ferenczi and how the analyst has to be a love object. I don't know if you read it that way, but it may be a danger about which I'm unduly sensitive. I don't think it's a new object; it's a new relationship with an object.

SRR: Could you say more about that? It sounds like a critical point.

RS: It seems very critical to me because it's easy to say I'm going to be a new object, I'm going to love this patient in a way that he or she was never loved. I discussed this with him, and he's agreed with me but not agreed with me. The way I see it, if I judge my own experiences, I'm not a new object. I don't love this patient. I'm not somebody in his or her life at all. It's quite different. But what I offer my patients or try to offer them is an opportunity to understand what they are struggling with and to have a relationship with me that's going to be different. I'm not going to argue with them, I'm not going to berate them, I'm not going to tell them how they have to behave. It's a new relationship, one that they've never had. And by virtue of their not being caught in those old ways, they can arrive at their own growth. That's why I see it as growth promoting and as a new relationship.

SRR: It's tricky because a relationship involves two people.

RS: It's extremely tricky, that's why I play with it so much. Just because it is tricky, I like to emphasize when I teach and when I think about it, that it's not me as an object, it's me as an object as an analyst, but different from any other object the person has. If you say new relationship, you think that somebody could have that with somebody else. I think that only with another analyst could one have that relationship.

SRR: Are you saying that it has less to do with your—the analyst's—way of relating to the patient, and more to do with his or her being able to relate in a different way to you?

RS: Well, I'm relating to them as I relate to no other person in my life except another analysand, because, certainly, I don't relate to other people with this kind of gentle objectivity or distance. That would be impossible; so I am relating to them differently.

LR: That reminds me of what you said about attachment in your essay. You wrote: "Attachment is the soil on which identifications grow and psychic structures are built. But attachment alone is insufficient for psychic growth. In fact, it can be the source of so much gratification that it impedes growth. The cognitive input which is essential for growth is mediated through the clarifications and interpretations of the analyst. In an atmosphere of optimal gratification, the patient is able to accept and integrate the understanding and insights offered by the analyst. These insights may lead to the dissolution of old structures and the formation of new ones. The latter are often the result of the rearrangement of the elements of existing structures. Parental ties are not dissolved as a result of analysis, but parents are viewed differently."

RS: That's what I was trying to say.

LR: I really like that description.

RS: That's right. We don't dissolve them. There's that famous statement by Mark Twain—do you remember that? A man that went away to college came back after two years. He hadn't seen his father during that time, and he said, "My father's grown enormously in these last two years." It's that kind of thing—how they change, how they've grown.

SRR: Do you see a distinction between therapeutic analysis and training analysis?

RS: I don't see any. I don't think there is any. It's just that the training analysis is for somebody in training, that's all. The one difference is that candidates might be introduced to their associations or other aspects that have to do with training. Just like a banker might introduce issues that have to do with banking. But I don't really see any difference as far as technique.

SRR: Some of the analysts we've interviewed have described a difference in terms of—I'm not sure if responsibility is exactly the right term, but something—perhaps about the nature of knowledge....

RS: Feeling more pedagogic about it.

SRR: Well, knowing that the candidate is going to be learning from....

RS: How would that influence the process?

SRR: It's not clear. That's why I'm asking you. You don't make a differentiation?

RS: No, I don't.

SRR: It doesn't feel different to you?

RS: No, it really doesn't. No. The problems don't seem to be, except as I say, in the content. We're back again to differences in times and history, but I don't see it as different.

LR: When training analysis is discussed in the literature, the problem of candidates identifying with their analyst for defensive reasons often is raised. What has your experience been of this issue? Is it more of a theoretical concern?

RS: I would think so. Patients want to identify with you in whatever ways they feel could be beneficial to them. Again, I think I would look to the defenses, to overidentification and idealization as ones which all patients are going to use. They're going to idealize you and want to be like you or not and fight it, which would be the other side of it. But that's not a special problem, for me at least. I'm trying to think of candidates whom I've had in analysis. Perhaps some idealize me more than another person might, but two candidates might idealize me differently and for different reasons. I don't find those things to be as prominent in analysis as I do the underlying issue with which we're dealing, that is the personality structure.

LR: What about the fact that termination is very different for candidates?

RS: Well, that is a little different, not terribly different, but different to the extent that you know you are going to see the person again. Your goodbye is not as final, as absolute. But, I think we talk about that. That comes up in the termination. And it can be a bomb. The patient will say, "Well, I'm not really saying goodbye because I want to see you, but I'm going to see you in a different way." Of course, that's true, too. They are not going to see you in the same way, they are going to have to put on a different front. They do, because we all do. They are going to present themselves differently, so to that extent it is different.

As I think about the termination with a candidate, you do really finish something. It's as sad and as rewarding as any other termination. Again, it does change. But when I think about my own experience with seeing my analyst, who has since departed, I felt awkward with him. It wasn't as if I was still in analysis with him. It was a whole different thing. I think it's a fantasy, really, which I've also talked about in relation to termination. The fantasy is that this is going to continue because you and I are going to have contact. It's the wish for the everlasting parental relationship, which is the way I hear it in analysis.

SRR: Is there anything else you might feel free to tell us about your analytic experience, how it affected your work or your way of seeing things?

RS: Well, I think in the way I've talked about it. My analytic experience was extremely helpful in allowing me to see things in a different light. I was like all of us, playing with all kinds of stereotypes and fallacies. As the result of the analysis, I saw that they didn't apply, which enhanced and enlarged my point of view. I had all these stereotypes, for example, about being a woman, which just weren't true as I came to analyze them. They were a composite of a lot of my experiences, but I realized that my fear of the strength or the weakness of women was fantasy, largely. There are certain sociological truths, but largely that was the thing I got out of my analysis. I learned how I had woven myths, as I think we all do. That's why I think when I see them in my patients that we are all wanting myths all of the time. Like this man who can't give up the conviction that he has to run back to his mother to save himself. It's a total myth. From what I hear of her, she's a totally incompetent lady. Really. She's agoraphobic, she can't leave her house, and this is a person from whom he's afraid to detach himself—which, from one point of view, is ridiculous, but from another point of view tells us how strong cathexes are.

SRR: Do you find that your style of working as it evolved was in large part shaped by your analysis or your work with certain supervisors?

RS: It was both. It evolved very much during my analysis, and I still think of what I learned in my analysis as a way of trying to understand things. But of course it has evolved; it's involved and evolved. It's involved with a lot of other people, too. And I've spent lots of time in classes with colleagues talking about the way they do things. So it's not the only factor, but it certainly was important. I think that speaks for the importance of the analysis. It's such an affectively laden experience with all its "transferences and countertransferences." It is tremendously important, but not the whole thing.

SRR: What other people have influenced you over the years?

RS: Well, the persons I have mentioned in the Analytic Institute, Knight and Rapaport.

SRR: Was either of them a supervisor?

RS: Knight was. He was a very important supervisor of mine; I've been influenced by him very much. Of course, there were many other people who were very important at the Western New England, by whom I wasn't directly supervised, but with whom I had a lot of talks—Sam Ritvo, Jay Katz;, there were a lot of those people. It's hard for me to say from whom I received what. Rapaport wasn't a supervisor, but Loewald was one of my supervisors.

SRR: Oh. What was that like?

RS: It was great, because he's such a feeling person. Feeling in the best sense of the word, feeling in the sense of being empathic and knowing what was going on. So, it was a good experience, very good. My analyst, of course, was very essential. Gross, who has since died, was one of my supervisors. Nobody in West New England really was of the old school of analysts, but he was a little bit like that, a little bit more rigid than some of the other people. So that was a good experience. I don't think Erikson ever directly supervised me, but I had classes with him. It came from so many sources. That's why I think one can't say I learned everything from the supervisors. What we do isn't all the mother or the father, you know.

LR: I note that they are all men.

RS: I did have one, Margaret Brenman. She was a supervisor of mine and teacher, too. Do you know her?

LR: I know of her. I believe she works at Austen-Riggs in Stockbridge, but she also supervises at Cambridge Hospital.

RS: This may be extremely personal, but if you are going to talk about male/female, she's more male than a lot of the male supervisors in the sense of being determined. I think she's very sensitive and very good, but she certainly has a strong point of view; some of these men that I'm talking about didn't. Now which is female? I don't know.

SRR: That brings up another question. Several of the men that we've met with talked about being very much in touch with their maternal identifications in their work. I was hoping for the opportunity to ask you, a woman, whether you feel aware of certain more masculine identifications?

RS: That's also one of the issues that I think I worked through in the course of my analysis. There was a time when, like many women,

I scorned female things, looked down on them. And so there was a time when I would, I think, look down on what was considered the feminine part of me. But as I've grown and had a lot of men in treatment and gotten to know a lot of men, I don't think that the differences are so sharp. Some of the men I know are a lot more maternal. They'll hide it, they won't let you in on it. But they are more maternal, if you want to use the stereotype—which I don't—in being caring and getting more easily hurt and wanting to protect. This is one of those things about being a man. If you're a good man, you'll protect the woman. It gets so mixed up. You'll come to her rescue and put her on your horse and ride away with her and shelter her.

SRR: Actually I was thinking of it more in terms of doing analysis, of getting a paternal transference and having to be aware in some way that you're put in the male role by your patient, more at that level. You know that some women analysts say they don't get a paternal transference and others say they do.

RS: It depends on how you define it. If you define the paternal transference as somebody who is going to protect and care for them and be strong, you do get that. That's what people look to you for. So that's organic; it gets so tricky.

SRR: But other people might describe that as a "mama bear" transference.

RS: Yes. So what would be a paternal one? That would be my question to you.

SRR: Maybe one that would be more phallic, somebody that would be very aggressive. Or, let's say that somebody had a very overbearing father, and you realize you're being responded to as that kind of person, whether you would identify that.

RS: Yes, it's there, but I think I'm aware of it.

SRR: But you may just not label it.

RS: I don't label it. I don't tend to, which may not be right, but I don't tend to. I say that this person is seeing me as somebody who is powerful and strong and overwhelming, and that that would come up. If you want to call that maternal or paternal, yes.

SRR: You might say it might come up, if you were to say, "You're experiencing me like your father."

RS: Yes. Well, that's true. Again, I don't think I'm so apt to make that kind of interpretation, because I'm not so sure how the person is experiencing his or her father. I say, "You're seeing me as this kind of person." I think that's one of the difficulties when we work with transferences, that we tend to label them as if I'm a person you're experiencing this way. I may have some of the characteristics that you attribute to your father and some to your mother. My bias is that these things are not so easily differentiated. I think that that's one of the tasks that we're struggling with, which is how do we really define masculinity and femininity apart from certain very definite biological phenomena, which do have psychological implications. For example, the issue of childbearing influences men and women, but just precisely how? You can't ignore it. But just precisely how do women welcome it, women resent it, men become envious of it, men resent it? Because one of the things that we see in our male colleagues, male persons, is how they resent the fact that we can have children. They really are mad about it, to put it mildly. So you know that it's there. We need to think more about it, but I don't think we can just label it with any real significance. Now our voices are different; you can tell that we are squeaking like a woman, not growling like a man. But I think we still need to find out how these biological differences have the real psychological implications they have.

SRR: Do you think of mourning as something that's usually part of an analysis?

RS: Mourning. Definitely; very much so; right from very early on, not just at the termination. The issue that I talk about, the giving up of these stereotypes about parents, it's why people get depressed. You're parting long before you terminate. It's very much part of analysis.

SRR: Can you say more about how you live with it in the analysis?

RS: How I as the analyst?

SRR: Yes.

RS: When I see a patient coming in depressed or discouraged, as I listen to the associations, one of the things that will occur to me is that this person is giving up something that's very important, a tie to whichever parent. And even though it may not reflect something that occurred in the past, it may evoke certain kinds of separation memories. But they are separating; you see this constantly in analysis, repeatedly, and I think that this can be overlooked too. Also in psychotherapy, I think one sees it. Just as a sideline, I think the tendency to give antidepressants to every patient who gets depressed is off the beam because this is certainly one reason. I think often with schizophrenic patients one sees this. They suddenly become depressed, and they don't know why because they are not enough in touch with themselves. I think that this can be awful. They are struggling with their separating. For them it's in a very painful way, painful for everybody because their ties are so tenuous. So yes, the answer is yes, it's a very important part of analysis; I think it has to be seen as a phenomenon, not a disease state, which unfortunately is too often the way we look at depression.

LR: That is increasingly true now with more pressure to medicate younger and younger patients. In the light of your experience, how do you view those changes in the use of medication?

RS: I know.

SRR: I'm curious, from your perspective, whether you think that that will lose its enchantment over time.

RS: Let me add, let me say that I think medication is very useful. I think it will even out. I think as people get discouraged, as they will, with the ineffectiveness of medication, it will drop off. I think right now, for example, in spite of all the antipublicity, that there is Prozac mania. Well it's got to die, because it can't be that good. Although it is amazing, I have to confess, what it has done for some patients, it hasn't done it for others. It's made them workable when they weren't. But you know, there have been fads in medicine forever—one panacea after another. There was a time when ECT was a panacea for everything, then the neuroleptics. I am old enough to have been around when Thorazine first came in, and they emptied out hospitals. Everybody thought that was the answer. I remember because I've been somewhat critical of medication in any field.

I remember there was a time that I was accused of being a lousy analyst, a lousy analyst person; I was cruel because I wouldn't give my patients neuroleptics. Well, I've lived to the point where I can say I'm pretty glad I didn't because look at the dyskinesia that they would get. I think these things do have an evolution. Sometimes they don't come quickly enough, or they don't go the way we'd expect them. But this tendency to medicate everybody has to die down, I think, because it just doesn't work to. Our colleagues who are doing it, are doing it because they think it's great, but most of them are not dumb enough to not appreciate that it doesn't always work. I've been accused of being a "pollyanna," too.

SRR: You've described the self as "a psychological organization that defines a person. It is akin to identity." I'm interested in your thoughts about the identity of the analyst and the process by which that becomes part of the self.

RS: That's a tough one. I'm not sure all that I said makes very good sense. I'm not so sure that my distinction between identity and self would hold up under metapsychological scrutiny. But what I had in mind just as an empirical issue is that by virtue of doing analysis and thinking about these issues we've been talking about, they become integrated. They get integrated within us, and we come to think of ourselves as persons who don't take things at face value, who look beneath the surface, who are willing to try to understand what seems impossible. And maybe we can understand. But I see the identity of the analyst as someone who is always willing to question, to try to understand, to not pass judgment summarily. And that, I think, is something that gets integrated as you listen, you realize how wrong you can be if you do make these summary judgments. So does that answer that?

SRR: Yes.

LR: You mentioned curiosity as a quality you recognize in yourself. I wonder how important you feel it is in the selection of candidates for analytic training?

RS: Very much so. Just today, I was talking to one of my colleagues, and we were talking about another colleague about whom we both had had great reservations, having been on an education committee together. This person about whom we had had all these reservations has really turned out to do very well and to be very understanding. So we were worrying and wondering, worrying and wondering, because we can make these summary judgments, but just exactly why were we wrong in the past? What happened to change our view or his view? So the curiosity goes on forever, every time you participate in a selection or an evaluation....

LR: So you ended up being curious about how you even assess a person over time.

RS: Right, the curiosity goes on forever, and it continues about a lot of other things. I love the theater, and I like movies too, somewhat. I go to a lot of things, and one of my friends keeps saying, "But how can you go?" My answer is just that I'm interested in how differently people see things. I don't want to go to see everything. I'm not indiscriminate; I don't mean that. But there are things at a certain level which I read about or hear about, and I like to go just because they are different.

LR: That raises the question of how you nurture yourself as an analyst. Do you find the work taxing at times?

RS: Sometimes I do, like everyone else. At times I have periods of feeling overwhelmed and wish I could do more. I need rest, so I'm taking a three-week vacation right now. This is a rest.

LR: How have your learned over time to take care of yourself, if that's not too personal a question?

RS: Well, no. One way is by turning off my analytic identity. I think I can say this—I don't analyze my friends or my family, you know—I don't keep the same hat on. You laugh because it is ridiculous, but there are people who do it. I just turn that off, and I won't do it.

LR: Is it hard to turn it off?

RS: Not for me, it isn't. I don't think so. I just don't do it. That may sound too simple, but I have a daughter and two grandchildren and a son-in-law. Things come up about which one could, but I just don't think I'm going to get into the business. And I have some intimate friends about whom I could easily think analytically if they were my patients. But I just don't do it. So we talk about other things—music, or books, or the weather, or flowers, or whatever—because there is no quicker way to lose friends, as I'm sure you've all learned, than if you try to talk to them as an analyst. And you know what? I don't want to do that. We don't take friends in analysis.

SRR: Right.

RS: Because I don't want to know about their problems. It's that kind of thing which is so different from a "doctor's" attitude, from one who is eager to know. I have a friend who is an orthopedist, and he's always getting involved in the personal lives of his patients. And he can't understand why I won't. I can't explain it to him, so

I don't. I just don't do it. He does it his way, and I do it mine. It's very different.

LR: Just this morning we were talking to James McLaughlin about his finding certain hobbies refueling.

RS: Well, I love to cook, so that's one of my hobbies. I used to like to garden, but I can't do that now; I don't have the physical wherewithal. I like to walk, but I think cooking has been my best way. That's one way, fixing food, as somebody else might turn to woodworking. I think Jim does that.

LR: When you're feeling stuck with a particular patient, what are your different ways of working it out with yourself?

RS: Well, I'll either go to a movie—now that I'm VCRing, I've got movies at my fingertips. That's one way. And music, I have records, or I'll turn the radio on, or the TV on. That's the way I would do it, or take a walk, or sometimes call up some close friends I have that I can talk to without revealing too much. I'll just blow off steam to them, just get rid of it and then hear what a jerk I am. Which is, I think, one of the main dynamics about what we call abreactions. You listen to yourself and you hear how jerky you can be.

SRR: You don't use self-analysis in any formal sense?

RS: No, no formal sense. As I say, sometimes I let it off to my friends, but they're not analysts. No, I don't. It's not formal at all, but just going over what I'm thinking. Often, you know, you come up to what I've been telling you about, these crazy—I say crazy advisably—but these fantasies that you have about how things should be, and they're not. One of the great mistakes I think we make, or I make and I hear about from my patients, is when we assume that everybody is going to be like us, and they're not. If we're disappointed, that's because we're starting with the wrong premise, which I think is also the advantage of talking about it. We realize that, which I think is different from Freud's idea of what abreaction was about. He thought he could decathect and get rid of energies, but it's really that we're putting things in a different perspective, I think, as we listen to our patients.

LR: Do you have many chances to get together with your analytic colleagues?

RS: I do. We get together. One of the ways we do it, is to go over applications all the time and progressions. We're constantly talking about people and exchanging ideas. I've been in several study groups, though right at the moment I'm not in one. And then coming here to meetings, you constantly hear people talking, doing hallway consultations and that kind of thing. So you have an opportunity to hear yourself, which sounds very autistic but very important, so long as you don't overvalue what you're hearing, but put it in perspective.

SRR: Do you see any patients for reanalysis?

RS: No, I haven't. I know some people do a lot of that. Dr. Horowitz was talking from the platform today, and I think he said his practice consisted largely of reanalyses. I'm in a small community, that makes a lot of difference. It's not Boston or New York, where there are a lot of analysts and a lot of reanalyses.

LR: Did you ever do any child psychiatry training?

RS: None in psychiatry. I did work as a child psychiatrist for a while in a child guidance clinic before I went into analysis, in my really old days.

LR: How did you like working with children?

RS: This was a state child guidance clinic. I liked it very much, and I remember a funny story. The clinic had its offices in the visiting nurses' association building, and the head of the visiting nurses was a good friend of mine. One day, she couldn't contain herself. I used to chase one patient in the hall; she said, "You know, Rebecca, you're the highest paid babysitter I ever met." I remember who the kid was, he was going up the stairs to dent somebody who was in the closet upstairs. I loved seeing kids. What one can learn from them I think is just fantastic. So that was a good experience, the variety was great. Children and psychotics and the nonpsychotics.

LR: What a tremendous breadth of experience.

RS: Yes, I had a good chance to be indulged.

LR: It sounds like you still enjoy doing analytic work, that it still challenges you.

RS: Yes. I still do it. I do less because I don't take on new patients; I don't think it's fair at my age. I do see patients in psychotherapy, but not in analysis, because I think the commitment isn't as big.

But I do feel it is a way of doing it without really doing analysis. I don't think the applied analysis which one does with books is terribly valid. I think it's very speculative and interesting, but I don't think it can be accepted as fact. That is, one's interpretation of a play is not a fact, it's just the way one is seeing it from an informed, analytic point of view. But there are certain kinds of persons who want to accept it as fact. People will say, "Well, what do you think of that?" as if I had some special insight. I don't, my insight is no more valid because I'm psychoanalytically informed, because I still don't really have psychoanalytic data. I'm just responding. In that situation, I don't know how the person would respond to me, which is a tremendously important part of being an analyst—what the patient does with me. So it's just like a very pleasant exercise to me.

LR: How would you advise beginning candidates to make optimal use of their training experience?

RS: I don't know how to optimize it. My advice would be just live it to the fullest and enjoy it. Be prepared to be disappointed, especially in this age. I again have an advantage because I grew up in the time when analysis was flourishing. There was a lot of encouragement for it. I don't think you people get that kind of encouragement at all. So, what I would say is that you've got to push against that. I was led to believe, and it was true for a while, that the world would open up to this. And you are being told, "Be careful, you are trapped in your world." So my only advice would be that there is a lot to be learned in it. You can still have fun with it because you can apply it or not, so long as you don't get too caught up and too disappointed. I think it offers a perspective that no other view that I know of can and the opportunity to listen to patients truly willing to reveal themselves. I think it's great, so long as one doesn't get carried away with it.

I think of another funny story. I went to see *La Boheme* with a friend of mine, a very unpsychologically minded person. I don't know if you know the opera, but Mimi is dying—that's the gal he loved. In the first scene, he throws her out. And I said, "Oh, the reason he did that is he wanted to protect himself against the loss." I think that was right, but the person I was talking to just couldn't hear it. I guess, as you can see, it's not hard for me to get enthusiastic. The people in the next seat were just laughing about it. I thought it was really obvious, he had to do that because he couldn't stand losing her. I don't know whether I was right or wrong, but it's that kind of thing that I would never have thought about if I hadn't known about loss and mourning. And it made it more interesting.

LR: It's wonderful to hear someone with your experience express so much vitality in your ongoing work. Thank you very much.

SELECTED BIBLIOGRAPHY

Solomon, R. Z. (1982). Man's reach. *Journal of the American Psychoanalytic Association,* Vol. 30, pp. 325–345.

Joyce McDougall

Joyce McDougall, Ed.D. graduated from Otago University in New Zealand. She underwent psychoanalytic training in London at the Hampstead Child Training Centre and completed her training at the Paris Psychoanalytical Society, where she is a supervising and training analyst. Dr. McDougall was interviewed December 21, 1991.

SRR: In *Plea for a Measure of Abnormality,* you ask: "Is it normal to put in doubt one's object choices, one's rules of behavior, one's religious and political beliefs, even one's esthetic tastes?" You observe that analysts do not readily fit into the normative norm of the normal others, that analysts at social gatherings do not talk like other people. You wonder whether analysis might provide a side benefit by enabling us (the analysts) to live with normal people. You conclude: "The analyst who believes himself to be 'normal,' and capable of deciding on 'norms' of behavior for his patients, runs the risk of being extremely detrimental to the creative unfolding and self-discovery they seek."

Could we conceive of analysts as people who grew up struggling with this dilemma, that of not feeling normal or of wanting to be normal? Do you observe this in analysts you have supervised? Are there residual problems? One of the things that is most striking to us in reading about your work is the freedom your patients experience to be themselves. How do you help beginning analysts to facilitate that kind of freedom, particularly given these issues concerning normality?

JM: I think one can create that space for the other person by being, oneself, open to everything coming in from the other. The most striking thing about any individual is her singularity, her uniqueness. This is partly, I think, what was in the back of my mind when I wrote those lines. In France, normality was talked about as a kind of ideal, but I find this is subtly present in United States also. It struck me as an aberration that there should be something called a normal personality or that there should be normal ways of making love or normal ways of going about anything. Whose norms? Whose reality is to decide these? Of course, when abnormalities hurt other people or run against the law, such as rape, or child abuse, and so on, we are, on the contrary, very closely identified with the ethics of the society we belong to with its lawgiving structures.

But setting aside those who seek to harm, there is room for every kind of personality structure, every kind of creativity; part of our work is to discover the creativity in every patient and to allow ourselves to become creative with them in return. This whole new experience must allow to come to life thoughts and feelings that have never been put into words before. Even if they are not the things that we would most wish for, we have to constantly ask ourselves, "*Why* do I want this for this person?" This is a problem I run across often with supervisees, "Why do I want this homosexual boy to become heterosexual if that's not what he wants?" It can be a problem of the analyst's. Yes, I would still stand behind the lines you quoted.

SRR: Do you find that that is an inhibition in most beginning analysts?

JM: Well, when we are beginning analysts, we are very scared of doing the wrong thing, whatever that is, something that is going to damage or narrow the possibility of our analysand's finding himself, his truth, and his path of creativity. It's natural to cling to the rule books as a young analyst and ask, "What's this coming up? Am I being led up the garden path by this patient?" One is oversuspicious, overanxious, and overcautious. It's like a beginning musician, you're very careful, and you practice a lot of scales. But as time goes on, we get to be more like free jazz musicians. You have to be an awfully good musician to play free jazz, and I think this is something we all aim at in ourselves, to really know everything that is knowable about ourselves, to really know everything that is knowable about the human psyche, and goodness knows, we don't know all that much. I think Freud's metapsychology is fascinating and interesting. Philosophers may look at it and say, "A lot of it doesn't hang together and so on." Theories don't. They're trial balloons. But we need to know all we can about what is included in the science of psychoanalysis and then begin to actually understand that half the changes that occur in analysis never even get put into words.

At the last International Psychoanalytic Congress in Buenos Aires, the theme was: "What are the agents of psychic change?" I was a discussant and expressed my feeling that the elements and agents of psychic change will always elude us. We will never be able to say, "It's because of this interpretation," or "Because I didn't interpret this" that this change can come about. We make theories about our work, and of course we make a theory about each patient, as well as listen to our patient's theories about himself or herself as best we can. And these theories change throughout the course of the analysis. It isn't necessarily our interpretations which cause psychic change. Otherwise, why would people effect such a fantastic change in their whole ways of being and feeling about themselves with analysts who have entirely different theoretical convictions and even different clinical approaches? The Kleinian and Lacanian analysts, for example, are almost opposite poles. People do effect very valuable psychic change with analysts of these schools as they do with Hartmannian, Sullivanian, or Kohutian analysts. It's something about the nature of the relationship, the respect for the psyche—ours and the other person's—that creates a situation that is propitious for new things coming into being. So, it's very difficult for a young analyst to say, "Well, I'm just going to let myself be creative." That would be rather terrifying. There is also the fear of acting out, which most psychoanalytic schools of thought—I was nearly going to say, most psychoanalytic religions, because there is danger of religiosity in our art and science—I lost the thread of what I was going to say....

SRR: Acting out.

JM: That's right. That it is one of the things all analysts are frightened of. Yet we are acting out in our technical handling and our interpretations, and even when we're not interpreting. You know the sort of complaints made by one analytic school against another: "Oh, the way you manage these short sessions, no one can regress;" "Ah, but the way you have everything worked out in advance, they can't think." There are dangers in any rigid school of psychoanalytic thought in which theories, which are, after all, a set of postulates that have never been proved, are treated as articles of faith. Then they become laws, and that stops creative thinking. So that what I'm really trying to say is that the young analyst, to whatever school he or she belongs, will in the beginning cling to the party line, whatever he or she feels is the way you should be doing it. But the hope is, as time goes on, that they will become more and more attuned to themselves in reaction to each individual patient and more appreciative of the unique quality of every human being that we have the privilege to have in analytic treatment.

LR: As an analytic candidate, I find your particular framing of things in terms of creativity versus normative/pathological processes very liberating and inspiring. You wrote: "The analytic process is itself a creative process, and these individuals carry within themselves all the elements for creating their analyst and the psychoanalytic adventure like everybody else. If once engaged in this adventure nothing happens to transform their way of experiencing themselves and the world, it may be that we have failed to understand their communication and to detect their cry of distress."

How do you specifically try to encourage creativity, play, and symbolization in your analysands and supervisees?

JM: Inside my own mind, this is what I am trying to do constantly, to open up the possibility for each analysand to have the courage to be, to possess their history and to see how many ways it can be experienced, as well as the extent to which one is constantly retraumatizing oneself because of the traumas of the past. Reality traumas do exist, quite apart from the fact that it's very difficult to be a human being anyway, and we have to remain aware of this. With regard to supervision, I do try to encourage my supervisees to see how they would see each analysand's story, and then, if they feel blocked, I will say, "Well, I could see it like this, or I could see it like that." I give perhaps three or four different floating associations, but I always say, "But you're the one who really knows." With each analysand we have to play it by ear. It's another music each time. Sometimes when they say, "Oh, when I heard myself say this horrible thing," I say, "Okay, you either work it out with your analyst, or, if you're not in analysis, work it out with your self-analysis; try to go a little further with it." I try never to make interpretations such as, "Ah, this is your inhibition," or, "This is your unconscious." I don't think this is the role of the supervisor.

By analyzing the problem themselves, candidates become fascinated with what's going on between themselves and their patients. And I do encourage them all when they have an interesting new idea, "Do write it down. Try to write it down." Quite a few of my supervisees do, after two or three years, write articles that they send me. And I feel very happy, as though they have given birth to an intellectual baby. Young analysts need a lot of encouragement because they don't always get it. They are often being told by old-age analysts, "Haven't you read Melanie Klein?," or, "Lacan never understood it like this." All concepts are interesting. These complicated religious leaders push us to think, and we're very grateful for anyone who pushes us to think even if we come up with quite different ideas. It's very important to encourage young analysts to read widely and also to write, if they want to.

LR: Can you say how your own personal experience of looking at the world might have contributed to your particular positive emphasis on a patient's creativity in solving their psychic problems?

JM: According to my parents, I was an absolute rebel, always dashing off after my own ideas, and, yes, putting into question the religious beliefs of my family very early on. That was probably helped by my father, because my mother went religiously to the Wesleyan church and my father said, "I worship God in my own way, in my garden." So, it was probably a feeling of freedom that my father gave us. Although they wanted boys and only got two girls, my father said, "Never forget that girls are just as good as boys, and maybe in some ways more interesting." My sister is a psychiatrist. My father was a businessman, an industrialist. I think he would have liked to see us create little businesses, so his daughters could be just as creative as he was. I'm giving more credit to my father than my mother. She would say, "There's something a little frightening about all this psychology stuff." I remember her saying, "As little as I can understand about psychoanalysis, what it really does is teach you how to hate your mother." I was a little shocked by this because I can't say I hated my mother. There was part of me that did. I had not had an analysis at that time, but I was planning to come to England in order to do this. And so, there were two or three mothers; one mother said "Maybe she should do it." I do love her for her attempt. She was herself, a displaced person, brought to New Zealand from England as a "prize of war" by my father after the First World War. And she was always a little disoriented. I talk a little about that in the beginning of *Theaters of the Body.*

I realize all she had to deal with in her New World. She was in fact in a pioneering country, a New World, and you see this with many people here who bring a wife or a husband from Europe and their struggle to adapt. But then, it's very stimulating, too, to come to the New World from the Old World, new things happen. So maybe it's partly being a New World citizen that stimulates me to do further research all the time, and to put new questions.

SRR: Yes, I think of you as a psychoanalyst pioneer.

JM: I'm a third generation New Zealander on my father's side, but first generation on my mother's side. She managed pretty well, all things considered.

LR: You also have lived in different countries; England, then France.

JM: My first husband, Jimmy McDougall, and I lived in England when we were in our early twenties with our babies under our arms, so to speak, because he wanted to go further with adult education and university extension work, which was his field. And I had wanted to study psychoanalysis since I was sixteen years old. He didn't find work when he got to London, except for a little job with the BBC in adult education programs, whereas I got a wonderful job at the Maudsley Hospital, which was exciting. Then I got accepted as a therapist in The London Child Therapy Clinic.

I wanted to study child analysis before adult analytic training, having two children of my own, but I came to realize that child analysis is much more complicated in many ways. That was the plan, but two years later, Jimmy McDougall was suddenly offered a job at UNESCO in Fundamental Education in Paris, which was a wonderful event. He became one of the leading spirits in UNICEF in control of the Middle Eastern sector. But our lives began to develop differently with our different orientations. So, I was catapulted in a sense to Paris, where I was destined to get my adult psychoanalytic training.

LR: Did you already speak French?

JM: Oh, I had some schoolgirl French.

LR: So you learned the language after you arrived?

JM: Yes, I really did. My children and my patients taught me, and I also went to the "Alliance Française." I did everything I could because I desperately wanted to go on with my analytic training.

SRR: How long was your training?

JM: In all, it was about eight years, but I was in London barely two years. I extended my child therapy training to the end of that year on the pretext that the children should finish up the school year. Actually, I didn't want to leave my analyst, I didn't want to leave the training, and I didn't want to leave my lovely job at the Maudsley Hospital.

LR: What was your work like at the Maudsley?

JM: Oh, very interesting. I thought I was lucky to get it. I was the clinical psychologist to Kenneth Cameron, who was the director of the Children's Department at the Maudsley. Among other tasks, I had to test children with Rorschach, TAT, and so on. I went to the Tavistock Clinic to learn more about them, but found, to my surprise, that we were actually quite well-taught in New Zealand. I can make a parenthesis there. When Anna Freud asked, "But how did you ever hear about my father?" I said, "But at the university, Miss Freud." "Ohhh, at the university no one talks about my father here in London," which they didn't in the early 1950s. I suddenly felt, "Oh, maybe the Kiwis aren't so bad." Then she said, "Do you have any experience with children?" I said, "Well, I have these little ones." She said she thought she could take me into the course, and of course, she was very disappointed when I went to say that I was leaving. "You're leaving the course?" "Well, my husband's got a job in Paris." Perhaps I got the feeling that it was not a valid excuse that I needed to be with my husband, so I added: "You see, Miss Freud, the children need their father." She said, "I will give you a letter to my friend, the Princess Marie." So I arrived in Paris with a letter for Marie Bonaparte. It was a wonderful introduction. Anna Freud was really gracious to give me this letter because I think she was genuinely disappointed that I was leaving. Oh, I was broken-hearted that I was leaving my London professional life.

I found a "progressive school" for the children where I thought they would have less pressure while learning French. With the help of Marie Bonaparte I was accepted at the Paris Institute of Psychoanalysis. She was a grand old lady, very different from Anna Freud. I had great admiration for Anna Freud, but she was just something quite different, or at least she appeared that way. I think she was probably in many ways very shy, too, which was not the case with Marie Bonaparte.

SRR: You must have read Elizabeth Young-Bruehl's book about her. What did you think? Did you already know about her analysis?

JM: No, no. I knew little bits and pieces, but rumors were so rife, and much of what we heard was probably apocryphal. You do get a picture of a live person, there's something sympathique about it. We had a lot of seminars with her alone, as with the others, and there she didn't show this side that the writer brings out so well. I did see her sense of humor, but she was a little uptight, you know. I still remember Freud's wife, Marthe Freud, was still alive, and one night, the door suddenly opened in the Freud Library. We were all sitting around discussing aggression or regression, and she saw us there and said in an offended tone, "Huh! Psychoanalysts!" then banged the door and off she went. The only time I ever saw her. She died shortly after that.

LR: How would you describe Marie Bonaparte?

JM: Oh, she was just fantastic. She wanted me to take her grandson, little Prince Charles, into analysis, and his father came to talk to me and said, "You know—I hope you don't mind my saying this—but I think all analysts are a little potty. I mean, they have to be, I do understand that. But take my mother-in-law, she's mad about criminals. She just loves them. And she's gone off to see Chessman to talk with him. She loves murderers, you see." But it's par for the course that a son-in-law can say what he wants about his famous mother-in-law and trying to explain that this might have affected Charlie. Charlie was about five or six, very funny, very intelligent. I was trying desperately to do very well with him. He was about my third or fourth child case after Sammy, who was my first psychoanalytic case. And of course, I astounded the French by seeing my child cases four or five times a week. They had never heard of such a thing. Anna Freud had told me: "There is no child analysis in France." They were doing psychotherapy analysis once a week, doing very good work, but there was no idea of full-scale child analysis in those days. It slowly evolved, of course, to become part of the Paris training, and children were taken into full analysis perhaps three times a week or four.

SRR: I'd like to return to some of our theoretical questions, since we are limited in time. In your 1985 interview with Baruch and Serrano, you stated: "There's something basically sexual, let's say, about one's way of listening and identifying with one's analysands. Perhaps something like the difference in the approach of each parent to his or her children."

You noted that you probably had deeper identification with your female patients and with the difficulties of growing into womanhood for the little girl. Could you tell us more about the differences between male and female ways of listening? Also, have you had a sense that your patients are aware, at times, of your identifying with them, or seeing them?

JM: No, very often you're the father or the hated brother, or the most beloved uncle or the incestuous grandfather. We have to play all the roles that are needed, and if you've got to settle accounts with the past, better let them be settled in the consulting room. So, there is always a sort of unconscious projection on the part of the future analysand, which may explain why they go to a woman rather than a man. Obviously, for very good reasons and for very bad reasons, too. Now I, in contrast to quite a number of my female colleagues, have a lot of demand from male analysands. So I have as many male patients as female patients, but I have had more male supervisory patients over the last few years than females. Probably the male analyst is trying to get some idea of how a female analyst listens.

Women candidates might want to have an analysis with a man, or do at least one supervision with a man to try to feel a man's way of looking at things too, because we've desperately got to use all of our psychic bisexuality to work with both sexes and be capable of identifying as fully as possible with the feminine part of a man and his terrified and delightful feminine feeling about it, just as much as we have to look out for the masculine part of the woman, her wish to be penetrating and phallic, as a man wishes for passive receptivity. I think that we're really trying to identify deeply with both sexes, but we can't get outside the biological realities that belong to one or the other. We will never *really* know to what extent this affects our way of being, talking, thinking, feeling, listening, interpreting, and whether we are reacting the same way or differently with male or female patients. I suppose that over the years I've come to feel that perhaps I understand female pain and suffering more deeply. Freud, of course, mainly understood male suffering. He claimed that the castration complex belongs to men, and women don't suffer it because they don't have a penis. This, you know, takes you a while to think through before you find the weaknesses in his outlook.

SRR: You've said, actually, that you've seen greater castration anxiety in women, than in men.

JM: I did, yes. In fact, that became a chapter in a book called *Between Analysand and Analyst.* I proposed that in many ways the "castration anxiety" of the little girl may make her feel her *whole* body is in danger. It doesn't mean to say that the little boy doesn't feel very fragile and exposed on the outside so that his anxiety is extremely acute. My quarrel with Freud is that he said that women don't suffer from oedipal castration anxiety because they don't have a penis. Therefore, they don't have perversions either! But we owe a lot to Freud, so I don't want to make too many criticisms. Anyway, to get back to your question, I don't know that I always feel that women listen differently. Some of my women patients feel I don't understand at all. Whereas some of my male patients feel I understand them most profoundly. And that's probably not so much to do with their psychosexual identity, but rather the uniqueness of their particular story. Some have learned to survive by never letting themselves be discovered, and this could apply to a man or woman. Whilst others, who had "good enough" parents in the Winnicottian sense, feel they can trust themselves. And you to hear their conflicts and mental pain, whether they be men or women.

LR: I am very interested in your conceptualization of primitive communication. In your *Plea for a Measure of Abnormality*, you wrote:

> "The eventual capacity of the growing infant to encode linguistically his bodily and emotional experiences is uniquely dependent on the nature of his tie to his mother, for it is she who, in the first instance, must interpret her baby's cries and gestures. The mother also gives her child meaning. She transmits the extent of fantasy space that the erogenous zones may occupy, and in particular, the nature of the relation between each zone and its complementary object. The latter is the cornerstone on which the psychosoma schema will be constructed.
>
> One further fundamental structuring element in the infant's psychosomatic organization is the mother's role in giving him the words for his affects. Lacking a language for his emotional states, he is incapable of dealing with them adequately. Thus it is within the unique mother-infant sphere that the child may hope to acquire a body which shall have symbolic meaning, and thus become conscious of its many messages and capable of elaborating symbolically, through verbal thought and imagination, the physical and emotional events that are truly his. This early psychic foundation will determine to a considerable extent the adult potentiality to capture and recognize one's personal psychic reality and to be able to communicate it to others. The gradual acquisition of an intact psychosomatic unity demands therefore that the body image, the erogenous zones and the affects and sensations belonging to these, be accessible to the symbolic process."

In these descriptions, you point out the vital role of the mother in providing a container for the infant's affects. Could you comment on the psychosomatic effects of the reverse situation, a mother using the infant as a container for her affects?

JM: There are not only psychosomatic effects. Sometimes a mother, because of her own internal problems, pain and traumas, is unaware of the fact that she needs to use her baby as either a narcissistic or a libidinal extension of herself. It might be her only love object, even more important to her than the father of the baby; or it may be a baby that unconsciously she has made with her father or her mother, or has replaced a dead baby. There are many factors that go into why a mother would communicate to her little baby that it is the infant's task to keep *her* together, and not the other way around; namely, that *she* is to help this little new human being to slowly grow together. And I have a number of patients who experienced their mothers in this way. The child grew up feeling very often the daughter—but not always—that she existed to keep her mother together. This, of course, is a source of pain and anger and hatred—"She ruined my life"—but underneath it, there's also a megalomanic satisfaction. Every child would like to be the only thing that keeps mother together, excluding the father. "Without me, she'd fall to pieces" is the message the child receives.

The other side of the coin is that "the moment she doesn't need me, I just don't exist. And even if she seems to need me all the time, I never got the chance of being my own person, of becoming an independent individual. My role, my identity, is to live for her, and I'm not going to do it. Yet, I've not the right to live for myself." It's a very painful situation, and it is very interesting to see this arising in the analysis. But I don't think of it as specific to psychosomatic illnesses; it's a part of the somatizing process in everybody. We can all regress to this stage where there was only one body for two, and the feeling that "Well, I have to keep her together. If she gets ill, I get ill," or, "If I stop, she will fall dead." These are undercurrent, completely unconscious fantasies that are active when we begin to somatize, when our defenses are overwhelmed. We all have some of these babylike, archaic longings and fears of facing the mother. A childlike need for one's mother, such as in accidents, may start off some outbreak of psychosomatic illness, but it can also lead to a more psychotic way of behaving for a while, or it can also stamp the whole character with the undercurrent feeling, "I don't belong to me. Part of me believes that my body, mind, and soul belong to my mother, and if I take them away something terrible will happen to her or to me." I'm oversimplifying, but I think it's an important fantasy in all psychosomatic manifestations.

LR: In reading your descriptions of addictive behavior, I wondered whether the gorging/purging cycle of bulimia or the tranquilizing/poisoning effects of alcoholism could be seen in terms of patients reenacting towards themselves an early kind of ambivalence they may have felt in their mother's nonverbal communication and attachment to them?

JM: I would say there's a particular maturational problem in the Winnicottian sense, that somehow there has not been a normal stage of transitional object development, that for some reason the child might never even have had any transitional objects or if he did, they didn't fulfill this function. This implies a lack of inner representation of a soothing mother with whom you could identify towards your own child-self and talk to it, "Poor kid, you've had a rotten day." There are ways that people can talk to themselves, like good mothers and good fathers. A good father might say, "Don't let them ride over you like that." And a good mother might say, "Well, anyone would feel a bit down in the dumps." But many people are totally incapable of identifying with good internal parental objects towards themselves. They are still on the outside, like the mothers and fathers of babyhood; then you search for these good objects in the external, so that the addictive search is always for something that is basically meant to fulfill a maternal and, very frequently, a paternal role as well.

There is a pattern in the bulimias, and the drug addictions, and so on, in which the object that you need because you have no way of self-soothing, is needed in order to feel safe, protected, or relaxed for a little while. But, of course, you can't complete an inner gap, something that's lacking an inner structure with an act or a person or a thing that's on the outside. It just has to be repeated again and again. There has been some breakdown in the introjection of the maternal and paternal caring. The transitional object represents an external and an internal object at the same time, mediated by this little toy or security blanket. It's discovered by the child, but it, too, contains the essence of the mother or sometimes the father. I've had patients whose transitional object was an object belonging to the father or mother.

So it stands for the mother's or father's presence and enables the child to feel it doesn't have to cry out for the *actual* presence of the parent. The child can go to sleep or go to stay with aunt Sadie, as long as he or she has that precious little object. This is a tremendous maturational step, of course. And some people have never been able to make this step, partly because the mother, or the father, could not allow it. "But I need *you*. You are my transitional object," perhaps using the child almost as a substitute for a maternal soothing substance. This lack of introjected caretaking objects must then be sought on the outside, as they were in early childhood.

LR: At one point in your writing, you described your stomach gurgling while listening to a "psychosomatic patient." I'm curious whether you have observed yourself responding more somatically while working with such patients and/or during phases of analyses in which patients are working through psychosomatic issues?

JM: Sometimes we capture something through the somatic feeling of our patients, the way they talk to us, reiterative, alexithymic, or operatory communications, which make you feel tight and tied up. It's actually a primitive communication in which they are talking to us, without realizing it, in a way *they* were talked to throughout their childhood.

Yes, I think we capture a lot just through the emotional tone of analytic discourse. Affects, of course, are always partly physical and partly mental. Many exchanges that are highly charged affectively are never even put into words. We don't know why we have a particular thought or feeling that might make us say, "Perhaps you felt paralyzed as a child?" "Oh, did I ever tell you that I had my leg in plaster for months and how they wouldn't let me move?" Or, "Yes, I did feel paralyzed. I didn't dare say, 'No, that's not what I want.'" I think we often experience countertransference affects that convey the somatic mode or affect mode of childhood. "This sounds like a frightened person talking. He's talking in this calm way, but I sense terror or fury behind it." An affect is never purely a bodily or purely a mental event. When you're angry, your heart is racing, and your mind is also filled with angry words. When you're terrified, something is, at the same time, happening in your body and your mind. But one can be psychosomatically vulnerable, or affect may increase character patterns which attempt to prevent certain events from occurring.

SRR: Also in *Plea for a Measure of Abnormality,* you describe masturbation as "a creative psychic activity whose aim, over and beyond its instinctual roots, serves narcissistic wishes of bisexual nature, and as such plays a role of considerable psychic importance." You also state, "In fact it may be said that the absence of masturbation fantasies, for whatever reason, in the analytic discourse of patients, is regrettable." Do you think the paucity of analytic reports about masturbation fantasies goes back to Freud?

JM: Freud's ambivalence about masturbation? He called it "the first addiction," and he thought it was the cause of many pathological conditions; yet, at other times he recognized that infantile masturbation exists. One of his great discoveries, apart from his discovery of the unconscious, was the revelation of infantile sexuality, which he attached to the oedipal phase, around three years of age. We would situate it much earlier today, thinking that infantile sexuality begins in the very first contact with the mother's body, her odor, her voice, which mobilizes a libidinal upsurge. Freud observed this at a slightly later stage, how sexually alive children were.

SRR: Why do you think masturbation isn't discussed more? You note that many work inhibitions and intellectual and artistic blocks are rooted in the unconscious refusal to accept bisexual wishes and conflicts. So it seems that if these kinds of fantasies don't emerge or can't be allowed, that it might inhibit the progression of the analytic work. How do you help analysands and also analysts that you supervise be more able to bring that material out?

JM: To bring that material out? First you have to make space for bisexual fantasies in your mind, and then help the patient to say, for example, "It seems as if you don't feel you have a right to both your feminine and masculine thoughts of yourself." I think that women, especially in the professional and artistic professions, accept more readily that they have a wish to be as powerful as their fathers as well as being as vitally important as their mothers. They don't feel so bad about saying, "Yes, there's a part of me that feels I could do this job as well as the male director who preceded me...."

But a man will often feel diffident about saying, "Well, I think there's a feminine part of me that would like to be receptive, and I, of course, accept this." Some men admit very readily their inner space and receptive wishes in sexual terms, as well as in work and professional terms. But I have observed that it seems more difficult for the men to admit to female longings than for the women to admit to masculine longings. But in either case, there's so often the feeling, "You're not supposed to have these." You're only supposed to be just one half of the sexual thing. That's what you are biologically. And so, you know, "just drop the rest." But you know, nothing ever gets dropped.

SRR: What are your thoughts as to why so little is written about masturbation fantasies?

JM: I've often wondered why. There's such a dearth of literature about masturbation, which is, after all, an important part of many adult people's lives; even people who have quite happy sexual lives will occasionally masturbate, perhaps some narcissistic need or anxiety-arousing circumstances, that's something interesting for us to understand. Leaving aside the people who only have autoerotic sexual lives—fetishistic situations and so on—we need to understand the person, who, for whatever reason, can have no love life or sexual life that is satisfactory. Some refuse even autoerotic pleasure, particularly women. I've often observed that we find in women a frequent equation of masturbation with death.

SRR: That's what I was going to ask next.

JM: Women's erotic sensations are mostly perceived on the inside of their bodies. And stemming from the clitoris, which Freud cast off as a little penis. His insistence on the importance of penis envy seems perhaps quite logical to a man: "If I were a woman, all I would want is a penis." The interdiction of masturbation starts so early in childhood, with the earliest of autoerotic manifestations, where the mother will not allow her baby to suck his thumb or have a pacifier or little pretransitional objects. When violently interfered with, this causes a gap in the slow coming together of the body image and the investment of the body as an erogenic and intact unity. We frequently overlook the fact that masturbation is the normal sexual life of children and of adults deprived of sexual relationships for whatever physical or psychological reasons. Some analysands claim that this is part of their problem, although for many people, it isn't a problem at all.

We have to be interested in the whole growth of the erogenic body as well as the way they slowly become integrated or fail to be integrated into genital functions. As you know, normal adult sexuality is markedly polymorphous. The more we try to understand all the different parts of the erogenic body that a patient is bringing us, trying to feel them in ourselves is sometimes very difficult. I find it difficult with the scatological people to identify with the wish to ingest somebody's fecal matter. We have to remind ourselves that babies smear and taste their feces and paint pictures with it. We have to be able to imagine that the child was so deprived of any right to its own body, its urine, and its feces, that all it could do was to try to erotize these functions to make the frustrations bearable.

SRR: It seems that you've given us the answer, that you really get into the other person's space, really try to do that, so that analysands must feel that.

JM: Yes, this makes them want to talk about their experience. Robert Stoller's latest book, *Pain and Passion,* is very interesting in that respect. He felt he did not understand enough about sadomasochistic pleasure. And people said, "Well, why don't you come to some of the S&M and B&D clubs?" which are clubs where people get together because otherwise they're so lonely. He was astounded to learn that they were pleased by his interest. They said, "Well, nobody cares about us. The gay world—everybody is interested in them—but everyone hates S&M people if they're not part of the club." We don't want to discover sadistic and masochistic problems inside ourselves. Stoller found that a certain number of these people who sought to receive pain had been hospitalized children, constantly receiving injections, having to stand the torment. It seems that some of these people survived by erotizing the pain. I've always been interested in the way in which erotization can make the most unbearable things more or less bearable. It's a triumph, in that it may enable traumatized people to survive psychically.

SRR: This is so helpful for understanding certain patients.

JM: We were lucky not to have been tortured, hospitalized children.

LR: You mentioned your interest in psychoanalysis started when you were still in New Zealand. Could you tell us more about how your interest developed?

JM: I read Freud's *The Psychopathology of Everyday Life* when I was fifteen in Penguin Books. When I told Anna Freud that, she was most surprised.

SRR: We would like to hear about the experiences which were the most formative, and the people—I remember your mentioning having had several analyses—the experiences which brought you the furthest in your development as a psychoanalyst.

JM: It's always very difficult to know what the inner psychic experiences stemming from early childhood were that might have led one to become more interested in one kind of profession rather than another.

SRR: The people who have influenced you? How did it affect you to read Freud's work at that age?

JM: It seemed to me overwhelming. And very early on I said, "I want to have an analysis." I didn't say, "I want to be an analyst." I wanted to know why I was so inhibited in certain areas. And of course, I held my mother responsible for these things. So, I wanted to know about that too. I think that most of us are drawn to this profession by a wish to understand our own psychological hang-ups and psychic pain. If we weren't, what are we doing in this profession? Some people have no idea what it is to be phobic or anxious or always doing the wrong things or creating the wrong relationships. Obviously, we're not only passionately interested in our own psychic pain, but also in other people's and in understanding how it works. Then it becomes a philosophical research as well: "How does the mind work?"

SRR: You had hope and awareness at that point, at such a young age.

JM: Yes, some hope of understanding all this.

LR: During your adolescence was your interest in psychoanalysis supported by anybody you knew? Did you pursue further reading at that point?

JM: Well, of course, I went to the University, and I took courses in philosophy and abnormal psychology because that fascinated me. And then we had to read Jung, Abraham, and Freud. It wasn't until I came to England and was able to begin training at the Hampstead Therapy Centre, that I really began to understand Freud. It was very exciting. But meeting Winnicott was probably one of the greatest experiences of my life.

SRR: Oh, can you tell us about that?

JM: Well, when I arrived in London, I wrote to everybody whose books or articles I had read, the sort of thing you do when you are very young. I wrote to Winnicott amongst others. They all invited me to come to consultation groups that they held. But as regards Winnicott, I was invited to the Paddington Green Children's Hospital. I went whenever I could. He loved having lots of people around. And there would be women and children in the background. Winnicott's consultation with mothers and children were fabulous. So I kept in touch with him when I went to France. In fact, I got the other students to invite him to Paris to talk, as well as Hannah Segal, John Klauber, and others I had met.

Other people who influenced me were Bion and Lacan. Lacan's theory is very interesting. I think it's worth struggling with, although he is difficult to follow.

LR: I find Lacan hard to read.

JM: Oh, he is difficult, but then he did not try to be clear. I got along well with him, but I could never practice analysis in the way he does. I have a lot of Lacanian analysts in continuing analysis because although I do not practice analysis as the Lacanians do, they know that I am not anti-Lacanian. I think Lacan was a very fine clinician, which many of his followers are not. They take on his tics and mannerisms and show little of his originality.

SRR: Could you tell us more about the influence of your analyses? You had more than one, so that you had different kinds of experiences?

JM: My first analysis got interrupted when my husband, James McDougall, was transferred to Paris, so I started off again. It was very upsetting to me to leave London and lose my analyst. I then continued with a Parisian analyst whom I became tremendously respectful of and fond of, although it never quite replaced that first transference experience. You put so much of yourself into the first analytic encounter. My analysis with Dr. Schlumberger went on for four years. And to my mind, he was a very fine man. Then years later, I wanted to go back into analysis with a woman.

SRR: I remember, you had discussed that you all knew the women analysts.

JM: Did I say this? Those I liked and admired were my friends, and those I couldn't bear were not the ones I wanted to go to. Finally, I did continue my analysis, but with another man.

LR: Was your first analyst a man?

JM: Yes, all three. It was a great sadness to me. I would have so liked to have had a woman analyst, even though to begin with, I only wanted a male analyst. As for the second, I had not much choice. I would have taken a male or female analyst, provided it was someone who could analyze in English. And then, many years later,

I discussed with my former analyst the idea of continuing my analysis—he was not encouraging about the woman analyst that I had thought of, or the few that I didn't know, so I chose another person whom I hardly knew, Dr. Michel Renard. This third analysis was very interesting. By then, you really have more precise aims about what you are seeking to understand about yourself. It doesn't mean that you're ever going to understand everything, but at least you know where your blind spots are, and one continues with self-analysis.

SRR: I wonder what it's like to be in analysis knowing as much as you do about the process. Not intellectually, but in a profound sense. What a different experience it must be.

JM: It's just so wonderful to suddenly be on the couch again. I sometimes think to myself that I'm jealous of my patients. I'd much rather be on the couch than in the chair. Just talking about yourself forever, it's wonderful. And otherwise, as the analyst, you have to make sense of it all, keep your mind on it. I think our patients have a more privileged place than we have! It's a tremendous pleasure to be on the couch and leave the worry to the other one.

SRR: The transference must be somewhat different, because earlier on there's so much less awareness of the nature and power of the process.

JM: I don't think we have as many idealizing projections. We are a little bit more realistic. We still feel he knows more than we do, otherwise, what are we doing there? And he psychologically knows more or should. I wanted someone whom I felt was a sensitive listener, sufficiently in touch with himself or herself to want to be in touch with somebody else's self. It's quite exciting to find yourself back on the couch, like at the beginning, investing things with a kind of childlike omnipotence, or belief, or longing, or pain; really quite surprising.

Silly things come back to my mind such as telling my analyst that for a very well-to-do analytic patient that I had, I had increased the fees. And I was wondering if this was the right thing to do. After all you don't pay more for your bread just because you've got more money. On the other hand, I felt this person needed to pay a higher fee, and the fee was in advance of what I was paying my analyst. And the next week, he put my fee up. I burst into tears. How childish can you get? On the other hand, I did wonder why he did it. I still wonder why he did it. He just said, "Well, you are asking this from an analytic patient." You take the truth, he didn't know. So I think we just go through all the normal regressions.

LR: As you look ahead, are there new areas of interest you want to pursue?

JM: Oh, I'm longing to have time to write the next book, which will be my fifth. But my patients won't give me a sabbatical.

SRR: We wondered about your patients. You write so personally about them.

JM: I always ask permission, but there are so few you can ask without perturbing the analysis. I give them the notes, usually notes that come from two or three years back. And they say, "Oh! I'm far better than that now. Oh! you've left out all my sterling qualities." And I say, "You know, it's not your sterling qualities that interest me, I'm only interested in your murky qualities. In any case, if you don't want me to use it, I certainly won't do so." Then, after reading the notes they often say, "Didn't I ever tell you? I can't understand why you didn't know this," and you get a lot of new material. But most of my patients say, "Why don't you ever quote *me*? Aren't I interesting enough?" "Why, I didn't find any mention of me. I give you all these mad things. I've got interesting psychosomatic illnesses. I'm weird as they come,"...and so on.

SRR: Oh, I wouldn't have thought of that. That's right.

JM: I don't write about patients if I feel that it would upset their analysis. Maybe I'm not as interested in them scientifically as they feel I could be. In the beginning, I would quote without permission because I never thought anybody would read anything I wrote. And then, as time went on, I realized I couldn't do that anymore, and that I really had to work that out with myself. It becomes an ethical question, and it's also difficult to decide whether or not to ask a patient for this permission. Sometimes I think, "I can't possibly ask this patient, even though it would be a wonderful insight into the theoretical ideas I'm putting forward."

The choice is very narrow. I can only ask people who have been a number of years in analysis, obviously, because it would be disruptive for someone who had been only a few years in analysis. Then I pass them the clinic notes that I have taken. Sometimes I say, "That dream is tremendously interesting. Would you mind if one day I asked you whether I could use it? Of course, I would let you know." Later, they may say, "You never used this dream," or,

"I hope you're writing this down, it would be interesting for an article." Such statements have to be analyzed too, of course.

Then I get good feedback, a whole lot of little details that I had not known before. There are many things that our patients think we know. "We ought to know everything, and shouldn't have to be told." The patient I call Georgette, for example [in *Theaters of the Body*], couldn't believe that I didn't know everything about her family background. What a discovery it was for her to find out that her father had been adopted. Or Benedict, I got a letter from her because I had written asking her permission. She had finished her analysis some time back. "I'm sending these clinic notes to you. If you don't want me to use them, I would quite understand. If you allow it, I would be very, very pleased." And she wrote back that she'd be delighted. She corrected all my errors in French, and she gave me some good advice because she's a writer, but she also said that there were important details that I didn't know about.

LR: She was the patient in "The Dead Father?"

JM: "The Dead Father"—yes, but this is a second essay, taken from sessions three years later, after she had had an ovariectomy, which was terrifying for her.

LR: "Sexual identity, trauma and creativity"...

JM: She told me, "But you've forgotten that I went to see 'City Lights' again and how dramatic it was for me?" I had completely forgotten that she had seen the film again, and in some way it had touched off the whole of her feeling of inner castration, and she had cried a lot, and then was furious with herself for crying.

SRR: When you were talking about the length of the analysis, I was thinking, we've heard about so many short analyses, and you do very deep analyses.

JM: Sometimes the analysis lasts for several years, but not all are that long, of course.

SRR: Could you talk about the resolution of analysis? I'm sure it differs in different treatments.

JM: Well,...the resolution. I think Freud was right when he said, "The analysis comes to an end when analyst and analysand stop seeing each other." There is never a real end. I sometimes feel that we've created new family romances throughout, that the analysand goes away with a better family romance than the original one. He or she will go on working with it and seeing it in different lights. I can't very well go along with the criteria for the termination of analysis. I think we have different criteria for each analysand, and the analysand has, too. The biggest problem are the people who never ever want to leave; then we have to ask whether there is something wrong with our work. These are the people I ungraciously called "antianalysands" at the time, but that was "countertransference" terminology. They cling to analysis like somebody clinging to a life belt.

LR: How do you handle that?

JM: It's a very delicate situation. We probably have to realize that every so often we will have people in analysis for life, like the family doctor. There are one or two patients whose whole capacity to go on living depends on having this contact. They're not cases that are well-chosen, let's say, for analysis. Freud would have said, "Throw them out. The gold of analysis can not be squandered on such desperately disturbed people." Today, we have many people who are far more disturbed than those Freud would have taken, according to his own criteria. We do have to accept that one or two of our patients can only keep together because of the analytic relationship, otherwise they would plunge into madness or suicide or psychopathic behavior. But, that's evading the question. Most patients, after three to four years of analysis, start to think they'd rather use their time differently. Maybe the problem with people who never want to leave might be a problem with me, I don't know. I want to take new patients.

I don't like this two-year waiting list that I have. On the other hand, one hates to feel one's rushing somebody out of their analysis. These days, so many patients have very long analyses. But I also have a lot of people who've had years of analysis before coming to me, and who want a short experience or want psychotherapy—not that we can always distinguish between the analytic processes in the two cases. I have quite a lot of people I see once a week sitting up, or even once a fortnight. I sometimes ask them to sit up when they want to throw themselves on the couch because they've been on it for ten years elsewhere. When I say, "Well, let's look things in the face," they're quite upset. They sometimes have a feeling of anxiety that wasn't there because they were lying down. It can be invested as a protective screen against allowing certain thoughts ever coming up, like being scared to look at someone in the eyes, a terror of being invaded or of invading, and other such fantasies. The face-to-face interview may be more traumatic potentially than lying on the couch, which can be soothing and defensive.

I'm very interested in the question of further analysis. I have a lot of people I see here in New York. Many are analysts of many years' experience. It's fascinating to see how analysts can use intermittent sessions of analysis with another person and go on working on their analysis creatively in between these intermittent sessions. I didn't seek a psychoanalytic clientele in New York, nor imagine that I would have ongoing psychoanalytic or psychotherapeutic patients. I have learned a lot about the psychoanalytic process through this work.

LR: It must be very gratifying to help colleagues in that way.

JM: For some, it has been. And then, also, to discover where it doesn't work, too, where I can't help this person. Or, it may be someone who's got to prove that no one can help her or him. And that, too, is a discovery that there's this desperate need to survive this way. So, to come back to the "resolution" of analysis. Maybe when we discover what the former solutions were, that may be enough. I know there's masses more to analyze, but I can deal with it myself. I get the feeling that the end of an analysis that feels satisfactory to both is when the analysand feels ready to be his or her own analyst. Sometimes *we* have to say, "I think you could go on your own now, and perhaps you haven't wanted to accept it." So I think that's about as close as I could come to saying when we can satisfactorily terminate an analysis. It's not a very satisfactory answer, I'm afraid.

LR: In your writing on symbolization and language, you point out that "the word creates a space between the mother and the infant" and that the father's increasing role in the mother-child dyad coincides developmentally with the child's learning to speak.

JM: Yes, but the father serves a vital function in helping the child even earlier than that, I would say, by protecting the infant against the omnipotent aspects of the relationship with the mother.

LR: In your case reports of Benedict [the writer whose father's early death had always been kept secret], it is fascinating that she draws some kind of parallel herself between words and her father by calling them "ghosts." I wondered whether you have found other examples in which a patient's use of words might reflect particular early mother/father dynamics? Do writers as analysands express any unique relationship to words in that respect?

JM: Writers have a special—but that's true for everybody. Writers are trying to get words to lie flat on the page, and they won't do it.

LR: What about the role of the father in the child's development of verbal language?

JM: Yes, I think it's important to realize that the *voice* is the fundamental element, and the words are like a third person coming between the intimate relationship between mother and baby. With regard to the origins of language, that is, prelanguage signifiers, perhaps I should get back to your question. Why am I so interested? In part, I think it's because I did my psychoanalytic training in France. French psychoanalytic thought is permeated with the theory of Lacan, even though many analysts would not say that they are Lacanian in their practice. Just as in England, psychoanalytic thought is permeated with Kleinian and post-Kleinian concepts. Yet, many who use these concepts say, "I'm not a Kleinian analyst," and they're not in their practice, but the whole permeation is there. The whole question of preverbal and nonverbal signifiers is very important to my mind, particularly as regards very early psychosomatic manifestations. These all go back to a time when the communications were nonverbal. Freud, like Lacan, clung to the power of language, and Freud admitted that he was totally insensitive to the charms of music.

LR: Is that right?

JM: Oh yes, he was very clear on this. But language and words meant everything to him. It's just as though language were something solid, and don't get entranced by the voice of the siren, where you no longer know where your limits are. Perhaps everybody clings to words, especially men. They serve a sort of phallic function. Words come in as a third dimension, although it's the mother who brings the words, and names the child's affects, and constructs the first meanings of things, but she's bringing this in from the outer world. That's why I criticize the theories of the psychosomaticists who tend to say there is no symbolic meaning to psychosomatic phenomena; they're just regressing, they're alexithymic, there's something wrong with the dopamine tracts, and so on. That's one theory of causality, but not analytic theories of causality.

We're interested in the infantile past and the origins that begin there. I am very interested in the early communications through voice, skin, body odor. Didier Anzieu, a very fine French analyst, calls it the "skin-self." I've made a plea for a respiratory self and a digestive self and an odor self, too. This concept helps us to understand many psychosomatic outbreaks such as allergies. People say the body has no language. I say, "Maybe it's the only one that can't lie!"

LR: In your writing, you frequently call attention to your patients' rich use of symbols. For example, in your case reports of Benedict, you mention that she had written an "opera" and that it had represented something about an "operation." I wondered whether her use of that medium in particular reflected her being drawn to voice with music. I also wondered whether at another symbolic level, unconscious or preconscious, "opera" to her represented a "word-thing" whose end, "-tion," she was eliminating, like an action of mastery over other "ends" she knew—her father had rectal cancer, her mother had performed enemas on her, and she had also undergone an ovariectomy.

In looking at how patients express themselves symbolically, how do you understand, in particular, patients who might resort to body gestures—facial expressions, holding their bodies in certain ways—to comfort themselves or to feel connected to others?

JM: This is an important question. Such patients might not have had enough transitional object experience, not enough introjected safety from the maternal environment.

LR: In your description of Benedict clinically, you noted how carefully she watched you. I wonder if her visual monitoring changed as she developed more verbal modes of symbolic representation and of relating to you during her treatment?

JM: Yes, it did, quite a lot. She was much less tense in her relationship to me. She didn't have to constantly be on watch nor monitor the end of each session. She was able to relax and let it be. She didn't need to have complete control of everything. We went for a long period of time when she'd say, "But I am so certain," and I'd say, "Certitude is certain." And then it struck her that people she had known who were psychotic were always "absolutely certain." Certitude had been important because nothing was real in the way events were presented to her in childhood. All essential things were made unreal. So she had to find out the truth for herself, like psychotic children do because of family secrets; things that can't be said, and so on. They have to make it all up for themselves. They know something is weird—"Where is my father?" Or, "Why did the uncle disappear?" Nobody says he committed a murder and was executed, or that there were cases of incest in the family. Reality is constructed by the parents, but sometimes they're not constructing it. Then there is often a lack of transitional space.

SRR: Do you find that the transitional emptiness changes with your patients, that they take something in from you?

JM: Oh, yes. How many of our patients begin for the first time to draw or to take dance classes or to do things with their bodies or their minds or their imagination that they've never done before? Beyond the symptomatic, they suddenly discover a whole other life. "Why have I never voyaged anywhere?" "Why have I never tried to write a song?" Yes, I think that's one of the most gratifying things that can happen in our work. And then, of course, there are those who don't finish their analysis because they decide to become analysts! That's another resolution.

LR: Does that happen often?

JM: Oh, I think so.

LR: Among your patients?

JM: Yes, particularly those who are candidates in analytic training.

SRR: Can you say more about that? Do you find that those who become analysts don't manage to finish some of the work?

JM: They act it out by becoming very good analysts. Then they find the necessity for going on with their self-analysis or going on with a second analysis somewhere, too.

SRR: But they can't do it still in the analysis with you?

JM: Perhaps they can't at that moment. There's a sort of deep timing rhythm in each person, I think. And I often feel that that should be respected. I might say to a patient, "Look, you may go on further with analysis in a few years' time," especially for those who are going to go into some of the professions in which they're going to use psychoanalytic knowledge. "And once you know more about your work in a few years' time, you might continue." "Are you trying to get rid of me?" "No, I'm just thinking that it might be we're coming to a moment when you might need to stop and carry on this new relation plan that you have." Sometimes analysands want to continue with an analyst of the other sex or who has another way of working. It is important to give them the right to leave because there is often an undercurrent feeling that we can't do without them, that we might fall apart. It's a terrible narcissistic wound, "You mean my analyst is going to go on living *without* me?" We dare not have other babies! But that the analyst is going to go on living perfectly well without them is a projection of baby omnipotence that's there in all of us. On the other hand, I'm very interested and concerned with somatizations that occur after a long analysis. I'm wondering to what extent. We can ever analyze deeply enough. We can't. It's our omnipotence that wants to help the patient to know everything, to prevent tragic or pathological things happening in the future.

We have to put up with our nonomnipotence. I am struck by the somatic symptoms which appear in people coming to talk about a second analysis that they have done with an analyst whom they have respected, whom I think is very estimable. That's why I always say a long time in advance, "We might think about terminating perhaps in a year's time," when the analysand seems to be prepared to stop, so that there really is a time to allow things to "come up." And that's something I'm still working on in my mind. It's very hard to conceptualize. I'm just struck by the clinical evidence.

LR: In some of the psychosomatic patients you describe, you talk of their occasional symptoms of psychosis as progressive steps towards health.

JM: Yes, psychosomatic manifestations are often the result of defense against psychotic kinds of anxiety, although there is no psychotic thought.

LR: Right, or they may be able to move into that or have a phase of that and then move on to something further developed.

JM: That you do find, of course. Some psychotic people start to get better when they start to somatize. And autistic children, who have impeccable health, as they begin to come out of it, catch colds, and they get other illnesses. This is another interesting aspect on the body/mind question that is difficult to theorize....It's another creative attempt at self-cure.

LR: What struck me is your capacity to tolerate psychotic symptoms in the analytic setting when other analysts might consider patients with such symptoms "unanalyzable," particularly in training institutes where they might be more protective of candidates.

JM: There are some crazy analysts, but they are often very gifted, too. I'm sure that today Ferenczi wouldn't get accepted at my institute!

LR: I actually had a quote from Ferenczi that we don't have time for, but he described a whole lot of somatic phenomena that he had....

JM: Oh, Ferenczi? Oh, please give it to me.

LR: It's "The Principle of Relaxation and Neocatharsis" from 1929. Here is the quote:

> "But after we had succeeded in a somewhat deeper manner than before in creating an atmosphere of confidence between physician and patient and in securing a fuller freedom of affect, hysterical physical symptoms would suddenly make their appearance, often for the first time in an analysis extending over years. These symptoms included paresthesias and spasms, definitely localized, violent emotional movements, like miniature hysterical attacks, sudden alterations of the state of consciousness, slight vertigo, and a clouding of consciousness, often with subsequent amnesia for what had taken place. Some patients actually begged me to tell them how they had behaved when in these states. It was easy to utilize these symptoms as fresh aids to reconstruction, as physical memory symbols, so to speak, but there was this difference, this time. The reconstructed past had much more of a feeling of reality and concreteness about it than heretofore, approximated much more closely to an actual recollection whereas 'til then, the patients had spoken only of possibilities or at most of varying degrees of probability and had yearned in vain for memories. In certain cases, these hysterical attacks actually assumed the character of trances in which the fragments of the past were relived, and the physician was the only bridge left between the patients and reality. I was able to question them and receive important information about dissociated parts of the personality. Without any such intention on my part and without my making the least attempt to

induce a condition of this sort, unusual states of consciousness manifested themselves which might also be termed auto-hypnotic."

My questions for you are the following: Did his description match any of your experiences of analysands with dissociated memories, or with episodes of reliving, reenacting physical memory symbols at certain affectively meaningful moments in their analyses? Why this type of regression in some patients and not others? Or any other thoughts, reactions you might have.

JM: Yes, this agrees very closely with my observations that psychosomatosis and psychosis have many features in common, as well as my belief that psychosomatic manifestations are an archaic form of hysteria, incorporation of early infantile experience before access to language has been achieved. The body has an astonishing memory.

Well, it's like the end of an analytic session, I'm afraid we have to stop now.

LR/SRR: Thank you so much.

SELECTED BIBLIOGRAPHY

McDougall, J. (1964). Homosexuality in women. In: *Female Sexuality,* ed. J. Chasseguet. Ann Arbor: University of Michigan Press, 1974.

McDougall, J. & Lebovici, S. (1969). *Dialogue with Sammy*. London: Hogarth Press.

McDougall, J. (1972). The anti-analysand in analysis. In: *Ten Years of Psychoanalysis in France.* New York: International Universities Press, 1980.

McDougall, J. (1972). Primal scene and sexual perversion. *International Journal of Psycho-Analysis*, Vol. 53, pp. 371–384.

McDougall, J. (1974). The psychosoma and the psychoanalytic process. *International Review of Psychoanalysis*, Vol. 1, pp. 437–459.

McDougall, J. (1980). *Plea for a Measure of Abnormality.* New York: International Universities Press.

McDougall, J. (1982). Alexithymia: A psychoanalytic viewpoint. *Psychotherapy and Psychosomatics,* Vol. 38, pp. 81–90.

McDougall, J. (1982). Alexithymia, psychosomatosis, and psychosis. *International Journal of Psychoanalysis and Psychotherapy*, Vol. 9, pp. 379–388.

McDougall, J. (1984). The dis-affected patient: Reflections on affect pathology. *Psychoanalytic Quarterly*, Vol. 53, pp. 386–409.

McDougall, J. (1985). *Theaters of the Mind: Illusion and Truth on the Psychoanalytic Stage.* New York: Basic Books.

McDougall, J. (1986). Identifications, neoneeds and neosexualities. *International Journal of Psycho-Analysis,* Vol. 67, 19, pp. 19–31.

McDougall, J. (1986). Parent loss. In: *The Reconstruction of Trauma,* ed. A. Rothstein. New York: International Universities Press.

Baruch, E. H. & Serrano, L. J. (1988). Joyce McDougall. In: *Women Analyze Women.* New York: New York University Press.

McDougall, J. (1988). Eve's reflection. In: *Between Analyst and Patient: New Views on Countertransference and Transference,* ed. H. Meyers. Hillsdale, NJ: The Analytic Press.

McDougall, J. (1989). *Theaters of the Body: A Psychoanalytic Approach to Psychosomatic Illness.* New York: Norton.

McDougall, J. (1989). The dead father: On early psychic trauma and its relation to disturbance in sexual identity and in creative activity. *International Journal of Psycho-Analysis,* Vol. 70, pp. 205–219.

McDougall, J. (1991). Sexual identity, trauma, and creativity. *Psychoanalytic Inquiry*, Vol. 11, No. 4, pp. 559–581.

M. Robert Gardner

M. Robert Gardner, M.D. is a founder and training analyst of the Psychoanalytic Institute of New England, East, and a member of the faculty of Harvard University. He is also a watercolorist and summer naturalist. Dr. Gardner was interviewed February 28, 1992.

LR/SRR: We're interested in hearing what role your writing has played in your life and in your analytic career.

RG: Writing? Yes. I imagine that anyone who begins to care about writing begins to favor an idiosyncratic approach. Mainly, I'm a journal writer. My journal is my home base. I began keeping a journal when I was eight or nine. I'm an early morning writer. Often I wake up with an essay in my head or with something that in the setting down becomes an essay. That first version often takes off both from a general subject I've been thinking about for several weeks and from a particular that I had thought about in passing on the previous day. Sometimes I'm also aware of having thought about some of this while drifting in and out of sleep during the night.

In these first bursts of morning writing, I usually feel a considerable enthusiasm. The main lines of the content and often some of the form seem promising. Later, however, when I look back at what I've written—often no more than a day or so later—I'm likely to be unsettled. More often than not, the content seems thin; and I can't believe I regarded any of the form acceptable, still less, promising. I've come to appreciate that this reaction is simply an overstated acknowledgment that something is wrong, not that the whole thing is beyond redemption. At any rate, at this point I resist the temptation to begin editing. I've learned that editing too early cools off the writing too quickly.

Still later, having set down other entries—most of them in similar early morning endeavors—and having gone through similar reversals of opinion about their worth, I begin to see a common theme or themes. I isolate the entries that most conspicuously reflect those themes, select large blocks, and arrange them quickly into a rough whole. At this point, I try not to rework smaller sections. I say I "try" because sometimes I can't resist polishing a phrase, and sometimes I even get carried away in weighing a single word. In the main, however, I wait for the polishing and weighing mania to subside and, in a relatively uncritical drift similar to the one in which I wrote the original entries, I arrange and rearrange the large sections. After this, I try to arrange and rearrange the smaller parts to give more emphasis to some and less to others. Overall, I move slowly from setting down the first overview, to arranging and rearranging large blocks, to arranging and rearranging smaller blocks.

Now I generally go over the materials again, this time arranging, rearranging, and polishing both larger and smaller parts in whatever unpredictable way—orderly or erratic—I feel inclined. And, of course, one change, small or large, often triggers another.

I keep this up till what I have written begins to say what I want to say and begins to say it the way I want to say it. Somewhere along the way I usually begin to see ways in which I have been engaged in a favorite preoccupation: trying in one way and another to shape the form so it reflects and illustrates the content. I try, then, to expand these particular harmonies of content and form, and to add others. I generally begin also to see that I have been shaping and reshaping the writing so that I am speaking in a consistent and friendly voice to a consistent and friendly reader. For me, that's very important and never easy—writing to the right reader in the right voice. One other thing. I keep working and reworking till the writing looks and sounds—especially till it sounds—as if I hadn't worked and reworked it. I try, that is, for an illusion of spontaneity and ease. For these and many other reasons, I'm a slow writer. Extremely slow.

SRR: It's reassuring to know that so much effort goes into something that looks so like an art piece. I'm curious about that process. At what point did you realize that way of working was something that was part of a whole progression?

RG: Perhaps last year. Surely not much earlier. Though I had been a journal keeper since I was a child, I was unaware till quite recently that I was journal-keeping in any particular way or for any particular purpose. Indeed, I don't remember ever thinking of myself as a journal keeper any more than as a talker, walker, or breather.

Having recently given the matter some consideration, I have come to the preliminary conclusion that the main purpose of my chronic journal-keeping has not been to serve the writing process about which you have asked but to help to keep my head screwed on straight; that is, to keep it screwed on as straight as I can. Until quite recently, I gave little thought to my way of writing or to its relationship to my journal keeping. I took it for granted that I would keep a journal and would work and rework the entries in the ways I have described. In so far as I thought about my way of writing at all—that is, about my way of writing for public reading or for publication—I thought of it as reflecting the lack of an organized approach to writing. The journal writing hand didn't seem to know what the other writing hand was doing and vice versa. Only lately have I thought of the steps in my writing, as you put it, as a part of a whole and characteristic progression. Not until quite recently have I managed to convince myself that there's method to my writing madness. I suppose this reflects my having reached the stage that Erikson has characterized as the struggle for integrity. I prefer to think of it, however, as the stage when one is even more than ever concerned with trying to make necessities into virtues.

In recent years, my way of journal keeping, and of other writing, has been aided and abetted by the use of a computer. And I imagine that the organized and organizing qualities of the computer have helped me to see a little more clearly some of the characteristics of my way of proceeding. At the very least, my computer has allowed me to set things down more easily and quickly in my journal in the first place and then in the second and whatever number more, to rework things till they look as if they might have been set down that way in the first place. I have often wondered whether the last drafts are that much better than the first to justify all the rewriting. I cannot imagine that they are. But I like to proceed that way. I need to proceed that way. In any case, though I've tried to answer your questions about my writing I want to stress that while I am actually writing, I have little or no conscious idea of what I'm aiming at or how I am proceeding. I don't know where I'm going; I don't know how I'm going to get there. I do usually know when I have gotten there. And that's where I stop.

LR: You're describing an intuitive sense of what sounds right to you. You work with it until it gets to that point.

RG: Yes. A lot has to do with sound. I think early training in music may have shaped my attention to sound and to composition, that is to that way of composing in which you touch on a theme, then drop it, then bring it back in a slightly different key, then try to resolve it at the end with something that weaves the theme and variations together. That reminds me: Often, while I'm writing, I find it very helpful to have music playing in the background. But all of this about how I write is mainly retrospective reasoning. I'm not aware while writing of trying to do anything in particular. I feel certain that my reasons for proceeding, however I proceed, are a good deal more complex than I can grasp. Indeed, I'm one of those persons who prefers not to look too carefully at the inner workings of his ways of writing, even though I'm addicted to trying to observe the inner workings of my ways of analyzing.

SRR: I would like now to ask you to move from how you write to what you have written and to your vision of analysis. This is a very recent quote: "As we grow less content to view analysis as a process in which the patient projects inner worlds onto a blank screen, especially a relatively blank analyst, we feel more and more the need for visions that do fuller justice to the joint contributions of analysts and patients." You begin to propose, it seems, an intrapsychic and interpersonal vision. You also say, "that might well assume that both analysts and patients are always enacting their currently lived conflicts in efforts both at blind repetition and at resolution, that this double duplicity influences the unfolding of all analyses, and, when things go well, some aspects of the analyzing play of the analyst and the patient's imagination lead to mutual growth."

I have several questions. Are you suggesting that the urges towards blind repetition never disappear, but are, hopefully, modified and restrained enough to lose their power? Do you conceive of the match between the analyst and patient as of central importance, a pairing of two people whose conflicts previously resolved and not yet resolved have a certain similarity or resonance? Also, do you think of analysts as persons more needing or choosing to continually resolve these kinds of conflicts through their work? Perhaps like artists.

RG: First question, I think that we never get rid of the inclination towards blind repetition of many tensions—perhaps to some degree, of all tensions—and that we also struggle over and over toward resolution of those tensions. I believe that when we speak of resolution we speak, at most, of re-solution, temporary solution, a solution at best a bit better in some ways than earlier solutions. I think we assume with fair reason that all our solutions and resolutions are, like all structures, never fixed, only relatively abiding. I see these unfoldings, as I imagine most analysts do, as occupying an endless and everchanging series. As to the inclinations toward blind repetition losing their power, I doubt it. Perhaps a little of their power. Rather I think we hope for an expanded play between inclinations toward blind repetition and inclinations toward more adaptive solutions.

I see a personal analysis as an effort to advance that expanded play in ways that help the analysand—and to some degree the analyst—to continue the play after the analysis. Which brings me to your question about the analyst's position. I would think that anything that any person becomes consistently and passionately involved in, whether as a psychoanalyst, a painter, a writer, or a baseball player, serves as a stage—a playground—for unending attempts both blindly to repeat the past and to bring some aspects to new, and currently better, conclusions.

I would think this backward and forward struggle is characteristic of all human endeavors but a trifle more characteristic of some. And I would think—I would hope—that psychoanalysis is one of those endeavors of which it's a trifle more characteristic. I see psychoanalysis as a process in which two persons agree to try to advance the development of one and, in so doing, end up struggling in many ways both to advance and to block the development of two. This encompasses many resonances and many dissonances. I don't think such a view excuses the analyst's intrusions; it only concedes their high probability and invites persistent exploration of their vicissitudes.

I hope it is clear that I don't tout the expression of the analyst's tensions on the analytic scene. It's all too easy to tout such happenings or to take the position, on the other hand, that a good-enough analyst's intrusions are, with rare exceptions, insignificant, or if not insignificant, speedily modifiable. I have found it useful to assume that my own inner workings are always powerfully at stake, and, therefore, my own inclinations both to advance and to retard explorations, my patient's and my own. I have tried to pursue a persistent self-inquiry both to increase the chances of keeping the expressions of my own tensions relatively subtle, relatively well-tempered, and in so far as possible, in the service of analytic aims and means. Beyond that, I have tried to pursue a persistent self-inquiry in the hope of studying a few ways in which my own workings shape and are shaped by the events of an analysis.

I believe that these habits of inquiry pursued for this mix of prophylactic, corrective, and academic aims has here and there, and from time to time, helped to transform a few expressions of my inner workings, if not into blessings in disguise, at least into useful shadings, verbal nuances, and so forth, rather than disruptive, runaway activities. And to the degree this has proved useful, I think it has proved a bit more useful when my self-inquiries have focused after hours on the visual images formed during hours. I am not one of those analysts who can pursue self-inquiry very far within hours without it distracting me from the workings of my patient. This after-the-hour exploration of visual images seems also to allow me to pick up and to explore some of my tensions when they are still relatively small rather than after they have taken the form of larger and potentially more counteranalytic enactments.

By the way, you mention a possible analogy to how an artist works; but if we were to follow through on that analogy, we might have to say that in analysis there are two artists at work, two artists who sometimes work cooperatively and sometimes at cross-purposes, and usually both at once. As to your third question, I'm still working on that.

SRR: As to the match.

RG: Yes. I'm uneasy about two current trends that go under two dreadful names and seem to have not unrelated dreadful manipulative possibilities. One is "converting" patients to analysis. The other is "matching." Each, I believe, is often the expression of a good intention gone far astray.

I do think it's well to recognize that no analyst is a universal analyst. One analyst is a little better on the average analyzing some personalities and some problems than another. And I can see that certain traits, interests, and values shared in common by patient and analyst can facilitate analysis in various ways. I can even see how, in one or another regard, it's possible to make an educated, but limited, guess about an analytic match. I don't deny that. But I do think we are seldom in a position to match conflicts of patient and analyst, to avoid matching conflicts, or to find the right mix of the matched and the unmatched. Nor do I think we need to. And even if we needed to, and even if we knew how, who would select the matchmaker best suited to do the matchmaking in a particular instance?

It seems to me fortunate that in usual circumstances there are enough useful resonances and dissonances mobilized by the free association method to enable effective analysis. I suspect that a good-enough analyst and a good-enough patient, exceptions notwithstanding, can usually find in him- or herself a sufficient supply of lively resonant and dissonant tensions for a good-enough match. In any case, I think the matching usually is best left a part of the more or less intuitive, and surely amateur efforts of the patient and analyst to decide, however they decide it, whether they can work together.

SRR: And then the last part was whether analysts are people who have more of an inclination, choosing to spend time in kind of resolving....

RG: I'm wary about generalizing in this matter. Ours is a big field. We have widely different temperaments. I've talked to some analysts who seem to do very little self-conscious self-inquiry. I think there are some analysts who are disrupted by too much self-inquiry, that is, by too much self-conscious self-inquiry. I have mentioned before that I have not found ways to explore the workings of my writing without disruptive consequences. Some of us can explore some of our activities; some can explore others. By the way, I believe you were not at that New York panel on self-analysis, or what I call self-inquiry. Somebody gave me what I guess was intended as a compliment. He said: "Most people can't do any self-inquiry. Only a few talented people can." And then he added: "If you find it interesting and useful, good for you. But it's not a generalizable activity." What could I say? I said, "I think the really talented ones are those who can conduct an analysis without all that self-analysis."

For my part, as I have said, I don't think I could conduct analysis without persistent self-inquiry, couldn't listen or respond the way I think I listen and respond best. And this is not merely a matter of tempering countertransference tensions. I find I must practice getting into states of evenly hovering attention in one situation and another—states in which I shift fluidly from the awake to the more dream-like—and I must practice observing those states in one situation and another, in order to do it the way I want to do it in the analytic situation. I don't think that's true of everybody. Analysts listen differently. They need to listen differently. They prepare themselves differently.

In my own case, as far as my visual images are concerned, I find that if I don't pursue frequent extra-analytic exercises in self-inquiry—warm-up exercises—I cannot catch my visual images as well, or I cannot make use of them as well, inside the analytic situation, or outside. All of which, I believe, is one part of my need and desire to approach analysis as a double inquiry, an inquiry for my patient and for me. To come back more specifically to your question, you asked whether I think of analysts as persons who need to use their work to resolve their conflicts. I think that is probably true in general but not in all cases, and not equally true in those cases in which it is true. I know it is true of me. I think it is very true of me. But I think that some analysts—like some artists, and for that matter, like some scientists—may work best at a slightly larger remove from their conflicts. I think I have seen both ways of working—the one, nearer to conflict and the other, more distant—and have seen each used well and badly.

SRR: This is from *Self-Inquiry:* "Outside psychoanalysis as well as inside, each person tries through his or her special medium and means to inquire into large questions of mutuality and tries in nodal moments both to preserve old answers and to find better. Each search is repeatedly for someone or something with whom or which to live out in these moments the lead questions with which he or she is now concerned." I think you have answered the first part of the question…

RG: Anyway, I touched on it.

SRR: …which has to do with the compatibility of searches. You might have some other thoughts about that. To continue: "Though it is better as a rule that some of my reliving be a shade more forward-looking where my patients may be a shade more backward-looking, and better that some of the consensual conflict of my character be less central and compelling, nothing happens to the one, I find, without something happening to the other. Such moments of parallelism of my patient and me might be regarded, might be, a special disorder that can surely cause trouble, but when on looking carefully I see no signs at all of such parallelism, I find we're in greater trouble."

I am very interested in this parallelism, what it is and what the trouble can be, and the times that you are stifled,…

RG: As far as parallelism is concerned, it goes back in some ways to matching. That is, it goes back to the inevitable and relatively spontaneous matching that takes place in what I regard a good-enough analysis. I would stress two aspects. One is an inherent parallelism in the developmental endeavors of any two persons. This expectation of a parallelism rests on a notion of Pekinese that runs through modern biology and runs in analytic thinking from

Abraham through Freud through Erikson and on—the notion that everybody goes over the same—almost the same—epigenetic ground plan, and everybody goes back repeatedly to past stations. Accordingly, there is a strong probability that there will be many epigenetic resonances between any two persons.

The second aspect of this "spontaneous" matching is that in the analytic situation, there's a strong probability that the many stimulations and accommodations brought about in the joint exercise of the free association method, bring forward and intensify particular epigenetic resonances between patient and analyst.

To speak more personally, I find I need to get in touch with some of my own struggles that parallel some of those of my patient in order to understand that patient in more than a rudimentary way. I believe analysts differ in this respect, too. Some need to work closer to these aspects of their own experience—to be more directly aware of them—and some need to proceed at a greater remove.

You asked about pitfalls. I hope it's clear that I am not saying what others should do. I'm saying what I have found to work best in my case; that is, what I think works best in my case. I think the job of an analyst includes an unending struggle to discover a little of what tends to work best in his or her case. In my case, if I cannot find currently lively resonances between my patient's tensions and my own, I am in trouble. But if in searching for resonances, I get the impression that my resonances are not merely clues to, but exact representations of my patient's tensions, if I get the impression that what is in me and what is in my patient is identical, I have lost my way. I find I must have a currently lively sense—often a hard-won sense—of similarities and of differences. And I find I must keep discovering similarities and differences afresh; otherwise my understanding, my comments, and the analysis become sluggish. In analysis, as in writing, I find I must struggle to become the right person with the right person.

SRR: Just the last part of that. How did you come to these ideas?

RG: I don't know. Do I have a special challenge, problem, fascination with self-object differentiation? I don't know. I do know that I have long been interested in the relationship between the observer and the observed, whether in the realm of the animate or the inanimate. But even in so far as early self-object differentiations are concerned—and later voyeuristic inclinations—I cannot explain the leap from these to the observation in the analytical situation of the wider range of similarities and differences of which we are presumably now speaking.

LR: I'm thinking about what you're describing in terms of the observer and the observed and wondering if you follow a parallel process while you paint, for example finding interest in the figure/ground or edge/boundary resonances?

RG: Yes. I think I have a special interest in the similarities and differences between one element and another—shape, hue, intensity, clarity, size, edge, and so on. It's hard to paint without having a special interest in balancing and opposing them. Still, in painting, I think my main interest lies in fluidity and transparency, and especially in capturing the look of light and space.

When I was stationed in Texas, it struck me one day that something was reminding me of home. That idea seemed odd since home was New York City. But then I realized that one piece of what had allowed me to accomplish this presumably wishful connection of Texas and home was that in many places in Texas, you see that vast unobstructed overhead bowl of sky all around to the horizon; and in my childhood I had gone often to and been fascinated by the vast unobstructed overhead bowl of the Hayden Planetarium. In that sense, the Hayden Planetarium had been my Texas, or Texas had become my Hayden Planetarium.

LR: I think of a fishbowl.

RG: That's one possibility.

LR: Actually, my association was to your being an only child and wondering if you often felt the object of a lot of observation?

RG: Yes. I don't know how it could have been otherwise. I think of myself, however, as having been more the observer as a child than the observed. It's all in the eye of the observer. Looked at one way, I was observed a lot. Looked at another way, I was observing a lot. But you will forgive me, I hope, if I decline to pursue further the relationship between my sense of space and my sense of enclosure, between my sense of being an observer and my sense of being observed, and the relationship between these and my fascination with the broad skies and celestial events of Texas, the Hayden Planetarium, and other locations.

LR: It's interesting that you went into the question before about empathy, because that was actually one of my questions. You describe in your book on self-inquiry how discord between a patient and analyst can be "mutually liberating." You wrote about the example of the "dog in the man-house": "And like my patient, I struggled between old urges to a forced accord and new urges to a mutually liberating discord. I was faced with ways I had colluded with my patient to blur borders between cooperation and conciliation. I was faced with my own tendencies toward trick-performing and gift-bringing, and the welcoming of them with others."

I thought your concept of discord put a positive light on the struggles between the analyst and patient to understand one another and dispels to some extent the "ideal" of always searching for the closest empathic attunement. How did you arrive at that idea?

RG: I think originally it may have come partly in opposition to the notion that empathy implies a perfect understanding, a perfect harmony of some kind. That idealized—or is it depreciated?—vision of empathy struck me as smacking of a perpetuation of some myths of the early mother-child relationship. That emphasis on harmony—lovely and useful as harmony may be—seems to ignore the large part that friction, the right kind and right amount of friction at the right time, plays in development.

I refer, for example, to the obvious role of friction in stirring capacities for adaptation, cooperation, and collaboration. I doubt there's any serious risk of too much harmony between one person and another, whether a mother and an infant, or others. Still, it doesn't seem to me useful to idealize harmony and to denigrate friction, and, in particular, to ignore the everchanging qualities of the balance between harmony and friction necessary to support and spur development. So, I think that's where my conscious ideas about similarities and differences began. They took off, however, mainly in the personal observations of which we were speaking a few moments ago. In the instance you quoted, I needed to see certain similarities between my patient and me. I needed to see that he had been bringing me dreams and other things as gifts. And to understand him—and myself—I had to dig down into ways in which I, too, had been a gift-bearer, both in the past and in the present. But to understand him—and myself—I had also to dig down into differences; for example, into ways I had spent more effort than he in rebelling against such gift-bearing proclivities.

And when I had grasped these differences, I began to recognize ways in which my patient had rebelled, though those ways had been different from my own. And that recognition helped me to see that his ways were not entirely different from my own. And so it went:

back and forth between recognitions of similarities and recognitions of differences. Perhaps I could have gotten at these matters another way—logical or other—without exploring these similarities and differences. Still, I find I often do proceed by finding similarity and difference; and I think I do so more speedily and fully when working at what I regard to be my best.

LR: Let me read another description of yours of this concept of "disorder" in your self-inquiry book, so that readers of this interview will have a sense of your language: "Without joint disorder we make little order, and less progress. When our self-inquiries meet, join, and mingle in shared repetition and optimal turmoil, when maintenance and metamorphosis seem to vie—till we find ways they do not—these are the moments of the most radical possibility. For my patient and me, 'The best of times and the worst of times.' In these moments, the dare at the crossroads is double."

RG: I believe that many of our efforts, analytic and other, are, in our best moments, very close to trouble. These peak efforts can advance our aims; or they can obstruct. I take this to be another specialized instance of a general phenomenon. I was talking in particular of those moments of high possibility when an individual, whether an analyst, a patient, or somebody pursuing another endeavor, is trying something creative. By creative, I don't mean novel or radical by ordinary standards. I mean a personally innovative response to the challenges at hand it may, by ordinary standards, be novel or conventional; but for the person involved, it's an attempt to face something new or to face something old in new ways.

In the analytic situation, these are often moments in which transference and countertransference—or other heightened conjunctions—produce simultaneously for patient and for analyst, in different ways and different degrees, opportunities to go backward or forward in development. This is not to say that development in analysis or elsewhere proceeds always or usually in dramatic events of crisis; "Sturm und Drang," and so on. It's rather to say that development often proceeds in barely perceptible events of minicrisis; minicrisis for more than one person.

LR: You also describe in *Self-Inquiry* how analytic work involves "matching subjectivities": "When things go well, my patient's self-inquiry meets mine in complex and seamless connection. And having found a good fit between my patient's self-inquiry and my own, I may say I have been objective. But I can only mean—and I should be pleased to mean—I've been objective in matching subjectivities."

You laugh, so I'm curious what you're struck by.

RG: I mean it's a paradox. That's what makes me laugh. One can place one's subjectivity in a slightly different position. This may involve a valuable shift in perspective. But to call it objective is a contradiction in terms. I was trying through this irony—objective matching of subjectivities—to highlight a notion of informed, relatively informed, subjectivity, a notion different from what we sometimes think of as neutrality or objectivity. In this regard, we are like modern mathematicians and physicists; we need and espouse concepts of relativity and concepts that help us to think of the relationship of the observer to the observed. And yet, holdovers from our previous theories keep breaking through in ways that might suggest—and I suppose we never stop wanting to suggest—that there is such a thing as a purely objective observer, an observer who observes things out there just as they are. It's very hard—perhaps impossible—fully to accept that we are, whether artists, scientists, or whatever mix—always taking temporary, limited, and highly personal sightings in endlessly changing circumstances, sightings marked not only by new corrections but by new errors.

SRR: It seems as if there could be several levels to the subjectivities you're working on with a patient; for example, the content of what questions you are both pursuing or the process of how you both think and talk about those questions. I imagine cultural differences also might make it more complex. How do you think about those different levels?

RG: The hidden questions that patients, analysts, and others pursue seem to me remarkably similar. In that sense, they are universal questions. Which is perhaps only to say that the fundamental human dilemmas are similar. But the ways in which those questions are advanced—what I think of as the genres of inquiry—or what you have just called the processes by which they are advanced—are highly idiosyncratic. As an analysis advances it is possible to observe remarkable consistencies between contents and forms of inquiry. And, over time, there are remarkable confluences between the content and genres of inquiry of the two persons.

I think that is one aspect of what we mean when we say that the patient and analyst tend to develop a common language. Vocabulary becomes similar, grammar becomes similar, cadences become similar, rhythms become similar. And much more. Recently, I was working with a patient, and I noticed I was constructing sentences in which the strongest word in the sentence was often at the end; and so the word, and the sense of the sentence, often came as a surprise. Later, remembering what my patient had earlier said that members of his family had said, I suddenly realized that in this respect I had begun to talk as his family had talked. I had become family.

LR: That's powerful.

RG: That was very startling to me. After the hour, I thought, That's his side of it; that's where this way of talking was in his past. And it's something he tends to use when he's advancing his most pressing hidden questions. But where does this way of talking come from in my past? By a roundabout route, I then remembered several persons from my childhood—persons with whom I had been deeply involved—who spoke with a similar end of the sentence tilt when expressing their pleasures, pains, humor, and much else. Which reminded me also that when I was a teenager I had been especially charmed by O. Henry's stories with their surprise endings. And now my interpretations had become like little O. Henry stories. Which realization led me by another roundabout route—this time, a particular O. Henry story—to a previously unrecognized aspect of my reactions to my patient. Which, in turn, led me to recognize a previously unrecognized question that both my patient and I had been trying both to advance and to obstruct.

I think we need to know much more about the ways in which our patients and we, through our mannerisms of speech, and much else, join in hidden conversations. We know too little, and we lack an adequate vocabulary for characterizing what little we know. Recently, a colleague reported to me that his patient was increasingly afraid he was going to seduce her. As he went on to tell the details of several analytic hours I discovered that when he spoke to her, his sentences did seem in a number of ways to chase her, to catch her, and to press her to expose whatever he wanted her to expose. When she would demur, he would pin her down till she would finally give in and follow the proposed analytic, though erotized, agendas. And so, within the formal quality of their discourses were repetitions on both sides of those very matters they were talking about and were trying relatively successfully to explore. These linguistic pursuits—pursuits in both senses of the word—were subtle—I have caricatured them for emphasis—and they took place within the broad bounds of acceptable analytic procedure.

One could quarrel with some ways in which the analyst was pushing the patient to acknowledge one matter or another. But one could also argue that the ways in which his verbal behavior joined and stimulated the patient's phantasies, and vice versa, proved a useful contribution to the analysis. I assume such mutual expressions of unconscious shared tensions often provide useful grist for the analytic mill, provided, that is, that they do not provide too much grist for either or both the millers. I believe that what we call neutrality often includes just such relatively well-disguised expressions, expressions compatible with analytic aims and means. Is that the kind of thing you're interested in?

LR: Yes. And that example of the analyst who was in relatively controlled pursuit of his patient raises the issue of the more silent, curative effects of therapy that may not be fully conscious. In that enactment, which is so much milder than what she feared, she might be learning a different, less frightening way to be caught and contacted. If that could be made more conscious and discussed between them, it might give her some sense of mastery over that type of experience.

RG: Yes, it might. But the question of what needs to be made explicit and what is better unsaid and left to a preconscious working through, is always a difficult one. In thinking about analysis, it seems to me that those of us who prize insight sometimes underestimate the complexity of the ways in which conscious and preconscious observations, insight, and corrective experience interact.

SRR: Do you think there's a difference in the impact of this kind of enactment when the analyst is aware? I don't know how exactly to say aware, maybe aware in some general way, or having some consciousness, versus when the analyst doesn't think in these terms?

RG: If we don't become aware because of a resistance in us, I think that could be—or lead to—trouble. But apart from resistance is the inevitable limitation that we can only follow so many—perhaps I should say so few—variables at any one time. We can only track a small fragment of what is going on in our patients, in ourselves, and between us. No matter how much we prize insight in general, and no matter how valuable that emphasis may be, we can't say that an analyst's or a patient's awareness of a particular element in a particular instance is necessarily a good thing or that a lack of such awareness is necessarily bad. These aspects of analysis—optimum awareness—for one patient and another and for one analyst and another are hard to observe. And we haven't talked enough to each other about the idiosyncrasies of our approaches in so far as we can observe them.

SRR: Would you tell us about how you came to be an analyst?

RG: I imagined you were going to ask that. I found something the other day, and I thought I'd show you this, and then you'd know how I came to be an analyst. [Shows us a photograph of himself as a one-year-old sitting on a porch rail with his mother holding him and leaning toward him.] I had a mother who was very attuned to me and to others and was highly psychologically-minded. I cannot speak to my infancy, but I do remember that throughout my childhood my mother often made insightful remarks—usually respectful—about people, and about the things going on between people. In turn, and I imagine partly as a consequence, I remember thinking about people, wondering why so-and-so did this or that, and remarking on these matters to my mother. I imagine these conversations satisfied some of my wishes for intimate exchange with my mother and frustrated others, stirred my curiosity, and provided my earliest memorable analytical supervision.

I don't suggest that when I was a child I wanted to be an analyst. I wanted to be a doctor. I had an uncle who was a pediatrician. Perhaps it is not insignificant that he was held in high regard for having gone to a far-off place called Vienna for his postgraduate training. In any event, he was my uncle and he was my pediatrician. And when I got sick, he would come to the house. I remember he would examine me carefully and when he was finished, he would give me a piece of gum. Sometimes he would give me a whole package of gum. It was always Dentyne gum. I took that to be important. The giving of that gum was a pronouncement that I couldn't be terribly sick; you wouldn't give a piece of gum to somebody—especially a child—who was terribly sick. The cure began with the giving of the Dentyne gum. I looked forward to the giving of the gum. I knew I would feel better as soon as I was given the gum. And I remember sometimes wondering if it was the medicine that made me feel better or the gum. I think that question hovered at the edge between science and humanism. It was also a piece of my confusion as to whether I wanted to be a doctor, like my uncle, or something else. I don't recall specifically what the something else might have been, but I think it was something in the humanities, and maybe, like my father, a teacher.

I'll jump ahead to later determinants of my becoming an analyst. I read a lot of Freud in college. But it never dawned on me that analysis was a profession. It seemed a literary endeavor, a very impressive literary endeavor. Freud wrote well, and his ideas were fascinating. But I didn't take seriously the possibility that psychoanalysis was a form of treatment. Even when Freud talked specifically about treatment, it didn't grab me as treatment. I did not, at that time, think about becoming an analyst. By the same token, though I had done a lot of writing in my journals, I never thought about becoming a writer. I have had patients who wanted to be writers but didn't want to write. I wanted to write, but I didn't want to be a writer. It never occurred to me to be a writer any more than to be an analyst. Both lines of work seemed more play than work. During my first undergraduate year, I finally decided I wanted to be a doctor, a body doctor. So, I took the requisite premedical courses. I didn't enjoy most of those courses. I enjoyed other subjects more, especially literature and history. But I finished my premedical studies, went to medical school, and tried my best to be a gung ho medical student, though I didn't really enjoy most of my medical studies either.

Somewhere along the way, I became very involved in what I regarded to be research. I decided to develop a spot test for the level of blood sugar. In those days, there was only a spot test—and that was qualitative—to see whether or not there was sugar in the urine. I didn't know much about that test except that it used a bismuth salt. I figured, however, that there must be some way you could remove and spin down a sample of blood, separate the plasma, dilute it out, and find a level at which the qualitative test for sugar in the urine could become a quantitative test for the level of sugar in the blood. I don't know where I got this idea—this conviction—that qualitative tests at some point must become quantitative. But I went ahead with it. And I did it by trial and error.

SRR: It makes me think of your making palettes, making Turner's palettes, totally confident that you will physically figure it out.

RG: I'm not sure how confident I felt. I think in both instances I felt that I wanted to, or had to, figure something out. And in both instances I was determined to, or had to, figure it out for myself. I suspect this reflected a mix of independence, shaky confidence, and an exaggerated need for self-sufficiency. I suspect it was also a piece of an only child pattern: initial solitary play followed by efforts to engage others in that play. For almost a year, I did this solitary "research" in my spare time. I would run around Presbyterian Hospital and when anybody was given the Folin-Wu test—you may remember this was a very sophisticated test for the level of blood sugar, very elaborate, very accurate—I would take a little of that blood, spin it, thin it, and try my spot test. Finally I found the range of dilution where it was accurate to 5 mg per 100 cc. This seemed to me an important discovery. I told my chief resident. My chief resident arranged an appointment for me to see one of the head honchos, a man who had gained a worldwide reputation for applying hard science to internal medicine and was, therefore, considered a guru in such matters.

When I was admitted at last to his presence—I believe it took several weeks before the meeting could take place—I told Dr. L. what I had done and awaited questions about the details of the test. Instead, he asked, "What's it good for?" I said: "Well, sometimes you need to know the blood sugar in a hurry, and you don't have the Folin-Wu." He said, "We have the Folin-Wu." I said, "Yes, I know, sir, but outside the hospital there are lots of places where doctors don't have it." He said: "We have the Folin-Wu." We went around this way for what seemed a very long time, though I don't suppose it could have taken more than a few minutes because Dr. L. was not a man inclined to waste time on trivia.

I was considerably taken aback by this blow to my claim to fame. I was even more taken aback—or at least I was more comfortable being more taken aback—with what I began to see as a widespread indifference in that institution to the welfare of patients. Partly in pique and partly in search of a field in which the struggle might be more prominent to blend the ideals and practices of humanism and science—what Benson was later to call the necessary blend of kindliness and science—I soon after began going across the street to conferences at the Psychiatric Institute. At the time, that seemed about as far as you could go from internal medicine. To understand how far that was, you need to know that the Dean of the Medical Center had several times made it clear that he considered psychiatrists, and especially psychoanalysts, charlatans.

Mixed reasons for my being at the P.I. notwithstanding, I found those conferences very exciting. I remember old Nolan D. C. Lewis looking at patients' paintings and telling a remarkable amount about their lives, personalities, and disorders just from the details of their paintings. I later learned that he had known a little more about the patients in advance than he had let on and therefore his conjectures were not quite so miraculous as they seemed. But that did not take away from the challenge and the possibility of finding macrocosms in microcosms.

I spent quite a lot of time around the P.I. In those days, the staff engaged in a lot of psychotherapy with fascinating patients. Today, many of those patients might be called borderline; then and there they were called pseudoneurotic schizophrenics. Whatever they were, most of them were very artsy-craftsy. Indeed, in those days a patient wasn't likely to be admitted to the P.I. unless very artsy-craftsy.

By my fourth year in medical school, I was allowed to volunteer to do something called psychotherapy. I didn't know exactly or even roughly what that enterprise might involve so I went back and read Freud, and tried to "psychoanalyze" patients—neurotic, psychotic, and borderline—using Freud's 1900–1905 methods. It was very exciting. If you want, I'll come back to that in a moment.

After a general rotating internship, I returned to P.I. as a resident in psychiatry. Nowadays, of course, residents sometimes have a little supervision. At least, they did till quite recently. In those days, we did not. That is, we were supervised in a particular way. Each of us was seen once a month by the director of the service. We would tell what we had done, and he would say, "Yes." He had an extraordinary range of tones and rhythms in which he said "Yes." And that range was the supervision. I remember in particular one of my patients. He was a weight lifter, quite paranoid, and with a number of elaborate delusions. I was hypnotizing him, inducing dreams, and "analyzing" his dreams. Perhaps you wonder at this procedure. I knew that Freud had analyzed dreams; my patient said he didn't have any dreams; so I hypnotized him and suggested that he dream. And then I would wake him up and we would analyze his dreams. Looking back, I'm surprised that I could have been so intrepid and so misguided, but I'm even more surprised at how well the man held up. We met five or six times per week. Mainly, we would get going about the symbolism of his dreams. And despite it all, he pulled himself together and was discharged from the hospital as cured. Years later, I visited the hospital. I was told by one of the staff that my former patient had since relapsed and had come looking for me. He refused to see anybody else. He said I was a very good doctor. They asked him why. He said it was because I was the only one who showed a consistent interest in his thighs. Indeed, I remember to this day that he had talked a great deal about—and I had shown considerable interest in—the mysterious "signals" he was receiving in his thighs. So that's how I began to be a psychiatrist and, in particular, a practitioner of talking treatment.

Despite that background of solid experience, I decided I needed a bit more supervision. Accordingly, I went next to the old Boston Psychopathic Hospital, later to become the Massachusetts Mental Health Center. There, you either engaged your patients in psychotherapy, or you hooked them up to the electric company. The choice was fairly simple. From then on, I was hooked on psychotherapy and psychoanalysis.

SRR: Could you tell us about some of the people who were important to you?

RG: In the Psychiatric Institute, where, as I said, we were left largely on our own, the residents had very important relationships with each other. We taught each other. We supported each other. We talked endlessly. We shared ideas. And we shared a passion for trying to understand our patients. Though there were many others, Paul Ecker and Lothar Gidro-Frank stand out in particular. But there came a time when it seemed reasonable to try to talk to people who might know a bit more. And I was given that opportunity when I arrived in Boston.

There, the most important person for me in the early years was Ives Hendrick. Ives was an unusual person: extremely bright, intuitive, and in uncanny touch with his own interior workings and those of others. What Ives taught us in particular was the virtue of moving back and forth between states of listening in a foggy drift and states of thinking rigorously about what one had observed of oneself and one's patient in those drifts. I can recall that he would often seem to go into a trance or to fall asleep while a case was being presented, and then wake up and offer an elegant and intelligent formulation of the whole case. And for all his unpredictable characteristics, Ives was in many ways extremely well organized, a very interesting balance between organization and fluidity.

This fascinated me and also touched on what I thought I needed to learn—to be scientific, which to me meant organized, and humanistic, which meant fluid, in the days when the sciences seemed sciences, and the arts seemed arts. Later, I joined Hendrick's teaching unit where he stirred and supported my interest in teaching. Whatever else he did, and it was not always easy to be with him, Hendricks drew us—students and teachers alike—into the world of the unconscious.

I also had some very good experiences with Elvin Semrad. I had the privilege of serving as his chief of service and of discussing many patients with him, my own and those of others. He had a wonderful way of seeing and appealing to the better possibilities in very disturbed patients. I remember once we were going through the ward, and we came upon a flagrantly psychotic patient who was holding an upside down paper as if he were reading it. In actuality, he was hiding. Or, so it seemed to me. And he had so far spoken to no one on the ward. Semrad asked in his characteristic mix of sympathy and challenge, "Who are you looking for?"—Elvin would never have said "Whom." He was intent on preserving his image of a country boy. The man looked up, stared at Semrad, and began to talk. He explained that he was looking for a member of his family whom he had recently lost. And he began to cry. Semrad got him to agree to talk to his doctor about his loss.

Indeed, Semrad seemed convinced that every patient needed to talk to his or her doctor about a recent loss, or as he often put it, "needed to grieve." Which need proved a safe and useful bet, or at least not a bad way to get started with many persons. I found it an even more promising starting point than hypnotizing patients and inducing them to dream.

When I finally began my studies at the Boston Psychoanalytic Institute, my most important experience was my analysis with John Murray. I found him an excellent listener; and that was a great help in fostering my abilities to listen to myself and to others. I also had some very important experiences with Felix Deutsch, Helen Tartakoff, and Beata Rank, who were my supervisors. Felix Deutsch liked to practice magic. My first analytic patient was a woman who often talked about the bathroom adjacent to her parents' bedroom, and often mentioned that the bathroom was pink. When Felix heard this, he said "Next time she talks about the pink bathroom, you say, 'Are you sure it wasn't brown?'" In those days, it wasn't unusual for supervisors to call in plays from the sidelines. I went in. I said what I had been instructed to say. Sure enough, within an hour the patient was talking of all sorts of cloacal fantasies and fantasies of rectal-vaginal intercourse.

Whatever the shortcomings of such dramatic intervention, and, among other things the abrupt bypassing of defense, it helped to sharpen one's hearing for the workings of the unconscious. Deutsch taught a great many ways to listen to everything in an analytic hour as if it were a piece of a dream; ways to hear; ways in which everything—so-called reality or not—is metaphor. He was superb at demonstrating that. And though he suggested a few interventions here and there, he made it clear that his suggestions were only temporary measures. Mainly, he held fast to the idea that if you understood your patient you didn't need to be told what to do. I don't remember his ever commenting directly on what I had said or failed to say. He assumed you would find your own way. He seemed confident you would find your way. After a few years, he said one day, "You do all right, doctor." That was all he ever said directly about my work.

Then, there was Helen Tartakoff. She was exactly the opposite of Felix Deutsch. She was practical, direct, very concerned with the best things to say and the best ways to say them. She stressed tact and timing. At least that's what she did with me. She once said, "You see an unusual amount; you'll have to be patient till you can find out how to use it." That, I believe, was her tactful and well-timed way of advising me to pay more attention to the requirements of tact and timing. She and Felix Deutsch were a nice combination. Deutsch tried to help me to listen more carefully. Tartakoff tried to help me to speak more carefully.

Felix Deutsch talked as if he figured everything out. Beata Rank, another supervisor, talked as if everything came to her from somewhere on high. If you asked her how she got wherever she got, she never knew. At least she purported never to know. It "came" to her. Deutsch figured everything out; Rank was all intuition. At least, that's how I perceived them. I often saw them back-to-back. I rushed across Cambridge to see the one right after the other. For me, they were like the two Hendricks. I realized in time that Deutsch was more comfortable stressing logic, and Rank more comfortable stressing intuition. And though neither showed me how to combine the two, or allowed me to see how they did it—how could they?—they heightened my attention to the challenge of putting them together. Looking back, they remind me of the Romantics and the Realists in the humanities.

Speaking of different vantage points, in those days many analysts were still caught between id-analysis on one hand and ego-analysis on the other. Tartakoff focused on the workings of the ego. Deutsch and Hendricks were all—almost all—id. Rank wandered about in a language of her own.

I think another important experience in my becoming an analyst was my work with adolescents in the Harvard Health Services. I became interested in what happens between early and late adolescence and between late adolescence and early adulthood. And that stirred my interest in development in general and played a large part in my decision to spend a year in child psychiatry at the Psycho. There I had a wonderful experience with Greg Rochlin. Rochlin was a gifted clinician, a superb thinker, and an inspiring teacher—they don't always go together. He helped me to recognize and support my patients' efforts to express themselves in displacement, whether with words or toys or something else. He helped me to avoid intruding on their theater, and instead to join it. Much of which, along with my continuing work with late adolescents, proved very useful in the analysis of adults.

Around 1960, having graduated from the Boston Psychoanalytic Institute, I opened a private office at 51 Brattle Street. I was determined to practice as much analysis as I could. And it was not a problem then as it is now to find patients. I soon had a full analytic practice.

SRR: It's amazing, isn't it?

RG: Yes, but of course this was still in the aftermath of World War II and in the era when analysts were playing a very large part in psychiatric education in particular, and medical education in general. There was a substantial belief in some circles that analysis would save, if not the world, a significant part. In any case, an analyzing life was easier to arrange in those days than it is for most analysts starting out now. And I liked analyzing; I liked it a lot. I still do. I sometimes wonder what would have happened if I had not had the good fortune to have my career as a Bismuth salt researcher nipped in the bud.

SRR: Is there anything you would like to say about the impact of your analysis or anything about the style of it?

RG: Not much. But I will tell you a bit more. My analyst's way of working struck me as reflecting a remarkable economy of means, economical in the sense of mainly staying out of the way and yet, at the same time, making a comment here and there that gave me the sense that he was always—almost always—with me. I have since talked to others who experienced John Murray as much more active. But that was not my experience. Mainly I found him a facilitator, a spare facilitator. I would start to talk about something;

I wouldn't know where it was going or whether it was going anywhere. He would echo an element of what I had said and add a question. Gently add a question. And often it would surprise me that when I would answer—that is, when I would say what came to mind in response to his response—I would often see both that I had already been talking about something worth talking about more and that I had not talked about something that needed to be talked about more.

I remember very few dramatic interventions or sequences. Mainly things moved in small steps. I believe my analysis helped to give me more access to my inner life, left me with the conviction that I should and could gain more access, and, in so far as it illustrated one way of analyzing, illustrated a way that was active but not intrusive, and that pulled things together here and there without "now hear this!" interventions. I think my fantasy—more fearful than wishful—had been that my analyst would be silent for very long periods and then would make sweeping oracular pronouncements, probably with a Viennese accent.

You asked about impact. I'll tell you about one. I had just left an analytic hour. I was walking down Marlborough Street. I looked at the brick buildings across the street. And at that moment, though I had seen those very same buildings many times before, I suddenly saw many more colors in the brick than I had ever seen before, and, in particular, I saw many more colors in the shadows. That was very startling. I had earlier thought that the impressionist painters had made up all that stuff about colors in the shadows. And there it was. I had not yet begun to paint at that time nor was I interested in doing so. Nor did I know what had happened in that analytic hour, or in earlier hours that might account for this breakthrough that allowed me to see better.

Still, I was struck by this example of how one can be radically influenced by one's state of mind. And I suspect this experience was part of what encouraged my much later studies in the nature of my visual images. To this day, though I am aware of several metaphorical reverberations of the notion of colors in the shadows, I don't know why my ability to see colors in the shadows broke through on that particular day. At any rate, I credit my analysis and my analyst with helping to add a lot of color to my life. And I credit my analyst with working in many ways that I found congenial. I suppose we were well-matched. I can think of some other analysts with whom I would not have been.

SRR: Did you choose him? I've heard about people sometimes being assigned. Did you choose your analyst?

RG: Oh, yes, I chose my analyst. I cannot imagine not choosing one's analyst. I chose my analyst in a very particular way. I had been accepted at the Boston Psychoanalytic Institute, but I had not yet begun analysis when the Korean War broke out. Those were the days when physicians either were drafted or they "volunteered" in order to have some say over what they would do. I "volunteered" for duty in the Air Force and was sent to San Antonio to work in psychiatry at the Lackland Air Force Hospital. Somewhere along the military way, I met a psychiatrist who said, "Oh, you're from Boston," and asked if I knew Jock Murray. I said I did not. He said he did. I asked what he thought of him. He said, "Oh, he's great."

I remember to this day that he stressed a remarkable quality that Jock Murray had shown as a consultant to the Air Force. He said that other consultants would come around and pontificate, but Jock would come down and work; "he'd talk to patients, talk to us, see us all day long, get a sense of what we were doing, and discuss things with us." When I got back to Boston, I went to see Dr. Murray. I liked what I saw. And I found no reason to disagree with what my colleague had said. Dr. Murray was a worker. He got down to work with me and discussed what he saw. So that's my analysis and that's my analyst.

LR: During different periods of your life, how have your creative outlets, such as painting and writing, been connected to your analytic work?

RG: For the first ten years of my analytic work, I did no writing or painting. That is, I did no painting; and I wrote in my journal, but nothing for publication. And even when I had begun writing for publication, I wrote little. As I have said, I write slowly. I have written a few essays here and there. And I now have almost finished the first draft of my second book. I don't know how long it will be before it sees the light of day, but I've got the hardest part done. And that has taken me only three or four years. The first book took me at least ten. They say short books take longer to write. My second book will be a bit longer, so perhaps it won't take quite so long. Someday I might be able to write a book in a year or two. Wouldn't that be something?

SRR: Could you tell us about it, because it's quite different from your first book?

RG: It is and it isn't. The second is really derived from the first book. In a way, it's an extension of the first—a piece of applied analysis. It's about my experiences as a teacher: what I've felt, thought about, struggled with. I've talked with many teachers. I come from a background of teachers. But the book is mainly an effort to speak about the teaching experience from the vantage point of the one teacher I know best. So that's not so different from the first book. And in the second book I am trying to tell what I do to get into what I regard a proper teaching state; so that's not so different from my effort in the first book to tell what I do to get into what I regard a proper analyzing state. At any rate, in this second book, I plan to call it *On Trying to Teach,* I am trying mainly to raise questions about teaching and about the dilemmas of teaching, and trying to propose a few personal answers.

LR: Are there any parallels between the inner play of your creative process while painting and while listening to patients? Are there any similarities in your capacities to visualize in those two activities?

RG: ...At first, unlikely as it seems, I experienced my analyzing and painting experiences as completely unrelated. And even when I had recognized that I was seeing many visual images in the analytic situation, I saw no connection between this sort of image-making and what I took to be the direct visualizing in which I found myself involved in the painting situation. The two experiences seemed to involve entirely different and unconnected worlds. To the degree I compared and contrasted these worlds, I thought, When I'm painting, I'm painting. When I'm analyzing, I'm analyzing.

Now, however, I do find certain parallels in the two situations. I might even say I find myself sometimes in similar states when painting and analyzing. And the more I have extended my self-inquiries to include the painting situation—that is, the more I have tried to explore my associations to what seem direct perceptions in the painting situation—the more clear it has become that what I experience as a direct visualization while painting and what I experience as a piece of image-making while analyzing are closer together, and bear more of the imprints of my inner worlds, than I would earlier have anticipated.

LR: I'm interested in whether your being inspired to paint relates at all to the creative associative process of listening analytically?

RG: I don't know. It seems plausible that my earlier experience of being analyzed and my later experience of listening analytically have helped to free me to paint and to paint more freely, and perhaps even to blend some of the elements of freedom and discipline necessary to painting. Whether there has also been a more or less direct connection between the processes of listening analytically and the processes of painting, I can't say. Mainly what I've been aware of is that painting has helped me to become more attentive to my visual images in the analytic situation, and exploring my visual images in the one situation has helped me to explore the visual images in the other.

SRR: It sounds as if it has helped you to tap into that inner place where you can find a visual image?

RG: Yes. I think I may have gotten a little better at drifting rapidly in and out of states that aid and abet the production and awareness of my images both in the analytic and in the painting situation. It sometimes helps if I'm a little sleepy. Not too sleepy, just a little. Usually I do nothing special to get into the right state. Looking at the scene to be painted or listening to my patient does it. Occasionally, I look about and I see something that has a hypnotic—a slightly hypnotic—effect. Sometimes a light will do that. Sometimes I look rapidly upward and see something at the edge of my visual field that helps to trigger a burst of visual images. At the very least, the upward look seems to soften the distracting influence of whatever is directly before me. I have wondered whether some persons of a more religious nature may be doing something similar, whatever else they are doing, when they cast their eyes upward toward something they regard divine.

In the analytic situation, many things can interfere with my seeing images or with my recalling them for after-the-hour exploration. Some patients consistently make it difficult for me to get into the right state. They keep waking me up. And note-taking makes me too wakeful. For me, note-taking and "dreaming awake" just don't go together. Some analysts seem able to achieve something close to automatic writing. Their note-taking seems to facilitate the drifts necessary both to their evenly hovering attention and to the particular sensory experiences they favor. For my part, the most I can do to stay in the right frame is to doodle. What notes

I make, I make after hours. The notes I make during hours are my visual images.

In the early years of my analytic work, however, I rarely, if ever, saw visual images. I cannot really account for the later heightening of my visual experience, or for the relationship between my painting and my analyzing, any more than I can account for that moment many years ago when colors appeared in the shadows.

SRR: Have there been other people or experiences since you've been settled as an analyst, during more recent years, other people who have influenced you?

RG: Yes. Many. I couldn't begin to mention them all. Collegial exchanges have been very important. I have received much help from these. I'll try to mention a few. For something on the order of thirty years, I have belonged to a CAPS group. We have met for two weekends each year in Princeton. We are from different parts of the country; we have the inevitable similarities and differences of outlook. It has been very useful to discover and discuss the similarities and differences in our approach to patients, to theory, to teaching, and to much else. The atmosphere of friendship and trust in that group has been especially important. It has also provided an opportunity to meet other colleagues who joined us from time to time to discuss their particular interests. I especially remember several extraordinary weekends with Robert Waelder, Erik Erikson, Rudy Loewenstein, Heinz Kohut, and Hans Loewald. Another group that stands out in my memory is a study group of the American in which for many years we considered our various approaches to supervision.

I have also had the benefit over the years of many valuable one-on-one consultations, exchanges, and correspondences. One that stands out in particular has been with John Gedo. On the local scene, I have belonged to several PINE study groups that have meant a great deal to me, and I have been especially lucky to have had many chances to discuss analysis with many persons outside the analytic field; Cambridge is a very good place to discuss almost anything anyone might want to discuss in any way with anyone. I've felt these latter exchanges—exchanges with persons outside the analytic field—have been important in helping me to see some things about analysis that I might otherwise not have seen and to see some things about the relationship of analysis to several other fields.

LR: What strikes me about what you're saying is how your thoughts about analysis have changed in your lifetime. You said that when you first read Freud, you couldn't imagine analysis ever being work. Now having done analysis as work, you talk of seeking other sources for refueling yourself.

RG: I suppose it's all part of a long interest, preoccupation, and compulsion to find connections between seemingly disparate worlds.

SRR: This is another quote: "I believe that the nature of the analytic situation, and the state that it requires, has the effect of pulling us over and over, a little bit or a lot, away from the stance we regard ideal. When things go well, we manage to observe some of these departures, and our in-hour and after-hour inquiries into those events lead to a fuller understanding of self and other, and sometimes to useful changes in method and theory."

One of the rationales for training analysis is to become able to observe those parts of oneself. I am interested in any of your thoughts about that, in particular about how the experience of training analysis, in your observations, helps to promote or inhibit or shape one's capacities for later self-inquiry?

RG: I don't know what I can say briefly. It seems clear that our personal analyses are helpful in many ways to our later efforts at self-inquiry. I believe many of us have seen many examples of such benefits for our colleagues, patients, and ourselves. It seems clear that when things go reasonably well an analysis helps to make the limited possibilities of self-inquiry a trifle less limited. That gain in capacity for self-inquiry may not seem much, but often it's a "not much" that counts considerably. Still, there's another side to the story, and it may be a side worth considering. As far as I can tell from my own experience and from what colleagues have told me of theirs, the road from analysis to self-inquiry is rarely direct. Post-analytic self-inquiry—at least some aspects—may require some perspectives and methods different from those we have found useful in our analyses.

In part, this depends on differences between what we experience—or the predominances of what we experience—when alone and in the presence of another. It appears also to be a matter of each person having better access to his or her inner worlds through his or her own idiosyncratic routes, routes that may differ in analysis and in self-inquiry. I think I somewhere tried to sum that up by saying that we have different holes in our heads. At any rate, our own best, or good-enough, approaches to self-inquiry take time to discover, and sometimes that discovery may be slowed by the too ready assumption that what worked best in our analyses will work best in self-inquiry. In my case, for example, even after I had become aware of the frequency of my visual images, it took time before I could take those images as seriously as the images in my dreams and could find ways to recall and explore them.

I do not minimize the limitations of self-inquiry. I do think, however, that self-inquiry involves both limitations and opportunities—some opportunities different from those of the two-party analytic endeavors. I find the search for more effective means of self-inquiry necessary to my analytic work and especially for effecting changes in my analytic work; and I don't think I would find analysis as interesting if I did not have a sense of changing, of trying to change, my approach both to self-inquiry and to analysis, and to moving between the one and the other. The wonderful thing about practicing an impossible profession like analysis is that it offers so many and such unending opportunities to discover one's mistakes. A few of one's mistakes.

SRR: Like painting watercolors?

RG: Exactly. You may know that some painters refer to watercolor painting as the art of taking advantage of one's mistakes.

LR: When you spoke of the importance of trying to consider different perspectives, I was reminded that earlier you mentioned meeting in Paris with French analysts. I understand you spent some time there. What was your experience like?

RG: Wonderful. Despite our differences of method and theory, I felt very much at home with my French colleagues. I was surprised by that. The particular analysts with whom I met were Lacanians, anti-Lacanians, anti-anti-Lacanians, and others. And they seemed at first a bit like the French parliament—every man, every woman a movement unto him- or herself. But when we got down to discussing actual analytic work, even though we often came to different conclusions, and even though we used different vocabularies, we seemed to have much in common. This was particularly true when we centered on what we inferred to be the patients' unconscious fantasies. Beyond that, I was struck that my French colleagues, whatever their differences from each other and from others, appeared to have in common that they approached analytic matters very much in the spirit of the pre-1920 days. They were very big on metaphor, id analysis, and linguistic nuances. And that was refreshing.

I think you might agree that whatever the virtues of the advances of ego psychology in this country and elsewhere, these developments have sometimes been misused in ways that make analysis sound more like social science than analysis, particularly when what passes for ego psychology becomes mainly an effort to make analysis a pop psychology. At any rate, I found it a pleasure to hear my French colleagues tell how they tried to plumb the depths. I don't mean that such efforts struck me as consistently better than those we associate with ego psychology. Indeed, I generally prefer to proceed in the much smaller steps that an ego psychological approach tends to encourage. But my experience with my French colleagues highlighted for me that with every gain in psychoanalysis, as in other fields, there are inevitable losses. In so far as their approaches resembled pre-1920 approaches, their profound attention to the workings of the unconscious pointed up some of the losses that have sometimes accompanied other analysts' efforts to make analysis a general psychology. All of which served to rekindle my interest in old and current problems—my own and those of others—that still confront us in trying to integrate id psychology with ego psychology. In that sense, our efforts in these meetings to bridge the gaps between a few analysts of different nations turned out to be, for me, efforts to bridge familiar gaps in my own experience and thinking. In addition, I was struck by ways in which the culture in which analysis takes place tend, sometimes usefully and sometimes not, to shape its methods and its theories. But that's another story.

Perhaps most of all, I was impressed that my French colleagues displayed both a passion for analysis and a tolerance for differences that is not always a prominent combination among American analysts. This may have been that we were all on our best behavior. Or, it may have been that linguistic limitations softened the possibilities for clear and harsh confrontation. In any case, these experiences heightened my interest in what we might do in PINE to encourage—or, at least not to intrude upon—both such a passion and a tolerance.

LR: Over time, do you think PINE has stayed true to your original vision for it?

RG: More than I would have thought possible. It's hard to assess any organization, especially one in which you have long been deeply involved. Every institute has inevitable frictions and tensions. Every institute has the bureaucratic complexities that reflect, aid, and abet those frictions and tensions. And within a very few years of its origins, an institute reveals many of the familiar problems that accompany our proclivities for elaborating bylaws and for running things by committees, subcommittees, and sub-subcommittees. Every institute is in part the prisoner of the administrative structures it has fashioned.

When we were forming PINE, we often joked that every five years there should be provisions to dismantle the existing bylaws and structures and to begin anew. We have not entirely lived up to the serious implications of that joke. Nevertheless, I believe we have tried relatively successfully to curtail the impulse to expand administrative structures, and we have managed to stay relatively flexible. Perhaps more important, we have developed an organization in which the mania to administer, and the mania to bicker about who shall administer what and how, does not play an inordinately large part. And so far we have been able to delegate authority to small groups without suffering paroxysms of the distresses of exclusion.

Another and not unrelated aspect of our vision was to develop and maintain a small institute. This was not based on any assumption that small is necessarily better, but rather on the assumption that there's an optimal size for everything. We believed and still believe that a good climate for learning and teaching analysis requires an intimacy more likely to be possible in a small organization in which candidates are deeply interested in analysis and in which the bulk of the teaching is done by analysts whose central interests are in the practice of analysis, in the study and development of analytic theory, and in the teaching of analytic practice and theory. I believe we have been true to those intentions.

My own experiences as a teacher in PINE have been very pleasing. I have had exciting times with candidates and exciting times with fellow teachers. I think PINE is a good place to begin to learn about analysis—good for the candidates and good for those of us who claim to be teachers. I think there's a persistent spirit of inquiry in PINE. And I think it remains a place where inquiry is encouraged. Which is what at the outset we hoped it would be.

On its worst days, and on my own worst days, I'm delighted to be in PINE. I think its atmosphere has been, with rare exceptions, one of proper respect for candidates, patients, and teachers. As to our curriculum, if I had my druthers, I'd change it. I would have fewer courses. I would make those fewer courses longer. From my point of view, there's too much uniformity—a curious uniformity—in what many of our institutes in this country teach, and the ways and sequences in which they teach it. I would encourage the development of a few courses that were highly organized—especially those that deal with the history of psychoanalysis—and many that were more freewheeling. The former would "cover" a few required subjects; the latter would be courses in search of a subject. I would especially want to see a program with much more tutorial teaching. In fact, if I had my druthers, I would make the core of our program tutorial. This might allow us to shape our teaching with fuller regard for the specific needs and strengths of our candidates and our teachers and their individual ways of learning and teaching.

Still, it's possible to place too much stress both on the content and on the form of the planned program, whether mainly tutorial or mainly seminar. I imagine that most students and teachers would agree that what counts most is the quality of the candidates and the teachers. And I think the quality of our candidates and teachers at PINE is, and promises to be, excellent. Partly that is the consequence of keeping the organization small and partly of recognizing that the particular qualities and eccentricities needed by an analyst are not in wide supply. In this respect of the problems of selection, PINE has exceeded my expectations.

SRR: That's wonderful. Speaking of a spirit of inquiry, I'd like to return now to an aspect of the subject of self-inquiry. I'm interested in your own affective experience in self-inquiry versus analysis. What fascinated me was the emergence of childhood memories. I wonder whether affectively that was similar or what that was like?

RG: Whether the recovery of memories in analysis and in self-inquiry has seemed similar?

SRR: Yes, the recall of forgotten memories or the experiencing of new memories.

RG: In self-inquiry I have found it sometimes possible, as in analysis, to recall forgotten happenings—affect-laden happenings—possible to see familiar memories in new lights, and possible to arrive at new combinations of old and new memories and of the underlying tensions they both reveal and conceal. And, though the pacing and intensity of these aspects of analysis and self-inquiry differ considerably, I have found that in self-inquiry as in analysis the recovery of such memories and the clarification of the tensions they embody sometimes encourages significant changes in attitude and activity. In that respect, although analysis and self-inquiry are different in many respects—importantly different—I don't find them completely different. By the same token, self-inquiry, like analysis, may proceed for long stretches without explicit recovery of memories, and in both cases, the recovery of memories, however fascinating, does not have a one-to-one relationship to utility. Also, if what you are asking is whether the subjective experience of recovering memories in self-inquiry resembles that in analysis, I would say I have often found it to do so.

Some analysts consider self-inquiry a contradiction in terms. I have talked to some who say of the memories that come of self-inquiry, "They're screen memories." I agree they're screen memories. How could they not be? All memory is screen memory. Some say: "How can you see past your own defenses? It's impossible." I agree that we cannot see past our own defenses. But neither are our defenses as solid as we sometimes imagine them to be. There are moments when even the most solid defenses tremble, moments when, for good or ill, our defenses don't work as effectively as usual. It's possible in these moments to expand awareness—whether of memories or something else—both in analysis and in self-inquiry. I see no reason why a recognition of the larger possibilities of psychoanalysis—those made possible through transference analysis and through other aspects of the two-party situation—makes it necessary to minimize the possibilities of self-inquiry, modest as those possibilities may be. Indeed, with all its limitations, and they are surely many, self-inquiry might afford access to some experiences—some aspects of solitude and creativity, for example—into which the two-party endeavor of psychoanalysis offers less. It seems to me odd to expect a training analysis to enable analysts later to practice useful self-inquiry into their countertransference reactions and yet to expect so little to come of their other efforts at self-inquiry, and so little to come of other persons' efforts at self-inquiry, before, during, and after analysis.

LR: I was interested in your description of the state of mind you get into where you're most fluid in your analytic reflecting, somewhere between dreaming and being awake. You wrote in your essay, "On Talking To Ourselves": "And they reflect, I think, the evocative and organizing effects of the special configurations one recovers, wants to recover, and can't help but recover in particular states of self-analysis: configurations formed and reformed in dreamlike states, and in the recall or reexperiencing, evocative of fresh dreamlike states. I mean, of course, slightly dreamlike states."

You also described in that paper the relationship between boundary, confusion, and creativity which reminded me of your interest in the observer and self-object dynamics: "I believe—which means I have a hunch—that in self-analysis, as in other arts, when we descend into those states in which our preferred metaphors, images, and perceptions shift most fluidly from the one to the other, we are most where for us 'the action is.' Which is also to say, I suspect that, for most of us, creativity is liveliest where the boundary narrows most between creativity and confusion. We cannot choose the terms of our creativity."

I would like now to juxtapose what you said with a passage from Ferenczi's "The Principle of Relaxation and Neocatharsis," to see how you might relate your ideas to what he described in his analytic work:

> "But after we had succeeded in a somewhat deeper manner than before in creating an atmosphere of confidence between physician and patient and in securing a fuller freedom of affect, hysterical physical symptoms would suddenly make their appearance often for the first time in an analysis extending over years. These symptoms included paresthesias and spasms, definitely localized, violent emotional movements like miniature hysterical attacks, sudden alterations of the state of consciousness, slight vertigo, and a clouding of consciousness often with subsequent amnesia for what had taken place. Some patients actually begged me to tell them how they had behaved when in these states. It was easy to utilize these symptoms as fresh aids to reconstruction, as physical memory symbols, so to speak, but there was this difference. This time the reconstructed past had much more of a feeling of reality and concreteness about it than heretofore, approximated much more closely to an actual recollection, whereas till then the patients had spoken only of possibilities or at most of varying degrees of probability and had yearned in vain for memories. In certain cases, these hysterical attacks actually assumed the character of trances in which fragments

of the past were relived and the physician was the only bridge left between the patients and reality. I was able to question them and received important information about dissociated parts of the personality. Without any such intention on my part and without my making the least attempt to induce a condition of this sort, unusual states of consciousness manifested themselves which might also be termed autohypnotic."

RG: I find it difficult to be sure where the similarities and differences may be between Ferenczi's experience and mine. I don't read Ferenczi with that in mind. I read him for his evocative quality. I don't think there's any question that we often observe the development of hysterical and other symptoms, and often observe changes of consciousness, in the analytic situation. Some of the fundamental observations regarding similarities in the mechanisms of dream and symptom formation have arisen in this context. I believe the moments to which Ferenczi here refers can be among the moments of which I was speaking, and which you quote, moments of high possibility in the narrow corridor between trouble and creativity. But there is always the question of optimum form and intensity. I have the impression that Ferenczi may be describing phenomena that are what I would regard, given the ways I prefer to work, too close to trouble. But I don't know how much this difference may reflect a problem of translation. I don't know how much Ferenczi's permitting himself a bit of poetic license in his use of words like "violent," "attacks," and "trances."

In any case, I believe that when the phenomena of which Ferenczi is speaking are relatively spontaneous and relatively temperate, their significance may be very different from those encountered when we have somehow encouraged, colluded with, or otherwise fostered a runaway regression, and, in particular, a runaway transference and countertransference regression. I do not say this to indulge in the familiar Ferenczi-bashing long popular in some circles. Nor do I intend to indulge in the equally familiar Ferenczi-celebrating. I want simply to say that Ferenczi expresses himself in ways that make it difficult for me to gauge matters of degree. But then I don't think it was his purpose to make that possible.

From my own work and from reports of the work of other analysts, I have the impression that the intensity, form, and frequency of these sorts of happenings depend partly on what an analyst considers an optimum level of regression in his or her patient, and in him- or herself, and in turn, how that judgment, other conscious and unconscious aspects of the analyst's character, ways of analyzing, and so on, influence the level and kind of regression a patient is likely to attain. I'm not sure what Ferenczi means when he disavows "any intention to induce a condition of this sort." I believe we always have lively intentions, recognized or not, both to increase and to decrease the level of regression. And I believe we have many ways of expressing those intentions and of influencing the level of regression, whether we recognize them or not. My belief in the ubiquity of those intentions and ways is one reason I find it necessary to pursue persistent self-inquiry.

To put the matter another way, I begin from the assumption that an important aspect of the free association method depends upon subtle and continuous adjustments on our part that help a patient to attain, and that interfere with a patient attaining, the kinds and degrees of regression that advance the analytic process. This is another of those areas that I think could benefit from added study by analysts—a study of the varieties of ways in which analysts influence the "spontaneous" unfolding of regressive phenomena, some of those ways bordering on "regressophilia" and some on "regressophobia."

SRR: You have described a tension between the patient and analyst which is often present when you have a visual image. Have you noticed any differences between men and women in working with these tensions?

RG: No. The differences between one person and another in, as you say "working with these tensions," seem to me linked to elements of character that do not seem specific to men or women.

SRR: There has been so much written about how few women become artists. Do you see any difference between men and women's capacity for visual images?

RG: No. I am one of those persons who thinks it's not so much a matter of so few women becoming artists as of so many women becoming artists without their efforts being recognized, appreciated, and encouraged. So often women have served in this regard, as in others, as the culture bearers. For example, women who have been unrecognized artists have often had sons who have become recognized artists. Winslow Homer and his mother are one example; I don't know enough to know what elements of identification may have been involved.

It's difficult to predict what specific propensities—neurophysiological and other—will some day be properly identified as specific to men and women, but it seems to me there is good reason to suspect that whatever the differences between men and women may be, women, if given sufficient opportunity in the world of art and elsewhere, will sooner or later match or surpass many of the best and the worst endeavors of men. In respect to visual images, I can only say that my rough and ready observations in the analytic situation have afforded no evidence that women have a lesser or a larger capacity than men to form and to make use of visual images—whether dreams or visual images in waking states—or lesser or larger capacity to slide back and forth between images and words.

LR: In several of your writings, I was struck by your capacity to frame dynamic issues in one way, but then to play with that frame and its elements to create new questions or perspectives. This is an example from your book on self-inquiry: "Beyond the urge to inquire and the urge to subvert inquiry, and the urge to advance and to obstruct mutuality, may be the urge to inquire into the tension between the one urge and the other." Do you think your capacity to shift frames has always been there or do you think your analytic work has helped shape it?

RG: I think I may have mentioned in that same book that British watercolorists often were taught to look at the scene upside down because looking that way provides an opportunity to see things that are difficult to see when one looks at things rightside up. To put it another way, the upside down look helps to disrupt habits that come of looking at things the familiar way. I am intrigued by the image of British watercolorists wandering about looking at things upside down. I think I find it intriguing because I have always wandered about looking at things upside down and am pleased to learn of these kindred spirits. And I suspect the reasons for my tilt toward the upside down go even deeper than the obvious contrarian. I suspect that opportunities to analyze, to paint, and to write have not originated in, but rather reinforced a long-standing preexisting physio-psycho-social tilt.

LR: Were you aware of your capacity to play with frames at an earlier age, before your analytic work?

RG: Yes. I think I can remember something of the sort at a very young age. I say I think I can remember, because I'm well aware of the tendency—especially when one has reached a "certain age"—to rewrite history. Still, I remember that I had a kaleidoscope. You looked through it. Then you turned it. Each time you turned it, a completely new design would fall into place. And that seemed very congenial to me. I think I already had a kaleidoscope. I suppose most children do. But I don't know why I have persisted in those childish ways. As long as I can remember, I've taken a keen pleasure in playing "What would it look like if you tilted it or turned it upside down?" "What would it look like if instead of putting it this way, you put it that way?" That's a very automatic part of my thinking.

There's something about persistently turning things around that offers assurance that the process will never end. I think this habit of turning things round may deal, among other things, with some wish for continuance. It's ironic that a reassuring constancy may lie in the unending change. In any case, I think this "shifting the frames" has become connected to what I like to think is a useful wondering. I can also remember as a child coming to the end of a book and thinking, "I wish this book were longer." And I can remember constructing sequelae with different endings and different consequences, another form of wondering how things would look if turned around.

LR: The image that occurs to me is one of mirrors. You turn them a certain way, and there will be hundreds of images.

SRR: I think of a looking glass.

RG: Yes. By the way, another device painters sometimes use is to look at the scene in a mirror, especially a black mirror that serves to remove some perceptual elements and to highlight others. But all these devices and all these ways of looking at things—these changes of "frame"—can serve creativity on the one hand or confusion on the other. So we're brought back again, or so it seems to me, to shimmerings between one state and another.

LR: That reminds me of a very powerful statement you made in your book on self-inquiry about how the limitations of language in describing the continuities of visual imagery may actually restrict what we see: "Unfortunately, however, our language for considering these matters is a pidgin English of isolated words and phrases that make a useful sense for some purposes, but are as unsuited for describing continuities as it would be to call the shimmering and shifting light at twilight 'gray.' More unfortunately, the constrictions of our language impose constrictions on our vision." Could you say more about that?

RG: Before answering our question, let me back up and say a bit about the notion of words and images out of which that comment arose. I don't have any quarrel with the notion that some aspects of our visual image-making precede some aspects of our other thinking. Nor do I doubt that some aspects of our early image-making tend to be more directly influenced by instinctual forces and in various respects to be more primitive than the more lexical thinking that develops later on. But that's not the same as equating the visual images of a very young infant—and their relatively primitive qualities—with the visual images of an older child or an adult. Such an equation would, as Parsons said, "confuse roots with fruits."

I think most of us would agree that over time our visual image-making is influenced by our lexical thinking and vice versa, and that over time we expand our capacities to shift back and forth from the lexical to the visual, from poesis to picture. Over time, therefore, the distinction becomes less sharp between visual and lexical thinking. What I think I meant especially to say in the passage you quoted is that sometimes in our psychologies we risk overestimating the word and underestimating the image and the subtleties of play between the word and the image. I think I meant also to suggest that, to the degree that some thinking is predominantly lexical and some predominantly visual, each may prove better for catching some things that the other cannot, and in the translation of one into the other something important can be lost in translation. Speaking of the value of one kind of thinking and another, reminds me that not only are some kinds of thinking better for addressing some problems, but for some of us, one kind of thinking is more useful for addressing a particular problem and for others, another kind is more valuable for addressing the very same problem. I remember some studies at MIT some years ago; it was found that if you asked what time it would be a certain number of minutes past a particular time, some persons would proceed by imagining a clock set to that particular time and would then move the hands around in their heads while others would arrive at their answers through numerical manipulations. And for some persons, one or the other approach was decidedly more efficient.

In my case, I know that I often cannot find connections between seemingly disconnected associations—that is, cannot synthesize—as clearly or rapidly with words as I can with a visual image.

Or at least I cannot synthesize as effectively with words till I have first done it with a visual image.

LR: One thing that struck me as you were describing your own mental process of images and how they are so condensed is the remarkable efficiency of the mind, to package things in that way. It's as if the mind almost relieves itself of the tension of multiple images. Boom! It condenses down, and it gives you something that can then be a shorthand, like words.

RG: That's how I experience it subjectively; suddenly a vast panorama is compressed into a snapshot. I experience that in two steps; not only, as you suggest, in the transition of images to words, but before that, in the transition of multiple images to one particular image. In both cases, the result seems a fix in time and space the way a still photo is, a capturing of something—there's that idea of continuance or permanence again—something to hold onto.

But at some point we must figure out what that snapshot means. It does not speak for itself. Often an interpretation comes to me in the form of a cartoon, not infrequently a *New Yorker*-like cartoon—yesterday's *New Yorker* cartoons, not today's—and then I have to translate it into words in order to consider its relevance to the immediate analytic situation, in order to communicate it to my patient, and in order to remove some of the cartoonlike qualities of condensation that might make it seem facetious.

SRR: That brings us to questions about technique. In supervision, you explained your thoughts about what we might call the problem of "what to do while you're waiting"—in other words, how to stay with a patient until he or she is ready to face something. I thought that might be a topic for elaboration.

I have several quotes, too, which seem to follow this theme. First: "We cannot go where we would have gone in the first place until we discover in the second place why we could not or would not go there in the first place." And that leads me to your essay "Indirection," in which you discuss the patient who gave you the weather reports. There you asked: "How shall we regard such long ways around from inner to outer to inner? Is there a better way?" Just how do you help the person on his or her journey?

RG: Well, for me many of them are ways of trying to help myself to get into the right state. Take one example. Over the years, I have become convinced that it's not wise to decide too quickly what's central and what's distraction, what's direct engagement and what's evasion or avoidance. I have come to the view that even when we are trying conspicuously to evade something we are often—perhaps always—trying to get at that very same something. I have come also to the view that if I listen carefully enough I'll probably be able—sooner or later—to see a bit of the inner struggle between the urges to evade and the urges to get at something. So one thing I don't do as much of as I once did is to arrive quickly at the view that a patient is trying exclusively or predominantly to avoid something. That does not mean that I find defense analysis less important, but rather that I find it more important to approach defense analysis with an appreciation of the patient's immediate ways of—and reasons for—trying both to advance and to retard exploration.

I find I don't work well if I begin to develop a vision of my patient as exclusively or even mainly obstructive. Besides, I think that such a narrow vision of a patient—a vision of the patient as trying only to obstruct—is not truthful; it fails to do justice to the complexities of conflict, conflict both in the general sense of the word and conflict in the narrow psychoanalytic sense. Therefore, when I find myself beginning to view my patient as only, or mainly, obstructive, I try to look inward. That's one thing I try to do "in the meantime." I try to get into a better analyzing position. I try to catch a glimpse of how and why I might be inclined to minimize my patient's exploratory inclinations. As I said before, I find it necessary to pursue most of my inward looks outside the analytic hour. But I find that an occasional inward look—usually fairly brief—during the hour often helps me to give my patient a little more room when I otherwise might be inclined to be impatient in my efforts at defense, or other, analysis.

LR: As you're talking about you and your patient, I'm thinking about the parallel process among analysts as colleagues. In your essay, "On Talking to Ourselves," you raised the question, "I wonder, especially, if a fuller sharing of our observations of our preferences of perception and of representation, and of our accompanying fantasies, might tell us more about those functions, about the intricacies of separation and restitution, and about the elusive workings of the creativity of everyday life. I refer to the earliest creativities of our childhood and to those later creativities that repeat, elaborate, and transcend the earlier." However, you point out the difficulties of analysts sharing their more private experiences: "If we could bear telling more and hearing more, it seems plausible to expect an advance in our common knowledge."

What do you think contributes to that reluctance among colleagues? In your experience, what helps facilitate fuller sharing between analysts of these aspects of their analytic work?

RG: Our reluctances to share the more intimate aspects of our work seem to me quite understandable. We want to protect our patients, and we want to protect ourselves. When we describe our analytic work, even in a relatively fragmentary way, we describe much about our patients and much about ourselves. We are unlikely to risk those descriptions and revelations unless the circumstances are particularly propitious. And they rarely are likely to be so. There are many problems of presentation. For example, besides the analyst's problems of balancing considerations of candor against those of protection of patient and self are the problems of balancing the requirements for candor against the considerations of protecting the audience or reader against the distractions of inappropriate revelation. Candor is one thing. Inappropriate stress on one's own reactions is another.

When an analyst is analyzing, he or she struggles to find a balance between the observations of his or her own experiences and the observation of the experiences of the patient. Similarly, the presentation of the analyst's feelings, thoughts, fantasies, actions, and so on, to colleagues must be part of what I have referred to as a well-tempered hypochondriasis. The same balance and temperance must be struggled for in presentation. And it's not easy to attain. Rather, it's easy to tip the balance too much in either direction, and in so doing, to obscure the important play between what is going on in the patient and what is going on in the analyst. To facilitate a better sharing of our analyzing experiences, we must not only attain a good-enough balance of these elements in the analytic work under consideration, but in the ways in which we present that work. In trying to present, I have found it helpful to try to subject to scrutiny both my analytic reactions and my reactions to presentation under the particular conditions at hand.

There seem to me to be three general aspects to our efforts to facilitate better communication. One is the effort to examine our reactions to analyzing and presenting. A second is the effort to examine our ways of reacting to our colleagues when they present their findings. A third is the effort to examine our ways of organizing seminars, panels, and other occasions intended to facilitate good presenting and good listening. In respect to that organizing, I can only say that it seems to me that often—and perhaps increasingly—we have copied the forms conventional for presentation in other fields but not as satisfactory in our own. For example, large panels of too many persons, who speak too briefly, tend to offer too little time for the participants to address the complexities with which an analyst actually deals, and tend to encourage the production of sound bites, and, therefore, of overstatements and understatements that encourage poorly framed arguments. We are in that drift toward soundbitism, perhaps the product of the television age and other aspects of our times.

In any case, though I think it might be worthwhile to study as carefully as we can how we might better the conditions for sharing our experiences, I think we must be careful not to expect too much of ourselves. Communications within any group of professionals, especially professionals who work in areas where it's so difficult to be sure of one's ground, are not likely ever to be free of that wide variety of tensions that threaten constructive agreement and disagreement.

SRR: Can I ask one more question? It's about your way of looking at adolescence, the adolescent process in analysis.

LR: Oh, that's right. We were talking earlier about how it might not be optimal if the analyst had not had an adolescent regression of his or her own.

RG: I have found that when an analysis is well-advanced, many aspects of my patients' behavior resemble many aspects of their own and others' adolescent behavior. But I have an easily discernible bias in this matter. You may recall that Jack Benny remained thirty-nine. I have remained seventeen. Perhaps I should explain. I would not want to lose my license because I am underage. When an analysis is well along, and in other circumstances, my experiences often bring back with special intensity my thoughts, feelings, questions, fantasies, events, hopes, ideals, and much else from that age. Clearly, this has influenced my readiness to accept the notion that analysis offers a chance at a second adolescence, a second chance both for my patients and for me.

Indeed, this may be another of those efforts to make a virtue of a necessity. Still, I tend to agree with those observers who say that many efforts at creative activity—in analysis and elsewhere—involve recreations and reorganizations of adolescent processes. Dr.

Raymond raised the question of whether it might be problematic if an analyst had never experienced an adolescent regression of his or her own. I suspect so. I suspect that such rigidity of character would be likely to prove burdensome in many ways. But I would not want to deny the possibility that there are many routes to creative activity, analytical and other. And I can imagine that even the handicaps of an analyst's lack of an adolescent regression might be overcome.

In addition, some adolescent regressions and some latter day recreations and reorganizations of those regressions are quite subtle and bear little resemblance to more dramatic and more easily observable versions of adolescent "Sturm und Drang." It can be difficult, therefore, to identify persons who have failed to undergo an adolescent regression. I do not want to speak for other analysts; only to say that I have the distinct impression, I hope not the delusion, that when I am working well enough, and sometimes when I am not, I am very often seventeen.

SRR: I was amazed when I read that. I totally understand what you mean, and I've never heard anyone talk about it.

RG: I know a few details of my own seventeendom. I shall speak only of one. There's a limit to my tolerance for autobiography. I went off to college when I was seventeen, off to a brave new world. I think that for me "seventeen" is a metaphor for moments of high promise and confusion, moments of going back to my past to discover who and where I am, what I might be becoming, and where I might be going. I would like to know about other analysts' peculiarities of "age" and how these might connect with the particularities and peculiarities of their analytic approaches.

I have operated on the assumption that if on some occasions I speak directly and indirectly of some of my peculiarities, some of my colleagues will speak directly and indirectly of some of theirs. Which is another piece of my answer to your question of what we can do—if we can do anything at all—to contribute, or try to contribute, to a climate in which we can learn a bit more about some workings of our own and each other's approaches.

LR/SRR: Thank you very much.

SELECTED BIBLIOGRAPHY

Gardner, M. R. (1961). On psychiatry and other schooling. In: *Psychiatry Education Today*, by I. Hendrick. New York: International Universities Press.

Gardner, M. R. (1983). *Self Inquiry*. Hillsdale, NJ: The Analytic Press.

Gardner, M. R. (1984). Apres. *Etudes Freudiennes,* Vol. 24, No. 2.

Gardner, M. R. (1984). Analysis and self-analysis: Looking two ways at once. Discussion of Vann Spruiell's "The analyst at work." *International Journal of Psycho-Analysis*, Vol. 65, pp. 39–44.

Gardner, M. R. (1989). On talking to ourselves: Some self-analytical reflections on self-analysis. In: *Self-Analysis: Critical Inquiries, Personal Visons,* ed. J. Barron. Hillsdale, NJ: The Analytic Press.

Gardner, M. R. (1994). *On Trying to Teach: The Mind in Correspondence*. Hillsdale, NJ: The Analytic Press.

Gardner, M. R. (1995). *Hidden Questions, Clinical Musings.* Hillsdale, NJ: The Analytic Press.

JANINE CHASSEGUET-SMIRGEL

Janine Chasseguet-Smirgel holds a Ph.D. in psychology and is a Docteur d'Etat et Lettres et Sciences Humaines of the Sorbonne. She is a training analyst at the Paris Psychoanalytical Society. Dr. Chasseguet-Smirgel has occupied the Freud Memorial Chair at University College, London and has been André Ballard Lecturer at Columbia University. She is a past vice president of the International Psychoanalytical Association. Dr. Chasseguet-Smirgel was interviewed May 21, 1994.

SRR: You have conceptualized the ego ideal as a specific anthropological phenomenon in the broadest sense of the term, which takes man beyond the simple quest for instinctual satisfaction. And, you have emphasized the developmental role of the ego ideal addressing the notions of hope and project, describing how the mother initially encourages her child to project his ego ideal onto successfully more evolved models. You have stated that the ego ideal naturally promotes maturation, and you have proposed "the existence of an innate program of psychosexual development that follows laws comparable to those that govern biological phenomena. This program is in some sense underpinned at each stage by the fantasy of the reunification of ego and ideal, which is merged with that of fusion with the primary object through realization of the incestuous wish."

Do you think that possibilities for growth through new ego ideal development continue into adulthood? And do you think that, in addition to analysis, there can be other opportunities in adult life, such as certain kinds of marriages or other personal experiences, which can enable some reshaping or modification of the ego ideal?

JC-S: The ego ideal is always there whenever one performs anything. For instance, when one gives a presentation, one wants to feed or gratify one's ego in order to bring it closer to one's ideal. But you spoke about changes in the ego ideal, and you gave the example of marriage. Of course, when a person becomes involved with someone else, it's never by mere chance. One begins to share some of the other's ideals as far as they are congruent with one's own. One can also have an encounter which changes deeply held political views, for example. I can think of people who are politically militant and then changed their ideals. Of course, they can also be disappointed, which occurred so often in France. There, most of the intellectuals were communist or were close to the communist party after the end of the war, in the 50s and through the beginning of the 60s. Little by little, their ideals fell. Disappointed, they had to make an entire reorganization of their ideals. Some were simply depressed, others denied, and others tried to reconstruct something from this. In a certain number of cases, this led to a kind of rethinking of their political ideals, and they became more humble. That meant that they tried to understand what had happened to them, and they converted, so to speak, to the fight for human rights. This happened in the late 70s and 80s, when a lot of intellectuals went through this evolution.

Of course, one may ask what happened to them when they had cathected, invested so much in their political ideal, this ideal which had shrunk, in a way, because the ideal of human rights is a great one, but it lacks the fanaticism of communism. No longer the ideal of a new world happening suddenly; everybody now working for human rights knows that change happens in small steps. "Le Grand Soir," the Great Evening as it's called in French, will not happen. They know—or learn at a certain level—that in all human undertakings, there are advances and retreats. It would be interesting but quite difficult to understand what happened to individuals' psychic economies, what happened to this huge investment where narcissism had played the main role, because it could not be entirely replaced by the fight for human rights. This could only really be understood if one had somebody of that kind on your couch. It's difficult to know. I suppose that great love can provide that investment. I say that in my book.

SRR: Yes, I know.

JC-S: It can be very important for the ego ideal, for this meeting of the ego with the ideal, which is never an entire fusion.

SRR: You noted how some people would get depressed and other people would somehow transfer or readapt.

JC-S: Or deny, which is worse.

SRR: Yes. Do you have any thoughts about what distinguishes people's capacities to adopt those different alternatives.

JC-S: It depends upon the entire previous organization of the self. Many of those who had chosen the path towards communism were very fragile, so it was very difficult for them, and, of course, some became depressed. I am a professor at a university where psychology is now almost entirely in the hands of the cognitive psychologists. I can't imagine that this is the case in the U.S. These people, at my university, are fanatics; extremely intolerant. They employ fascistic methods against all trends but their own, most particularly against psychodynamic thinking. They are trying to destroy the psychoanalytic trend. They are killers; they can psychically annihilate people. I was informed that in the past they were communists, Stalinistic communists. The communist party in France was the most Stalinistic of Western Europe. These particular individuals were among the most zealously Stalinistic. So, with the demise of communism, these people have converted to cognitivism, committing themselves to it as if it were a political machine—a war machine, or "Machine de guerre" in French.

SRR: I have to say that there are psychologies, psychologists like that here. There are those schools here.

LR: In your interview with Elaine Baruch and Lucienne Serrano, you raise an interesting question about women who were Russian nihilists and Nazi concentration camp guards. You said, "Because he doesn't have the capacity for motherhood, the man perhaps fixes his ego ideal on the extremist ideologies more often and that leads him to revolutionary groups which want to sweep away the superego, to make all culpability disappear totally. However, among the Russian nihilists, there were many women, and among the Nazis, there were female guards in the concentration camps. What in their structure made them choose this more masculine mode of resolving the ego ideal? Not all ego ideals lead simply to destruction." I wonder how you might answer your own question.

JC-S: Certain women demonstrated the greatest violence; they can be compared to the cognitivists that I just described. One should say "woman" in quotation marks, because, perhaps, we are not truly describing a woman. While it is normal for a woman to have masculine parts, here we find an unusually masculine quality. It is a difficult question, requiring the psychoanalytic study of such women in order to truly understand them. From a psychoanalytic vantage point, I would not describe these women in terms of masculine identifications. I think that the Nazis, men and women, have an identification with a very archaic undifferentiated maternal imago, one which is not clearly male or female, but which is very primitive, aggressive and dangerous. I think this is true with female Nazis, as well as with men.

As I described in my writings, I don't think that Hitler was a father figure. I think that he served as a much more archaic image. If one observes him, he had none of the attributes of a real man. Rather, he played on very primitive narcissistic needs related to the very early maternal imago, a mother who was not very clearly a mother. I think this imago is represented by spider fantasies, probably also by the Sphinx. Sophocles depicts her as female. Representations of the Sphinx are a type of chimera; they have both female and animal features. All of these aspects concern that obscure world of the early imago.

SRR: I wanted to introduce the reader to your writings on Nazism. This is from your essay on the Nazi biocracy and genocide. Your thesis is that Nazism is based on the fantasy of fusion with the mother, that in fact, the archaic matrix of the oedipus complex lies at the heart of all extreme idealogies, but that National Socialist ideology gave a more concrete expression of it than ever before. You note how Hitler had accused the Jews of inventing reason and you recount that, "according to Vermeil, for Rosenberg, the flaw in the Jews is their intellectualism, that fatal separation which comes between our natural instinctive roots composed of blood and race, and our soul, our thoughts and our actions. In other words, thought is an obstacle to the fusion of mother and child. Perhaps, in the last analysis, this hatred of Jews is linked to everything in their religion and their concept of the world which pertains to separation."

And then, following this, in your reflections on the Hamburg Congress, you state that "Nazism furnishes us with staggering insight into the human soul. What incredible split could allow an analyst to remain indifferent to the Jewish problem and to the events of the Second World War." You note how in France, while psychoanalytic patients include a much higher proportion of Jews than the average population, many analysts, Jewish and non-Jewish, are unable to recognize material connected with the Shoah and the antisemitism of Jewish patients, the analysis of which is even more important than that of non-Jews. In most cases, it is never brought to life.

I am curious about that. How do you try to counteract it? Is there course work?

JC-S: Of course, I try to show this when I supervise. I am reminded of an analyst I like very much, who is very interested in the Jewish question. Though not a Jew, he claims some Jewish blood. He reported at a meeting about a candidate who presented his work to him as his supervisor. The candidate's patient related many dreams about fire and burning corpses; it was extremely disquieting material. Yet, when the candidate mentioned that the patient was a Jew, the supervisor made no connection between this material and his Jewishness. While of course any patient could produce material of this nature, when a Jew presents such material it certainly refers to his fantasies about what happened to his family. In this case, nothing was mentioned about the family, so it is a good example. I have often found that this kind of imagery is ignored. I had a discussion with an American analyst, whose name I will not disclose. He presented striking material about a patient's fears of being killed in a particular, very precise way. The analyst described the case in a detailed presentation, neglecting to mention, until asked by a colleague, that the patient had been in the Warsaw Ghetto. So you see, it was not connected.

Although gradually, little by little, the psychoanalytic community is accepting the idea that the Shoah retains an importance for later generations. However, not long ago I attended a colloquium in which case material was presented by American colleagues. It concerned a young patient whose mother had been in a concentration camp. According to the patient, her mother had received almost no food, but probably survived by being a prostitute for the SS. The mother killed herself when the patient was eighteen, but this history was not discussed in connection with her suicide. It's evident that this patient's primal scene fantasies, her notion of coitus between a man and a woman, were based on the mother's prostituting herself to the SS. I stated that in the discussion, but this idea was rejected.

LR: What dynamic factors do you think contribute to people not feeling free to talk about it?

JC-S: I think it's too frightening. I have never written about this, but I've thought about Melanie Klein's work in this context. I think her first book was published in 1932. She was in Berlin at that time, while she was in analysis with Karl Abraham, so that she witnessed the growth of Nazism. While she never discussed this, it appears that the fantasies that she discovered in people have a deep connection with what was to happen some years after.

SRR: That's amazing.

JC-S: For instance, she described burning the body with urine, choking from gas, all of these fantasies about the body. The idea of the destruction of the body through teeth, through the anus, these are considered to be fantasies she discovered or created. I am not suggesting that she denied what was happening in the outer world, which then emerged in her findings, as we do not know about her feelings at that time. But when you read the *Freud-Klein Controversies,* that huge volume, you also discover amazing facts. For example, the British society met during the war when London was submitting to dreadful bombing. At one point, they mention that the meeting was interrupted so that everyone could go to the bomb shelter, but nothing more about it is discussed. However, if you consider the entire material Klein presents, it reflects so closely what was happening and about to happen in the world, especially in Europe where her loved ones were—family and friends. Europe was in a kinetic state. While it was not as tragic in London as elsewhere, since people were not gassed and there were no concentration camps or burnings, still the bombings were awful. And nothing of this was referred to in the *Controversies*. I think, however, that Klein's entire theoretical work was impregnated by world events at that time.

SRR: That's fascinating.

LR: Do you think that your training in political science allows you a unique perspective or have you always been interested in the interplay between the external context and the intrapsychic?

JC-S: Probably I chose political science because I was already interested in the psychology of politics. That approach is not that different from the analytic method. For example, the way the events of the world produce ideologies can be seen as very similar to the way day residues enter into our dreams.

SRR: While we're still somewhat on the subject of Europe and Germany, I want to include your statement, "I cannot overemphasize the strength of my belief that the Germans suffer from unconscious persecutory guilt which impels them to verbal and intellectual violence and actual terrorism." And you assert that the problem is one of identification. "What is one to do with a Nazi father? Apparently the only solution is to reject him. If you speak of the need to integrate your identifications of that father, you are immediately treated as a Nazi yourself. But in the absence of identification, where there is only counteridentification, there can be no genuine choice between acceptance and rejection, and sublimation becomes totally impossible. In order to become a human being in the full sense of the term, we have to be able to discover and confront Hitler in us, otherwise the repressed will return and the disavow will come back in various guises."

Do you have any thoughts about what could be done to help people face these identifications?

JC-S: I wrote about this some years ago, and the return of the repressed has occurred exactly as described.

SRR: I know.

JC-S: I don't mean that it is exactly the same people who so violently disowned their identifications with their fathers that in identification with these fathers, they now behave again as the Germans did earlier. However, in each country in Europe we are again finding people burning foreigners. While it is not on such a large scale, it is absolutely frightening. I think that the younger generation, which is no longer so young, should have been helped to face the past. While some German politicians and some writers did make efforts to do this, many did not. Rather, they tried to cover it up. This work of facing the past could only have been done by leaders, by politicians, thinkers, writers, and never in the very violent way that was frequently attempted. I think that von Weizsacker has played a proper role as Germany's president. For example, recently people demonstrated with swastikas. They were arrested and then immediately released.

And von Weizsacker made a protest and said they should not have been. So, I think that he plays a good role, but while there should be many people playing that role, the opposite is true. Many remain who have not changed; I met people from the extreme left who are the same. It is not better on the left than the right, both may be sadistic and cruel, projecting guilt onto the other and, if possible, onto the Jews. I was the chairman of the International Psychoanalytic Association's Hamburg Congress which focused on the Nazi phenomenon. A newspaper from the left, the *Frankfurter Rundshau*, wrote that this conference was an attempt to take distance and cover things up and entitled the article devoted to the congress "From Bitburg to Hamburg." If you remember, Bitburg was the place where Kohl received Reagan, and they went to a cemetery where Allied troops were buried. Kohl wanted Reagan to pay homage to the SS as well as the American troops who were killed in Germany. The title of the article meant that the purpose of the congress was the same. These people's main victory is when they can accuse Jews of being those who want to cover up the whole issue. I was so infuriated when I read that! I wrote a letter to that journalist and told him to stop putting his Lady Macbeth-bloody hands in my face.

LR: That was a very good retort. It reminds me of your discussion of projection and incorporation in your interview with Elaine Baruch and Lucienne Serrano. You were noting that men more frequently use projection as a defense, whereas women more frequently use incorporation. You said of incorporation, "This mechanism consists of taking something into oneself, of swallowing, absorbing and not of going out from the self. This mechanism exists in both sexes, and is necessary for the enrichment of the ego, but there is a preponderance in the woman, which is without doubt bound to her capacity for maternity, and for incorporating the penis to create an infant. This concrete incorporation extends to more abstract mechanisms. That women use this mechanism more frequently than men explains the quantitative difference between women and men's psychic problems. For example, the great number of depressions in women are bound up with introjection."

Are you thinking of incorporation as a process for dealing with affects or as a process of identification with objects? Could you elaborate more?

JC-S: Depression often occurs when the incorporated object is believed to have been destroyed or damaged by the subject him or herself, in this case by the woman. Statistics testify that women experience more depression than men; I think that this is because of women's propensity for "taking in" things.

LR: I was wondering more about women perhaps feeling less entitlement to express anger or to assert themselves.

JC-S: That is also possible. Women experience more feelings of guilt and more unconscious guilt than men, which indicates that their aggression is less free than males'. This leads to the question concerning the female superego. I agree with Melanie Klein that women's superegos are stronger than those of men, which is, of course, the opposite of what Freud believes.

LR: In the United States, there is a growing literature on the psychology of women, suggesting that women's identity and sense of self-esteem comes often from mutual connection to one another, whereas men tend to have more hierarchical, counterdependent relationships with each other. I don't know whether there is a parallel literature developing in France, but I'm trying to think about how your view of the gender differences in the use of projection and incorporation might fit in.

JC-S: I have not heard this theory expounded in France, perhaps it is specific to the United States. It's difficult for me to object, not having read it, but I do have an objection. I think that men have stronger homosexual relationships, not necessarily, but sometimes, manifest. Latent homosexuality plays a more important role for men than for women. Women have always complained of men having another milieu, whether club, pub, or cafe. Men prefer being with male friends participating in activities such as watching football games, where only men play, and so on. There is, I think, great complicity between men in many, many circles. For example, there are the Lacanians, who have become so numerous. I'm not sure what is happening with them now, but when Lacan was alive he was surrounded by a clearly male cult.

LR: That's interesting.

JC-S: Women were hardly allowed to enter the circle.

SRR: I didn't know that.

JC-S: Oh, yes.

SRR: Speaking of women, you have described how the two sexes "are marked at the psychic level by the integrations of their identifications with two parents, an identification with a mother, experienced from the beginning as possessing a vagina and a fertile womb" and that this plays a fundamental role in the psychosexuality of men and women. And you propose that "it is the primacy and the wish for a child combined with the presence of the female receptacle, which produces the oral conception of coitus and pregnancy, and the primacy of orality over genitality. Motherhood is cosubstantial with female psychosexuality whether or not it results in the birth of a child."

I have several questions. You state that the capacity for motherhood enables the woman to realize in fantasy her dual incestuous wish to recover the state of primary fusion with the mother and to keep the love object, the father or his penis inside herself. You describe the woman's disappointment with the birth of her actual child, because it is not the wished-for baby of her father. What are your thoughts about Melanie Klein's ideas about motherhood, particularly her belief that becoming a mother enables the woman to feel equal with her mother, in this way resolving the oedipal trauma? Also, do you conceive of the experience of being a mother, the actual experience of mothering, as providing opportunity for making new identifications, with one's mother and father, and at different phases of parenting?

JC-S: I said that there was, at least sometimes for certain women, a disappointment in the child who is not the imagined, incestuous child of the father. Klein says that this is the normal way of solving the conflict with the mother. It is true, that the woman does become like her mother. Your second question was, "Does being a parent change the ego because of new identifications?"

SRR: Yes, my question is whether being a parent provides new opportunities to identify with one's mother or father at different stages as one's child gets older. In other words, that doing the parenting can allow for a different kind of empathy with one's parents. I can give an example. I have a seventeen-year-old daughter, and I can find myself jealous of her in a way I never was when she was younger. Being aware of this has made me sympathetic towards my mother for the first time, in respect to her envy of me. I realize I really have a much better life than my mother's was and here I am feeling envious at moments of my child, so I am able to appreciate in a new way what my mother must have been struggling with and feeling.

JC-S: It's interesting. The envy of the mother towards a growing child has not been described in the psychoanalytic literature, yet, I think that it plays a great role. You are aware of it, but how many mothers who are not analysts are not conscious of this envy, but instead enact something against their children, particularly their daughters? I think that this happens very often. So, you suggest that it has had a positive effect, that you can better understand your mother.

SRR: Yes, I feel more forgiving. I feel sympathetic towards her because as much as she hurt me at that time, I now believe that some of what happened was inevitable and that she could have been so much worse towards me. I see how my daughter ignores me or demands a great deal and then dismisses me. And I can see that I did that to my mother, and she did many things to me, but she didn't retaliate as she might have done. She did stand by me. So, I have appreciation for just what a tough stage it is.

JC-S: It seems quite important. Probably it changes something deep inside you. Your maternal imago is probably better.

SRR: Yes.

JC-S: If this imago is better, probably your envy towards your daughter is helped. You can deal with it better.

SRR: Yes. Of course, analysis made me able to tolerate that I have envy. Years earlier, I would have been horrified or very guilty about it.

JC-S: I can remember having experienced this envy when I was young. I was lucky, I was not yet twenty-five when I began my analysis.

SRR: Oh, you were lucky.

JC-S: So I began analysis when I was young. And I began my first book, *Female Sexuality*, by writing two articles on human sexuality. That was thirty years ago. I was thirty-something, still young. At that time the book had a certain success. It still has. It will soon be republished again in France and Italy, and there have been three English editions. So, at that time I became known and had a fair amount of attention, and I experienced the envy, and even hatred, of certain female analysts.

LR: That seems similar to the phenomenon of older women doctors, who had more obstacles getting through their medical training, at times being hard on younger female medical students.

JC-S: I won't give examples, but I experienced real hostility from these women. I had no way to understand why one, especially well-known analyst attacked me. At least until now, I have not experienced those feelings towards young analysts, but who knows?

SRR: It's like the fairy tales with the stepmother.

JC-S: Yes.

SRR: One more part to that question. I think of motherhood as influencing a woman's creativity, which leads to the more fundamental issue of women's creativity in general. Could you tell us how you think about women's creativity outside of motherhood, whether you think of it as essentially the same as men's, or do you see differences?

JC-S: That is a very difficult question. I wrote about this in 1971, in a collection of articles on creativity. It has been republished in France, and published in Germany, and a few other languages. I was writing about the inhibition of women's creativity at about the same time that I wrote about women's sexuality. The subjects are related. I described how women feel the need to protect the father and by extension, by a kind of transference, the male. This is because males experience women's creativity, when it's not the biological, as a kind of usurpation of their powers. Thus, women experience their creativity as a castration of men, through entering their domain. The woman's creativity is inhibited by her belief: "I am doing something wrong, forbidden, I am harming men." This is probably not the only reason. I think that even if you are very feminist, you have to admit that women's creativity is not as great as men's, although there are some very bright exceptions. For example, in psychoanalysis, whether or not you are a Kleinian, I think that you must confess her to be a great discoverer. And, of course, there are poets. I don't know Sylvia Plath's work very well, but I know that she's a great poet. And for great writers, there are Virginia Woolf and the Brontë sisters. In truth, it can't be said that women have been as creative. I think it's due to inhibition, not to a lack of some essential quality. I think it is a problem of inhibition.

LR: In your interview with Elaine Baruch and Lucienne Serrano, you describe "successful love" as "love which accepts the limits that are inherent in the human condition." You also write about perversion as the wish to annihilate genital differences, to return to pregenital anality with a destructiveness and devaluation of the "genital father."

In your clinical experience, what allows people to accept loss and disappointment to reach "successful love" and to avoid perversion? What contributes to a person's ability to accept some narcissistic renunciation in the resolution of the Oedipus, to not experience it as an annihilation of oneself, but instead to have the capacity to accept loss and compensate in some other way? How do you help increase a person's capacity to accept those limits and work towards a mature kind of acceptance of themselves?

JC-S: Of course, it has to do with narcissism.

LR: Do you think there are any general differences in the way men and women handle those narcissistic injuries or compensate for them, or do you see it more as a function of individual dynamics?

JC-S: I have not been the only one to describe perversion as linked to the mother's attitude towards her male child, to whom she conveys a message: "You are my favorite, you need not grow in order to become like your father. I like you and love you as you are and as long as you are." In certain extreme cases, this attitude leads to the child developing a kind of grandiosity which prevents him from accepting limitations. Usually, girls are not raised this way; their mothers do not convey this message to them. Therefore, they lack this grand illusion and are more able to accept limitations. When one has experienced such a grand illusion for a certain time, one must try at all costs to maintain it, because without sustained effort it will break down. The little girl, I think, has no opportunity to develop this illusion. I know it may seem reactionary to say, but it is a fact that the young woman's life is more regulated biologically than her male counterpart; this provides her with a very important link to reality and to the reality principle. She is less grandiose.

LR: In your essay, "Loss of Reality in Perversions—With Special Reference to Fetishism," you note that male perversion can result from the mother being seductive with the male child. You also mention that perversion is less frequent in women than in men. Is there any increase in perversion, however, with women whose fathers have been seductive with them? Do you see them as parallel dynamic situations?

JC-S: The seduction theory. There is a revival of it. But things are less simple.

LR: Yes, with current interest in how to sort out the psychic consequences of actual trauma from fantasied seduction. I'm curious because you described situations in which the mother was seductive with the male child. What about those in which the father or mother was seductive with the female child?

JC-S: First of all, I don't think it's parallel. In certain cases, although no incest occurs, the father treats his little girl as very, very precious, more precious than his wife, her mother. This situation does not usually lead to perversion, rather to hysterical and phobic symptoms and organization. The little girl cannot have the illusion that she can give birth to a child. I think this fact is very important, almost from the beginning. In contrast, the little boy can be misled by his mother. As small as he is, he can think he is a perfect sexual object for her. But unless the little girl is delusional, she cannot believe that she can give birth to a child. In very bad cases, actual incest sometimes leads to psychosis, but it does not lead to perversion in women. Perhaps it may in rare cases, but not very often. Once again, I think this is because the father is not the original object.

The real incest is with the mother. In the rare case, when a little girl has a sexual relationship with her mother, the mother is really psychotic. The incestuous mother is not like the incestuous father, who is a pervert rather than psychotic. And this usually leads to psychosis in the girl rather than perversion, because it forces a return to the place where one was before birth. I think it has another unconscious meaning. I think, also, that in the United States there is an exaggerated emphasis on incest, the notion that so many women had incestuous fathers. I don't believe that. Perhaps we closed our eyes too much at one time. The larger society, as well as psychoanalysts, denied that there incestuous fathers. But I think that it's crazy to now believe that all fathers were incestuous, and all males are horrible.

SRR: In the interest of time, I'll skip over the first part of my question, but I'm thinking about what you've just said and am reminded of describing your essay about your patient Franca. This next question, I think, concerns the same problems. You describe how "the lack of manifestation of feelings of grief, which are necessary to the maintenance of bonds with the mother, bonds recognized as tenuous and fragile but all the more vital to psychic survival, is accompanied by a proportional distortion of the development of psychic mechanisms and of the sense of reality. In particular, the bad character of the object is denied and the object is idealized." And you question "whether this need linked to the very ancient experience becomes paradoxically more important than life itself."

I'm very interested in your thinking as to whether and how much psychoanalysis can help an individual relinquish this kind of object. In Franca's case, you talked about the particular difficulties with the countertransference. I hoped you could say more about your countertransference and your use of it in working with patients with these very deep disturbances. Also, whether you think that Freud may have had the problem of treating these kinds of patients in mind in writing "Analysis Terminable and Interminable?"

JC-S: I think that there are special technical problems which are partly, though not entirely, due to the countertransference. Such a patient was very difficult to bear because she was always like a small child, who is...[gestures].

LR: Tugs at your skirt?

JC-S: Yes, and whatever you do, it's never enough. There is a deep dissatisfaction that never goes away. One feels impotent in the face of it. At the same time, one sometimes also feels angry, like the mother of such a child. The technical problems in such cases are related at least in part to these feelings; it is very difficult to deal with these emotions. One has the impression that one is trying to fill something which has a hole, so that whatever is put in eventually comes out. But the wish is there, the hope of being able to help. I think that one has to have several patients like this before one is really able to help. One must be able to tolerate these feelings in order to understand these patients, to use the feelings, to make something out of them. I think that one way is to speak or write about such a patient. If it is helpful to us, then it helps the patient.

It's possible that this kind of case is a new version of "Analysis Terminable and Interminable." In certain cases, it appears to be something interminable, bedrock, as Freud described it. Although I don't think that he was right in describing penis envy as bedrock. We have discussed this, the idea of the male's passivity in front of other men as being bedrock. But it's probably a new version which we see in certain difficult analyses, which seem to be more frequent nowadays. This is probably due to the scattering of the family. It's a crisis, at least in the West, for which we have no solution. Perhaps we will find one, I don't know. But for now, we see more and more people from scattered families. Although this patient did not come from one; rather, she came from a crazy family. She had a mother and father, but her father was crazy, not psychotic. Neither were appropriate patients. We have more and more of these cases because we have less and less fathers; the role of the father is a very important one. Now we have more mothers with a child and no third party.

SRR: You said that it becomes easier after treating a number of these cases. Is it that one doesn't get as upset by them?

JC-S: Oh, yes, but you must not have several at the same time. Once you have experienced your countertransference, you begin to understand a little more what is at stake. There are moments when you simply want to give up, you are convinced the work will not progress, and you feel really tired. You are truly tired, they are very tiresome patients.

SRR: Thank you.

LR: Can you tell us about your work at the university?

JC-S: Yes, I teach in the psychology department. There is a specialization combining the study of clinical psychology and psychopathology.

SRR: That's excellent.

JC-S: It's terrific, except that the cognitives are taking over, and they are computerizing everything.

LR: There is a similar phenomenon in American psychiatry of analysis being pushed out of the medical academic environment with increasing emphasis on neurobiology and psychopharmacology. Hopefully, both perspectives can eventually be better integrated.

JC-S: According to a colleague with whom I spoke yesterday, he says that cognitivism is decreasing here. Is that true?

SRR: Is he a psychologist?

JC-S: No, he's probably an M.D., a psychiatrist.

SRR: I'm a psychologist by training. As you know, while there are many psychoanalytically informed psychologists, we are definitely the minority of the membership of the American Psychological Association. There are more cognitive psychologists or behaviorists, and so forth. I didn't really appreciate that clinical psychology existed when I was an undergraduate; the psychology department at my college was noted for rat psychology.

JC-S: There exists a struggle against psychoanalysis which is one with the struggle against thought itself. A denial of the unconscious is in keeping with the dehumanized world in which we live. A postgraduate student in cognitive sciences, after a presentation of mine on hallucination was over, told me: "We can't measure it." Another added, "Dreams do not interest us since computers don't dream." It was not a joke....

LR/SRR: Thank you very much

SELECTED BIBLIOGRAPHY

Chasseguet-Smirgel, J. (1970). *Female Sexuality: New Psychoanalytic Views*. London: Karnac, 1985.

Chasseguet-Smirgel, J. (1973). *The Ego Ideal.* New York: Norton, 1985.

Chasseguet-Smirgel, J. (1974). Perversion, idealization and sublimation. *International Journal of Psycho-Analysis,* Vol. 55, pp. 349–357.

Chasseguet-Smirgel, J. (1976). Some thoughts on the ego ideal: A contribution to the study of the "illness of ideality." *Psychoanalytic Quarterly,* Vol. 45, pp. 345–373.

Chasseguet-Smirgel, J. (1978). Reflexions on the connexions between perversion and sadism. *International Journal of Psycho-Analysis,* Vol. 59, pp. 27–35.

Chasseguet-Smirgel, J. (1981). Loss of reality in perversions—with special reference to fetishism. *Journal of the American Psychoanalytic Association,* Vol. 29, pp. 511–534.

Chasseguet-Smirgel, J. (1983). Perversion and the universal law. *International Review of Psychoanalysis,* Vol. 10, pp. 293–307.

Chasseguet-Smirgel, J. (1984). The femininity of the analyst in professional practice. *International Journal of Psycho-Analysis,* Vol. 65, pp. 169–178.

Chasseguet-Smirgel, J. (1984). *Creativity and Perversion.* New York: Norton.

Chasseguet-Smirgel, J. (1986). The archaic matrix of the Oedipus complex. In: *Sexuality and Mind.* New York: New York University Press.

Chasseguet-Smirgel, J. (1987). "Time's white hair we ruffle," Reflections on the Hamburg Congress. *International Review of Psychoanalysis,* Vol. 14, pp. 433–444.

Baruch, E. H. & Serrano, L. J. (1988). Janine Chasseguet-Smirgel. In: *Women Analyze Women*, New York: New York University Press.

Chasseguet-Smirgel, J. (1988). A woman's attempt at a perverse solution and its failure. *International Journal of Psycho-Analysis,* Vol. 69, pp. 149–161.

Chasseguet-Smirgel, J. (1988). A short essay on the Apocalypse. In: *Psychoanalysis and the Nuclear Threat*, ed. H. B. Levine, D. Jacobs & L. J. Rubin. Hillsdale, NJ: The Analytic Press.

Chasseguet-Smirgel, J. (1990). Reflections of a psychoanalyst upon the Nazi biocracy and genocide. *International Review of Psychoanalysis,* Vol. 17, pp. 167–176.

Chasseguet-Smirgel, J. (1990). On acting out. *International Journal of Psycho-Analysis,* Vol. 71, pp. 77–86.

INDEX